D0407316

Korean Endgame

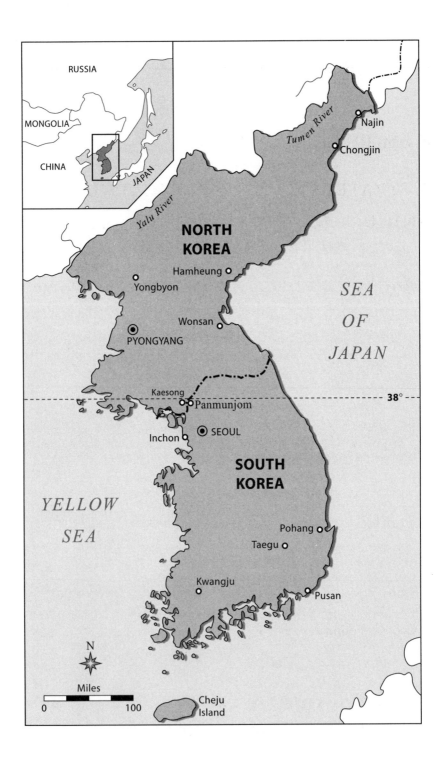

Korean Endgame

A STRATEGY FOR REUNIFICATION AND U.S. DISENGAGEMENT

Selig S. Harrison

A Century Foundation Book

PRINCETON UNIVERSITY PRESS

PRINCETON AND OXFORD

The Century Foundation

The Century Foundation, formerly the Twentieth Century Fund, sponsors and supervises timely analyses of economic policy, foreign affairs, and domestic political issues. Not-for-profit and nonpartisan, it was founded in 1919 and endowed by Edward A. Filene.

Copyright © 2002 by The Century Foundation
Published by Princeton University Press, 41 William Street, Princeton, New Jersey 08540
In the United Kingdom: Princeton University Press, 3 Market Place, Woodstock, Oxfordshire OX20 1SY
All Rights Reserved

Library of Congress Cataloging-in-Publication Data

Harrison, Selig S.
Korean endgame : a strategy for reunification and U.S. disengagement / Selig Harrison.
p. cm.
Includes bibliographical references and index.
ISBN 0-691-09604-X
1. United States—Foreign relations—Korea (North) 2. Korea (North)—Foreign relations—United States. 3. United States—Military relations—Korea (South).
4. Korea (South)—Military relations—United States. 5. East Asia—Strategic aspects.
6. Korean reunification question (1945–) I. Title.

E183.8.K7 H34 2002
327 .7305193—dc21   2001055186

British Library Cataloging-in-Publication Data is available

This book has been composed in Galliard

Printed on acid-free paper. ∞

www.pup.princeton.edu

Printed in the United States of America

1 3 5 7 9 10 8 6 4 2

Contents

Foreword

FOR MORE than a decade, scholars and analysts of U.S. foreign policy have labored under enormous handicaps. In many ways, the unexpected breakup of the Soviet Union complicated the basic work of understanding and explaining world affairs, making the task of prescribing policies even more difficult. There were numerous good reasons, for example, to be uncertain about the stability of both the regimes and policies of the formerly Communist states. One simply could not know what the near-term future held for the so-called Commonwealth of Independent States or even for the Russian Federation itself. And, on the fringes among the far-flung allies of the old Communist bloc, the questions about the future were even more vexing.

One prominent example of the problem facing analysts is the involvement of the United States in Korea, a story that reflects many of the main currents of American foreign policy over the past fifty years. After the defeat of Japan in World War II, the United States found itself simultaneously engaged in several missions in Asia: large-scale humanitarian aid programs, reconstructing (or creating) civil and political institutions, and a nascent effort to create a firewall against the spread of communism. In Korea, these activities led to support for a relatively undemocratic regime, a long-term military presence, and, in 1950, a bitter and costly war against both the North Korean invaders of the south and the so-called Chinese volunteers. For good or ill, this has meant that all postwar U.S. governments have considered the relationship with Korea to be a vital national concern. Now that the success of a reform-minded political movement finally has removed one continuing cause for concern—the lack of true democracy in South Korea—U.S. policy has been focused appropriately on the dangers posed by the Stalinist regime in the North. Today, the threat posed by North Korea is especially worrisome because there is evidence that this poor but belligerent state has the potential to develop nuclear devices and a means to deliver them.

Although our understanding of these complex issues has increased as 2001 draws to a close, the recent terrorist attacks on America's homeland are a stinging reminder that those who confront these new global realities still have much to learn. Since the end of the cold war, The Century Foundation has been sponsoring a wide variety of studies on U.S. foreign policy, as well as several task forces on the need to increase the effectiveness of American intelligence agencies. Our general view has been that, given the many imponderables in the new situation confronting the United States, we could serve a useful purpose by sponsoring the work of scholars, journalists, and former policymakers who hold a range of views about the future. Initially, we produced a number of books that dealt with the immediate breakup of the Communist bloc, including Elizabeth Pond's 1990 report, *After the Wall*, and her 1993 book, *Beyond the Wall*. In those early years after the end of the cold war, we also sponsored Richard Ullman's *Securing Europe*, James Chace's *The Consequences of the Peace*, Murray Weidenbaum's *Small Wars, Big Defense*, and Jeffrey Garten's *A Cold Peace*. Later, as the new outlines in post–cold war international affairs began to emerge more clearly, we supported Jonathan Dean's *Ending Europe's Wars*, John Gerard Ruggie's *Winning the Peace*, Michael Mandelbaum's *The Dawn of Peace in Europe*, and a number of examinations of the role of the United Nations in the new world order. Our most recent studies of U.S. policy and world affairs are Walter Russell Mead's *Special Providence*, David Calleo's *Rethinking Europe's Future*, and Gregory Treverton's *Reshaping National Intelligence for an Age of Information*. In the near future, books examining these issues by Henry Nau and Robert Art will be appearing. In addition to these broader studies, however, we have been supporting a number of studies exploring U.S. relations with specific countries, including a volume of essays on Turkey edited by Morton Abramowitz, Lincoln Gordon's examination of Brazil, Leon Sigal's study of Russia after the breakup, Patrick Tyler's examination of China, Richard Kauzlarich's analysis of the situation in the Transcaucasus. Now this important volume by Selig Harrison on Korea joins that distinguished list.

Selig Harrison, a scholar (with, at various times, the Brookings Institution, the East-West Center, the Carnegie Endowment for International Peace, and the Woodrow Wilson International Center for Scholars) and a former journalist (with, over the years, the Associated Press, *New Republic*, and the *Washington Post*), has been covering, analyzing, and writing about Asian issues for half a century. Author of numerous important studies of the region, including *India: The Most Dangerous Decades; The Widening Gulf: Asian Nationalism and American Policy;* and *In Afghanistan's Shadow*, he presents a provocative look at a topic that is sure to stay in the news. Harrison has had extraordinary access not only to the makers of U.S. foreign policy for the region and those in the government of South Korea, but with North Korean leaders as well, including Kim Il Sung. As a result, he foresaw the likelihood that the North Korean regime, given its internal harsh controls, would endure after the death of Kim Il Sung and even in the face of widespread famine. He also reported on the possibilities for changes in policy before the visit of Secretary of State Madeleine Albright to North Korea in 2000.

But Harrison, who was present at numerous meetings and discussions with officials of the United States and of both Koreas, does more than report and analyze the issues involved in U.S.- Korean relations. He offers his proposals for increasing the prospects for a peaceful evolution from the currently stalemated efforts to reunify the peninsula and contain the dangerous belligerency of the North Korean regime. He goes on to outline a strategy designed to bring about a neutral Korea and to disentangle the United States from its long, direct military involvement. Wherever one stands on debates about American policy toward Korea, these are important ideas worthy of serious attention and debate.

In the aftermath of September 11, we are in the midst of another sea change in our view of the threats to our peace—and our domestic security. In that light, North Korea poses a risk not simply as a rogue state that might cause much mischief in Asia, but also as a possible supplier of dangerous weapons to terrorists. In its role as one of a number of such potential trouble spots, it will remain a high priority for scholars and policymakers alike. On behalf of the Trustees of the Century Foundation, I want to thank Harrison for his extensive research and lucid writing on this important topic.

Richard C. Leone, President
The Century Foundation
November 2001

OVERVIEW: The United States and Korea

IN AUGUST 1945, the United States and the Soviet Union divided Korea and set up client regimes in the South and the North that immediately dedicated themselves to undoing the division. Both Syngman Rhee in the South and Kim Il Sung in the North repeatedly pressured their superpower patrons to help them reunify the peninsula militarily. The United States resisted Rhee, but in early 1950, after initially restraining Kim Il Sung, Josef Stalin agreed to support a North Korean invasion of the South. When the Korean War finally ended with the 1953 armistice, some 800,000 Koreans on both sides of the thirty-eighth parallel had lost their lives, together with 115,000 Chinese and 36,400 Americans.

PUPPETS, PUPPETEERS, AND THE KOREAN WAR

Mounting historical evidence makes it increasingly clear that the meaning of the Korean War has been widely misunderstood. The original assumption underlying U.S. intervention was that the North had acted as a puppet of the Soviet Union in the opening thrust of a worldwide Communist expansionist offensive. This assumption led to an image of the conflict as a mere extension of the superpower rivalry, with its fundamental character as a civil war largely obscured. But historians have now established beyond doubt that it was Kim Il Sung, not Stalin, who instigated the invasion primarily in response to an internal factional challenge from his most significant rival for control of the ruling Workers Party in the North, Pak Hon Yong, who was later purged. Pak had been the leader of the Korean Communist organization in the South before fleeing north following the division and the U.S. occupation. Having left his party base behind, he wanted to liberate the South to enhance his power in the Workers Party. Pak used the rallying cry of unification to challenge Kim for party control, and Kim responded by assuming the leadership of the unification cause himself.

Recent research in the Soviet Union and China has unearthed extensive documentation that shows how hesitant Stalin was in responding to Kim's pressures for an invasion. When Kim first raised the issue in March 1949, Stalin told him not to invade the South unless Rhee attacked first. In October, Moscow reprimanded Pyongyang for provocative military operations. In January 1950, Kim stepped up his pleas for permission to attack, warning that the South was rapidly upgrading its military capabilities and would soon be too strong to challenge. But Stalin was noncommittal. It was not until his second meeting with Kim in April that the Soviet leader authorized a major escalation of military aid to the North, and not until Kim had sent forty-eight telegrams appealing for a decision that Stalin gave his go-ahead, on May 14, for the fateful attack six weeks later. Stalin finally yielded to Kim because he mistakenly concluded that the war would not take long and would not lead to conflict with the United States.[1]

The central conclusion emerging from a study of the Korean War and its consequences is that the cold war was dominated by the superpower rivalry but not by the superpowers. Moscow and Washington saw themselves as the puppeteers pulling the strings. More often than not, however, they were manipulated by clients who had their own agendas. In the case of Korea, Kim Il Sung skillfully exploited Sino-Soviet tensions to get Soviet support for his reunification adventure. Kim visited Beijing as well as Moscow in April 1950. He secured Mao Tse-tung's blessing for an invasion, which greatly strengthened his hand in dealing with Stalin, who feared a Chinese challenge for leadership of the world Communist movement. Far from being a puppet of either Moscow or Beijing in subsequent decades, Kim systematically played one against the other throughout the cold war, securing at least $18 billion in economic and military aid grants and credits, not to mention trade subsidies.[2] Pyongyang's current economic difficulties started when the cold war ended and Moscow and Beijing no longer needed to compete for its support.

The United States, for its part, has been manipulated by a succession of South Korean leaders, starting with Syngman Rhee. It was Rhee's refusal to sign the 1953 armistice and his threats to "march North" that forced the United States to buy him off with economic and military commitments much more extensive and much more binding than it originally had in mind. For eighteen months after the armistice, relations between Seoul and Washington grew so embittered that the United States finally cut off civilian oil supplies to the South. Seoul never did sign the armistice, a major complication in current efforts to replace it with a permanent peace treaty. Rhee finally agreed to respect its provisions only after President Eisenhower promised long-term economic assistance, starting with $1 billion in the first four years; military aid sufficient to give the South military superiority over North Korea; a mutual security treaty; and an open-ended U.S. military presence.[3]

Initially modest, the resulting influx of U.S. economic and military aid to South Korea totaled some $19.07 billion by 1997, including $11.05 billion in grant aid, of which $6.44 billion was military hardware. The only countries that have received more American assistance have been Israel ($56.1 billion), Egypt ($36.7 billion), and South Vietnam ($21.8 billion). Government-subsidized U.S. military sales to the South reached a total of $11.7 billion in 1999, and commercial export licenses for military sales reached $2 billion in 1996 and 1997 alone. In addition to this cornucopia of bilateral aid, the United States has encouraged the multilateral aid agencies to extend $11.42 billion in credits to South Korea and to provide a $17 billion bailout package when its economy was on the verge of collapse in 1998.[4]

Nearly five decades after the armistice, the United States is still committed to one side in an unfinished civil war in Korea that could erupt at any time into another major conflagration. This commitment originated in the context of cold war alignments in Korea that no longer exist. The United States agreed to Rhee's demands for a military alliance because it viewed North Korea as a projection of Soviet and Chinese power. By 1961, both Moscow and Beijing had concluded alliances of their own with Pyongyang. But now Moscow has nullified its security treaty with Pyongyang and is selling its most advanced military equipment and technology to Seoul. Beijing, while retaining its security treaty, has phased out its military aid to Pyongyang and is seeking to promote a reduction of military tensions between North and South by playing the role of honest broker. Equally important, both Russia and China have forged much more important economic links with the South than with the North.

Since 1958, there have been no Soviet or Chinese forces in North Korea. Nevertheless, the United States continues to maintain 37,000 U.S. troops in the South at a direct cost of $2 billion per year, plus an indirect cost of $42 billion per year for the maintenance of the supporting forces in the Pacific that would be needed to back up any U.S. military intervention in Korea. The United States said in 1991 that it had removed its tactical nuclear weapons from Korea and from Pacific fleet aircraft carriers but did not rule out their reintroduction in a crisis. At the same time, it has retained its submarine-launched strategic nuclear capability in the Pacific and has pointedly refrained from ruling out the first use of nuclear weapons against what it considers to be aggression by North Korean conventional forces.

The relaxation of tensions in Korea following the unprecedented June 2000 summit meeting between South Korean president Kim Dae Jung and North Korean leader Kim Jong Il has not altered U.S. plans to keep an American military presence in the peninsula indefinitely. Pentagon officials contend that the North Korean military threat to the South and to U.S. interests in Northeast Asia is undiminished. If anything, they say—pointing to Pyongyang's missile program, its chemical and biological weapons capabilities, and the possibility of a covert nuclear weapons program—the threat could well increase. The U.S. military presence should be maintained at existing or higher levels, in this view, both to confront the North Korean threat and to play a larger "stabilizing" and "balancing" role in Northeast Asia.

The need for a comprehensive reassessment of U.S. policy in Korea has been steadily growing since the end of the cold war. It has become more urgent in the context of a divergence between South Korean and U.S. policies toward Pyongyang. While South Korean policies have softened since the North-South summit, the U.S. policy posture has remained largely unchanged, except for a brief but notable thaw during the final year of the Clinton administration. As I will show, such a reassessment has been blocked, in part, by entrenched military and industrial vested interests in Washington and Seoul alike with a stake in sustaining North-South tensions and in keeping the specter of a North Korean threat alive as a justification for maintaining the present level of U.S. force deployments in Asia. Another factor that impedes a new and more balanced approach to the two Koreas is the American preoccupation with a North Korean "rogue state" perceived as a threat to the global nonproliferation regime and other norms of international behavior. The emotional intensity of this preoccupation on the part of many Americans is partly a visceral reaction to the brutality of an Orwellian totalitarian regime insensitive to human rights. But it also reflects the fact that North Korea challenges two pervasive American assumptions: that the United States is entitled to be treated with deference as the "only superpower," and that Western-style democracy, together with economic globalization based on market principles, is now the natural, universal order of things.

Pyongyang refuses to defer to the United States and seeks to deal with Washington on a basis of sovereign equality despite its inferior power position. Although anxious to obtain foreign capital and technology, it is seeking to do so selectively on its own terms, resisting pressure for basic political and economic reform that might weaken the control of the Workers Party regime. Above all, what exasperates many Americans about North Korea is the very fact that it continues to exist at all and has not gone the way of the Soviet Union and the East European Communist states, thus finally confirming the ideological victory of the West in the cold war.

The Collapse Scenario

The death of Kim Il Sung in 1994 and the onset of endemic food short-ages strengthened the widespread belief that the North is doomed to collapse. The persistence of this belief on the part of many U.S. officials is the main reason why the United States has failed to develop a coherent long-term policy toward the Korean peninsula, relying on short-term fixes while waiting to see what happens.

The incoherence and ad hoc character of U.S. policy was exemplified by the 1994 agreement between Washington and Pyongyang in which North Korea agreed to freeze its nuclear weapons program. Many offi-cials of the Clinton administration and many members of Congress made the implicit assumption that the Pyongyang regime would collapse and be absorbed by South Korea before the key provisions of the accord would have to be carried out. Yet the terms of the agreement treat North Korea as an established state and envisage the normalization of economic and political relations, starting with the gradual removal of the economic sanctions imposed against Pyongyang since the Korean War. In North Korean eyes, normalization necessarily presupposed the conclusion of a peace treaty ending the war. The freeze agreement was acceptable to Pyongyang primarily because the prospect of an end to sanctions and of normalized relations offered hope that the United States was ready for coexistence, notwithstanding differing ideologies, and would not seek to bring about its collapse.

It was the failure of the United States to begin easing sanctions until six years after the conclusion of the accord that led to heightened ten-sions between Washington and Pyongyang despite the 1994 freeze. By the same token, the visit of Secretary of State Madeleine Albright to Pyongyang in November 2000 opened up a hopeful opportunity to move toward full normalization and an end to military confrontation precisely because it reflected U.S. readiness to deal with North Korea as an estab-lished state for the first time. The explicit commitment to normalization as the ultimate goal of U.S. policy that was central to the 1994 freeze agreement was conspicuously absent in initial Bush administration policy declarations. Expectations of a collapse were still widespread in Washing-ton in 2001. Opponents of normalization with Pyongyang argued that it would prop up a moribund regime that would otherwise implode or explode.

Is North Korea indeed on the verge of collapse? Or is it likely to sur-vive by moving toward a liberalization of its economy broadly similar to what has been happening in China since the death of Mao? Would its collapse and absorption by South Korea be desirable? Or would American interests be better served by a "soft landing"—a gradual process of unification in which neither side is swallowed up by the other? Is North Korea a military threat to South Korea and the United States, and is a continued U.S. military presence in Korea necessary?

This book begins with an examination in part 1 of North Korea's prospects for survival, conducted without ideological blinders. My conclusion is that although it is not likely to implode or explode in the foreseeable future, it could well gradually erode, leading to major leadership upheavals and systemic changes but not necessarily to the demise of the North Korean state.

Based on this assessment, I consider in part 2 whether and how the peninsula might be peacefully reunified. This discussion underlines the differences between Korea and Germany and the heavy economic burdens that would be imposed on the South by the collapse and absorption of the North. My conclusion is that the most promising route to peace and reunification in Korea lies in the proposal for a loose confederation made by Presidents Roh Tae Woo and Kim Dae Jung. The prospects for eventual agreement between North and South on the form of a confederation improved after the first Kim Dae Jung–Kim Jong Il summit.

I also discuss in part 2 the prospects for confederation and reunification in the context of U.S. policy options, showing how U.S. alignment with the South (and the present form of the U.S. military presence) prolongs the civil war in Korea and impedes reunification by providing an economic subsidy that enables the South to have a maximum of security with a minimum of sacrifice. The South's upper- and middle-income minority, in particular, has acquired a vested interest in the status quo. So long as the South has the U.S. military presence as a cushion, it is under no compulsion to make the compromises with the North necessary to reach agreement on coexistence and eventual reunification.

Much of this book focuses in detail on the key issues relevant to the future of U.S. forces in Korea. I examine in part 3 the balance of conventional forces between North and South and assess each of the arguments made in favor of the U.S. presence with one notable exception: that the North's declining ability to maintain its existing conventional force levels compels it, willy-nilly, to develop nuclear weapons and a missile delivery system. Part 4 deals separately with this critical issue. Part 5 examines the attitude of Korea's neighbors toward the future of the U.S. presence and the impact that U.S. disengagement would have on regional stability in Northeast Asia.

THE CASE FOR THE U.S. MILITARY PRESENCE

The rationale for continued American military involvement in Korea is based on some arguments that have been advanced for many years and others that are relatively new, some arguments made only in private and others made in official pronouncements.

In private, American officials say frankly that the American presence is needed in part to make sure that the South does not drag the United States into a new Korean war by seeking to reunify the peninsula militarily as Rhee wanted to do. The American desire to keep a firm grip on Seoul is apparent in the fact that an American general retains wartime operational control over South Korean forces within a joint command structure, despite periodic South Korean pressures for a transfer of authority.

The principal publicly stated premise underlying the American presence has long been that the North has never given up its goal of "liberating" the South militarily. As a totalitarian state, it is argued, Pyongyang can devote a greater share of its resources to military purposes than a democratic electorate will permit in the South. The malign intentions of the North are demonstrated, in this view, by the forward deployment of forces and artillery within easy striking distance of Seoul that could inflict massive damage at the outset of an offensive. Thus, the South needs a U.S. military presence to provide timely military support in a crisis, even though there are no Russian or Chinese forces based in the North. Since Russia and China border Korea, Moscow and Beijing could reintroduce their forces quickly, while Washington would have to transport forces over long distances.

Apart from Korea-specific military considerations, the need for American forces has been justified for many years in terms of regional stability. In this argument, the removal of American forces while Korea remains divided could result in a new war that would lead at the very least to large-scale refugee flows into China and Japan, if not to direct intervention by Moscow or Beijing or both, notwithstanding their professed desire to avoid military entanglement in the peninsula. Even in the absence of a new conflict, an American withdrawal either before or after the unification of Korea would create a power vacuum, inviting a competition between neighboring powers for dominance in Korea reminiscent of the late nineteenth century.

American strategists view the U.S. presence in the South as part of a regional military posture in which U.S. forces and bases in Korea and Japan are complementary and backed up by the Pacific fleet. In the event of a Korean conflict, Marine battalions based on the Japanese island of Okinawa would be dispatched to Korea, and Japan would be required under the new U.S.–Japan Defense Guidelines to permit the use of U.S. and Japanese military facilities in Japan as well as civilian airports and hospitals. The possibility of a new conflict in Korea has been the major justification for continuing to maintain U.S. forces in Japan since the end of the cold war. However, an additional argument now advanced is that U.S. forces in Korea and Japan alike help to balance the rising power of China.

During most of the cold war, the case for the American presence rested on fears of a militarily powerful North that had stronger forces than the South and might feel emboldened to attack in the absence of U.S. forces, especially U.S. airpower. In recent years, however, as the North has become an orphan of the cold war, bereft of its Russian and Chinese economic support, a new and very different argument has emerged. Given its shortages of food and fuel and the resulting decline in its military readiness, it is said, North Korea is more dangerous than ever because its desperate leaders might regard their armed forces as a wasting asset and decide to "use them or lose them" now.

The most important new argument advanced in support of the American presence is that North Korea's declining ability to maintain the readiness of its conventional forces has compelled it to shift its strategic emphasis to nuclear weapons and missile development. This argument is based primarily on the fact that Pyongyang has successfully tested intermediate-range missiles capable of reaching Japan and is seeking to develop longer-range missiles. It would make no sense to develop missile delivery systems, in this view, unless Pyongyang possesses or is seeking to acquire enough fissile material to make nuclear warheads. Proponents of this argument minimize the importance of the agreement concluded by the United States with North Korea in 1994 to freeze what were then its known nuclear facilities. Although the freeze agreement barred the production of new fissile material, they point out, it left unclear how much North Korea had accumulated before the accord went into effect. In any case, it is alleged, Pyongyang has cheated on the agreement, and North Korean missiles with nuclear warheads will soon be able to reach not only

The United States and Korea • xxi

South Korea and Japan but the United States as well. The American presence in South Korea and Japan must therefore be upgraded and supplemented with theater missile defense capabilities, together with a missile defense system for the United States itself.

U.S. DISENGAGEMENT: WHY, HOW, AND HOW SOON

In answering the argument that North Korea has not given up the goal of "liberating" the South militarily, I focus in part 3 on three key factors:

- First, the change in the Russian and Chinese role in Korea since the end of the cold war and the very low odds that either Moscow or Beijing would intervene in Korea militarily again, barring a U.S.-supported South Korean invasion of the North.
- Second, the severe deterioration in North Korea's military readiness and its resulting inability to sustain a protracted war.
- Third, the fundamental change in the North Korean worldview that has taken place during the past three decades.

Despite its military setback in the Korean War, North Korea remained confident during the early years after the armistice that it would eventually achieve reunification under its control through political means. Now Pyongyang is on the defensive, fearful of South Korean, U.S., and Japanese pressures to bring about its absorption by Seoul. The loss of its massive cold war Soviet and Chinese subsidies was a traumatic blow that has left a deep sense of economic and military vulnerability. The North is acutely aware that the South would be able to sustain a long war even without U.S. combat forces, given the strength of its economy, the technological sophistication of its armed forces, and the dynamism of its military-industrial complex.

In dealing with the argument that North Korea's forward military deployment proves its aggressive intentions, I take into account in part 3 the North Korean counterargument that these are defensive deployments necessitated by the overwhelming superiority of forward-deployed U.S. and South Korean forces. My analysis of the North Korean position goes beyond formal pronouncements, drawing on a series of discussions I have had with North Korean generals, including one together with Gen. Edward C. Meyer, former U.S. Army chief of staff. The burden of the North Korean position is that U.S. airpower gives the South a critical advantage and a capacity for "leapfrogging" the North's defenses that can only be offset by forward deployments. This is a plausible rationale, but it does not alter the magnitude of the threat posed by such large forward deployments so close to Seoul, especially the North's deployments of heavy artillery and multiple rocket launchers.

After putting the threat posed by North Korean conventional forces into a balanced perspective, I suggest a basic change in the nature of the U.S. military role in the peninsula. At present, the mission of U.S. forces in Korea is limited to the defense of the South. North Korea has put forward a peace proposal in which the United States would become an honest broker, like Russia and China, playing a role designed "to prevent any threat to the peace either from the South against the North or the North against the South." Drawing on elements of this plan, I propose in part 3 U.S. participation in a trilateral mutual security commission consisting of North Korean, South Korean, and U.S. generals. The new commission would replace the Military Armistice Commission and the United Nations Command, both Korean War relics that symbolize an adversarial relationship. This would be accompanied or preceded by conclusion of U.S.–North Korean and U.S.–Chinese peace treaties ending the Korean War. The new commission would carry on the same peace-monitoring functions now performed by the Military Armistice Commission while assuming a new and broader role as a forum for negotiations on tension-reduction and arms-control measures.

The arms-control agenda with Pyongyang discussed in part 3 would link the pullback of forward-deployed North Korean forces with the gradual redeployment and reduction of those aspects of the U.S. combat force presence in Korea regarded as threatening by Pyongyang, such as combat aircraft. How much of the U.S. presence would be withdrawn, and how soon, would depend on what the United States asks of North Korea. If, for example, Washington wants Pyongyang to discontinue all or part of its missile program, which is designed to deter any U.S. military threat to Pyongyang, North Korea would no doubt press for more U.S. concessions than would otherwise be the case. In a private exchange during their summit meeting, Kim Jong Il agreed with Kim Dae Jung that a U.S. presence helps Korea keep China, Russia, and Japan at bay. In its direct dealings with the United States, however, Pyongyang has been more ambivalent. On the one hand, it does not want the issue of U.S. forces to interfere with the full normalization of relations and an end to the Korean War. On the other, Kim Jong Il has not given the United States carte blanche to maintain the present level and character of U.S. forces in perpetuity, especially in the context of an adversarial relationship.

Many of the arms-control and tension-reduction proposals that have been put forward by Washington and Seoul have ignored Pyongyang's security concerns, especially its fear of U.S. combat aircraft. I suggest in part 3 specific scenarios for tension reduction that take these concerns into account and are thus likely to be acceptable to North Korea. The degree to which the United States would agree to the force reductions and withdrawals sought by Pyongyang would depend on what reciprocal concessions Pyongyang is prepared to make on such key issues as the pullback of its forward-deployed forces and the testing, development, production, and deployment of its missiles. A negotiated timetable would make steps by each side conditional on parallel moves by the other. The United States would seek to promote separate negotiations between the North and South on issues involving South Korean forces alone, such as mutual North-South force reductions. However, since these negotiations could take many years and involve factors beyond American control, the United States would not condition its own concessions on their outcome.

Since Pyongyang is under much greater economic pressure than Seoul to reduce military spending, the North could prove more amenable than the South to significant force reductions and arms-control compromises. Hard-liners in Seoul, anxious to keep U.S. forces in the South at present levels, might turn out to be the principal obstacle to arms-control agreements. If, in fact, hard-liners in Pyongyang should prove to be the major obstacle, the United States could find it difficult to extricate its forces from Korea. By the same token, Washington should not become a hostage to Seoul if it is the South that throws roadblocks in the path of tension reduction.

I conclude that the goal of the United States should be to disengage most of its forces from Korea gradually during a transition period of roughly ten years while seeking to encourage a confederation diplomatically by shifting to a new role as an honest broker. The eventual withdrawal of all U.S. forces would promote stability in Northeast Asia if it could be combined with a regional neutralization agreement in which China, Russia, the United States, and Japan would all pledge to keep out of the peninsula militarily. The United States would agree to end its security treaty with South Korea if China would terminate its treaty with Pyongyang and if Russia would pledge not to restore its former treaty commitment. Pending such a neutralization agreement, the U.S.–South Korean security treaty would remain in force, and a limited, noncombat U.S. force presence would stay in the South to facilitate the reintroduction of U.S. combat forces in a crisis.

In contrast to some proposals for a relatively quick disengagement driven primarily by budgetary considerations, I emphasize in part 3 the need for a gradual process. This is primarily because a U.S. withdrawal would mean a surrender of U.S. wartime operational control over South Korean forces. Such a shift of authority could conceivably lead to a South Korean military invasion of the North in which Seoul would seek to involve the United States. While acknowledging this risk, I conclude that it can be minimized by linking the disengagement process to parallel arms-control and tension-reduction measures. By the time operational control has been transferred and the last U.S. combat forces have left, the United States will have made its best effort to reduce North-South tensions. The South would then be on its own if it is responsible for provoking a new conflict.

The argument that a U.S. presence is needed to preserve regional stability is addressed in both part 3, in relation to the regional military environment, and part 5, which assesses Japanese, Chinese, and Russian interests in Korea in the context of historical experience. I explain in part 5 why Korea would not be a "power vacuum" in the absence of U.S. forces and why it need not again become a flash point of regional rivalries. My conclusion is that a gradual U.S. withdrawal linked to the reduction of North-South tensions would enhance regional stability by setting the stage for a regional agreement with U.S. participation to neutralize the peninsula militarily. China, in particular, wants to see a U.S. withdrawal. Pending unification, Beijing is ready to tolerate U.S. forces in Korea, but a postunification U.S. presence would be a red flag. Korea would be a constant focus of Sino–U.S. and Sino-Japanese tensions, since Beijing would view the U.S. presence as part of a concerted U.S.–Japanese containment posture.

A NUCLEAR-FREE KOREA?

A neutralization agreement barring the introduction of U.S., Japanese, Chinese, and Russian conventional forces in Korea would be an essential prerequisite for meaningful efforts to negotiate some form of six-power denuclearization agreement such as the one proposed in part 4. In such an agreement, the North and South would commit themselves not to make or deploy nuclear weapons or other weapons of mass destruction and to accept international inspection safeguards. In the event that the agreement is negotiated after either or both already possess declared arsenals, both would agree to a timetable for dismantling their nuclear stockpiles. In addition to ruling out intervention with conventional forces, the United States and the three neighboring powers would pledge not to use nuclear weapons against either the North or the South; not to deploy them in the peninsula; and not to visit Korean ports with nuclear-armed ships and submarines.

The possibility of achieving such an agreement is progressively declining. In the absence of a U.S. rapprochement with Pyongyang, the balance of forces within North Korea is shifting with each passing year in favor of the pro-nuclear lobby, and the opportunity for a nuclear-free Korea that existed in 1994 may have slipped away. I note in part 5 that if the opportunity for a denuclearization agreement still exists, it depends on the willingness of the United States to remove both its conventional forces and its nuclear umbrella from the Korean peninsula.

China and Russia both say they would join such an accord if the United States does. Given the depth of its suspicions of both Japan and the United States, the North might be the last to join. But my assessment is that Pyongyang would participate, in the end, if Tokyo and Washington do. Japan, for its part, is deeply divided between supporters and opponents of a nuclear weapons program. Since the pro-nuclear forces justify their position by pointing to the North Korean threat, Pyongyang's participation in a denuclearization agreement would tip the balance in favor of the anti-nuclear forces, especially if the United States joins the accord. There is also a strong lobby in South Korea pushing for reprocessing facilities comparable to those of Japan that would give Seoul, like Tokyo, a nuclear weapons option. However, I show in part 4 that the South would be likely to join in a denuclearization agreement if the United States, Japan, and North Korea all do.

Part 4 begins with a review of what is known and not known about North Korean nuclear and missile capabilities and why they have been developed. My conclusion is that the North initiated both its nuclear and missile programs primarily as a response to the U.S. deployment of tactical nuclear weapons in South Korea. Even though Washington says that it no longer bases such weapons in the South, the North has continued to pursue these programs for four reasons:

- First, because Washington reserves the right to use nuclear weapons first to repel what it considers to be aggression by North Korean conventional forces. China has long had a no-first-use policy, and Russia, while retaining the option of first use, has never threatened to invoke it in Korea.

- Second, because the United States continues to maintain a conventional force presence in the South that the North regards as a potential threat to its survival.
- Third, because nuclear weapons cost less than high levels of conventional forces.
- Fourth, and most important, because the United States has been slow in honoring the key provisions of the 1994 freeze agreement. In North Korean eyes, the full normalization of relations envisaged in the agreement, together with an end to the Korean War, would make the U.S. military presence less threatening and would make it possible to follow up the freeze with measures foreclosing nuclear weapons development altogether.

My analysis presents new evidence showing that the long U.S. delay in honoring the 1994 accord directly strengthened the proponents of nuclear and missile development in Pyongyang. For example, article 2, section 1 states without conditions that within six months "both sides will take steps to reduce barriers to trade and investment." The U.S. failure to implement even a partial relaxation of the embargo until June 2000, despite this clear commitment, vindicated the pro-nuclear hawks in Pyongyang, who cited it as proof that the United States wants to force a North Korean collapse. By the same token, it undermined efforts by moderate elements to keep the freeze intact and to fend off pressures for the resumption of nuclear weapons development and missile testing.

For four years after the conclusion of the accord, Pyongyang demonstrated good faith not only by maintaining the freeze of the facilities specified in the agreement but also by suspending missile tests unilaterally. By 1998, however, the pro-nuclear hawks were on the ascendant in the North Korean nuclear policy debate. Pointing to the continuance of the embargo and to continuing delays in implementing other pledges in the freeze agreement, Pyongyang resumed missile testing and warned that it would resume its nuclear program unless the United States took steps to honor the accord.

The angry reaction in the United States and Japan to the resumption of missile testing ignored the fact that Pyongyang had unilaterally suspended testing for four years. Later, when U.S. satellites found evidence that the North was making preparations for a possible resumption of its nuclear development, the resulting debate in Washington revealed fundamental confusion concerning the nature of the 1994 agreement. Contrary to the impression created in the United States when the freeze was negotiated, North Korea did not unconditionally give up the option of resuming its nuclear program by concluding the agreement. From the start, Pyongyang suspected that the United States might not honor the agreement and conditioned the final surrender of its nuclear option on U.S. compliance with the accord. The late President Kim Il Sung expressed these North Korean suspicions to me in a three-hour discussion on June 8, 1994, detailed in part 4, in which he agreed to the concept of a freeze for the first time. This meeting set the stage for the visit by former president Jimmy Carter a week later that led, in turn, to the freeze agreement in October.

In negotiating the freeze, Pyongyang insisted on retaining its nuclear weapons option primarily to bolster its overall bargaining position in dealing with the United States and Japan. Thus, Pyongyang is not yet irrevocably committed to a costly and risky program of nuclear and missile development. Nevertheless, while urging exploration of a denuclearization accord, I consider in part 4 what the United States should do in the event that Pyongyang does develop a nuclear arsenal and is not prepared to abandon it in return for U.S. participation in neutralization and denuclearization agreements.

My conclusion is that the United States can live with a nuclear-armed North Korea, just as it does with a nuclear-armed China, given its strategic nuclear retaliatory capabilities in the Pacific. Similarly, in proposing the withdrawal of the U.S. nuclear umbrella from Korea, my underlying assumption is that Washington will and should continue to deploy its Pacific-based nuclear retaliatory capabilities pending global nuclear arms-control agreements to phase them out, together with a Pacific naval presence and the strategic mobility capabilities necessary to intervene quickly in Asia with conventional forces in the unlikely event that North Korea, China, or another Asian power should, in fact, ever pose a military threat to the United States.

As I show in part 4, the most compelling argument for pursuing a denuclearization agreement is that living with a nuclear-armed North Korea would in all likelihood mean living not only with a nuclear-armed South Korea but also with a nuclear-armed Japan. The denuclearization of Korea offers the best way to contain pro-nuclear hawks in Tokyo who are steadily gaining in strength. A detailed examination of the many factors relevant to the future of the U.S. nuclear umbrella in Japan and other aspects of the U.S. military presence there is beyond the scope of this study. However, in analyzing how Japan views its relations with Korea and the U.S. role in the peninsula, I explain in part 5 why a redefinition of U.S. interests in Korea and the withdrawal of U.S. forces would be consistent with U.S. interests in Japan.

The Economic Dimension

The focus of this book is primarily on the security issues confronting the United States in Korea because these issues have a more direct bearing on U.S. interests than the economic aspects of U.S. relations with both the North and the South. Given the economic problems of the North, it is often assumed that economic incentives would be sufficient to exact concessions from Pyongyang relating to its security posture. But the bottom line of this book is that North Korea can only be expected to limit or end its nuclear and missile development and the forward deployment of its conventional forces to the extent that the United States agrees to make changes in its own security posture designed to remove North Korean security concerns.

Critical economic issues relevant to U.S. policy in both the North and South are discussed throughout this book. For example, while emphasizing the political factors that enhance the staying power of North Korea as a state, I warn in part 1 that political cohesion in Pyongyang would be progressively eroded by the failure of Kim Jong Il or his successors to adopt pragmatic economic policies. In making the case for a loose confederation, I stress in part 2 the economic burdens that would be imposed on the South by a precipitate absorption of the North. In discussing mutual North-South force reductions, I underline in part 3 the differing economic factors in the North and South that explain why Pyongyang wants force reductions and Seoul does not. My analysis shows that the North, with per capita defense spending five times greater than that of the South, views force reductions as the key to resolving its economic problems, while the South, with a population twice as large, much greater economic strength, and the economic cushion of a U.S. force presence, has been able to maintain high defense-spending levels without comparable economic hardship. In the case of the South, the U.S. military presence helps support a standard of living that could not be sustained at present levels if Seoul should attempt to maintain its existing level of defense spending in the absence of U.S. forces.

In proposing U.S. military disengagement, I point out in part 3 that the $17 billion, U.S.–supported financial bailout of South Korea in 1998 was sold to the U.S. Congress largely in terms of U.S. security interests

despite doubts about whether it served U.S. economic interests. The bailout no doubt did serve the interests of private commercial lenders who
faced default on their loans. Whether it served broader U.S. economic
interests remains to be seen. In return for the bailout, Seoul pledged to
implement basic economic reforms that would lead to the end of its inequitable, mercantilist trade and foreign investment policies. Since 1997,
Seoul has liberalized its foreign investment policies to some extent but
has continued to pursue mercantilist trade policies promoted by conglomerates that have successfully resisted basic restructuring reforms. Yet
the United States is so entangled in its obsolete cold war security links
with the South that it is unable to pursue its economic interests there
aggressively and might well be drawn into new bailouts in the event of
future economic crises.

Many books on the American role in the world begin with a preconceived definition of U.S. interests and goals and offer policy prescriptions
that fit this definition whether or not they square with local realities. This
book considers American interests and options in terms of Korea-specific
factors and of the Northeast Asian environment, but it does so with a full
recognition that future U.S. decisions relating to Korea will be affected
by the larger global direction of U.S. policy.

Thus, so long as the United States is driven by a self-image as the
"only superpower," it will be indifferent to Korean nationalist pressures
in both the North and South alike for an eventual withdrawal of U.S.
conventional forces and of the U.S. nuclear umbrella. Similarly, if the
United States believes that it is entitled to decide the terms of power
relationships in Asia, it will discount China's aspirations for regional primacy and cling to a military foothold in Korea whether or not this poisons U.S. relations with Beijing. By the same token, to the extent that
American policy at the global level becomes more sensitive to the emerging reality of multipolarity, the need for a new approach to the Korean
peninsula will gradually become apparent as part of a larger reassessment
of the U.S. role in Asia. Sooner or later, the cold war will inevitably come
to an end in Korea, its last and most petrified bastion.

despite doubts about whether it served U.S. economic interests. The bailout no doubt did serve the interests of private commercial lenders who faced default on their loans. Whether it served broader U.S. economic interests remains to be seen. In return for the bailout, Seoul pledged to implement basic economic reforms that would lead to the end of its inequitable, mercantilist trade and foreign investment policies. Since 1997, Seoul has liberalized its foreign investment policies to some extent but has continued to pursue mercantilist trade policies promoted by conglomerates that have successfully resisted basic restructuring reforms. Yet the United States is so entangled in its obsolete cold war security links with the South that it is unable to pursue its economic interests there aggressively and might well be drawn into new bailouts in the event of future economic crises.

Many books on the American role in the world begin with a preconceived definition of U.S. interests and goals and offer policy prescriptions that fit this definition whether or not they square with local realities. This book considers American interests and options in terms of Korea-specific factors and of the Northeast Asian environment, but it does so with a full recognition that future U.S. decisions relating to Korea will be affected by the larger global direction of U.S. policy.

Thus, so long as the United States is driven by a self-image as the "only superpower," it will be indifferent to Korean nationalist pressures in both the North and South alike for an eventual withdrawal of U.S. conventional forces and of the U.S. nuclear umbrella. Similarly, if the United States believes that it is entitled to decide the terms of power relationships in Asia, it will discount China's aspirations for regional primacy and cling to a military foothold in Korea whether or not this poisons U.S. relations with Beijing. By the same token, to the extent that American policy at the global level becomes more sensitive to the emerging reality of multipolarity, the need for a new approach to the Korean peninsula will gradually become apparent as part of a larger reassessment of the U.S. role in Asia. Sooner or later, the cold war will inevitably come to an end in Korea, its last and most petrified bastion.

PART I

Will North Korea Collapse?

CHAPTER 1

The Paralysis of American Policy

> The question is not will this country disintegrate, but rather
> how it will disintegrate, by implosion or explosion, and when.
> —Gen. Gary Luck, commander of U.S. forces in Korea,
> in testimony before the House Armed Services
> Committee, March 16, 1996

> When you hear about starvation in North Korea, a lot of very
> level-headed people think, "There is no way a country like that
> can survive." Well, I can guarantee you this: I'm here to tell
> you with absolute certainty those guys will tough it out for
> centuries just the way they are. Neither the United States nor
> any other country is going to be able to force a collapse of that
> government in North Korea.
> —Eason Jordan, president, CNN International Networks,
> in a lecture at Harvard University, March 10, 1999,
> reporting on nine visits to North Korea

THE DEBATE over whether North Korea will collapse—and whether the United States should promote its collapse—has paralyzed American policymaking relating to Korea. Unable to resolve this debate, the United States has been marking time, watching to see what develops in Pyongyang and keeping its options open with a policy of "limited engagement." In the absence of coherent, long-term goals, successive administrations have improvised ad hoc responses to a series of crises precipitated by Pyongyang in pursuit of its own objectives.

The debate has been framed simplistically in terms of a stark choice: on the one hand, implosion or explosion, leading to the collapse of the North Korean state; on the other, the survival of the Kim Jong Il regime unaltered. Yet a realistic assessment conducted without ideological blinders suggests that the most likely outcome is an intermediate one in which the North Korean state survives, but only after major changes in the character of the Workers Party regime and its leadership. In the chapters that follow I explain the four key factors underlying this assessment.

Against this background, it will then be possible to define the policy choices confronting the United States with respect to the unification of Korea, the future of the American military presence, and the prevention of a nuclear arms race in Northeast Asia.

Expectations of a collapse increased steadily during the eight years of the Clinton administration, stimulated first by the death of Kim Il Sung and thereafter by famine and industrial stagnation in the North. When the United States concluded its nuclear freeze agreement with Pyongyang in October 1994, the White House and State Department openly defended the accord against Republican attacks by predicting a collapse. To critics who objected to building civilian nuclear power reactors for Pyongyang in return for the freeze, one official responded that it would take a decade to build the reactors "and that is almost certainly a sufficient period of time for their regime to have collapsed. The country simply won't exist then because it will have been absorbed by South Korea."[1] Ten months later, *Washington Post* columnist Jim Hoagland wrote that "although they don't say so publicly, Clinton foreign policy aides assume that the isolated, destitute regime of North Korea will collapse before the promised reactors are built, taking the United States off the hook."[2]

On January 21, 1996, National Security Adviser Anthony Lake invited six nongovernment specialists to a discussion in the White House Situation Room. Lake was preparing for a trip to South Korea. Eight U.S. officials dealing with Korea participated, and all of them, including Lake, rejected my view that North Korea would survive as a separate state for the indefinite future. Most of them scoffed at my warning that the U.S. failure to honor the freeze agreement by lifting economic sanctions might lead North Korea to resume its nuclear weapons program, arguing that its economic plight and fear of a collapse make it dependent on the United States.

One of those present at the White House meeting, Stanley Roth, who served as director for East Asian affairs in the National Security Council during 1994 and 1995, told a *Los Angeles Times* reporter soon after leaving this post that U.S. policy was being formulated "in the context of an imminent collapse."[3] Roth bet a former assistant secretary of state for East Asian and Pacific affairs, Richard Solomon, that the collapse would come within a year.[4] In March 1997, Vice President Albert Gore exemplified the thinking then prevailing in Washington when he pointed northward during a photo-op at Panmunjom, declaring that "the cold war survives here, but not for long because their system is collapsing."[5]

Well before the death of Kim Il Sung and the famine, anticipation of a collapse had increasingly dominated thinking about Korea in the United States, South Korea, and Japan following the demise of the Soviet Union and the Communist regimes of Eastern Europe. Facile comparisons with East Germany led to the widespread belief that sooner or later North Korea, too, would crumble and be absorbed by the South in a repetition of the German unification process. But such comparisons ignored the central historical reality that the two Koreas had fought a fratricidal war. West German chancellor Willy Brandt did not have to overcome the bitter legacy of such a conflict when he initiated his Ostpolitik. It was the network of contacts and economic linkages between East and West Germany made possible by Ostpolitik over a twenty-five-year period that set the stage for the upheaval triggered in the East by Gorbachev's relaxation of the Soviet grip. By the same token, it is the paucity of North-South interchange that freezes the situation on the Korean peninsula.

For all of its repression, East Germany did not achieve the Orwellian thoroughness of North Korea, where children begin to spend six days a week away from their parents at the age of three and often earlier. Well-equipped and well-staffed, the lavish child-care centers that one sees even in rural areas teach children above all else that Kim Jong Il personifies the patriotic virtue exemplified by his father. Unlike Eastern Europe, where television, short-wave radios, and cassettes have leapfrogged national frontiers, North Korea is tightly insulated from outside influences. All television and radio sets must be registered and have fixed channels. Only the top echelon of the Workers Party has more than an inkling of what the rest of the world is like. To be sure, as foreign contacts increase, the system is gradually becoming more penetrable. This is precisely why the Kim Jong Il regime continues to restrict contact with the outside world, permitting only the minimum necessary to meet specific economic needs.

The fact that North Korea has a repressive totalitarian system and is insulated from outside influences does not in itself support the conclusion that it will survive for an indefinite period. In the absence of other reasons for predicting its survival, it could be plausibly argued that the North Korean system will inevitably come apart sooner or later as outside influences creep in. But there are, in fact, other equally important factors that also make its collapse unlikely, and it is these critical but little-recognized factors that I will discuss in detail in the following chapters.

Chapter 2 focuses on the siege mentality and intense nationalism that have resulted from the distinctive historical experience of North Korea, especially from the devastating impact of U.S. bombing during the Korean War and from the cold war alliance between the United States, South Korea, and Japan, which Pyongyang has perceived as aggressive in character. The quasi-religious nationalist mystique associated with the memory of Kim Il Sung explains, at bottom, why the Workers Party is able to command such a broad popular acceptance of its totalitarian discipline.

This discipline is reinforced by a second factor discussed in chapter 3: the powerful Confucian traditions of political centralization and obedience to authority that date back more than six centuries in Korea and were consciously appropriated by Kim Il Sung.

Many observers acknowledge that nationalism and Confucian traditions give the regime in Pyongyang durability. But they ask, understandably, how long the regime will be able to keep control if it fails to deal effectively with profound economic problems resulting from built-in systemic weaknesses that were aggravated by the end of the cold war and the demise of the Soviet Union. In this view, it is assumed that the regime will be unable, or unwilling, to introduce the incentive-based economic reforms that would be necessary for its economic survival.

In contrast to the conventional wisdom, my analysis of North Korea's economic prospects in chapters 4 and 5 emphasizes the steady liberalization of economic life that has already occurred there, especially the growth of private farm markets in response to the famine with the blessing of the regime. At the same time, it does not prejudge whether Kim Jong Il will be able to move the process of reform forward fast enough to forestall growing economic discontent and challenges to his authority. The early years of his regime have been marked by bitter internecine divisions over economic policy. Lacking the unchallenged control exercised by his father, Kim Jong Il has settled for carefully calibrated liberalization measures that have gone just far enough to produce large-scale corruption and destabilizing disparities of wealth, but not far enough to bring broad-based economic benefits.

In the sixth and final chapter in part 1 I assess the durability of Kim Jong Il and the possibility of a stable transition to a new leadership committed to more meaningful economic reform. It does not rule out the possibility that he will gradually lose effective authority to a collective leadership of generals, secret police barons, technocrats, and Workers Party warlords. However, my conclusion is that with or without Kim Jong Il, North Korea is likely to make the changes in economic policy necessary for the survival of the state and the present ruling elite. Predictions of a collapse underrate the determination of this elite to preserve its privileges and vested interests. It is often taken for granted that a collective leadership would inevitably succumb to self-destructive factionalism. But an equally cold-blooded view of human nature suggests that it would decide to hang together rather than hang separately.

The North's proposal for a loose confederation as the first step toward unification is motivated primarily by a desire to keep the present power structure in Pyongyang intact within a controlled process of North-South interchange. Far from collapsing, North Korea is likely to survive until the differences between the economic systems in the North and South are narrowed through such interchange and until the emergence of a unification formula that minimizes the damage to vested interests in the North and South alike.

CHAPTER 2

Nationalism and the "Permanent Siege Mentality"

THE PSYCHOLOGICAL cement that holds North Korea together is nationalism, and the key to understanding the strength of nationalist feeling in the North lies in a recognition of the traumatic impact of the Korean War. Kim Il Sung skillfully utilized his totalitarian control to enshrine himself as the defender of Korean sovereignty and honor in the eyes of his people, but he was able to do so primarily because memories of the war made his nationalist message credible.

The American visitor is reminded constantly that the scars left by the war are unusually deep in the North. The South suffered brutal but relatively brief anguish during the latter part of 1950, with Pyongyang using little close air support in its operations there. The North, by contrast, endured three years of heavy U.S. bombing in addition to the Yalu offensive on the ground. This crippled the North economically and added to its short-run dependence on Moscow and Beijing. More important, it led to a new Korean self-image based on pride in having survived an encounter with the most technically advanced power in the world. A Japanese visitor, struck by the cocky nationalist spirit of the North, found the roots of this pride in the American defeat at Taejon and the capture of Maj. Gen. William F. Dean.[1] In North Korean imagery, the war was an American invasion designed to forestall a unified Korea for American strategic reasons, and in frustrating this design North Korea had emerged not only as the victor but as the proven champion of Korean nationalism.

THE TRAUMA OF THE KOREAN WAR

Explaining the "permanent siege mentality" rooted in the war, Carter Eckert, director of the Korea Institute at Harvard, emphasizes that "virtually the whole population worked and lived in artificial underground caves for three years to escape the relentless attack of American planes, any one of which, from the North Korean perspective, might have been carrying an atomic bomb."[2] These underground caverns had schools, hospitals, and small factories in addition to barracks where people were housed, though gradually, as the air campaign dragged on, many of those who survived fled across the Yalu to Manchuria. Pyongyang was bombed until almost no buildings were left standing, and an entirely new capital had to be rebuilt after the war.

When China first came to the defense of the North in October 1950, Gen. Douglas MacArthur intensified the bombing campaign in an attempt to clear the way to the border. The U.S. Air Force was ordered to destroy "every means of communication, every installation, factory, city and village" between the Chongchon and Yalu Rivers, which meant that all of North Pyongyang and Chagang Provinces were a free-fire zone.[3] The devastation intensified during the retreat in December. According to the war diaries of the Twenty-Fourth Infantry Division, "razing of villages along our withdrawal routes and destruction of food staples became the order of the day." The diaries of the First Cavalry Division reported that the reason for the systematic destruction of the cities of Pyongyang, Hungnam, and Wonsan was to deny them both to enemy troops and to Korean civilians who chose to remain behind.[4] Another official account said that from the very beginning, pilots "napalmed villages and strafed refugee columns" because they were assumed to conceal enemy troops.[5]

Far from reducing the intensity of the air campaign, the United States stepped up its air attacks after armistice negotiations began in 1953 in order to put pressure on Kim Il Sung for favorable terms. During World War II, the Nazi bombing of the dikes in Holland was pronounced a war crime, but in May 1953 the United States bombed the Kusong and Toksan reservoirs in North Korea with impunity. At Toksan, recalled an Air Force officer involved, "the subsequent flash flood scooped clean 27 miles of the valley below, and the plunging flood waters wiped out rice paddies, railroad lines, bridges and highways. The Westerner can little conceive the awesome meaning which the loss of rice has for the Asian— starvation and slow death."[6]

North Korea and China have long accused the United States of using biological weapons during the war. Recent research has established that U.S. forces did not carry out systematic biological warfare but in all likelihood did conduct large-scale field experiments with biological weapons in North Korea and China. The purpose of these experiments was to test capabilities that had been developed following Defense Secretary Robert Lovett's December 21, 1951, directive ordering the joint chiefs of staff to achieve "actual readiness" in biological warfare "in the earliest practicable time." In their meticulously documented 1998 study, *The United States and Biological Warfare: Secrets from the Early Cold War and Korea*, Stephen Endicott and Edward Hagemann draw on U.S. official sources and extensive interviews with Chinese scientists who were involved in the Korean War. Their findings strongly point to the conclusion that U.S. planes dropped infected fleas, ticks, and spiders in the Chorwan, Kumhwa, and Pyongyang areas of North Korea during February and March 1952, leading to outbreaks of plague and anthrax.[7]

Apart from the horrific impact of the air campaign and the indiscriminate violence inflicted by U.S. forces against civilians during their northward march, North Korean memories of the war focus on the vicious civil strife that occurred throughout the countryside between North Koreans and South Korean occupation forces operating under the United Nations flag. It is often forgotten that the U.N. occupation of liberated areas in the North was administered primarily by South Korean military units and political commissars. The anti-Communist zeal of the South Koreans acting under the U.N. mandate led to widespread atrocities.[8] Even today, the visitor who watches North Korean television dramas of the Korean War finds that it is the South Koreans, not the Americans, who are the worst villains, because they are regarded as traitors who sided with foreigners against their own brethren at the expense of national unity. In North Korean eyes, China intervened in the war to support Korean reunification, while the purpose of American intervention was to keep Korea divided.

The defiant distrust of the outside world that persists in North Korea today recalls the first American flag, unfurled by John Paul Jones in 1775, which bore the motto "Don't Tread on Me" and depicted a rattlesnake poised to strike. Soon after winning the Revolutionary War, however, the United States adopted a confident posture toward the world, while North Korea continues to feel defensive and embattled five decades after the armistice. This "permanent siege mentality" has been systematically kept alive by Kim Il Sung and Kim Jong Il to fortify their domestic power. North Korean leaders have been able to appeal for support in the face of a foreign threat by pointing to the many reminders that the Korean War is not yet over: the continuance of the U.S. economic sanctions imposed during the war until a partial relaxation began in 1999; the presence of U.S. forces in the South, still operating under the same U.N. command structure used during the war and still conducting regular military exercises with South Korean forces; and above all, the legal reality that the Korean War has not ended.

To the United States, the fact that the armistice has not been replaced with a permanent peace settlement is a mere technicality. But to North Korea, the unresolved stalemate with Washington over the terms of a settlement reflects an American-Japanese plot to stall for time while promoting the collapse of the North and its absorption by the South.

KIM IL SUNG AS THE LIBERATOR

The central theme of North Korean nationalist symbolism is that the United States is helping Japan restore its lost dominance in Korea for U.S. strategic reasons and that South Korea, as a U.S. "flunky," supinely permits Japanese inroads into the peninsula for the sake of short-term economic gain. This theme finds powerful support in a historical catechism that all Koreans share. North Koreans and South Koreans alike blame the United States for acquiescing in the Japanese annexation of Korea in 1905 in exchange for Japanese support of American hegemony in the Philippines, and for joining with the Russians five decades later to divide the peninsula. From a North Korean perspective, however, South Korea has betrayed the national cause since the division by opening the gates to American and Japanese influence. This was only to be expected, Pyongyang argues, since so many of the Koreans who led the South in its early years had collaborated with the Japanese, in contrast to a North Korean leadership with unsullied nationalist credentials as anti-Japanese guerrilla fighters.

In applying a broad brush to all South Korean leaders as former collaborators, Pyongyang ignores the anti-Japanese record of some South Korean notables such as Syngman Rhee. But it is true that many of those who had collaborated with Japanese colonialism were quick to hitch their wagon to the American star and become the leaders of the South Korean government set up under the U.S. aegis. The most striking example was the late Park Chung Hee, the U.S.–supported military dictator who had served the Japanese Army in Manchuria. It was Park who presided over the 1965 South Korean normalization treaty with Japan that marked the start of its economic penetration of the South. Park's domestic political opponents, echoed by North Korean propagandists, frequently used his Japanese name, attacking "Lieutenant Masao Takagi, the distinguished graduate of the Emperor's military academy." Park's opponent in the 1963 presidential election asked "how a decent and patriotic Korean could become a soldier for the Japanese oppressor, shooting his own people." Park acknowledged his military service under the Japanese, but denied North Korean charges that he helped to repress anti-Japanese Korean guerrilla units in Manchuria led by Kim Il Sung.[9]

In creating Kim's charisma as a symbol of Korean nationalism, North Korean propagandists have inflated his role as leader of an anti-Japanese guerrilla band linked to the Chinese People's Army and have papered over the fact that he was installed in power by Soviet forces. But the fact remains that he did fight against the Japanese and that once in power, he adopted a freewheeling nationalist posture, playing off Moscow and Beijing against each other.

Born near Pyongyang, Kim grew up on a farm in Manchuria, where his father had emigrated during the wave of political persecution following the 1919 Korean uprising against Japanese rule. Kim went to Chinese schools and became fluent in Chinese, a fact that was to prove of material importance in shaping his early guerrilla activity. Beginning in 1932, he became a protégé of the Chinese Communist military in Manchuria, leading a detachment of some three hundred men in a Chinese guerrilla force known as the Northeastern People's Revolutionary Army. Then in 1941, or possibly earlier, he fled into Siberia with his followers to escape an advancing Japanese column and joined forces with the Soviet Army in time to emerge as Moscow's man in Pyongyang when the Soviet Union occupied North Korea in 1945.

Kim can lay claim to a part in the Korean nationalist struggle because the men under his command were Koreans, drawn primarily from Korean émigrés in Manchuria, and they were indeed engaged in fighting the Japanese, largely in Korean-majority areas. On one occasion, while battling Japanese police just inside the northern border of Korea at Po-ch'onbo on June 4, 1937, Kim banded together with a non-Communist nationalist group, the Korean Fatherland Restoration Association. To put his nationalist record in perspective, however, Kim spent most of his guerrilla years fighting as part of the Chinese Communist effort to rid Chinese territory of the Japanese, rather than as a leader of a Korean nationalist movement in Korea. Like other guerrilla leaders who were active in Korea and Manchuria during the Japanese period, Kim Il Sung won a fleeting notoriety, especially after successful encounters such as the battle of Poch'onbo. Many Koreans had never heard of him, however, when he turned up in Pyongyang in 1945. His major claim to popular acceptance when he emerged as the leader of the new, Soviet-sponsored regime was his cloudy identification in the minds of some older Koreans with the legend of a turn-of-the-century folk hero named Kim Il Sung. Many a young revolutionary had adopted the pseudonym of this vaguely remembered, possibly imaginary Korean Robin Hood, and this appears to have been the case with Kim, whose original name was Kim Song Ju.

Those who had heard of a Kim Il Sung and who turned out to receive him at a public rally in Pyongyang on October 14, 1945, expected to see a gray-haired old patriot of Rhee's generation. Instead, they found a pudgy young man in his thirties who bore no resemblance to the legendary hero. One account suggesting the flavor of the popular response to Kim's first public appearance has been given by O Yong Jin, a leading non-Communist who was present on the dais. He relates in his memoirs that Kim "wore a blue suit which was a bit too small for him, and he had a haircut like a Chinese waiter. He is a fake! All the people gathered in the athletic ground felt an electrifying disgust, disappointment, discontent and anger. But oblivious to the sudden change in the mass psychology, Kim Il Sung continued with his monotonous, plain and duck-like voice to praise the heroic liberating struggle of the Red Army."[10]

Even if one allows for the animus pervading the writings of exiles from North Korea, it is clear from a wide variety of sources that Kim Il Sung was relatively little known at the time of his initial appearance and deeply handicapped by his lack of a widely known nationalist record. For this reason, his propagandists concentrated from the start on building his image as the liberator who vanquished the Japanese oppressor. The origins of the struggle for Korean independence are traced back to an underground group said to have been established by Kim's father in 1917, and the day on which this group was founded is now commemorated as a national holiday. North Koreans also celebrate the anniversary of a 1936 gathering at the Manchurian town of Nanhu-t'ou, where Kim first enunciated a united-front strategy for the anti-Japanese struggle. They are exhorted to study an unending succession of historical tracts on the minutiae of Kim's Manchurian years. The two hardy perennials at the Pyongyang Opera House are *Sea of Blood* and *Speak, Ye Forest*, both depicting anti-Japanese guerrilla exploits. Publications directed to Korean residents in Japan solemnly describe the inauguration of nationwide study classes in industrial installations, informing the reader that in the Pyongyang thermal power plant, "before adjusting the heat regulator of the Sixth Boiler, the chief boilerman never forgets to read the *Reminiscences of the Anti-Japanese Partisan Fighters*."

By far the most important focus of the Kim legend is the Poch'onbo episode. A one-hundred-twenty-six-foot-high monument showing Kim and a group of guerrillas locked in combat with the Japanese was unveiled there on the anniversary of the battle in 1967, and June 4 has now become a North Korean Fourth of July and Memorial Day rolled into one. The streets of Kaesong were alive with jubilant thousands staging a torchlight parade when I visited the North Korean city on Poch'onbo Day in 1972. Two decades later, in the Revolutionary Museum, the most dramatic exhibit was an amphitheater with a life-sized reproduction of the Japanese stockade at Poch'onbo under siege by Kim's forces. Hushed audiences sighed, wept, and cheered as shifting photo montages were projected onto the stockade backdrop and patriotic songs blared, creating the illusion of a battle in progress followed by Kim's adoration on the shoulders of triumphant villagers. The special utility of Poch'onbo lies not only in the fact that a clash did take place there but also that it was the one encounter of any consequence between Kim and the Japanese that occurred in part, at least, on the Korean side of the Korean-Manchurian border.

The North Korean populace has been brainwashed into uncritical acceptance of the Kim legend by a propaganda machine that has utilized not only Workers Party indoctrination, a state-controlled educational system, and a monopoly of radio and television but also a highly developed motion picture industry. The average North Korean views at least ten of the thirty new feature films produced each year, plus three times as many documentaries.[11] Shown in factories, collective farms, and schools as well as in theaters, these films are endlessly replayed on television. I have seen dozens of them during my visits to the North and have noted a steady improvement in their entertainment value. The propaganda message is generally woven into the North Korean equivalent of soap operas or into sagas about the Korean War and the struggle against Japan comparable to Westerns and war movies in the West.

The success of the leadership in its indoctrination has been facilitated by a comprehensive reconstruction of the social fabric that has gone far beyond comparable social engineering efforts in other Communist countries. Kim Il Sung had a relatively clean slate on which to write his nationalist message because he has systematically relegated much of the pre-1945 educated elite and its descendants to the margins of society. When Kim took over, the big landowners of the old order were excluded from power and the "good" people, in Communist terms, were factory workers, laborers, poor farmers, clerks, small traders, and low-level bureaucrats. The Workers Party, built around this proletarian majority of North Korean society and their descendants, had little or no pre–Kim Il Sung educational exposure and thus readily soaked up the message of the regime.

For all of its importance, the effectiveness of his propaganda harking back to his past glories does not adequately explain how Kim Il Sung acquired charisma and legitimacy. What gave his nationalist message credibility and immediacy was his determined defense of North Korean interests in dealing with Russia and China throughout the cold war. His freewheeling stance in playing off Moscow and Beijing against each other is detailed in my discussion of North and South Korean relations with other Northeast Asian states in part 5. Kim Il Sung was the first leader of any Communist Party in the world to repudiate the concept of a "leading party" in the international Communist movement. In a defiant manifesto on August 12, 1966, "Let Us Declare Our Independence," the Workers Party declared that "all fraternal parties are equal and independent. There may be a large party and a small party but not a higher party and a lower party. . . . No centralized discipline is applicable to relations among fraternal parties." This pronouncement outraged both Moscow and Beijing, but it dramatized Kim's nationalist posture in the eyes of his people.

JUCHE AND THE HOLY TRINITY

Behind Kim's assertion of independence at the rhetorical level lay the reality that North Korea became profoundly dependent on its Communist patrons, especially for food and fuel. By manipulating the Sino-Soviet rivalry as skillfully as he did, he was able to keep economic and military aid flowing. Ironically, however, notwithstanding this dependence, Kim promulgated a nationalist ideology, known as *juche*, that elevated the goal of self-reliance to a national religion and submerged the ideology of Marxist class consciousness that he had nominally embraced when Moscow installed him in power.

The term *juche* is not easy to translate. It is often rendered in other languages as literally meaning "self-reliance" or "independence." In North Korean usage, however, it has a broad range of political, social, economic, cultural, and philosophical connotations connected to an all-embracing concept of self-defined national autonomy. "It is less an idea than a state of mind," observes Bruce Cumings. "The term literally means being subjective where Korean matters are concerned, putting Korea first in everything."[12] Han S. Park has cautioned, though, that it is "far more than a form of anti-foreignism. It has acquired a quality of self-affirmation. The 'self' in this case is the nation as an indivisible and deified sacred entity. The notion that individuals are not worthy of living if they are deprived of their nation has been promoted so persuasively that complete loyalty to the nation is considered natural."[13] Historically, notes

Carter Eckert, the term literally referred to "the body of the emperor or monarch." Eckert has offered perhaps the best definition of *juche* as a product of Korea's historical experience: "*Juche* was, in effect, a passionate and unrestrained *cri de coeur* against centuries of perceived incursion or subjugation by external forces that had sought to weaken or destroy the country. It was also, in that sense, an unequivocal reassertion of Korea's will to national greatness."[14]

In place of the class struggle, *juche* emphasizes the importance of cooperative national struggle and categorical loyalty to the Workers Party as necessary for progress and survival. Marveling at the success of the North Korean leadership in inculcating a spirit of communal effort, American journalist Bernard Krisher, who has visited both North Korea and Israel, recalled the kibbutz cooperatives in Israel. North Korea, he wrote, is like "one big *kibbutz*."[15]

Long before his death in 1994, Kim Il Sung had been deified as the personification of Korean national pride, and "Kim Il Sungism" had become the national faith. The holy trinity in North Korea still consists of Kim the father, Kim Jong Il the son, and *juche* the holy spirit. *New York Times* correspondent Nicholas Kristof aptly reported that "North Korea is not so much a nation as a religion. A Westerner visiting North Korea inevitably feels like an atheist at a convention of evangelists. . . . Perhaps the best metaphor for North Korea is the medieval church. Much of the population consists of genuine believers, and no one pays enormous attention to the minority of heretics who are tortured or killed the way witches or Christians of a dissident sect were killed during the Middle Ages."[16] To carry this metaphor further, just as penniless congregations in medieval England or France accepted lavish spending on the Crusades and on towering cathedrals, so North Koreans tolerate costly monuments and marble-lined subway stations in the midst of economic privation as symbols of their faith.

The obvious flaw in likening North Korean worship of "Kim Il Sungism" to a religious faith in the Western sense is that the Workers Party regime imposes comprehensive totalitarian controls on the populace. While the medieval church exercised a variety of social controls on its followers, these controls can hardly be compared to the totalitarian grip of the North Korean regime. This basic difference makes it impossible to judge how much of its potency "Kim Il Sungism" might lose if and when the system should loosen up. Nevertheless, most observers with experience in North Korea, myself included, share Kristof's assessment that in the existing North Korean context, "Kim Il Sungism" is in effect a national religion and commands reverence on a nationwide scale comparable in intensity to the fervent support enjoyed by evangelical Christian denominations.

After spending four hours with Kim Il Sung in 1992, Rev. Kwon Ho Hyung, president of the Christian Broadcasting System in South Korea, concluded that Kim's childhood exposure to Christianity had a significant impact on his thinking and his leadership style. His father became a Presbyterian elder in Pyongyang after attending the select Sungshil Christian Academy there operated by an American missionary. When the family fled to Manchuria to escape reprisals for anti-Japanese activity, his mother was active in the Namri Presbyterian Church established by missionaries. As a result, Reverend Kwon told me, Kim "understood messianic themes in Christian doctrine, and he ruled the country like a religious leader, casting himself as the fatherly shepherd of his people. It is often said that he utilized the feudal traditions and Confucian respect for authority inherited from the Korean past. But another reason for his effectiveness and the longevity of his rule was that he founded his own religion." During their meeting, Reverend Kwon said, "Kim knew the book of Levi when I quoted from it. He talked respectfully of his own experiences in Bible School. When we parted, he said, 'Well, Reverend Kwon, we're both getting older, why don't we go to the Kingdom of God together?' "[17]

In his memoirs, Kim acknowledged receiving "a great deal of humanitarian assistance" from Korean Christians in hiding out from the Japanese forces during his guerrilla years in Manchuria. Significantly, he said that "I do not think the Spirit of Christianity that preaches universal peace and harmony contradicts my ideas advocating an independent life for man."[18]

In references to Kim Il Sung, the North Koreans frequently use the term *urora patta*, which they translate as "to hold in respect." But as Bruce Cumings points out, the term literally means "to look up and to receive" and is used by Korean Christians in liturgical references to receiving Christ. The first statue of Kim erected in the North, Cumings writes, was unveiled on Christmas Day 1949, "something that suggests a conscious attempt to present him as a secular Christ, or Christ substitute."[19]

The importance of Kim's childhood exposure to Christianity is a subject of debate among Korean specialists. Based on my conversations with Reverend Kwon and a variety of North Koreans, I find it credible that this exposure helped make Kim aware of the need to replace the cold class-warfare tenets of Marxism with a more emotionally satisfying ideology. K. A. Namkung, former director of the Atlantic Council Korea Program, believes that *juche*, with its fusion of a humanist emphasis on the individual and a broader appeal for communal self-sacrifice, was inspired in part by Christian doctrine. He points out that Kim Il Sung and other Korean leaders of his generation grew up in an atmosphere greatly influenced by American missionaries who provided the only contact with outside thought during the Japanese colonial period. In his view, *juche* has echoes of the Wilsonian emphasis on self-determination as well as of the Christian emphasis on self-reliance. Namkung grew up in Tokyo, where he attended an evangelical Christian missionary school. "It helps in understanding North Korea if you have lived in a fundamentalist Christian community," he recalled at a National Defense University seminar on Korea. "Just like the North Koreans, we believed in the absolute purity of our doctrine. We focused inward and didn't want to be tainted by the outside world."[20]

The word "nationalism" is often equated with anti-foreignism. But in North Korea, the brand of nationalism preached by Kim Il Sung was primarily inspirational and uplifting. For all of their anti-American and anti-Japanese coating, the North Korean films and television dramas about the Korean War and the anti-Japanese struggle that I have seen during my visits were not designed to arouse xenophobic hatred of foreigners. Their keynote was rather the glorification of Korean virtue. In the case of the Korean War, the American imperialist was the fall guy, frustrated in his designs on Korea, who proved the bravery and invincibility of Korean antagonists fortunate enough to be led by Kim Il Sung.

Shifting the Focus to Japan

Since the death of the Great Leader, there has been a subtle change in the tone of official appeals to nationalist sentiment. Kim Jong Il echoes the uplift message of his father, but he has added to it with a new emphasis on North Korea's "greatness" as a military power and with the selective use of anti-foreignism focused on Japan. When Tokyo issued threats of retaliation after Pyongyang demonstrated its long-range missile potential in 1998, Kim Jong Il unleashed a sustained and virulent anti-Japanese campaign that not only recalled the horrors of Japanese colonialism but also charged that Tokyo, with missile capabilities of its own much greater than those of Pyongyang, is the real threat to peace in

Northeast Asia. At the same time, Kim carefully minimized anti-American rhetoric and successfully used the missile issue to push the United States toward a normalization of relations.

Kim Jong Il has consciously attempted to soften the impact of economic problems by pointing to satellite and missile capabilities as symbols of national pride. On one occasion, he explicitly declared that he had considered "whether it is justifiable to spend scarce resources on our missile and satellite program when many of us are suffering economically," but had concluded that it was "unavoidable, for the sake of defending our honor and sovereignty."[21]

In calling on his people to stand together despite food shortages, Kim Jong Il uses symbolism evocative of past periods of hardship. The present crisis, he declares, will go down in the nation's history as the "Forced March." He exhorts the country to show the same stamina displayed by Kim Il Sung's guerrilla forces when they were pursued by Japanese troops during their "Arduous March" from November 1938 through February 1939, which North Korea compares to Mao Tse-tung's "Long March." Above all he reminds them of how they endured the Korean War years and the austere reconstruction period afterward. But it was one thing for Kim Il Sung to evoke the past, since he himself had suffered so much, and it is quite another for his sheltered son to do so.

Born in 1942, Kim Jong Il grew up after the anti-Japanese guerrilla struggles were over. To give him nationalist luster, the legend built up around him holds that his birthplace was a secret guerrilla camp on Mount Paekdu, inside Korea, a sacred peak revered by all Koreans as the site of the founding of the nation some five thousand years ago by the mythical King Tangun. But this is not taken seriously by North Koreans, in contrast to the widespread acceptance of Kim Il Sung's nationalist credentials. In reality, Kim Jong Il was born in Khabarovsk in the Soviet Union after Kim Il Sung took refuge there.

Although he is respected as a custodian of his father's legacy, Kim Jong Il lacks charisma and is not a revered figure. During the food crisis, the country has continued to rally around the flag in response to his appeals, but it is uncertain how long the Kim Il Sung mystique will last if economic hardship persists.

Even before the Great Leader's death, I had noticed a contrast between the exultant nationalism of 1972, when I first visited the North, and the more subdued atmosphere that marked my last several visits. Pride in national economic achievements, such as the giant Nampo reclamation project along the Japan Sea, is now tempered by anxiety about economic prospects and a desire for solutions rather than rhetoric. At the same time, it would be a mistake to underrate the underlying strength of nationalist feeling in North Korea, if only because Kim Jong Il can still point to credible foreign threats.

The durability of nationalism as a unifying factor will not be put to a definitive test until fears of the United States and Japan begin to subside. In particular, given the centrality of the Korean War in nationalist symbolism, the real test will come only when there is a final end to the war leading to the eventual withdrawal of U.S. forces. The "permanent siege mentality" will then give way to a more complex nationalist psychology, one in which the fear of foreign threats to the survival of North Korea is mixed with a hunger for the realization of a completed Korean national identity through unification.

The absence of U.S forces would not fully erase memories of the Korean War, especially on the part of the older generation. Moreover, fears of a more nationalistic Japan are likely to grow in both North and South Korea in the face of increasingly formidable Japanese armed forces that are likely to include nuclear capabilities for reasons spelled out in part 4. North Korean leaders will continue to use nationalism to hold their country together for some years to come by placing a new emphasis on the danger of a revived Japanese expansionism, while steadily moving closer to South Korea as the gap between their economic systems narrows.

CHAPTER 3

The Confucian Legacy

IN PREDICTING a collapse, many observers who compare North Korea to East Germany ignore the cultural and historical differences that set the two cases apart. In East Germany, the Soviet occupation imposed an alien totalitarian model in a cultural environment more hospitable to democratic concepts. In Korea, the Confucian ethos and the traditions of absolute centralized rule that go with it have facilitated totalitarianism in the North and authoritarian rule in the South. Together with the power of nationalism, these basic differences explain why the fate suffered by the East European Communist states is not likely to be repeated in North Korea.

Kim Il Sung consciously attempted to wrap himself in the mantle of the Confucian virtues. The tightly controlled system that he founded has lasted longer than any other twentieth-century dictatorship because he carried over traditions of centralized authority inherited from the Confucian-influenced Korean dynasties of the past. The North's system is much more in tune with long-established Korean political norms than the hopeful democratic transition initiated during the past decade in the South after three decades of authoritarian rule under Syngman Rhee and a series of U.S.–supported generals.

The Confucian virtues are filial piety, benevolence, respect for parents and elders, and reciprocity between a commanding, kindly leader, sensitive to the needs of his people, and obedient followers. Kim Il Sung and Kim Jong Il are constantly depicted, accordingly, in the role of benevolent father of the nation, with the nation compared to one large family. Their appeals for support use metaphors designed to draw on the feelings of duty toward one's parents, seeking to transfer these feelings to a national father figure.

A Korean student of Confucianism, Hosuck Kang, has observed that young Koreans developed a "dual personality" during the Japanese colonial period. Family-centered Confucian values were still dominant, but a new nationalism aroused by the severity of Japanese rule was boiling under the surface. One of the keys to Kim Il Sung's success as a leader, Kang concludes, was his ability to fuse these two currents. "The familialism of the old Korean society has been transformed into the nationalism of North Korea," writes Kang. "What was once the striving of a family for its own social status has been refashioned into efforts for achievement as a nation. The change is clear-cut but not revolutionary because it occurred within the Confucian framework. The father-son relationship and the brother-brother relationship in the family system were merely changed into the relationship of the fatherly ruler and filial subjects in the state, and of brotherly comradeship in society."[1]

Shaped by Confucian values, the Korean tradition of unified government with a centralized bureaucracy dates back more than twelve hundred years. Deep-seated regional animosities that persist today led to intervals of disunity, interrupting centralized rule, but Korean nationalism invariably reasserted itself. Germany had been unified for less than a century when it was divided in 1945. Its cultural and political makeup was highly localized, with every major city vying to have the best brand of sausage and the finest opera house. Homogeneous Korea, by contrast, had a pyramidal administrative structure with the king at its apex in which local governments were merely branch offices of the monarchy and cultural standards were ordained by Seoul. The ruling State Council during the Yi dynasty amassed much more power than the Chinese Ming and Ching prototypes after which it was modeled. All government jobs were centrally controlled through a civil service examination system, similar to the one in China, that reached down to scoop up the best talent in every village. The principal clans that made up the nobility lived permanently in the capital unless forced out in intra-dynastic conflicts. There was no concept of sacrosanct private property. The long arm of the monarchy intruded into economic life whenever the whims of the monarch so decreed.

"As Paris was for France," Gregory Henderson writes, "Seoul was not simply Korea's largest town; it was Korea. Government was a great vortex summoning men rapidly into it, placing them briefly near the summitry of ambition and then sweeping them out, often ruthlessly into execution or exile." For crimes as minor as spilling wine on the king's robe or taking the "incorrect" side in a royal dispute, "officials would be tortured, beheaded, dismembered, gibbeted; their property was confiscated, their homes torn down, the sites ploughed over, their brothers beaten, their wives and families turned into public slaves."[2]

The dictionary defines a vortex as a force that "draws to the center all surrounding it." In his 1968 study of Korean political history, Henderson aptly likens the Korean governmental institutions of earlier centuries to "a great vortex." He then goes on to show that "the politics of the vortex" led to the rise of military rule in the South and to Kim Il Sung's totalitarianism in the North.

This suggestive way of looking at Korean political dynamics has been of continuing value in interpreting subsequent developments. In the case of the South, it helps explain why efforts to loosen Seoul's grip on local governance meet such strong resistance and why it has been so difficult to uproot vestiges of authoritarian rule that have marred progress toward democracy under Presidents Roh Tae Woo, Kim Young Sam, and, to a lesser extent, Kim Dae Jung. In the case of the North, the vortex analogy is even more compelling. The acquiescence of the North Korean populace in such a rigid system for so many years, despite intermittent economic hardship, becomes more comprehensible when one recognizes the historically rooted strength of centripetal forces in Korean political culture.

The ideal leader in the Confucian ethos rules through the moral power of his exemplary behavior and the wisdom of his teachings, not through brutal coercion. Wisdom is handed down from the leader to the people, who learn what is "correct" through the rote mastery of received truth. Kim Il Sung, like many of the Korean monarchs of earlier dynasties, did rely on the systematic use of brutal coercion. At the same time, the built-in readiness of his people to accept as truth what is dispensed from higher authority made it possible for him to win widespread voluntary acceptance of his rule. His most serious repressive excesses were committed during the early years of his regime when he was liquidating his rivals for leadership of the Workers Party. Once his control was established, Kim ruled through a political machine dominated by his comrades-in-arms from Manchurian guerrilla days and their families. The personal bonds that held this group together had an intensity suggestive of the traditions of chivalry rooted in Korea's feudal past. Kim successfully combined the democratic centralism learned from his Soviet sponsors with Confucian values and other Korean cultural legacies to produce a system that does not fit neatly into conventional political science categories.

Western observers initially looked on the North Korean system during the cold war as a replica of the Soviet Union and East European "people's democracies" because it had been established under the aegis of Soviet advisers. In reality, however, as Bruce Cumings argues, if it must be assigned to any Western political science category, the appropriate one is "corporatism." This loosely defined concept covers a variety of political forms throughout history that have been the antithesis of liberal politics, starting with Western monarchical traditions and culminating in European fascism, Soviet and Chinese communism, and Japanese emperor worship.

Thus, in medieval models of corporatism, the body politic was "a living organism, literally corporeal." The king or prince was father of his people, who were joined with him organically in a functional whole, "with love and protection descending," as the earl of Stratford put it, "and loyalty ascending."[3] In interwar Japan, Masao Maruyama writes, the emperor was the father of his people, and the state was always "considered as an extension of the family; more concretely, as a nation of families composed of the Imperial House as the main family and of the people as the branch family." The nation was bound together under the emperor by the principle of eternal Japanese unity—*kokutai*, literally meaning "national essence," which bears a striking resemblance to North Korea's *juche*.[4]

Although Japan joined with the European fascist powers, Cumings points out, the Japanese imperial system was not really fascism because it lacked a mass party and a coherent ideology. It was an "Asian corporatism" deeply influenced by Japan's Confucian heritage, and North Korea can best be described as "a peculiar and fascinating form of socialist corporatism" mingling Marxism-Leninism with the Confucian legacy inherited from Korean political history.[5]

CHAPTER 4

Reform by Stealth

THE UNIFYING power of nationalism and the Confucian legacy of absolute centralized rule help explain why North Korea has held together for the past five decades and is not likely to collapse. But another crucial factor contributed to its stability during four of these five decades: the massive and wide-ranging economic subsidies provided by the Soviet Union and China. The sudden termination of these subsidies following the end of the cold war triggered a precipitous decline in the North Korean economy that has imposed unprecedented strains on the political system. As economic hardship has increased, so has a long-standing policy struggle between pragmatic technocrats and Workers Party ideologues over whether to move toward market-oriented economic reforms and a liberalization of foreign economic policy designed to stimulate foreign trade and investment. The outcome of this struggle and the success of North Korea in dealing with its economic problems will undoubtedly have a critical impact on its political cohesion.

Many predictions of an imminent collapse rest on the incorrect perception of a monolithic North Korean leadership implacably resistant to economic reform. In reality, however, behind the façade of a monolithic power structure, the struggle between reformers and the Old Guard has been steadily growing in intensity. Even before the loss of Soviet and Chinese aid, the pressures for reform were starting to build up. The reformers won their first victories in the form of a cautious opening to foreign investment in the Rajin-Songbong free trade and investment zone. Ironically, however, they were unable to make much headway in liberalizing the domestic economy until the food crisis starting in 1995 led to the widespread, spontaneous eruption of private farm markets. Faced with a breakdown in its machinery of government food procurement and distribution, the Kim Jong Il regime had two options: close down the private markets by force or look the other way. Kim Jong Il chose to look the other way. In doing so, he sided with reform-minded officials who argued that the private markets would not only ease the food shortage for some sections of the population but would also jump-start movement toward a market economy.

Since 1996, there has been a steady increase in the number of private markets, together with a diversification of their merchandise, which now embraces consumer goods as well as farm produce. Yet no Workers Party doctrinal pronouncements have acknowledged or legitimized this significant sea change in North Korean economic life. Kim Jong Il is presiding over a process that might be called reform by stealth. He is tacitly encouraging change in the domestic economy without incurring the political costs of confronting the Old Guard in a formal doctrinal debate. At the same time, he is openly sponsoring newly flexible policies toward South Korean and foreign investment as part of the broader moves toward greater openness that were symbolized by the June 2000 North-South summit and the subsequent Albright visit to Pyongyang.

By all conventional economic indicators, North Korea is a hopeless basket case, destined for inevitable collapse under the weight of its economic problems unless the pace of systematic remedial action is greatly accelerated. Pointing to the experience of Romania, however, Marcus Noland suggests "caution in drawing too deterministic a link between economic hardship and political failure." In Noland's analysis, "between the extremes of reform and collapse lies muddling through."[1] In this chapter and the next I show why North Korea is indeed likely to muddle through despite its economic problems. In this chapter I focus on the process of reform by stealth that has been building up over the past decade. In chapter 5 I discuss North Korea's rich, largely unexploited natural resources, including gold and other minerals and possibly seabed petroleum. Above all, an important assumption underlying this analysis is that the totalitarian North Korean leadership is ready to incur horrendous human costs in order to assure its survival. Food shortages will not lead to a political collapse because the regime clearly gives priority in the allocation of scarce food resources to the armed forces and other elite groups that constitute the pillars of its support.

REVERSAL OF FORTUNE

The striking contrast today between a near-bankrupt North and an economically vital South is a complete reversal of the situation that existed during the first three decades after the division of the peninsula. Until the early 1980s, the South did not catch up to the North in per capita income, even though Seoul started out with several important economic advantages. The South got most of the good agricultural land while the

North, with mountains covering 80 percent of its territory, was forced to supplement domestic food production with costly imports. The North did inherit 65 percent of the heavy industry built during the Japanese colonial period. But as George McCune has observed, "Industry in Korea was such an integral part of the economy of Greater Japan that most of the industrial plant existing in Korea at the end of the war was incapable of independent existence."[2] Salvaging what it could from the industrial infrastructure bequeathed by Japan, Pyongyang made significant strides during the 1950s and 1960s with a forced-march industrialization strategy supported by Moscow and Beijing. This progress was unmistakable during my first visit in May 1972. Harrison Salisbury of the *New York Times*, who also visited the North at the same time, wrote of "a tremendous technical and industrial achievement . . . on a per capita basis, North Korea is the most intensively industrialized country in Asia, with the exception of Japan."[3] In agriculture, too, the North made the most of its totalitarian control. Seeking to compensate for its shortage of arable land, Pyongyang introduced terracing to grow crops on hillsides, reclaimed saltwater tidelands, and built an extensive irrigation system fed by a network of dams and pumping stations. With abundant Soviet and Chinese petroleum imports readily available, the North went all-out to mechanize its agriculture and to maximize the use of fertilizer made in factories that relied on imported petroleum as their key raw material. This heavy dependence on Moscow and Beijing had disastrous consequences when they cut off their aid. North Korean fertilizer factories, tractors, irrigation pumps, and coal mines were immobilized, leading to economic stagnation and to famine conditions in many parts of the country following two successive years of flooding in 1995 and 1996.

From the start, the North had suffered from the standard problems of socialist economies, such as inflexible centralized planning, the inefficient use of capital equipment, low productivity, poor quality control, and the lack of incentives for farmers and workers. An even more important constraint on its economic development was a high level of defense spending resulting from its military confrontation with the South. With a population less than half that of the South, Pyongyang felt compelled to spend more than five times as much of its gross national product on defense. This diverted both labor and resources from the development of consumer-oriented light industries. Perhaps the most serious built-in weakness of the North's economy was its wide-ranging dependence on the Soviet Union and China not only for petroleum but also for coking coal, rubber, and light metals. Pyongyang rationalized this one-sided dependence as a regrettable but unavoidable by-product of the superpower rivalry. At the same time, despite its commitment to self-reliance, the North made little effort to forge offsetting economic ties with the West and Japan until the last years of the cold war.

By the late 1970s, the first significant pressures for reform were starting to surface, generated by pragmatic bureaucrats; like-minded elements in the Workers Party hierarchy; students who had returned from foreign exposure in Eastern Europe, the Soviet Union and China; former Korean residents of Japan living in the North; and diplomats, aid workers, and military personnel who had been posted abroad. In 1979, North Korea made its first overture for foreign aid, inviting the United Nations Development Program (UNDP) to open an office in Pyongyang. This led to an initial $8.5 million technical assistance grant and a total of $73.8 million in UNDP assistance by 2000. In its first report on North Korea, the UNDP warned in 1981 that Pyongyang's industrial technology was becoming increasingly obsolescent. North Korea had established "a broad-based industrial infrastructure through gigantic efforts," the report declared, "but further development of basic industrial subsectors is constrained because of the growing need for advanced technologies available only from abroad, which are essential for achieving improved productivity and product quality."[4]

The Beginnings of Reform

While not dismissing the UNDP warning, North Korean leaders were uncertain how far and how fast they could safely go in opening up to greater foreign contact without jeopardizing their control. This ambivalence led to cautious, experimental reform steps taken with an ever-watchful eye on the political consequences. The first tentative move toward the liberalization of foreign economic policy came after visits by Kim Il Sung to China in 1982 and 1983, followed by the appointment of a leading reformer, Kang Song San, as prime minister and a 1984 visit to China by Kim Jong Il, who had already been designated by his father as his successor. Following Kim Jong Il's return from China, a joint venture law was promulgated, signaling a new readiness for foreign investment. In its initial form it was not precise enough with respect to key details to evoke much immediate interest in the West, but it did lead to a spurt of forty-four carefully controlled joint ventures with affluent Koreans resident in Japan in which Pyongyang dealt with all of its Tokyo-based partners through a single government holding company. In 1987, reflecting the changing mood, an article in the Workers Party theoretical journal *Kulloja* echoed the UNDP report. Obliquely suggesting the need for increased foreign economic contacts, the writer declared that "we can only enhance the productivity and quality of consumer goods by bringing our equipment and facilities into conformity with the scientific and technological trends of the world."[5]

On my second visit to Pyongyang in 1987, I found signs that popular pressures for more and better consumer goods were contributing to the official reappraisal of economic policies then getting underway. I had been struck during my 1972 visit by the listless crowds in Pyongyang's one department store and the high prices and poor quality of consumer goods available. By 1987, the popular hunger for a wider range of improved products was unmistakable on visits to six bustling department stores and a popular underground shopping arcade where 17,000 people poured through daily and 30,000 on weekends. Asking questions irreverently about the goods on display, shoppers gravitated to new items, especially improved clothing styles, while contemptuously criticizing prices they considered too high. Intent crowds pushed and shoved, skeptically appraising housewares, clothing, foodstuffs, and appliances that were better and more varied than those I had seen in 1972 but were still too expensive for most North Korean workers and poor in quality by international standards.

The atmospherics during my 1987 visit all suggested the beginnings of a turn outward. Photos and statues of Kim Il Sung depicted him not in a Mao jacket but in a Western suit. Eight hotels, among them the thirty-seven-story Pyongyang Koryo, punctuated a skyline previously monopolized by museums and monuments, and four new hotels were under construction. Tour groups from Australia, Hong Kong, and Britain were beginning to trickle in. There were discos in three hotels, and rock music blared out of the loudspeakers in hotel dining rooms along with North Korean patriotic anthems. In the grim atmosphere of Pyongyang in 1972, I was under relentless surveillance. Consigned to an isolated villa, I ate in solitary splendor in a private dining room and was prevented from talking to other foreigners in the same villa as well as resident diplomats in the capital. In 1987 I found a less restrictive climate in which I was permitted to meet diplomats and foreign businessmen and to stroll alone in the vicinity of my hotel.

To my surprise, I found that under the 1984 joint venture law the government had permitted the establishment of a new chain of ten luxury department stores and shops where North Koreans were able to see the contrast between the quality of their own indigenously produced consumer goods and imports from Japan, Western Europe, and in a few cases even the United States. These Rakwon ("Paradise") stores, which were among the forty-four joint ventures with "Japanese-Koreans," were a focus of controversy within the leadership. The rationale used by reform-minded officials to get approval for the stores was that they would help the government acquire the hard currency brought back by North Korean diplomatic personnel and foreign aid technicians from overseas assignments. Purchases in these stores were limited to resident foreign diplomats and returned travelers in possession of a special form of currency obtainable only with hard currency. Significantly, however, access to these stores was not restricted to those who could actually spend the special currency, known as the red won. Hundreds of people were lined up at the entrance to the Manyang store in central Pyongyang on several random occasions when I visited, and hundreds more were filing through the aisles examining Gucci purses, gauzy Paris frocks, Savile Row suits, and Japanese frozen foods.

One of my guides loosened up in talking about the Rakwon stores after I "loaned" him forty dollars to buy a new pair of Japanese-made eyeglasses at the Manyang store that were of much better quality than the locally manufactured brand. He explained that some of the officials who were promoting an expansion of joint ventures with foreigners were consciously attempting to use the Rakwon stores to whet popular appetites for higher quality consumer goods. Old Guard elements, wise to what they were doing, had failed to block the Rakwon joint venture because the stores were popular with the Workers Party and military elite.

I met a German businessman during my 1987 visit who alerted me to a distinctive format for foreign economic collaboration that North Korea was then developing on an experimental basis. In an effort to get foreign technology and capital without foreign ownership in a formal joint venture, Pyongyang had initiated a system of production contracts in which the foreign company supplies needed raw materials and equipment and is committed to purchase what is produced at an agreed price with payment in dollars. Lebek, a West German manufacturer of women's apparel, had equipped a factory near Pyongyang and purchased 90,000 jackets in 1987 for $200,000. My informant, Frank Zeigler, a technical adviser sent to supervise quality control, said that "the workers have the same skills and diligence as those in South Korea, and in five or six years they will be able to make products just as good as those we now get from the South."[6]

The bottleneck that was holding back expanded arrangements, he said, was a lack of reliable transport facilities from the factory to the port and resultant shipment delays. Similar complaints have been expressed in subsequent years by Japanese and South Korean firms concerning similar "processing by commission" arrangements in North Korea, but the number of such links has nevertheless steadily grown.

Some of the more bizarre examples of joint ventures that I learned about in 1987 were motion pictures jointly produced by foreign film producers and the North Korean International Film Co-Producing Agency. Flying into Pyongyang from Beijing, I sat next to a British actor who showed me the script of *Tenzan: Valley of Hell*, co-produced with an Italian company, which defied the stereotype of a reclusive, doctrinaire, and humorless North Korean regime. The opening scene took place in a Hong Kong massage parlor. Mavi, a raven-haired Eurasian beauty, was recruiting mercenaries for the bad guys, a consortium of scientists who were seeking to develop a master race at a heavily guarded secret laboratory operated by an unnamed power. In the guise of research on new aphrodisiacs, the scientists conducted experiments on abducted teenagers that grew ever more depraved until Mavi, conscience-stricken, decided to reveal what they were doing. Enter the good guys, a group of European scientists who stormed the laboratory with their own force of mercenaries. *Tenzan* was of special interest because Kim Jong Il, a film enthusiast, was then personally supervising North Korean motion picture production.

A revealing debate over orthodoxy versus reform was touched off by a 1986 policy change that permitted local enterprises to retain 20 to 50 percent of any earnings over and above their minimum required contribution to the national government. For the first time, local enterprises could have autonomous accounting systems, but an official commentary stressed that although "the independent accounting system heightens the responsibility and initiative of enterprises, the state's centralized planned management must be firmly guaranteed."[7] By January 1990, the Central Committee of the Workers Party shifted emphasis markedly when it omitted any reference to centralized management in a policy statement calling for "correct enforcement of the cost-accounting system in keeping with the transitional characteristics of our socialist system." "Transitional" is a doctrinal code word in Pyongyang that is used to rationalize reform measures branded by opponents as "capitalist vestiges." Pledging a "radical improvement in the people's standard of living," a Central Committee plenum declared that greater efficiency is imperative in order to "utilize fully the already-created production capacity in light industries."

Several articles in *Kulloja* during 1989 and 1990 argued that autonomous cost accounting and incentives reinforce each other by enabling enterprises that exceed their quotas to keep part of the surplus and then choose between reinvesting it or distributing it as bonuses. While the reformers wanted to use all of the surpluses for bonuses to encourage productivity, the orthodox view held that surpluses should be used in ways that would benefit all of the workers, such as recreational facilities.[8] The fact that the reform view on local autonomy was permitted to surface at all reflected the changing climate, but it was only when Kim Jong Il presided over adoption of a new constitution in 1998 that it finally received official sanction.

Following another visit to China by Kim Jong Il in 1991, North Korea announced the creation of a special free trade and investment zone in the Rajin-Songbong area of the Tumen River delta in the northeast corner of the country. This was followed by the enactment of thirteen laws that spelled out the legal framework for foreign investment in the new zone and for joint ventures elsewhere in North Korea. These laws went far beyond the loosely defined 1984 joint venture law. With respect to the new zone, they specified the sectors open to foreign investment; permitted investors to have full ownership of their enterprises; gave them a guarantee against nationalization; promised the right to lease land for up to fifty years and to repatriate profits; and offered a three-year tax holiday, followed by an income tax rate of 14 percent. When I questioned officials, it became clear that many of these provisions did not apply to other parts of North Korea and that an internal policy debate continued to rage over how far to go in courting South Korean and foreign investment in areas other than the new zone.

Rajin-Songbong had deliberately been located in an isolated area so that the expected foreign influx would not unsettle the rest of the country. "We no longer have an iron curtain," a leading reformer, Deputy Premier Kim Dal Hyon, told me during my 1992 visit, "but we still do have a mosquito net. It can let in breezes, and it can also defend against mosquitoes."

North Korea's caution in copying Chinese economic reforms was understandable in economic terms. When China began its reforms, the Chinese economy was more agrarian in character than that of North Korea, and Beijing could shift workers out of agriculture and into the emerging private light industrial sector without disruptive effects. For a more industrialized economy such as that of North Korea, a similar transition would require more unsettling changes in existing economic patterns.

On the surface, the terms being offered in Rajin-Songbong appeared more favorable than those in China's special zones, but the anticipated influx of foreign investments failed to materialize. In addition to infrastructural bottlenecks, especially poor transportation access to the remote zone, the wage rate for North Korean workers, although lower than the rate in South Korea, was higher than for comparable skilled labor in China and Vietnam, and foreign firms could not hire workers directly. They were required to go through the North Korean government, which skimmed off part of the wages before paying them.

In part, the tepid response of foreign investors to Rajin-Songbong reflected the fact that U.S. economic sanctions against North Korea made it impossible for goods produced in the zone to be exported to the United States. Reform-minded officials were well aware that the removal of sanctions and the normalization of relations with Washington would be a prerequisite for increased foreign investment from South Korea and Japan as well as from the United States itself.

Stepping Up the Pace

As the controversy over North Korea's nuclear program intensified, it became increasingly clear to the reformers that the nuclear issue was the principal obstacle to normalization and thus to a liberalization of foreign economic policy. In December 1991, they forced a showdown over nuclear policy in the Workers Party Central Committee and won a significant victory. With Kim Il Sung's blessing, the committee gave the go-ahead for the inspection of North Korean nuclear facilities by the International Atomic Energy Agency (IAEA), then a key U.S. demand. North Korean informants have subsequently told me of the bitterness that marked the intra-party debate over the IAEA issue. The reformers argued that economic survival required an economic opening to the United States, Japan, and South Korea. Hard-liners ridiculed the idea that Pyongyang would get any help from Washington, Tokyo, and Seoul, insisting that they wanted to bring about the collapse of North Korea.

The result was an uneasy compromise. The reformers were authorized to pursue normalization with the United States, but the debate between reformers and hard-liners continued to rage behind the scenes, with the shifting course of the North Korean policy struggle directly attuned to the evolving U.S. posture toward Pyongyang. During the tense standoff over the nuclear issue that resulted during the next two years, the reformers in Pyongyang were on the defensive. The nuclear freeze agreement of 1994 temporarily gave them the upper hand, but the U.S. failure to relax economic sanctions for the next five years soon undermined them, and the struggle continued unabated.

Since Kim Il Sung's death in 1994, Kim Jong Il has not had the tight centralized control that his father had. Turf fights over economic policy, often reflecting ideological conflicts, have increased. In April 1996, Kim Jong Il's director of External Economic Cooperation, Kim Jong U, was dispatched to Washington, where he made a major appeal for foreign investment. "We recognize that the world market has been unified into a single capitalist market," he said, "and we are ready to plunge into it. In order to introduce the high technology and foreign capital investment so urgently needed by our national economy, we are introducing across the board the business forms and modes that are taken as universal on the international market."[9] In May 1997, Kim Jong U made a similar appeal for investment at the annual conference of world business leaders in Davos, Switzerland. But when the reformers have promoted visits by foreign business delegations, the Old Guard elements have done their best to throw roadblocks in the way.

At least three U.S. business missions have been unceremoniously canceled at the last minute. Still, during my visits in 1992, 1994, and 1996, I found a small but steady increase in the number of foreign businessmen looking things over. The North Koreans were not as uptight about foreigners as in past years and were learning how to cope with them. The hotels were set up to cash dollar travelers checks. There were direct-dial telephone and fax facilities in hotel lobbies. In contrast to earlier years, you no longer awoke to the sound of loudspeakers blaring out revolutionary songs. The number of Rakwon stores scattered around the country had grown to thirty by 1996. I wandered more freely outside of my hotel than in 1987 without apparent surveillance. A *Wall Street Journal* reporter wrote in 1992 that "Pyongyang no longer feels the need to supervise and control every activity by foreigners. Unlike during previous visits to the capital by foreign reporters, North Korean 'handlers' assigned to the reporters often allow them to roam alone."[10]

Although Kim Il Sung had supported the 1994 nuclear freeze, his attitude toward the liberalization of foreign economic policy was more cautious than that of Kim Jong Il. In my three-hour conversation with Kim Il Sung one month before his death, I found his answers to questions about economic reforms vague and defensive, in contrast to his forthright responses on other issues. As Kim Jong Il has consolidated his control following his father's death, he has gradually signaled his sympathy for reform with several modest but significant steps, starting with his bid for North Korean membership in the Asian Development Bank (ADB) in 1997 and culminating in his bold decision in June 2000 to permit Hyundai to establish an industrial investment zone at Kaesong.

In April 1997, North Korea wrote to the ADB formally requesting admission, following up on a suggestion by former senator Sam Nunn, who visited Pyongyang in August 1996. Nunn said that the United States would support North Korean membership in the ADB, the International Monetary Fund (IMF), and the World Bank if Pyongyang would participate in the four-power Geneva talks on a Korean War peace settlement that had been proposed by Washington and Seoul. When Pyongyang submitted its ADB application, however, Japan quickly vetoed it, a major embarrassment for Kim Jong Il and the reformers.

Despite this rebuff, Pyongyang conveyed its interest in exploring membership in the IMF and the World Bank. This led to an IMF fact-finding mission to Pyongyang in September 1997, followed by a similar World Bank mission in February 1998. Bradley O. Babson, a senior adviser to the bank who led the 1998 mission, conducted a full week of intensive meetings with officials of the Finance Ministry, the Central Bank, and the Foreign Trade Bank. "They were amazed to learn what membership would entail," he recalled, "especially the extent of the information they would have to share, and I was amazed at how little they knew or comprehended about the workings of the international economy. They were willing and eager to learn, but it was clear that they would have to educate a lot of people in their bureaucracy and their leadership before they would be ready to join. Their experience with the ADB had left a bad taste. You know, once bitten, twice shy."[11]

When South Korea attempted to get North Korea into the ADB in May 2000, the United States and Japan both vetoed the idea. North Korea is on the State Department list of terrorist states, a U.S. spokesman explained, but even if it were removed from the list, "as long as the North Korean regime is one which is fundamentally incompatible with the principles of institutions such as the ADB, we would oppose membership."[12] Similarly, in April 2001, when North Korea wanted to send observers to the ADB annual meeting in Hawaii, the United States refused to issue visas despite South Korean intervention on behalf of Pyongyang.[13]

Babson, who had represented the World Bank in opening up ties with Vietnam, has pointed out that Japanese colonialism had left North Korea ignorant of how market economies operated, in contrast to the legacy of French colonialism in Vietnam. While the Vietnamese were exploited, he said, many received education in Europe, where they assimilated Western intellectual history and were exposed to Western commercial practices. In North Korea, by contrast, the Japanese occupation was designed mainly to extract raw materials and exploit Korean labor to help build up industries linked to Japan. Koreans had little practical contact with market economies elsewhere. Babson found the Vietnamese "much better equipped to design economic reforms and adapt to new economic policies than the North Koreans, who are terribly handicapped by a widespread ignorance of even the most fundamental concepts of market economics and finance."[14]

Conscious of this handicap, North Korea started sending officials abroad in late 1997 for training courses in market economics and international law supported by the UNDP. By mid-1998, the number of trainees had reached thirty. Although the defection of a trainee in Beijing led to the program's temporary suspension, its international law component was resumed in late 1999, reflecting a quiet but persistent effort on the part of reform-minded technocrats to make the adaptations to international practices needed to get an influx of foreign aid and investment.

A striking example of this effort was the unstinted cooperation that North Korea gave to the UNDP in developing a program for agricultural self-sufficiency in early 1998. The program was designed to phase out the dependence on the humanitarian food aid initiated after the 1995–96 famine. A detailed outline of the plan prepared jointly by the UNDP and North Korean agricultural officials contained a wealth of detail concerning the North's rural economy that had never before been made public, prompting the UNDP to observe in its introduction that "the extensive statistical data and information contained herein should assuage prevailing concerns that virtually all economic and social data are somehow regarded as 'state secrets.' "[15] North Korea pledged matching funds of $2 billion in local currency to complement the $300 million in foreign exchange needed to cover such activities as the rehabilitation of irrigation pumps and fertilizer factories and the introduction of double-cropping. At a Geneva meeting in May 1998 called to seek support for the program from governmental and private donors, North Korean delegates were attentive and conciliatory despite a barrage of ideologically colored attacks on their system as an impediment to any effective action. Babson described the meeting as "perhaps the most dramatic example of North Korea's willingness to engage the international community in new ways."[16] In the end the United States and other donors failed to fund the proposed program, and the more costly humanitarian aid effort has continued. But the key technocrats involved in shaping the program with the UNDP persuaded Kim Jong Il to support many of its reforms, such as double-cropping and the cultivation of potatoes, which he put forward as his own innovations in his 1998 "New Theory of Agriculture."

In September 1998, when Kim Jong Il introduced a new constitution and revamped the North Korean governmental structure, many observers focused solely on the fact that the new structure gave greater power to the armed forces. But an equally important feature of his restructuring of the government apparatus was a separation of Workers Party and governmental functions that reduced the power of party ideologues over economic policy. This was accompanied by a sweeping reshuffle of key ministries to make way for a more technocratic bureaucracy. Out of twenty-three vice-ministers and deputy ministers in ministries dealing with the economy in late 1998, sixteen were new appointees.

The preamble to the 1998 constitution talked of "making the socialist fatherland rich, powerful and prosperous," omitting the references to the country's "independent development" that had marked earlier versions. Other changes in the new constitution left the door open for reforms in domestic and foreign economic policy alike. Article 16 guaranteed "the legitimate rights and interests of foreigners in the territory of the Republic." Article 37 said that "the state encourages joint ventures and business collaboration between our country's agencies and enterprises and foreign corporations and individuals, as well as the establishment and operation of various forms of enterprises in the special economic zones." Article 24 relaxed previous limits on the ownership of private property. In addition to private garden plots at their residences, which had previously been permitted, article 24 added a statement that "the products from the private subsidiary economy and income derived from other legal economic activities are also private property." While article 21 reaffirmed that the state "plays a leading role" in the economy, article 22 relaxed restrictions on the possession of the means of production by nongovernmental "public and cooperative organizations," which may "own land, farm machinery, boats and small and medium-sized plants and enterprises." Article 33 pledged to introduce cost accounting in economic management and "ensure that such economic levers as cost, price and profits are properly used." Hailing these changes, South Korean President Kim Dae Jung declared that "there is a change going on in North Korea similar to what happened during the initial stages of the opening in China and the Soviet Union."[17]

One of the more significant stratagems adopted by Kim Jong Il to outflank Old Guard opposition to economic liberalization has been the creation of a "second economy" or "special sector" attacked by its critics as a "court economy." Bypassing the formal economic bureaucracy controlled by Old Guard party functionaries, Kim has set up a conglomerate under his own direct control modeled after the South Korea *chaebol* and the Japanese *zaibatsu*. At first, it was limited to foreign trade in gold bullion through the Daesong and Bonghwa banks and to joint ventures with the "Japanese Koreans." Gradually, however, it has evolved into an extensive network of trading companies operated primarily by Kim loyalists in the armed forces. Powerful generals now control the Mabong, Rungra 888, Bong Hwa, Dae Hung, Bu Heung, and Kunsung trading firms, which handle most of North Korea's covert opium trade as well as commercial exports of zinc, anthracite, gold, and other mineral resources. The biggest of these, Chung Woon San, controlled by Vice-Marshal Jo Myong Rok, deputy chairman of the National Defense Commission, oversees all economic activities related to the production, distribution, and consumption of goods utilized by the armed forces, everything from rice and military uniforms to the production of weapons, including missiles, which are exported to earn foreign exchange.

There is an increasing recognition in the North Korean leadership that opening up to greater foreign economic contacts is not only necessary to revive the North Korean economy but also offers opportunities for personal profit. This might be called the "smell of money" factor. North Korean leaders have watched the sons of Deng Xiao Peng in China grow wealthy overnight running giant import-export companies. North Korean generals, in particular, are aware that their counterparts in the armed forces of China, Indonesia, Thailand, and other Asian countries have claimed a profitable role in economic development. By giving key military supporters a share in the benefits of the "court economy," Kim Jong Il has won substantial military support for the liberalization of foreign economic policy.

Private Markets: Looking the Other Way

Step by step, North Korea is overcoming the paranoid fears of the outside world that have inhibited foreign economic contacts. Beginning in

1997, U.S. military aircraft have been permitted to land in Pyongyang to bring in U.S. official and congressional delegations. When a U.S. Army mission went to North Korea to negotiate arrangements for the return of the remains of GIs killed in the Korean War, Pyongyang agreed to the installation of a powerful Army radio transmitter to facilitate communication with Washington. In 1999, to earn foreign exchange, Pyongyang authorized overflights by foreign and South Korean airlines in its airspace.

Kim Jong Il's ambivalence about how far and how fast to go in opening up has been exemplified by his approach to the Internet. Keenly aware of the importance of computers, he told Japanese visitors that he has three computers in his residence and surfs the Internet for two hours or more a day.[18] His propagandists credit him with setting up four computer training centers beginning in 1985 and for ordering universities and high schools in 1998 to start computer courses. When he went to China in May 2000, he made a point of touring the Legend Company, China's biggest personal computer factory, where he asked "surprisingly well-informed questions about information technology."[19] Kim has been systematically increasing North Korean access to the Internet. In May 2001, Pyongyang joined the International Telecommunications Satellite Program (Intelsat),[20] and in June, the Chosun Computer Center in Pyongyang concluded an agreement with a leading South Korean information technology firm, BIT Computer, to set up satellite access in place of previous North Korean reliance on limited, telephone-based access to the Internet through China.[21] At the same time, while North Korea has an extensive "Intranet" linking government departments, Kim has carefully insulated the populace from the Internet. This contrasts markedly with China, which had some nine million people online in 1999, albeit subject to government restrictions on "dangerous sites."[22]

In order to obtain large-scale foreign food aid, North Korea was forced to permit more than one hundred representatives of international food relief and humanitarian aid agencies to live in Pyongyang. In contrast to the tight restrictions of earlier decades, I found on a 1998 visit that foreign residents were free to drive their own cars around the city and to meet and telephone each other. There were six restaurants and several karaoke bars operated by "Japanese Koreans" where foreigners and North Korean officials mingled without surveillance. Faced with demands for permission to monitor food distribution in the countryside, Pyongyang made its most important concession to the food aid organizations, authorizing regular, escorted visits to 163 out of 210 counties. Although 47 counties were barred in the name of security considerations, these monitoring visits have provided an unprecedented window into rural life in much of North Korea.

Driving through the countryside with their "handlers," foreign food aid officials have seen more and more private roadside farm markets where food is sold for cash or bartered for consumer goods. The consensus of six different officials interviewed during 2001 was that at least three hundred of these markets have now been identified.

Farmers in North Korea have long been permitted to grow food in private garden plots next to their homes in addition to what they produce in state farms or cooperatives. Any surplus from these private plots could be sold once a month in a small number of widely scattered private markets. Visiting the Onchon-Sindok cooperative east of Nampo in 1987, I was told that farmers there often traded their surplus of corn and rice for wheat and soybeans at a nearby monthly private market. The deterioration of the rural economy that began with the cutoff of Russian and Chinese aid led to pressures for more markets, pressures that were intensified by the food crisis following the floods of 1995 and 1996. Visiting North Korea in 1996, China's leading specialist on North Korea, Tao Bing Wei, reported that "markets for agricultural products, which used to be very few, are now emerging in great numbers. There are many such markets even in Pyongyang, and about 10,000 people can be seen trading in the Qilbok market, the biggest of such markets there."[23] In December 1999, U.N. food aid official Erich Weingartner reported "an increasing number of farmer's markets and street vendors, visible and out in the open, not under bridges or behind walls as we used to see them. One can often see small stalls along the highway or on the main roads of cities, selling everything from fruit in season to home-baked goods to hand-made household supplies to even furniture."[24]

At first, Kim Jong Il appeared alarmed by this new phenomenon. In a speech to a Workers Party audience that the North Korean defector Hwang Chang Yop later made public, Kim lamented that food shortages were leading to "anarchy." The mushrooming farmers' markets, he said, "could eventually undermine the base of support of our party." But the breakdown of the official food procurement and distribution system resulting from the famine left the government with no alternative but to acquiesce both in private markets and in widespread illegal private cultivation by farmers in areas beyond their allotted garden plots. When I asked North Korean officials about the private markets in 1996 they were clearly uncomfortable, but two years later they seemed less defensive. One reform-minded bureaucrat I had met frequently over the years said with a wink that "there are many ways of doing things. The respected General, Kim Jong Il, knows best, and he has decided not to interfere with the heroic efforts of our people to survive this difficult period."

For the reformers, the new markets offered a shortcut to a partial privatization of commerce that would have been difficult or impossible to achieve through a formal doctrinal change. By late 1998, Professor Ri Dong Gu, a leading pro-reform economist, put forward an open rationalization for the markets in the *Kim Il Sung University Gazette*. In a series of awkward doctrinal contortions, Professor Ri explained that while "a farm products market is an outdated commercial style in the socialist system, it does contribute to a certain degree to upgrading living standards." Thus, "the task of the working-class party and the state is to correctly utilize this old-style market, correctly managing it through restrictions on the items sold and through a proper adjustment of prices." Forcibly closing the markets, he argued, would only "aggravate underground dealings," while "allowing farmers to freely trade or sell their agricultural produce will stimulate their zeal for production."[25]

While still maintaining the nominal requirement that farmers sell all of their food production to the government at fixed prices, Kim Jong II has been moving gradually toward a formal restructuring of agricultural policy. In Workers Party meetings following a visit to China in January 2001, he praised the Chinese system of permitting farmers to keep a contractually agreed portion of their production for their own use or for sale and initiated the system on a trial basis in Hanbuk Province as a step toward possible nationwide application.[26] Australian scholar Adrian Buzo has argued that "the expanding nature of unofficial markets and second economy activities have not only undermined belief in the socialist economy but have shown the existence of an alternative to the general populace." This presents "a growing challenge to the authority and credibility of the regime," Buzo said, that will lead to "a major systemic crisis."[27] Perhaps so, but a British North Korean specialist, Aidan Foster-Carter, has offered an assessment more in tune with my own observations in North Korea. "Pyongyang's reformers," he wrote, are using "the sheer desperation caused by two years' flooding to force even the diehards into tacitly allowing change on the ground. Just as an emergency, you understand. But the reformers realize that once market practices are in place, there'll be no going back." What is happening in North Korea, Foster-Carter added, reminded him of a ditty sung by student Communists during his university days to mock the social democrats. In the Communist parody, the social democratic theme song was:

> We'll change the country bit by bit,
> So nobody will notice it
> And just to show we're still sincere
> We'll sing "The Red Flag" once a year.

In those days it was meant as mockery, he commented, "but in this context it's a compliment."[28]

To the extent that the danger of a "systemic crisis" does exist in North Korea, it lies in the growth of inequities and corruption resulting from the food crisis and the breakdown of economic discipline. The most obvious example of officially sanctioned inequity is that scarce rice supplies go first to Pyongyang and to the armed forces, while the rest of the country, if it eats much at all, eats corn and potatoes. As for corruption, the new markets provide an outlet not only for food brought by farmers but also for consumer goods, as well as food, diverted from government stocks by local officials. This corruption at the local level is part of the larger pattern of "underground dealings" mentioned by Professor Ri. Smuggling networks are pervasive, operated by the "Japanese Koreans" and by a mafia of Chinese merchants known as Chungguk Hwakkyo, based in the ethnic Korean areas of Manchuria. An affluent elite is gradually emerging in supposedly egalitarian North Korea, made up of corrupt officials and party functionaries at all levels; generals in charge of import-export enterprises; returning diplomats and foreign aid officials who have accumulated hard currency; and other North Koreans with access to hard currency from relatives abroad. This elite has provided a market for subrosa imports of luxury goods—including a small number of automobiles—that are officially prohibited but tolerated if the payoff is high enough. A symbol of this high-living elite is a scattering of some twenty-five palatial villas on azalea-covered Mount Yaksan that are clearly visible from the highway linking Pyongyang with the nuclear complex at Yongbyon.

In earlier years, discontent over food shortages and other hardships has been cushioned in North Korea by the absence of visible economic disparities. Just as corruption in China helped trigger the Tienanmen tragedy, so the emergence of economic inequities on a large scale could prove to be destabilizing as Pyongyang gradually liberalizes its economy and opens up to the outside world.

OPENING TO THE SOUTH

The reformers in Pyongyang have long pushed for greater economic ties with the South as the quickest way to get a large-scale infusion of capital and technology. But they have faced obstacles both in the North, where the Old Guard has viewed such linkages as a Trojan horse, and in the South, where businessmen desiring to explore ties with the North were blocked by a ban on trade and investment with Pyongyang until 1988.

For the first four decades of their existence, both the North and South pursued economic self-sufficiency through the costly duplication of industrial structures. In 1970, the South was paying $125 per ton for pig iron imports, while the North was selling pig iron to Japan for $70 per ton. In the South, critics of the trade ban envisaged imports of North Korean raw materials in exchange for the South's food and manufactured goods. But the North's policy was dominated by fears that economic ties with Seoul might open the way to political absorption. Thus, in a series of exploratory talks on possible economic cooperation in 1984 and 1985 while the trade ban was still in effect, Pyongyang insisted on strict reciprocity. In the area of development, the South would develop iron mines in the North in parallel with the North's development of tungsten mines in the South. Raw materials would be exchanged for raw materials, agricultural products for agricultural products, and manufactured goods for manufactured goods. Given the North's fears of dependence, this was an understandable posture in political terms. But it made no economic sense, since the South had few raw materials of its own and the North had few high-quality manufactured goods.

The end of the cold war set in motion a thaw in attitudes in both Seoul and Pyongyang that has slowly progressed despite internecine opposition in both capitals. In October 1988, as the keystone of a broader shift to an Ostpolitik policy, President Roh Tae Woo ended the South's total ban on trade and investment in the North while still requiring case-by-case government approval for investment and for production contracts such as the one involving the German textile manufacturer mentioned earlier. North Korea, for its part, responded by gradually dropping its insistence on strict reciprocity in economic dealings. This relaxation of the North's posture coincided with the victory of the reformers at the December 1991 Workers Party Central Committee meeting that opened the way for IAEA nuclear inspections.

In early 1992, the appointment of reformer Kim Dal Hyon as deputy prime minister led to a spurt of North Korean exploratory contacts with South Korean businessmen culminating in a visit by Kim Dal Hyon to Seoul in July. Pyongyang's new readiness for economic cooperation with the South was demonstrated when Kim made a secret proposal during his visit for a joint nuclear energy development project that would supply electricity to both North and South. South Korean leaders summarily

rejected this proposal, which envisaged construction of a light water nuclear reactor in North Korean territory close to the border with the
South. Seoul did give the go-ahead, however, for South Korean companies to negotiate production contracts. This led to a steady increase
from 10 contracts in 1992 to 132 in 1999. Out of a North-South two-
way trade total of $333 million in 1999, some $111 million was in the
form of imports and exports related to these contractual arrangements. In
addition to garments, the goods produced included a wide range of items
from wigs to television components.

Progress toward formal equity investment relationships has been slow
and tortuous. In January 1992, Daewoo signed an agreement with Kim
Dal Hyon for the construction of an industrial estate near Nampo big
enough to accommodate ten factories. But opponents of the deal in both
capitals blocked its implementation for five years. Finally, in 1996,
Daewoo concluded negotiations with North Korea and the South gave
its final approval. Daewoo ended up with three factories, not ten, where
it started to produce garments and golf bags, mostly for export to Japan,
until its own financial difficulties and policy disputes with Pyongyang led
to a suspension of operations three years later.

Daewoo's pioneering experience in the North shows that it will take
time for Pyongyang to adjust to the realities of doing business with
South Korean and foreign investors. In a 1998 discussion, Choon Park,
vice president of the Daewoo joint venture, told me that while the $110
per month average wage is much lower than the $1,140 rate in a compa-
rable South Korean factory, productivity is roughly half that of South
Korean workers. The reason for this disparity, he explained, is that
Daewoo must route its wages through the government, which then pays
all workers at the same rate, leaving no room for incentives to reward
high productivity. Another serious problem faced by Daewoo, Park said,
is that the managers and technicians are often given only short-term visas,
with the term often arbitrarily altered, leading to disruptions in production. Moreover, given North Korea's antiquated economic infrastructure,
he added, "everything is a big headache." For example, sudden variations
in voltage cause damage to machinery, so that machinery with a normal
life expectancy of two years might last only a year in North Korea. At the
same time, he emphasized, the workers are capable and quality control
has not been a problem. In 1998, despite all of the handicaps he faced,
the Nampo complex produced two million shirts, many with the Pierre
Cardin label, 500,000 ladies' jackets and 50,000 golf bags, and Park said
that the company would recover its $5.1 million investment "soon" if it
could resume operations.

In order to make future joint ventures work, Park warned, the South Korean government would have to obtain assurances that managers and technicians will be given long-term residence permits. Still, even with such concessions on key operational issues, Park believes that it would be risky for small companies to go north in the foreseeable future, since they lack the economic and political clout that the big conglomerates can wield in dealing with Pyongyang. Smaller companies, he said, should start with production contracts, in which "the North has to worry about things like electricity and productivity."[29]

Although it will take time for Pyongyang to adjust to the way that capitalist countries do business, the learning process is under way, and Kim Jong Il has put his personal stamp of approval on increased economic links with the South as a key part of his reform effort. For example, in 1998, Hyundai magnate Chung Ju Yung visited Pyongyang to conclude a $942 million agreement for the tourist project subsequently established in the Mount Kumgang area on the east coast of North Korea. Instead of letting cabinet ministers deal with Chung, Kim Jong Il called on the octogenarian executive at his guest house, an unprecedented gesture for a North Korean leader. When Chung visited again in October 1999, he reported that Kim had expressed "strong personal interest" in a proposed investment zone for South Korean companies. More important, in symbolic terms, Kim made several statements implying a recognition of the South's economic progress, saying that "Seoul looks better than Tokyo in the movies, like an international city."

The reformers in the North recognize that the sprawling, isolated Rajin-Songbong zone, with its undeveloped infrastructure, might not attract a big influx of South Korean and foreign capital and technology. They want to give a higher priority to the establishment of big investment zones in areas with a more developed infrastructure, along with smaller, bonded processing areas in the port cities of Nampo and Wonsan, each allotted to a specific company, and above all, to production contracts.

In 2001, more than three hundred South Korean companies had production contracts with North Korean manufacturers. The South Korean partners provided raw materials and specialized equipment and paid for the finished products in dollars. The North Korean factories turned out consumer goods, mostly for the South Korean market and partly for export to Europe, China, and Russia. South Korean entrepreneurs like these arrangements, as Daewoo executive Park suggested, because they preclude the managerial headaches that would come with direct investment. The North Korean government likes production contracts because they provide jobs and foreign exchange without a politically sensitive influx of South Korean managers. In April 2001, the Supreme People's Assembly in Pyongyang enacted legislation codifying the procedures for these contracts, making them more attractive than ever in the South.

Hyundai got the go-ahead in August 2000 for an investment zone near Kaesong big enough to accommodate some seven hundred South Korean firms. More of such large zones are possible, but whether or not they materialize, more modest forms of accelerated North-South economic contacts that do not involve direct equity investment are likely. In Rajin-Songbong, North Korea had to start from scratch, building port and transport facilities and the rest of the infrastructure needed to support a large number of factories. By contrast, as a leading reformer, Kim Mun Song, told the Council on Foreign Relations in 1998, "In Nampo and Wonsan, where we have a scheme to set up bonded processing areas, the existing infrastructure is better than in Rajin-Songbong, with a favorable transport system, abundant labor, and robust existing industrial enterprises that can serve as suppliers."[30] As in Rajin-Songbong, the bonded processing areas would enable companies to import raw materials and components and assemble products for export, using North Korean labor. Customs duties and local taxes would be waived, provided that the production is solely for export. Nampo and Wonsan, on the east coast, are closer to South Korea and Japan than Rajin-Songbong, and another potential site for a bonding processing site on the west coast, Shinuiju, has convenient transport links to Manchuria.

The U.S. decision in June 2000 to begin relaxing economic sanctions against North Korea might well, in time, enable South Korean companies to export products made in the North to the American market. Thus, South Korean interest in taking advantage of North Korea's low-wage labor is likely to grow. Even though the $110 monthly wage rate at Daewoo's Nampo plant is higher than the 1998 rates for comparable work in China ($80) and Vietnam ($70), it still looks good to South Korean businessmen who are paying ten times as much. However, the pace of expansion in North-South economic contacts could well be slow and uneven, depending on the policies pursued by Kim Jong Il's successors and on Kim's ability to overcome Old Guard resistance in Pyongyang.

One of the most serious deterrents to South Korean and Western investment is North Korea's reputation as a deadbeat debtor. Lacking experience in the capitalistic world economy, Pyongyang went on a borrowing spree in the 1970s based on expectations of high profits from its raw materials exports that proved to be illusory when commodity prices collapsed. The result was debt obligations to Japanese and Western banks and five governments (Russia, China, France, Sweden, and Japan) that have been compounded by accumulating unpaid interest penalties and foreign exchange fluctuations. Estimates of these debts range from $4 to $7 billion, including some $1.6 billion in principal and interest due to Western banks.

One way out of this dilemma would be for South Korea to buy up the debt at a discount on the international financial market, as Marcus Noland has observed, thus acquiring powerful economic leverage over Pyongyang.[31] Another would be large-scale infusions of Japanese capital as part of the economic rescue package expected to accompany a normalization of relations between Pyongyang and Tokyo. British financial consultant Colin McAskill, who has acted periodically as a middleman between Pyongyang and the consortium of Western banks involved, believes that the only realistic way out would be for the banks to cut their losses and accept a heavily discounted settlement.[32] Many, but not enough, of the banks agree. In one way or another, North Korea will have to start liquidating its foreign debts or its ability to attract the foreign aid, trade, and investment needed for its economic reform efforts will be severely constrained.

CHAPTER 5

Gold, Oil, and the Basket-Case Image

THE STEREOTYPICAL image of North Korea as a hopeless economic basket case ignores the fact that there are extensive natural resources there. Gold, iron ore, anthracite coal, zinc, lead, magnesite, and tungsten mines have been operating in Korea for centuries, most of them in the northern part of the country. Since the creation of North Korea, these mines have provided the major source of Pyongyang's foreign exchange earnings. Production has declined or stopped altogether at many of them since 1990, reflecting the economic dislocations resulting from the termination of Soviet and Chinese aid, especially the breakdown of transportation links with the mountainous mining areas. One of Pyongyang's major goals following the removal of U.S. sanctions is long-term collaboration with U.S. and other foreign mining companies to modernize existing mines and to find and extract undeveloped mineral resources, with payment in minerals. Pyongyang also hopes that the removal of sanctions will lead to stepped-up petroleum exploration. Preliminary geological studies suggest the possibility of significant oil and gas reserves, especially along the west coast on the North Korean side of the Yellow Sea, where China has already found oil in the Bo Hai Gulf not far from where Pyongyang wants to encourage drilling.

GOLD: HOW MUCH IS LEFT?

In the case of gold, North Korea clearly has substantial reserves, though how much is left after past mining activities remains to be determined. China established gold mines in Korea as early as 1122 B.C., and an Arab traveler to the peninsula in the ninth century A.D. wrote that "gold abounds in this mountainous country." In 1897, when King Kojong, the last monarch of the Yi dynasty, parceled out economic concessions to appease the competing foreign powers contending for supremacy in Seoul, he gave the biggest gold mine to the American-controlled Oriental Consolidated Mining Company and lesser mines further north to Russia. At first, Japan did not disturb the American concession at Unsan during its colonial rule of Korea because it lacked the technology needed to operate the mine. As war clouds approached in the 1930s, however, Japan forced Oriental Consolidated to channel gold exports where they would best serve Japanese imperial aims, and in 1939 Tokyo compelled the company to sell out to Japanese interests.

After Japan surrendered in 1945, Oriental Consolidated immediately initiated efforts to get Unsan back, working through Syngman Rhee, who was the U.S. choice to become the first president of South Korea when a government was established there. During the transition period leading up to the formal creation of the Republic of Korea, Seoul newspapers reported that Rhee had promised to restore control of the mine to Oriental Consolidated when and if South Korea won control over the North, and he had accepted a payoff from the company for making this pledge. This touched off a major political scandal that almost destroyed Rhee. In March 1946, he was forced to step down for two months from the interim governing body in Seoul, known as the Representative Democratic Council. He acknowledged that he had set up a "Korean-American Institute" to study the restoration of the mines in which his U.S. partner happened to be Preston Goodfellow, a former CIA agent who had personally escorted Rhee back to Seoul from his exile in the United States and who had prewar ties with Oriental Consolidated. But Rhee denied ever accepting money for the Unsan rights. With American support, he survived the crisis and soon became president.

The amount of gold recovered by Oriental Consolidated was substantial. By 1916, after seventeen years of operation, the company had refined 2.6 million ounces of gold from the ore mined at Unsan with a gross value of $56 million at the price of $20.67 per ounce then prevailing.[1] At late 1999 prices, which hovered near $300 per ounce, 2.6 million ounces would have a gross value of $780 million, or an average of $45 million annually over a seventeen-year period. The production and price statistics available from company records for the ensuing years prior to its takeover by Japan are less complete but suggest a decline in the amount of gold obtained. Since the creation of North Korea, the Unsan mine has fallen into disrepair, with some of its shafts flooded and inoperable. North Korean data relating to its gold production are fragmentary. However, South Korean statistics show that Seoul imported gold bars from Pyongyang with a value of $193 million from 1995 through 1997.

Definitive estimates indicating the extent of North Korea's unexploited gold potential at Unsan and other locations must await new exploration. Foreign companies seeking access to North Korean gold would have to modernize existing mines and conduct new studies to locate undeveloped deposits. In addition to Unsan, the two other major gold mine complexes already operating are at Sangnong and Hochon, also in the northeast corner of the country.

The Unsan mine became the focus of a conflict between the United States and Israel in October 1992 when Pyongyang, desperate for a quick, large-scale infusion of foreign exchange, offered to sell it for $1 billion to Israeli investors as part of a broader investment and development aid package. Israel, hoping to get Pyongyang to stop missile exports to Iran and Syria in exchange for aid, sent its deputy foreign minister to inspect the mine and parley with the North Koreans. Later, Foreign Minister Shimon Peres was on the verge of flying to Pyongyang to wrap up a deal when the United States persuaded him to call off the trip, warning that any Israeli bargaining with North Korea relating to missiles would undercut the U.S. effort then under way to pressure Pyongyang into giving up its nuclear weapons program without a quid pro quo.

Along with gold, North Korea's principal sources of foreign exchange have been exports of anthracite coal, iron ore, and nonferrous metals. Most estimates suggest that the North's vast anthracite coal reserves exceed 10 billion tons. The Mabong trading company, operated by a group of generals, presides over exports of 500,000 tons per year, 200,000 to Japan. Iron ore reserves, centered in Musan, are estimated to be three billion tons; lead and zinc, concentrated in the Komdok area of the northeast, roughly 12 million tons each; tungsten, a strategic mineral needed in jet engines and missiles, 232,000 tons; and magnesite, found in Tanchon, Ryongyang, and Taehung, six billion tons.[2] Together with adjacent deposits in China, North Korea's magnesite reserves are among the world's largest. Steel manufacturers must have this fire-resistant mineral to line blast furnaces. Thus, when China jacked up its prices for magnesite, U.S. steelmakers lobbied the Clinton administration to permit imports from North Korea despite the Korean War economic sanctions still in force against Pyongyang. Article 2 of the 1994 U.S. nuclear freeze agreement committed the United States to a relaxation of sanctions, and the White House used this opening to lift restrictions on magnesite imports while maintaining sanctions on other trade with North Korea. But a British importer told me in 1998 that Pyongyang was too impoverished to operate many of the kilns needed to refine its magnesite and was beset by transportation bottlenecks that also limited its export earnings.

OIL AND THE SOUTH KOREAN CONNECTION

In contrast to the long history of mining activity in North Korea and the certain knowledge that there are substantial, unexploited mineral reserves there, serious petroleum exploration is just beginning. The seismic studies conducted with Soviet and Chinese help during the cold war decades were limited in scope and inconclusive. However, following the victory of the reformers at the December 1991 Workers Party Central Committee meeting, Pyongyang decided to invite the help of Western companies in an intensified search for oil and gas. With U.S. sanctions still in effect, American oil companies were barred from operating in North Korea. But Pyongyang concluded agreements with an Australian company, Beach Petroleum, in 1990; Taurus of Sweden in 1992; and SOCO International, a British subsidiary of the Snyder Oil Corporation of Fort Worth, Texas, in 1998. Beach says that its seismic studies show a potential of 500 million to one billion barrels in its seabed concessions along the east coast. SOCO, with west coast concessions straddling both onshore areas near Anju, northwest of Pyongyang, and adjacent seabed areas in the Yellow Sea, bases its hopes for major discoveries on the geological linkages connecting its seabed concessions with the nearby Bo Hai Gulf, where China has already found oil. There are proved recoverable reserves of 450 million barrels in Bo Hai. Production there was running at 68,500 barrels a day in 1998,[3] and is expected to increase following the discovery of new structures in the Peng Lai areas of the Gulf and a subsequent exploration agreement concluded by Beijing with the Phillips Petroleum Company.

North Korean hopes for seabed oil discoveries off the coast near Anju have been stimulated by successful drilling in nearby Sukchon, where an oil well began producing 2.2 million barrels annually in 1999.[4] More recently, an American petroleum specialist of Korean ancestry has identified five zones in the Yellow Sea seabed off Anju with a potential of 1.17 billion barrels of recoverable reserves, based on seismic surveys and aerial surveys utilizing a new, computer-controlled sensing technology that he has developed.[5]

Beach, Taurus, and SOCO are all small companies seeking to parlay a small initial investment in seismic surveys into something bigger by making partnership deals with more affluent companies that will make possible large-scale exploratory drilling. For example, SOCO and its North

Korean contractors were using an outdated Romanian rig in 1998 and could only drill to a depth of 3,600 feet, instead of the 4,300-foot depth required to make a meaningful assessment. In late 1999, North Korea, impatient for results and convinced that the foreign companies were not investing enough in seismic studies to make definitive findings, hired a Singapore-based firm, Veritas Geophysical Company, to conduct extensive seismic studies in a specified area thirty-five miles off the coast. The government-operated North Korean Oil Exploration Company took possession of the resulting data for processing on its own instead of letting Veritas do it, and the results are not known. Pyongyang is intensely suspicious of foreign oil companies and releases little information concerning its oil prospects.

Since neighboring South Korea, Japan, and China would provide easily accessible markets for any oil found in North Korea, oil companies in all three of these countries have shown interest in supporting the search for petroleum in the North. "North Korea's West [Yellow] Sea is presumed to contain abundant amounts of petroleum," said Hyundai chairman Chung Mong-hun in 1998 after a visit to Pyongyang. "If oil is found, North Korean leaders proposed that Hyundai build an oil pipeline over land to our refineries, instead of by sea."[6] South Korea would save significantly on shipping costs if it could get oil through such a pipeline rather than by tanker from the Middle East. North Korea, for its part, would not only get a bonanza of foreign exchange earnings if oil is found but would be able to get its agricultural and industrial economy back into full swing again after a decade of stagnation following the end of the cold war.

CHAPTER 6

Kim Jong Il and His Successors

PREDICTIONS of a collapse are often based on an either-or dichotomy: Kim Jong Il either proves to be a strong leader and pushes through systematic economic reforms or is so weak that the economy continues to stagnate, discontent grows, and rampant factionalism brings down the entire structure of the North Korean state. But the reality may well lie in a more nuanced assessment.

Kim Jong Il is not a charismatic leader like his father and is not even attempting to emulate the Kim Il Sung leadership model. He has created a new constitutional structure in which the armed forces provide his personal power base and have replaced the Workers Party as the focus of political authority. North Korea has already had a bloodless military coup. Thus, a stable transition from the Kim Jong Il regime to a successor regime could well occur without rampant factionalism, since the armed forces leadership would continue to provide the power base and political anchorage for the new leadership as it does for Kim Jong Il.

It is precisely because he does not have his father's charisma or monolithic personal control that Kim Jong Il is pursuing a cautious course of "reform by stealth." Pyongyang in 2001 was a jungle of turf fights between contending interest groups and ideological battles between hawks and doves seeking to influence Kim's policy decisions. Nevertheless, his measured reform process is likely to gain momentum during his tenure and set the stage for a more formal doctrinal shift to pragmatic economic policies either under his leadership or that of his successors. For the foreseeable future, regardless of the pace of reform, Kim Jong Il is needed as a legitimizing symbol of continuity with the Kim Il Sung era and is not likely to be replaced.

OUT OF THE SHADOW OF KIM IL SUNG

For the first six years after his father's death in 1994, Kim Jong Il remained a reclusive man of mystery. The Western media, parroting the disinformation disseminated by South Korean and U.S. intelligence agencies, depicted him as a flaky, dissolute dimwit, dangerously irrational and unpredictable. Then came his sudden emergence into the international media spotlight during his June 2000 summit meeting with South Korean President Kim Dae Jung, followed by the Pyongyang visit of U.S. secretary of state Albright.

Kim Dae Jung found him to be a man of "intellectual ability and discernment, reform-minded, the type of man we can talk with in a common sense fashion."[1] Secretary of State Albright, after meetings totaling six hours, described him as "a very good listener and a good interlocutor. He strikes me as very decisive and practical. And serious."[2] In Washington, the new conventional wisdom, reflected by a *Washington Post* columnist, was that he is "rational and even capable of supporting a sustained policy of opening to the world."[3] In Seoul, press reports of the summit and of a luncheon hosted by Kim Jong Il for forty-six South Korean editors in August emphasized his "pragmatic attitude,"[4] his "decorum and typically Korean manners,"[5] his "self-confident, free and easy," "frank"[6] personality, his "willingness to acknowledge his mistakes," and his "considerable knowledge about many fields, including world affairs,"[7] acquired in part, it was said, from listening to CNN, BBC, and Japanese radio and television broadcasts. As the *Financial Times* correspondent in South Korea reported, "what once made Kim Jong Il a butt of ridicule—his paunchy, diminutive figure, bouffant hairstyle and shoes with platform heels—have now become endearing qualities," with South Korean children emailing pictures of him as a "cute cartoon figure, comparing him to the Teletubbies because he has a pot belly and is cheerful."[8] The picture of Kim Jong Il that has now emerged does not conflict with the impressions of the few foreign visitors who have met him in earlier years and with what I have been able to find out about him by talking with North Koreans who know him well.

During his father's lifetime, Kim studiously avoided competing with him as a spokesman for North Korea, rarely receiving foreign dignitaries. However, on several occasions, he has agreed to meet with visiting foreigners in connection with business deals. In April 1992, apparently hoping to receive a massive investment from French business interests linked with the Rev. Sun Myung Moon, Kim received Antonio Betancourt, a Colombia-born American who works for Moon. " I found him to be very intelligent and sharp, very coherent, right to the point," Betancourt recalled. "He struck me as perfectly rational and stable."[9] In September 1992, Carlo Baeli, president of an Italian company that was selling critically needed gold-mining machinery to North Korea, spent five hours aboard Kim's private yacht. "The thing that struck me most about him was his simplicity," Baeli later observed. "He was very simple in how he met us, simple through the meal we had, simple when we said goodbye. He has versatile interests and a good sense of humor. Once the world meets the man, they'll realize that he is not the man described up to now. He wanted to have direct ties with the United States. He said, 'we are men and sooner or later we should come to an understanding. There is no reason for us to be enemies of the United States.'"[10] In December 1995 he met former Soviet defense minister Dmitri Yazov, who said that Kim made "a good impression." Refuting reports that Kim had a speech defect caused by an accident, Yazov said that "he had no difficulty speaking, looked healthy and was lucid."[11]

A frank and sympathetic appraisal of Kim Jong Il has come from his adopted daughter, Li Nam Ok, who was thirty-five in 2001. She lived in his household over a period of fifteen years beginning in 1979, when she was thirteen, except for periods of study abroad in boarding schools in Moscow and Geneva. Li's aunt, Seung He Rim, an actress, was Kim Jong Il's mistress. Their son, Kim Jong Nam, who was confined to their residential compound, had no playmates of his own age, and her aunt invited Li to live with them. The family had meals together, Li recalled, including Kim Jong Il, "almost everyday."[12] Although Kim Jong II was "a kind father to me," after an extended exposure to the West she decided to become an exile in 1992 while studying in Geneva. Emphasizing that she is not a defector to the South, Li says that " I departed my country to live my own life and to integrate my identity as a Korean with Western concepts of a woman's self-fulfillment intellectually and professionally." The event that precipitated her decision was an impending arranged marriage in North Korea. Now living in Paris, Li, who speaks fluent French and halting English, is married to the son of the French intelligence agent who arranged for her to elude North Korean surveillance after her decision not to go back.

Initially, Li avoided media exposure because "I didn't want to have my statements distorted to serve someone's political or propaganda agenda." However, appalled by what she considered Western callousness when famine hit North Korea, she granted several interviews and began collaborating on a book about her life that she said she hoped would improve understanding of the country. Her collaborator was Imogene O'Neill, a French-speaking author resident in Washington. After two years of collaboration Li withdrew from the project, and O'Neill has written her own book recounting what Li told her, *Breaking Silence*.

In a 1998 interview with Ray Suarez of National Public Radio, Li said that the image of Kim abroad is "a caricature. He is a very liberal and modern-thinking man, a brilliant man and not mentally unstable as I have seen it written. He works very hard until late at night in his office in the residence. There was a room with several TV monitors and special radios to get foreign news broadcasts. He's very open-minded, someone with broad interests, you know, like computers, music, cars, good food, you know. He's very funny. He's just like everybody, not very different from the rest of us." Suarez interrupted at this point to object that "you and I don't have ten-story tall portraits of ourselves in the cities and newspapers that come out every day to say that we can do things more perfectly than other human beings." "That's beyond him," she responded. "It's within the system for things like that to go on. It's beyond the man himself."[13] In a similar vein, she told the Japanese weekly *Bungei Shunju* that "he is not a pretentious person. For example, the famous 'Dear Leader' title. He couldn't stand it and it gave him gooseflesh to hear it. The people around him came up with such a title."[14]

When a listener on the call-in NPR program asked, "Well, what about the alcohol and the fast cars and the prostitutes?" she was quick to acknowledge, "Yes, he does like cars, that's true. And he is a heavy drinker, but the Japanese and all Asian men also drink a lot, so he's not unique in that respect." As for his relations with women, she remained silent at first when her *Bungei Shunju* interviewer asked what had happened to his first wife, Hong Il Chon, a fellow student at Kim Il Sung University, and his second, Kim Yong Suk, once one of his secretaries. Finally, her reply was that "I want to respect Kim Jong Il's private life. It might not be allowed for the President of the United States to have a private life, but we don't have the same mentality." The interviewer pressed on, asking about reports that Kim had a Japanese-born Korean mistress in the early 1980s who bore him a son, Kim Jong Chol, in addition to his other son, Li's cousin, Kim Jong Nam, and two daughters born during his marriages. She said only that "it is up to others to talk about his private life, including this lady."

Asked on the NPR program whether it is true that "he wears a bouffant hairdo, so that it exaggerates his height," Li said, "No, no, I don't know if Western people have the same problem, but many Asians have very thick and coarse hair and they can't manage with that. So not only Kim Jong Il, but many North Koreans and South Koreans and Japanese, they have a perm, you see." However, she did acknowledge that he was self-conscious about being short when asked by *Bungei Shunju* to confirm that he wears platform shoes "because he has an inferiority complex about his body." "He told us over and over to 'exercise to become taller,'" she replied. "He was proud of his son, because Jong Nam is tall."[15]

There are numerous anecdotes suggesting that Kim Jong Il's personality has been influenced by his short physical stature. Choe Eun Hee, a South Korean actress who is five foot two, and her husband, producer Shin Sang Ok, were kidnapped and taken to North Korea in 1978. They were given VIP treatment because Kim Jong Il wanted them to help him make better motion pictures. At a welcoming dinner, Choe recalled, Kim Jong Il immediately asked her with a chuckle, 'Well, Madame Choe, what do you think of my physique? Small as a midget's turd, aren't I?' When he laughed, his aides and I couldn't help but laugh with him. It was true. He appeared to be no taller than I." However, in photographs showing Choe and Kim side by side, Kim appears to be three inches taller.

Eight years after their kidnapping, Choe Eun Hee and Shin Sang Ok eluded their North Korean security guards while traveling on a mission to Europe for Kim Jong Il and remained under CIA custody for the next three years writing a book, *The Kingdom of Kim Jong Il*, published in Korean and Japanese.[16] I had several meetings with them, the longest a two-hour discussion on September 10, 1987. In their overall assessment, they rejected the image of Kim as a lazy lightweight, describing him as "very intelligent, ruthless, a micro-manager." They also questioned reports that his parties were wild orgies. At the many parties they attended, "Kim Jong Il never sang or danced. He would just listen and watch and enjoy himself" while his guests "would dance the fox trot or disco or gamble at blackjack or mahjong and sing South Korean popular songs." Kim Jong Il "used to have fun at the expense of the band. He would request a song, then after a few bars, tell them to play a different song, repeating this game over and over. Sometimes, when he was in a good mood, he would pick up the baton and conduct the band himself. He seemed to have a very good knowledge of music, running the gamut from popular songs to light music and even the classics."

Echoing Li Nam Ok's statement that Kim did not like the personality cult surrounding him, they described an incident when an all-male band had left and was being replaced by a band composed of "about ten young women in their twenties. They were coming out on the stage, jumping up and down and shouting, 'Long Live the Dear Comrade Leader.' Kim Jong Il waved at the band members and gestured for them to stop the shouting, but the yelling did not stop." At this point Kim Jong Il grabbed Shin's left hand and remarked, "Mr. Shin, all that is bogus. It's all just pretense."

Choe Eun Hee recounts several episodes that make him look rash and impulsive. After a picnic on a lake, Kim invited his guests for a ride in his motor launch, promptly taking the wheel himself "and maneuvering the boat around the lake recklessly at a very high speed, turning it this way and that, laughing and obviously enjoying himself. Everyone else seemed to be nervous about his rough maneuvers, but tried to be pleasant." In another incident, he invited her to ride with him in a golf cart around his fifteen-acre residential compound, "taking several turns recklessly, much like a child who was pleased to ride a new bike."

Describing his love for gambling, Choe tells of a blackjack game in which everyone was losing and the dealer "had all the money in the pot. Even Kim Jong Il lost everything. He then suggested that they play a single hand with the dealer and called for more chips. All the other players bailed out. He played one hand, winner-take-all, but he ended up losing his whole stack of chips. 'Put the chips on my account,' he said. I think I understood something of his personality as I watched from behind."

Since Choe and Shin were making movies for Kim, they had a close-up look at his passion for the cinema. They estimated that he had from 15,000 to 20,000 films in his personal film library and "thinks he knows the West through the movies." He is especially fond of horror and daredevil action movies, they said. I recalled this observation in March 1996, when a North Korean diplomat I knew at the United Nations had an urgent request—he asked me to help him obtain a copy of a movie that Kim wanted to see. The film was *Sudden Death*, made by Universal Pictures, featuring Jean-Claude Van Damme, known for his kung fu and martial arts exploits. Terrorists hold a U.S. vice president hostage in the film and threaten to blow up a stadium where ice hockey playoffs are in progress unless their demands are met. I said that I had no contacts in the film industry, but gave him the address of Universal Pictures.

Kim has private projection rooms in his many villas, Choe said, all of which had "furnishings that were luxurious and expensive, but somehow unrefined. For example, every room had crystal chandeliers dangling from the ceiling in an awkward, gauche manner."

Money was never a problem in budgeting the movies he made for Kim, Shin said, because Kim had a personal gold mine concession that he used to finance his movies, plays, music, and other artistic endeavors. An informed U.S. specialist on North Korea of Korean ancestry, K.A. Namkung, has an aunt who holds the exalted rank of "People's Actress" in Pyongyang and knows Kim Jong Il well. She once told Namkung that "his cultural work is really his first love and he often puts off political work if there is a problem in one of his film projects."[17]

A categorically negative assessment of Kim Jong Il has come from North Korea's highest-ranking defector, Hwang Chang Yop, former international secretary of the Workers Party, a longtime confidante of Kim Il Sung. I had met Hwang three times while he was still in Pyongyang. After he defected in April 1997, I had a three-hour discussion with him in Seoul in May 1998 and a two-hour meeting with him in May 1999. Hwang said that Kim Jong Il is "intelligent, but he is also arrogant, obsessively conspiratorial, and inflexible. He is very wily and manipulative. His only concern is to perpetuate his power. Everything is approached in terms of personal profit and loss." Of course, he conceded, Kim Il Sung "was also a dictator, but he asked for the opinions of others and showed flexibility. On the whole, I respected him. His one great weakness was nepotism, too much favoritism for his family. The trouble is that he completely spoiled his son by giving him absolute power to run the day-to-day affairs of the country as a relatively young man. Now, Kim Jong Il won't listen to anyone else. Unlike his father, he is not what you can call a political animal."[18]

The real question about Kim Jong Il is not whether he is rational but rather whether he is enough of a "political animal" to maintain the control he has inherited from his father and to mobilize an effective response to North Korea's problems. In my 1972 and 1994 meetings with Kim Il Sung, I found him to be a magnetic, imposing figure, with the outgoing personality of a born politician, complete with bear hugs and backslapping that reminded me of my encounters with Lyndon Johnson during his Senate days. Kim Il Sung clearly liked being a political leader and skillfully managed the competing interest groups within North Korea. Does Kim Jong Il have these political skills, or is he the arrogant, inflexible autocrat depicted by Hwang Chang Yop? I was unsure after studying his behavior in several film documentaries in Korean made for North Korean audiences. One of these, depicting the last year of Kim Il Sung's life, was given to me as a memento because I was shown in it meeting with the Great Leader. The 1994 documentary records at length numerous state and party occasions at which both father and son were present. Kim Il Sung reveled in greeting dignitaries and party functionaries, handshaking and chatting amiably. Kim Jong Il, standing on the sidelines and avoiding people, looked bored, distracted, and uncomfortable, as if he hoped it would all be over soon and he could leave.

Faced repeatedly with polite refusals to my requests to meet Kim Jong

Il, I have asked many North Koreans over a period of years to tell me about him. Along with the predictable canned answers, I have often sensed a difference between the authentic reverence shown toward Kim Il Sung and a more subdued, ambivalent attitude toward his son. My clear impression dating back to my 1987 visit has been that he is respected but not worshipped, reflecting a changing landscape dominated not by gods and demigods but by workaday problems requiring practical solutions.

The Bloodless Coup

Direct and indirect hints from North Korean officials suggest that there were serious tensions within the leadership and within Kim Il Sung's family over his determination to make Kim Jong Il his successor. Kim Jong Il is the son of Kim Il Sung's deceased first wife, Kim Jong Suk. Since childhood, he has reportedly resented his stepmother, Kim Song Ae, who attempted to promote her handsome elder son, Kim Pyong Il, eleven years junior to Kim Jong Il, as the heir to the throne. At first, Kim Il Sung let it appear that his younger brother Kim Yong Ju, director of the Organization Department of the Workers Party Central Committee, might become his successor. By replacing his brother in 1973 with Kim Jong Il in this key party post, he signaled the start of a systematic effort to give Kim Jong Il a secure power base both in the party and the armed forces.

Recognizing that Old Guard elements in the party resented the imposition of a dynastic succession in a Communist polity and distrusted his reform ideas, Kim Jong Il did not rely on his nominal control of the Workers Party organization. He has built a parallel organization of his own, comparable in some respects to Mao's Red Guards, known as the Three Revolution Teams (TRT) movement. Headed by his sister Kim Chong Hui's husband, Chong Song Taek, the TRT movement claimed some 80,000 members in 1999. At the same time, Kim's nominees have taken over control of the party's youth organization, the Socialist Youth League. With an estimated two million members, the league has its own machinery separate from the Workers Party, which, according to Hwang Chang Yop, has four million members, 30,000 of them full-time employees.

Although control of the TRT movement and the Youth League are important to him, Kim Jong Il, with the help of his father, has consciously attempted to make the armed forces his major power base. In

December 1991, Kim Il Sung appointed his son supreme commander of the People's Army. Between April 1993 when he became a marshal and chairman of the powerful National Defense Commission, and October 2000, Kim Jong Il had selected 966 officers for promotion to major general or above in a series of reshuffles. Even so, until the death of Defense Minister O Jin U in 1995 and of his successor, Marshal Choe Gwang, in 1997, the armed forces were dominated by a clique of Kim Il Sung's old cronies from Manchurian guerrilla days. As a well-informed Japanese observer, Wada Haruki, has noted, the passing of these two venerable figures marked the transition of North Korea from a "Guerrilla Unit State" to a "Regular Army State." Kim Jong Il, Haruki writes, "secured freedom of action after O Jin U's death,"[19] promptly naming two generals in their sixties to key positions. Vice-Marshal Jo Myong Rok, commander of the Air Force, was named director of the Political Department of the National Defense Commission and Gen. Kim Yong Chun as Army Chief of Staff. It was Jo who met Clinton as Kim's emissary in October 2000. There are still powerful Old Guard figures scattered in the military and intelligence hierarchy, notably Marshal Li Ul Sol. It is unclear whether Kim Jong Il is in unchallengeable control of the national security machinery or is merely the central figure in a more complex web of power relationships.

On the surface, he would appear to be well protected against a major coup. He has installed brothers of his sister's husband, Chong Song Taek, in three of the most sensitive positions in the power structure. The elder brother, Gen. Chang Sung Woo, commands one of the Army corps in control of Pyongyang; the second eldest, Gen. Chang Sung Kil, is political commissar of another corps in the capital; and the youngest, Gen. Chang Sung U, is director of the Political Department in the Ministry of Public Security. The only known case of an attempted uprising against the regime has been a localized revolt by elements of the Sixth Corps in 1995 in remote North Hamgyong Province, the area most seriously affected by the food crisis.

Without fanfare, even before adoption of his new constitution in September 1998, Kim Jong Il had started to treat the Military Committee of the Workers Party as equal in power to the Central Committee. The restructuring of the government that accompanied the new constitution explicitly gave the National Defense Commission—"the supreme military guidance organ of state sovereignty"—overriding authority in the North Korean system. Kim Jong Il was formally enshrined as chairman of the commission and concurrently general secretary of the Workers Party. The office of president held by Kim Il Sung was abolished. Nominally, the Supreme People's Assembly was to hold ultimate authority in the land. The chairman of its presidium, former foreign minister Kim Yong Nam, became a de facto ceremonial head of state, designated to represent North Korea in dealings with other national leaders. However, to make matters unambiguous, Kim Yong Nam, in his assembly address formally proposing the election of Kim Jong Il as chairman of the National Defense Commission, declared that " the office of the commission chairman is a very important position. It is in charge of the whole of our political, military, and economic powers and is the top post of the republic." In June 1999, two official organs of the Workers Party Central Committee, in a joint article, declared that "giving priority to the Army is the perfect mode of politics in the present times . . . a mode of leadership which solves all problems arising in the Revolution. Our revolutionary philosophy is that the Army is precisely the Party, people, and state."[20]

In a December 1996 speech attributed to Kim Jong Il, he implicitly acknowledged and defended the shift of power to the armed forces. "The functionaries of the Party Central Committee," he said, "do not possess as high a revolutionary spirit as the political functionaries of the People's Army." According to Hwang Chang Yop, who made a taped transcript public after his defection, Kim gave this speech to party cadres at Kim Il Sung University on the fiftieth anniversary of its founding. Its flavor and rambling style are credible, but its legitimacy is not certain. "I saw people lined up along the street trying to get grain," Kim said, "and I heard that the trains and stations are crowded with people trying to get grain. Heart-aching occurrences are happening everywhere, but the responsible provincial, city and county party functionaries merely get together in conferences or offices instead of making practical efforts. They are simply telling people to solve the problem on their own." Citing Army efforts to build vegetable greenhouses and mushroom farms, he excoriated "incompetent, listless" party functionaries for failing to stop "cooperative farms from hiding a substantial amount of grain, using this or that excuse, which means that we cannot properly supply provisions to the People's Army."

The most remarkable aspect of this transcript is that Kim implicitly casts himself as a detached figure, alone at the top, rather than as a hands-on administrator with tight centralized control. Referring to the party as if it were beyond his reach, he complained that instead of "going out among the masses and eliminating these phenomena, party functionaries merely mobilize agents from the Ministry of Public Security and other agencies to clamp down according to the letter of the law." Although he had assisted in his father's work since the 1960s, he said, "no functionary assists me effectively. I am working alone."[21]

Kim voiced a similar dissatisfaction with Workers Party functionaries during his August 2000 meeting with South Korean editors, saying, "I get irritated when I meet party officials. They're following the same old patterns. These people are stuck in a pattern, not trying to change." When one of the editors asked whether the Workers Party would amend the passages in its constitution calling for a Communist revolution in the South, Kim responded that "since the party charter was written in 1945, right after the liberation, it has many radical and militant expressions. Among the party cadres there are many who worked with the president [Kim Il Sung] and there are also many that are very old. That is why we cannot change it easily."[22]

When Kim assumed the post of general secretary of the Workers Party in October 1997, he was not elected at a plenary session of the Central Committee but on the basis of proclamations of support from provincial party conferences and from the armed forces. This strongly suggests that Kim is not in complete control of the Workers Party and decided to impose a new constitutional structure in 1998 to strengthen his position in combating party hard-liners opposed to reform.

KIM JONG IL AND KING KOJONG

Questioning whether Kim Jong Il is capable of leading North Korea toward reform, Carter Eckert has offered a suggestive comparison with King Kojong, who was the last monarch of the Yi dynasty during the decades leading up to Japan's annexation of Korea. Like Kim Jong Il, Eckert said, Kojong was not strong enough to overcome an entrenched conservative elite, which "retained a grip on many of the key levers of power and was often able to slow down or frustrate efforts at Westernization by reformist bureaucrats."[23] In late nineteenth-century Korea, writes Vipin Chandra, another historian of the period, "there was a pulsating, albeit latent, popular craving for reform" reflected in the modest reform measures of 1895 and the emergence of the Independence Club led by reformers So Chae Pil and Yun Chi Ho. But reform could only take place with "the monarch's patronage or even grudging tolerance." In the end, Chandra concludes, the king, with his "maddeningly inconsistent and arbitrary behavior, could not be counted on" and opposed the reformers.[24]

This analogy is complicated by the fact that the reformers were tarred by their identification with Japan as the spearhead of Westernization. Moreover, as Eckert points out, Kojong's "attitude toward Westernization was basically ambivalent and vacillating." Kim Jong Il, by contrast, recognizes the need for economic reforms. He is constrained not by intellectual ambivalence but by fears of destabilizing political consequences. Secretary of State Albright said that he told her he was "examining alternatives" to his Communist economy, referring specifically to "the Swedish model."[25]

Hwang Chang Yop is categorical in asserting that Kim Jong Il "understands the desirability of economic reform. What worries him is that it will open up a Pandora's box. If he could have reform and be sure of keeping his power, he would do it. Don't forget that what has happened in North Korea, all the killings, is much worse than in China or Vietnam. He's afraid it will all come out if he opens up too much." Hwang added that "all of the working-level officials in charge of different aspects of the economy favor reforms, especially those who have contact with the outside world. Some of the higher-ups, too, but most of those people are sycophants and yes-men. No one there is in favor of political reform, that is an end to the Kim family dictatorship, or for that matter a real market economy. In any case, it's not possible for like-minded people to have meetings of any kind, so there are no hard-line or moderate factions, just individuals who recognize the need for change."[26]

In her 1997 interviews, Li Nam Ok repeatedly pointed to "the many signs of change, the many signals he is sending that he is ready to change if the world will let him, if he doesn't feel threatened by doing so." The most important signal came on Korean Independence Day, August 15, 1997, when he said that "America is no longer North Korea's enemy. I think if someone knows a little about the regime and about North Korea's history, they must realize how big a change this is, how much more important it is, coming from him, than the routine anti-American propaganda. It was a big signal when he sent a representative to the World Economic Forum in Davos to say that he was ready for foreign investment. These were not easy things for him to do, if you know our history and the feelings of our people. But I don't think it would be good to open up too quickly. If he suddenly opens up, how will he deal with the enormous consequences?"[27]

As the process of "reform by stealth" proceeds, the readiness of Kim Jong Il and his successors to step up the pace of change is likely to depend on whether or not they perceive economic reform as a Trojan-horse strategy designed to dethrone them. To the extent that the United States can encourage reform, it can do so only by first demonstrating that it is ready to coexist with North Korea and has abandoned hopes for its collapse. The possibility of such a policy reversal is growing as American leaders become better informed. When he was defense secretary, William J. Perry said on September 26, 1993, that North Korea would collapse "some time in the next few years." Six years later, after his first visit to Pyongyang, Perry concluded that "the regime is very much in control, and it would be imprudent on our part to assume that this regime is going to collapse. We have to deal with the North Korean government not as we wish they'd be but as, in fact, they are."[28]

PART II

Reunification: Postponing the Dream

CHAPTER 7

Trading Places

How, when, and whether Korea can be reunified is the overarching issue that has confronted both the North and the South since the division of 1945. It is this issue, above all else, that shapes their attitudes toward the United States. Pyongyang and Seoul alike believe that the United States bears the principal responsibility for the division. Both believe that the United States should now accept the principal responsibility for helping them put the pieces back together. At the same time, there are profound differences between North and South, and within the South itself, concerning the role that the United States should play during the transition to reunification and thereafter, especially concerning the role of U.S. forces.

The dramatic reversal in the relative economic and political strength of North and South over the past five decades has led to a corresponding turnabout in the way each of them views reunification.

Initially, a confident North Korea believed that it would be able to reunify the South under its control because its economic and political institutions were more stable than those of the South. Kim Il Sung, who presided over an acquiescent populace that had been successfully repressed by his totalitarian system, saw a South Korea in which authoritarian military rulers faced seething popular opposition. No longer able to rely on Soviet and Chinese military support and facing a U.S. military presence in the South, he could not embark on a new Korean war. But he nevertheless expected to unify the peninsula through political means. Pyongyang saw itself as the custodian of a "pure" Korean nationalism unsullied by the South's dependence on U.S. forces and Japanese capital.

In proposing a confederation as an interim step toward reunification, Kim Il Sung assumed that the North, with its claim to the leadership of nationalism, could use interchange with the South within a confederal structure to win converts there. Conversely, the South, lacking a domestic political consensus, felt insecure in the face of the political and military challenge posed by the North. The South Korean military regimes that governed from 1961 to 1987 feared that a confederation would indeed be used by Pyongyang to prepare the ground for a unified Korea under its domination, not only through legitimate political competition but through terrorist tactics such as the unsuccessful attempt to assassinate Park Chung Hee in 1971 and the 1984 bombing attack on visiting South Korean officials in Rangoon.

Although popular pressures for better relations with the North boiled beneath the surface,[1] the Park Chung Hee and Chun Doo Hwan regimes were able to contain them with periodic cosmetic gestures toward Pyongyang, such as the 1972 North-South dialogue, coupled with a continual propaganda barrage designed to keep alive fears of another North Korean invasion. The military regimes consciously fanned tension with the North to justify their repressive rule. By the late 1980s, however, the North and South had traded places. In the new environment accompanying the end of the cold war, it was the North, not the South, that felt economically and politically vulnerable, especially after the death of Kim Il Sung.

The loss of Soviet and Chinese aid subsidies aggravated the built-in weaknesses of the North's overcentralized, over-autarkic, Marxist economy. By contrast, the South had made the most of its U.S. aid and the massive influx of foreign credits and investment that began with the normalization of its relations with Japan in 1965. Emulating the Japanese *zaibatsu* model, the military regimes had subsidized Korean-style conglomerates, known as *chaebol*, that presided over a remarkable, export-led surge of economic development. This pell-mell economic expansion gave the South an ever-widening margin of economic superiority over the North, accompanied by a new confidence in dealing with Pyongyang that led, in turn, to a series of overtures for better North-South relations following the overthrow of military rule in 1987 and the emergence of Roh Tae Woo as a democratically elected president. Ironically, it was their short-term economic success that proved to be the undoing of the generals, since it exacerbated inequities between rich and poor that fueled the rebellion against Chun Doo Hwan. But it was this economic success, together with the political stabilization of the South, that explains Seoul's increasingly confident posture in North-South relations since 1987, just as it is the North's economic troubles and Kim Il Sung's death that account for its mood of anxious insecurity in dealing with the South.

While still formally committed to a confederation as the prelude to reunification, Pyongyang is in reality obsessed with fears of a concerted U.S.-Japanese-South Korean effort to promote its collapse and absorption by the South in a replica of the German unification experience. In the immediate aftermath of Kim Il Sung's demise, the South did, in fact, believe that the likelihood of a collapse had increased. President Kim Young Sam, who followed Roh, did pursue policies designed to promote a gradual, "managed" collapse and an absorption of the North that would be less costly than the sudden absorption of East Germany by West Germany. This approach was repudiated by Kim Dae Jung when he assumed the presidency in 1998. Warning that a collapse would be undesirable for the South and is unlikely, in any case, Kim Dae Jung has pursued stepped-up cultural, economic, and political relations with the North. Significantly, however, he has soft-pedaled his long-standing advocacy of a loose confederation, partly for domestic political reasons and partly in the belief that the North feels too insecure to move in this direction soon.

Given its deep sense of insecurity, Pyongyang has remained wary of Seoul despite Kim Dae Jung's overtures for better relations. Pointing to his many statements that Seoul wants to promote market-based reforms in the North through economic ties, Pyongyang charges that the Kim Dae Jung "sunshine policy" masks what is still the South's intention to undermine and absorb the North, albeit more gradually than envisaged in previous absorption scenarios. By backing off from his confederation proposal, Kim Dae Jung has accentuated the North's suspicion of his motives. In the North's eyes, a confederation would assure its security, since it would institutionalize the coexistence of two separate states with differing systems until joint agreement on the terms for unification can be negotiated, thus precluding the absorption of either side by the other.

Two factors explain why the North has moved so cautiously and so selectively in opening up to the increased economic relations that Kim Dae Jung has promoted. One is a distrust of Seoul that has persisted despite the June 2000 summit. The other is the defensive psychology produced by its diplomatic isolation since the end of the cold war and the cutoff of its Soviet and Chinese economic subsidies. These factors also explain why Pyongyang has rejected proposals for the reunion of separated families, which it perceives as political, not humanitarian, in intent, designed to sow unrest in the North by demonstrating the affluence of the participating families from the South.

The sharp polarization of opinion in the South over the "sunshine policy" is likely to constrain movement by Kim Dae Jung and his immediate successors toward a confederation. North Korea, for its part, while ready for dialogue on a confederation, wants to postpone the actual establishment of one until it has rebuilt its economic strength. Meaningful progress toward unification could well remain on hold, in short, for a decade or more. During this period, if the North is able to stabilize its economy and gradually adopts market-based reforms, the ideological gap between Seoul and Pyongyang would narrow and a confederation would become more attractive to both sides as a way to structure systematic interchange. Once established, a confederation would release pent-up nationalist sentiment on both sides of the thirty-eighth parallel that would accelerate progress toward greater integration.

It would be a serious mistake to underrate the dynamism of the emotional drive for reunification on both sides of the thirty-eighth parallel and thus the possibility of unpredictable developments that could speed up the process. As Kim Dae Jung has observed, Korea's division since 1945 has been "a painful, brief anomaly compared with thirteen centuries of Korean unity."[2] The nation-states of Europe were only beginning to come together with settled borders when the Korean peninsula was unified in A.D. 668. Apart from a civil war from A.D. 890 to 935 and an interval of Mongol rule over the northwest corner of the country from A.D. 1259 to 1392, Korea has maintained a continuous political identity within the same boundaries since the seventh century. Germany, by contrast, had been unified for less than a century when it was divided in 1945.

Many Koreans believe that the origins of Korean identity date back well before recorded history to the founding of a Korean state 4,332 years ago in the northwest by a king named Tangun, legendary progenitor of the race. The supposed date of its founding, October 3, is officially celebrated in the South as National Foundation Day. The North erected a national shrine in Tangun's honor in 1993 at Kangdong, where it claimed to have discovered his tomb and to have unearthed his skeleton, which is displayed at the shrine.

With their vivid national historical memory and a degree of ethnic and linguistic homogeneity found in few other countries, Koreans exemplify the interdependence of individual and group identity emphasized by many psychiatrists and social psychologists. Erik H. Erikson wrote of "the mutual complementation of ethos and ego, of group identity and ego identity."[3] "In its most central ethnic sense," Erikson said, the ultimate discovery of identity involves the psychological interplay between the individual and his or her communal culture, "a process which establishes, in fact, the identity of these two identities."[4] It might be debatable whether this insight has universal applicability to all societies and cultures. In the case of divided Korea, however, I find it unmistakably relevant, as do many other observers who have had intensive contact over the years with Koreans in both North and South. Stephen Linton, who grew up in Korea in a missionary family, has observed that "the division has had the psychological effect of physical dismemberment" on many Koreans of his acquaintance. This statement reminded me of a similar analogy with reference to Vietnamese by Bernard B. Fall, who wrote that the division of their country has had a psychological impact on many Vietnamese "as drastic as the amputation of their own limbs."[5]

Life in both the North and South is suffused with deep feelings of national grievance and mourning known as *han*. The South Korean theologian C.H.S. Moon defined *han* as "the accumulated anger and resentment felt by the people of a small and weak nation who hate and resent the wrongs done to them by surrounding nations whose might they cannot overcome."[6] Sociologist Roy Grinker, describing *han* as "a complex of suppressed emotion," found in extensive interviews with South Koreans that their sense of *han* is focused in particular on the division of the country. The essence of *han*, he writes, is that "division and unification appear to be beyond Korean control because there are political forces, within the two Koreas and outside of Korea, that make unification and thus a resolution of *han* impossible." The resulting frustration "breeds additional *han*, making Koreans hate their perceived enemies," above all Japan and the United States.[7]

In the two chapters that follow I will analyze the evolution of reunification policy in the North and South, with special attention to the costs of a sudden absorption and to how the concept of a confederation would be implemented under their respective proposals. I will then explore why Koreans hold the United States primarily responsible for the division and turn finally to the ongoing impact of the U.S. role in Korea on the prospects for reunification, focusing on the impact of the U.S. military presence.

CHAPTER 8

Confederation or Absorption?

To MANY foreign observers, talk of a confederation in Korea sounds legalistic and academic. It seems more plausible that the South will absorb the North gradually or that the status quo will continue indefinitely until some explosion within the North, or between North and South, precipitates a sudden reunification of the peninsula. To North Korea, however, and to many Koreans in the South, including President Kim Dae Jung and former president Roh Tae Woo, the concept of a confederation has long been attractive as a realistic way to reduce North-South tensions and to formalize the de facto division of the peninsula while moving toward eventual reunification through structured interchange.

At first, the North and South had radically different concepts of how a confederation would work. The North proposed a unitary, centralized confederation that many Western political scientists would call a federation. Kim Dae Jung and Roh Tae Woo envisaged a much looser confederal structure. Gradually, however, the gulf between the two has narrowed. The declaration issued after their June 2000 summit meeting by Kim Dae Jung and Kim Jong Il "acknowledged that the different formulas that the North and South favor for reunification have common factors."

Given the economic difficulties that the North has faced since the end of the cold war, neither Pyongyang nor Seoul is in a hurry to talk seriously about moving toward a confederation. Pyongyang is not as confident as it once was that it could hold its own in a process of accelerated interchange. In the South, the North's economic vulnerability has strengthened hopes that the South can have unification sooner or later on its own terms without the compromises that a confederation would entail. Still, the climate for a confederation could well improve over time as the North stabilizes its economy and as nationalist pressures generated by the summit grow in the South. As I will seek to show, the future role of the United States will have a critical impact on the North-South climate and thus on the possibilities for a peaceful transition to reunification.

NORTH KOREA: CONFEDERATION AS THE "FINAL STAGE"

Although North Korea seeks to present itself as the leading champion of reunification, Pyongyang has gradually diluted its original goal of an integrated national state, shifting to the more limited objective of confederal institutions that would permit separate regimes to coexist in the North and South for an indefinite period.

The legitimacy of the Communist regime depends to a great extent on the credibility of its commitment to pursue the goal of reunification. Thus, as originally formulated, the confederation proposal was uncompromising. It projected an integrated political and economic system following reunification and envisaged a confederation as a temporary way station on the road to full reunification. Even at the confederal stage, Korea would have unified armed forces and conduct diplomacy jointly. In my first interview with Kim Il Sung on June 23, 1972, he spoke of a confederal structure that would "maintain the present different political systems of North and South as they are *for the time being*" (italics added). When I suggested that, as a practical matter, separate regimes with separate armed forces might have to continue for several decades, he replied vaguely that a "Korean consensus" would decide such questions and that the "people" in the South would determine what system would exist there and for how long. Five years later, however, when I met Vice Premier and Foreign Minister Ho Dam in New York on October 3, 1977, he did not flatly reject my suggestion that the confederation might have to last for as long as thirty years. "We are a homogenous nation," he said, "with a history of many centuries as one people. In this light, thirty years is a short period. But the main point is this: If the American troops go out of Korea, the period of solution will be greatly shortened."

Pyongyang prepared the juridical basis for a confederal framework in its revised 1972 constitution. One clause pointedly replaced Seoul with Pyongyang as the capital of the Democratic People's Republic of Korea (DPRK). Another said that the DPRK "strives to achieve the complete victory of socialism in the northern half" while seeking only to "drive out foreign forces on a nationwide scale."[1]

As the cold war drew to an end and North Korea faced the inescapable reality of an economically and politically stable South Korea, Pyongyang softened its terms for a confederation. Hwang Chang Yop, then international secretary of the Workers Party, told me in Pyongyang on October 10, 1987, that North Korea no longer considered a confederation as a transitional phase but as the "final stage" of unification. Similarly, in November 1988 when Harvard Korea specialist Edward J. Baker visited Pyongyang, North Korean officials "clearly and repeatedly stated that they would regard the establishment of the Democratic Confederal Republic of Koryo as unification—as the final step."[2] In my meetings with Hwang, I argued that the provision in the North's proposal for an integrated army was unrealistic. In principle, he replied, a combined army would be a long-term objective, but "if we can improve relations between the two Koreas, then having two armies would be acceptable, especially if their size can be reduced." Hwang's statements were echoed by other officials, including Kim Yong Sun, then a key official dealing with reunification policy.

Kim Il Sung repeatedly emphasized in formal pronouncements that the North's terms for a confederation are negotiable. Thus, citing Pyongyang's detailed 1980 proposal for an integrated "Confederal Republic of Koryo," he declared in his 1991 New Year's address that if this is not acceptable, "we are ready to discuss vesting the autonomous regional governments of the confederal republic with more rights on a tentative basis and then increasing the functions of the central government in the future."

During a visit to Washington in June 1991, former vice foreign minister Han Si Hae made an even more explicit North Korean statement elaborating what Pyongyang has in mind. "We envisage a loose confederal state," he said, in which "all ongoing entities in North and South would be kept intact as they are for the time being. Both would have independent military affairs and diplomatic relations, and the confederal state would be limited to a coordinating function."[3] On the critical doctrinal issue of when full reunification would be achieved, he volunteered that this would come "when the confederal government has the full power of diplomacy and defense." However, even then, he noted, the North and South would continue to have independent economic and cultural relations with foreign countries.[4]

Repeating several times that the North has "no intention or capability at all to communize South Korea," Han offered a new rationale in support of this position. "It would be strategically unfavorable for our side to change the Southern capitalist system into a Communist system," he argued, because "we want to improve our relations with many countries that have large investments in the South, especially the United States and Japan."[5]

The latest definitive North Korean statement on reunification policy,

Kim Il Sung's "Ten-Point Program of Great National Unity," issued on April 8, 1993, emphasized that the proposed confederation "should recognize private ownership and protect the capital and property of individual persons and organizations and common interests with foreign capital."[6] On the critical issue of whether the North and South could maintain their separate armed forces, it was pointedly silent, in contrast to formal statements a decade earlier that referred specifically to "combined" forces. The sensitivity of this issue in internal doctrinal debates was reflected in the qualified language of a 1995 policy statement. The North and South, it said, "could exercise tentatively the commanding power over their respective armed forces."[7]

Kim Jong Il has not gone beyond the Ten-Point Program in enunciating reunification policy except in one significant respect. His spokesmen make the case for the proposed confederation by arguing that it would provide more meaningful guarantees of autonomy than those enjoyed by Hong Kong under China's "one country, two systems" concept. "In our confederation, one side would not revert to the other side as in the case of Hong Kong, which is now a part of China," said Kim Byong Hong, director of policy planning in the Foreign Ministry. "The North and South would be on an equal footing, which means that our proposal inherently protects the autonomy of both sides, while China retains ultimate sovereignty in the 'One Country, Two Systems' approach."[8]

Prior to the June 2000 summit, Pyongyang expressed disappointment that Kim Dae Jung, as president, appeared to abandon his earlier commitment to pursue a confederation. In the North's eyes, the South's readiness to establish a confederation would signify the formal rejection of absorption as its ultimate goal. By insisting on "small steps first," in this perspective, Seoul is putting the cart before the horse. Since North-South tensions are rooted in mutual distrust, Pyongyang argues, the logical way to remove this distrust is to agree at the outset on a structure for peaceful coexistence that would guarantee both sides an equal say in deciding how much integration is desirable and how to achieve it.

South Korea: The Unresolved Debate

The crux of the opposition in the South to the differing confederation proposals put forward by the North and by South Korean leaders Kim Dae Jung and Roh Tae Woo is that they all envisage the equal representation of the North and South in the proposed confederal structure.

Pointing to the fact that the South has a much bigger population (46 million) than the North (25 million), most South Korean governments have advocated free elections in the North and South to choose a unified legislature that would be dominated by the South. In this approach, a change in the North's system would be necessary before movement toward unification could begin.

South Korea's first president, Syngman Rhee, was acutely sensitive to the potential of the reunification issue in domestic politics, seeking to preempt it with his refusal to sign the 1953 armistice and his "March North" slogan. When the dictatorial Rhee was overthrown in 1960, the South enjoyed a revealing interlude of free speech in which attitudes toward reunification received a rare public airing. The election of a democratic regime produced a polarization between newly emboldened reformist elements and militant anti-Communists that set the stage for the 1961 military coup. Pro-unification advocates received a major shot in the arm when U.S. Senator Mike Mansfield made a proposal—largely unnoticed in the American press—for Korean reunification "on the basis of neutralization on the Austrian pattern."[9] Neutralization became the intellectual fashion overnight. Unification rallies and torchlight parades attracted big crowds. Student groups called for postal, athletic, and trade exchanges with Pyongyang and extended an invitation to North Korea for a meeting of student representatives at Panmunjom on May 20 that the North promptly accepted. On May 14, a mass rally in Seoul urged the government to authorize the May 20 meeting, and on May 16, Gen. Park Chung Hee staged his coup. Military leaders made no secret of the fact that the reunification uproar was the critical factor precipitating their decision to act.[10]

Park cracked down hard on advocates of conciliation with the North by promulgating a sweeping National Security Law, still in force, that authorizes arbitrary arrests for any activity alleged to show sympathy or cooperation with Pyongyang. At the same time, the new military regime made periodic cosmetic gestures designed to appease pro-unification sentiment. In 1960, Park created a National Unification Board, hoping to divert the unification issue into safe channels. His nominee as head of the new board was a respected former president of Seoul National University, Sin Tae Wan, an economist who had drafted Park's first development plan in 1961. Park envisaged the chairmanship of the board as a symbolic, ceremonial role, only to find that Sin took it more seriously as a platform for provoking public discussion of ways to ease tensions with Pyongyang.

Sin's frequent open references to the need for a more "flexible" approach to the North gradually began to arouse public expectations of serious political initiatives that the Park government had no intention of undertaking. After a stormy year in office, Sin was abruptly dismissed after he published a poll disclosing significant support for personnel exchanges with the North. This occurred in February 1970, just when Chancellor Willy Brandt was about to initiate his first discussions with East German leaders, a development keenly watched by politically conscious South Koreans. Moreover, following his ouster, Sin continued to speak out for more open discussion of unification possibilities. In an interview with me that filtered back into South Korea despite press controls, Sin compared Korea and Germany, declaring that "we're in the same situation. We're both divided countries, and while we can't go as fast as the Germans are going, we've got to begin turning in the same direction. Without recognizing the existence of the North Koreans as a political force, we will never get anywhere. . . . If it is too soon for direct contacts, it is not too soon to begin preparing ground by modifying the National Security Law so that we can at least discuss developments in the North. We cannot even admit that they exist. We are risking arrest if we use any phrase other than 'Northern puppet.'"[11]

Sin was interrogated and placed under surveillance after this interview, but his views were vindicated in little more than a year as a rapid sequence of international developments forced Park to modify his posture. In addition to the peculiarly sharp impact in Seoul of Brandt's Ostpolitik, American troop reductions in Korea inspired mainly by budgetary considerations led to a desire in Washington for a relaxation of tensions to fit in with the new policy. This, in turn, emboldened opposition leaders in Seoul to use the issue of contacts with the North as a major weapon. Park made a dramatic attempt to escape from his defensive position on the reunification issue in 1972 by entering into talks with the North, nominally addressed to the establishment of a North-South Coordinating Committee at Panmunjom. However, the 1972 dialogue soon reached an impasse when Pyongyang made steps toward the mutual reduction of military force levels its top priority. Seoul argued that smaller and more manageable issues should be settled first.

Park defended the "small steps first" approach as necessary to develop mutual trust. However, his pronouncements made clear that his basic purpose was to buy time during which the South could build up its relative power in order to enforce reunification on the most advantageous terms. In his 1971 New Year's Press Conference, he declared that "the easiest road to unification is to strengthen our national power. When our power surpasses that of North Korea, and when the urge for freedom moves from the Republic to the north of Korea, Kim Il Sung's dictatorial system will surely collapse."[12] Six months later, he added that "by the mid-1970's, we should have become strong enough to achieve reunification."[13]

The Chun Doo Hwan military regime that took over after Park's assassination in 1979 made no changes in reunification policy. However, hoping to promote a North-South summit meeting that would strengthen his weak domestic political position, Chun supported a secret, back-channel dialogue between North and South initiated by a nationalistic official of the South Korean CIA, known as the KCIA, Jae Nang Sohn. Former North Korean foreign minister Ho Dam met with Chun secretly in Seoul in September 1985, paving the way for a softened policy toward the North by Roh Tae Woo.

Roh immediately began to show a more flexible policy toward Pyongyang when he took office in February 1988, permitting unprecedented freedom of speech and the press that made possible greater public discussion of reunification. On July 7, 1988, he urged greater American and Japanese contacts with Pyongyang and offered to engage in customs-free "internal" trade between North and South. In the South's perspective, Roh's policies were magnanimous, especially against the background of Seoul's belief that Pyongyang was responsible for the 1987 midair explosion of a Korean Airlines passenger jet, killing 115 passengers.

It was a significant departure when Roh advanced his proposal for a Korean Commonwealth or Korean National Community on September 11, 1989. The new plan explicitly accepted the principle of equal representation in a projected transitional, twenty-member council of ministers and a one-hundred-member council of representatives:

> The council of ministers would be co-chaired by the prime ministers of the North and South and would comprise around ten minister-level officials from each side. Under the council standing committees could be created to deal with humanitarian, political, diplomatic, economic, military, social, and cultural affairs. The council of ministers of the North and the South would discuss and adjust all pending North-South issues and National problems and would ensure their implementation.
>
> The North-South council of representatives will be composed of around 100 North-South parliamentarians, with equal numbers repre-

senting each side. It will draft a unified constitution, prepare methods and concrete procedures to realize reunification, and advise the North-South council of ministers at its request.

It also called for a joint secretariat to be located in the Panmunjom demilitarized zone and resident liaison missions in Seoul and Pyongyang. However, echoing the South's earlier policies, the plan continued to envisage the eventual integration of the two Korean states as a democratic republic following elections, and the new republic was to have a bicameral legislature in which the lower house would be based on population.[14]

Roh's plan was a copy in most respects of the proposal for a loose confederation that had long been advocated by Kim Dae Jung, then the principal opposition leader. The key difference was that Kim's plan did not call for eventual elections and thus accepted the indefinite continuance of coequal representation. At the same time, Kim's "confederation of Korean republics" would differ fundamentally from Pyongyang's single confederal republic because North and South would begin what is envisaged as a protracted confederating process, possibly over a period of decades, without surrendering any of their sovereignty.

Addressing the Council for the Promotion of Democracy in Seoul on August 15, 1987, Kim declared that

> As a first stage, we should recognize the North Korean communist regime as a communist regime which is an independent government and [they should] firmly recognize the Republic of Korea as a democratic government which is an independent government. Then both sides, for the sake of peaceful coexistence, should dispatch their representatives to make a confederal system with very weak powers. . . .
>
> The confederal republic proposed by Kim Il Sung in North Korea seeks to create, in a single stroke, a genuine single state in the form of a federation like the United States or Canada. But this is utterly impossible. I oppose this. What I have spoken of is a confederation of republics—even the name is the opposite. We must move forward on the road toward building, atop two independent republics, a confederal system having limited authority and functions.

In 1992, Kim added an important modification, stating that "perhaps up to a decade after beginning this confederation, both Koreas would build a national consensus toward establishment of a multiparty and open market system. We would then enter into a second stage of the unification process." In this second stage, "one federal government of two local autonomous governments would be formed, with foreign affairs and defense controlled by the federal government."[15]

In contrast to the explicit character of the Roh and Kim Dae Jung proposals, Kim Young Sam, who served as president from 1993 to 1998, outlined his approach to reunification in broad-brush terms with few specifics. In his inaugural address on February 25, 1993, he sounded a nationalistic note, declaring that "no ideology or political belief can bring greater happiness than national kinship." However, faced with a conservative backlash that was heightened by U.S.–North Korean tensions over the nuclear issue, he quickly retreated. When he put forward a three-stage reunification plan, it said vaguely that North and South would "move from the initial step of reconciliation and cooperation to the next phase of Korean commonwealth and to a final stage of a unified nation of one people and one state."[16] He never clarified how long the initial period of reconciliation would last, what form a commonwealth would take, and whether it would be based on coequality. In effect, he rejected the coexistence of differing systems central to the confederation concept by consistently calling for a "democratic unified Korea in which political and economic freedom must be guaranteed."[17]

Kim Il Sung's death in 1994 rekindled the hopes of hard-liners in Seoul for a collapse of North Korea. Kim Young Sam's pronouncements made clear that he envisaged a collapse followed by the South's absorption of the North. In his August 15, 1995, Independence Day address at Chonan, he declared that a reunified Korea would be "another ROK." Referring to the "miracle of the Han River," he said that "as an extension of all this, we should now create a new ROK—a reunified Fatherland enjoying democracy and prosperity." Angered by what he considered excessive U.S. concessions in its 1994 negotiations with Pyongyang on the nuclear issue, Kim told the *New York Times* on October 7, 1994, that the North Korean regime "is on the verge of an economic and political crisis that could sweep it from power," and U.S. compromises on the nuclear issue "might prolong its life." "He expected the collapse during his Administration," a U.S. intelligence assessment said, "and according to some reports, launched covert actions to facilitate it."[18]

KIM DAE JUNG AND THE "SUNSHINE POLICY"

In one of the best known of Aesop's fables, the North Wind and the Sun have a test of strength to determine which one "could strip the clothes off a traveler. The North Wind tried first. He blew violently. As the man clung on to his clothes, the North Wind attacked him with greater force. But the man, uncomfortable from the cold, put on more clothes. . . . The Sun now shone moderately, and the man removed his extra outer cloak. Then the sun darted beams which were more scorching until the man, not being able to withstand the heat, took off his clothes and went to take a dip in a nearby river."[19]

It was this sixth-century Greek fable that gave the "sunshine policy" its name. Kim Dae Jung frequently invoked Aesop to explain why he rejected the premise of previous South Korean presidents that pressure alone would make the North more conciliatory. When Pyongyang feels the warm sun of brotherly beneficence and cooperation, it will remove the straitjacket of a controlled economy, reform its system, and open up to increased dialogue and contacts with Seoul.

This was a simple and effective way of justifying his new policy to the South Korean public and to foreign public opinion. But his emphasis on reform proved to be a serious tactical error because it made his new policy initially suspect in the North. The essence of the new policy was a separation of economics from politics that would permit South Korean companies to pursue business relations with the North without regard to North-South political differences. In Kim Dae Jung's perspective, the impact of this approach would be felt gradually over a long period. North Korean leaders would modify their system at their own pace and in ways they deemed consistent with retaining political control. In the North's perspective, however, the "sunshine" policy was an unabashed attempt to subvert its system, more dangerous than previous attempts precisely because it was more subtle. It was designed to bring about dependent economic relations with the South, in the North's view, leading to the replacement of the present leadership in Pyongyang with new leaders beholden to Seoul and, in time, to absorption on the South's terms. For this reason, while Pyongyang is eager to get infusions of cash, investment, and other economic help from the South, it has scrutinized each transaction suspiciously to minimize any resulting dependency. Similarly, the North believes that Kim has pushed for the reunion of separated families not for humanitarian reasons but to sow discontent by showing off the affluence of the reunited family members who live in the South.

From the outset, Kim Dae Jung has been constrained in shaping his policies toward the North by the strength of hard-liners not only in opposition ranks within the South Korean National Assembly but also in his own ruling coalition. In order to win the presidency, he had to form an electoral coalition that combined his own strength in the southwest Cholla region with that of a veteran conservative leader in Chunchon, Kim Jong Pil, known for his rigid stance on North Korea policy, who served as prime minister in 1998 and 1999.

In a ninety-minute conversation on May 2, 1998, three weeks after his inauguration, Kim Dae Jung spoke with satisfaction of his success in overcoming the opposition of hard-liners to his new posture toward the North. "Kim Jong Pil has always been for absorption," he said, "but now, after his cooperation with us, he has changed his policy." To neutralize hard-line opposition to the "sunshine policy", Kim Dae Jung added, he had named as his unification minister Kang In Duk, a former top official of the KCIA. Kang had helped formulate the North Korean policies of earlier regimes but now said that "new developments in the North" had made Kim Dae Jung's approach realistic.

Asked why he had not mentioned the confederation goal in his inaugural address, Kim offered a frankly political explanation, saying that it was first necessary to build public support in the South for his new policy "by creating a better atmosphere" in relations with Pyongyang. This marked a departure from his pre-election stance. In 1997, citing differences between his position and that of President Kim Young Sam, he wrote that the government's proposed commonwealth stage, comparable to a confederation, "is entered into after a prior phase of reconciliation and cooperation. In our case, however, the confederal stage is itself one of reconciliation and cooperation, thus requiring no special preparatory period, and can be commenced forthwith."

Not only in his public utterances but also in private conversation over the years, Kim Dae Jung has displayed a degree of intellectual consistency rare for a political figure in his basic approach to dealing with North Korea. The "sunshine policy" has been germinating for three decades. My conversations with him about North Korea began in 1972 when Harrison Salisbury and I became the first Americans after the Korean War to visit Pyongyang. In twenty-three freewheeling exchanges with Kim since then, he has used me as a sounding board for his evolving policy ideas, as he has done with others on other issues, pumping me for information after each of my trips to Pyongyang and inviting give and take.

In our May 1998 meeting, with his first visit to Washington just a month away, my main objective was to add my views to those of others who were seeking to persuade him that the improvement of North-South relations required the simultaneous or prior normalization of U.S.–North Korean relations, starting with an end to sanctions on nonstrategic trade and investment. The arguments in support of this view were threefold. First, in the absence of normalization with Washington, the North felt that it would be in an inherently weak bargaining position in any dialogue with the South. Second, article 2 of the 1994 U.S.–North Korean nuclear freeze agreement provided for a relaxation of sanctions, and the United States was not living up to the agreement. Finally, of direct relevance to the "sunshine policy," South Korean companies operating in the North would benefit from such a relaxation, since the sanctions prevent them from exporting their products to the American market. By pressing for an end to sanctions, he could demonstrate his bonafides to Pyongyang. He peppered me with a series of technical questions about the nature of the existing sanctions, the extent to which President Clinton could remove them without congressional approval, and how he could raise the issue without seeming to interfere in U.S. affairs. Then he said that "my own mind has been running in this direction, and this will help us to focus our thoughts." Turning to his national security adviser, Lim Dong Won, he added, "We will deal with this actively in preparation for the visit."

Three days later in Pyongyang, Kim Yong Nam, then foreign minister and deputy prime minister, listened coldly to the suggestion that the advent of Kim Dae Jung offered an unprecedented opportunity for improved North-South relations on terms acceptable to the North but that the new government in Seoul needed a conciliatory response to its overtures from Pyongyang in order to win domestic acceptance of its new policies.

"We have had hopes that Kim Dae Jung would be different," Kim Yong Nam said, "but I must be frank and tell you that we are disappointed." The "real intent" of the "so-called 'new' South Korean policy," the foreign minister said, was revealed by Kim Dae Jung's failure to reaffirm his long-standing commitment to a confederation after taking office. While also criticizing Kim Dae Jung for his "unpatriotic" overtures to Japan for better relations and for his advocacy of a continued American military presence in Korea after reunification, Kim Yong Nam emphasized what he perceived as his "surrender" to entrenched hard-liners in Seoul on the confederation issue. "They all turn out to be the same, these South Korean leaders," he said. "They're all creatures of the same ruling group. Do you really expect someone like Kang In Duk to implement new policies toward us? Kim Dae Jung is merely following in the footsteps of his predecessors." I responded that I had known Kim Dae Jung well for thirty years and that he was more genuinely committed to equitable relations with the North, and more genuinely opposed to an absorption policy, than any previous South Korean leader. "I doubt that you will ever have a more reasonable negotiating partner in Seoul," I observed. "We know them better than you do," he countered, "but time will tell."

In conjunction with his U.S. visit, Kim Dae Jung did, in fact, call for an end to U.S. sanctions in a series of media statements. Lifting sanctions is "imperative," he said on *The News Hour with Jim Lehrer*, "in order to let North Korea open its doors to the outside. The hard-liners in the North are stronger than the moderates there, and such sanctions give a good excuse for hard-liners to maintain the present isolation of the North."[20] Later, when President Clinton named former defense secretary William Perry to review North Korea policy, Kim pushed the sanctions issue hard in his meetings with Perry. This was largely responsible for Perry's recommendation that sanctions be relaxed and for the White House pledge in September 1999 to move in this direction.

Pyongyang was surprised and impressed by Kim Dae Jung's stand on the sanctions issue. An equally important demonstration of his bonafides in North Korean eyes was his support for Hyundai president Chung Ju Yung's plan to develop a tourist resort in the North near Mount Kumgang (Diamond), especially his support for generous terms that gave Pyongyang quick infusions of hard currency.

The octogenarian Chung, who was born in the North, had lobbied for years in both Seoul and Pyongyang for expanded North-South economic cooperation, focusing especially on the Kumgang project. Both the Roh Tae Woo and Kim Young Sam governments in Seoul had thrown cold water on the idea, blocking Chung from offering any economic sweeteners to whet Pyongyang's interest in the idea. Kim Dae Jung, by contrast, encouraged Chung to offer terms attractive enough to open up Mount Kumgang as soon as possible. In Kim's calculations, this would be a psychological breakthrough that would give impetus to broader economic linkages. The result was a controversial, front-loaded deal in which Hyundai agreed to make a down payment of $942 million over a six-year period, starting with payments of $25 million monthly, for the exclusive right to operate tours on Mount Kumgang for thirty years. Further payments were to be made thereafter, depending on the volume of visitors. By April 2000, more than 190,000 South Koreans had gone on the Hyundai tours.

The entrenched power of the hard-liners in Pyongyang is clearly the critical obstacle to progress in improving North-South relations, and their strength lies, at bottom, in their ability to play on fears of absorption shared by the moderates. For this reason, it appeared in early 1999 that Kim Dae Jung's tactical retreat on the confederation issue, dictated by domestic political realities, would prove counterproductive in the North, giving credibility to the hard-line refrain that absorption is his ultimate goal.

Kim Dae Jung himself shrugged off this concern in a conversation on May 4, 1999, arguing that the North, with its internal difficulties, was not yet ready to pursue a confederation. He dismissed the suggestion that even if a direct proposal for discussions on a confederation might not yield results, he could improve North-South relations by talking once again about confederation as a desirable goal. Shaking his head, Kim replied, "That would be premature under present circumstances. The time is not ripe. If we don't get a positive response, that would be a problem for us. When we say something, we should be confident that they'll accept. We will make progress through deeds and actions, not words, and we must take care always that neither side loses face, which would have negative consequences internally for the side affected. But confederation should, of course, remain our goal, even though I might not be able to realize it while I am in office." Later, Lim Dong Won indicated that informal contacts had revealed a lack of interest on the part of the North in pursuing the confederation issue, which he attributed to the pervasive feelings of insecurity that made Pyongyang suspicious of the entire "sunshine policy."

A similar assessment of the North's mood was expressed by Prof. Lee Yueng Hi of Hanyang University, a courageous scholar and former journalist who was imprisoned by the Park Chung Hee regime for advocating a confederation. Professor Lee was given a warm reception on a 1999 visit to Pyongyang, where he had access to many key figures and engaged in extensive informal discussions in Korean. His impression was that the North wanted to stabilize its economy and normalize relations with Washington and Tokyo before starting the accelerated interchange that would be inherent in a confederation.

THE JUNE 2000 SUMMIT AND ITS AFTERMATH

The desire to improve its bargaining position with Seoul has been one of the key reasons why Pyongyang has been so reluctant over the years to engage in meaningful North-South dialogue or, at times, any dialogue at all. Thus, it was a remarkable reversal of strategy when Kim Jong Il accepted Kim Dae Jung's proposal for a summit in June 2000. In this case, Kim Jong Il wanted to use Seoul to increase his bargaining leverage in dealing with the United States at a time when the normalization dialogue with Washington was stalled. Pyongyang had agreed to suspend missile testing on September 17, 1999, in return for a White House announcement that "most" economic sanctions would be lifted. The White House, under pressure from Republican leaders in Congress, had failed to deliver on this pledge. Indeed, during abortive negotiations in New York on March 18, 2000, the United States had demanded new concessions relating to missiles. On April 13, climaxing months of behind-the-scenes negotiations, the two Kims announced agreement on their June summit meeting.

What were the decisive factors that led to Kim Jong Il's acceptance?

First, Kim Dae Jung skillfully prepared the climate for a summit with his February 29 description of Kim Jong Il in a television interview as a "pragmatist, a man of insight, a decisive leader with whom it is possible to negotiate."[21] Second, North Korea's urgent economic needs clearly made a summit attractive when Kim Dae Jung pledged economic help in his March 9 speech at the Free University of Berlin. Private sector economic cooperation based on the principle of separating economics from politics would not resolve North Korea's economic difficulties, he declared, calling for cooperation at the governmental level to expand "the social infrastructure, including highways, harbors, railroads and electrical and communications facilities."

According to respected Japanese Korea specialist Hajime Izumi, Kim Dae Jung promised to give ten million tons of surplus coal to North Korea during the back-channel Beijing negotiations that preceded Kim Jong Il's acceptance of the summit.[22] Ten million tons of coal would have supplied North Korean power stations for three years, so expectations of such a gift would undoubtedly have made a summit attractive. Several days before I heard this from Izumi, I met Kim Dae Jung in Seoul. When I emphasized the importance of North-South energy cooperation, he volunteered that he was considering giving ten million tons of surplus coal to the North but that Pyongyang had made this difficult to do by refusing to permit South Korean surveys of its power stations, which would be necessary to make such a munificent gesture acceptable to public opinion in the South.[23]

It is questionable whether Kim Jong Il accepted the summit invitation with expectations that South Korean aid would be on a massive scale, given Seoul's own economic problems and Kim Dae Jung's shaky domestic political base. Rather, the critical factor may well have been a calculation that a North-South summit would trigger U.S. action on economic sanctions. This is precisely what happened. The summit gave President Clinton the political cover needed to ignore Republican protests, and on June 19, 2000, four days after it ended, acceding to a personal plea from Kim Dae Jung, Clinton made good on his September 1999 pledge.

For Kim Jong Il, the relaxation of sanctions would remove one of the critical obstacles that had impeded his pursuit of his reform agenda. The relaxation of sanctions and the removal of North Korea from the U.S. list of terrorist states are both prerequisites not only for U.S. and Japanese diplomatic normalization but also for admission to the World Bank and other international financial institutions that can provide large-scale infrastructural aid. As it happened, despite Clinton's June 19 executive order, the relaxation of sanctions had only been partially implemented by 2001. On security grounds, both the Clinton and Bush administrations have circumscribed the scope of the executive order, in practice, more sharply than its language indicated, barring U.S. trade and investment with a sweeping list of North Korean entities allegedly linked with Pyongyang's nuclear and missile programs. However, the Executive Order was perceived internationally as a major shift in U.S. policy and did lead to the normalization of North Korean relations with U.S. allies in Europe and Asia.

By all accounts, the confederation concept was one of the most hotly debated and time-consuming topics discussed at the summit. Kim Jong Il initially made a determined defense of his father's 1991 version of a "provisional" loose confederation. But he agreed, in the end, that the 1989 Roh Tae Woo "Korean Commonwealth" proposal, with its institutionalized twenty-member council of ministers and its one-hundred-member council of representatives, "converges" with what Kim Il Sung had in mind.[24]

Despite the acknowledgment in the June 14, 2000, summit declaration that there are "common factors" in the two positions, the prospects for early movement toward a confederation appeared uncertain in 2001. Each side was watching to see whether the other would deliver on the promises and half-promises made at the summit. For the North, the overriding question was how much aid the South would actually provide, and how soon. The South, for its part, had a whole series of questions: Would the North agree to join in reducing military tensions? Would it carry out its pledge to cooperate in building new railroad links, and would it let them operate? Would it provide investment guarantees and accept realistic ground rules for investors in its projected investment zones? Would it broaden the exchanges of separated family members? Would Kim Jong Il visit Seoul for a second summit?

The two Kims, who both faced opposition from domestic hard-liners that restricted their freedom of action, were trapped in a vicious circle in which the failure of one to act restricted what the other could do. Kim Dae Jung confidently predicted that the summit would lead to "genuine discussions" on a confederation, though not necessarily before his departure from office.[25] But unification, he said, could take "several decades."[26] Significantly, when the South extended food aid to the North after the summit, it was on a loan basis—repayable in thirty years.

In the initial aftermath of the summit, a flurry of North-South ministerial exchanges led to hopes for rapid progress, especially a dialogue between the defense ministers of North and South and working-level discussions on clearing land mines from a two hundred fifty-yard corridor across the DMZ that would permit restoration of a North-South railroad link severed by the Korean War. But progress came to an abrupt halt when president-elect George W. Bush, despite nominal support of the "sunshine policy," voiced doubts about the possibility of meaningful engagement with North Korea following a meeting with Kim Dae Jung in Washington on March 2, 2001. "We're not certain as to whether or not they're keeping all terms of existing agreements," Bush said. "When you make an agreement with a country that is secretive," he declared, "how are you aware as to whether or not they are keeping the terms of the agreement?" Moreover, he added, "I do have some skepticism about the leader of North Korea."[27]

Since North Korea had expected the summit to produce improved relations with the United States, Pyongyang reacted by freezing most North-South contacts as a gesture of protest. On a visit to Pyongyang in late May, I argued that this response was self-defeating and would be cited by hard-liners in Washington as new evidence that North Korean commitments made at the summit were unreliable. General Ri Chan Bok, North Korean delegate at Panmunjom, told me on May 31 that the United States "has pulled the reins on Kim Dae Jung and won't let him deliver on the promises he made to us. We cannot take the risks involved in going forward unless the South shows that it is independent and can be relied upon." It was Seoul, not Pyongyang, he said, that had reneged on its promises, blaming U.S. pressure for the South's failure to provide electricity and other energy assistance that "we discussed in detail at the summit."

Although dramatic breakthroughs on key issues such as the restoration of the North-South railroad link were blocked during 2001 by the Bush administration's hard line toward North Korea, Pyongyang avoided military provocations, and quiet North-South cooperation continued on significant issues. For example, the Supreme People's Assembly in Pyongyang enacted legislation in April 2001 that codified the legal framework for production contracts between South Korean and North Korean companies. Slow but steady progress continued in Russian negotiations with North and South Korea on extension of the Trans-Siberian Railway to North Korea and thence to the South. Of even greater potential importance, in October 2001 North Korea permitted South Korean experts to survey the route of a projected natural gas pipeline that would go from Kovykta in western Siberia through China into North Korea and then to the South. In return, South Korea invited North Korean experts to join in a feasibility study of the project that the South Korean government gas monopoly, Ko Gas, is conducting with Russian and Chinese experts.[28]

Even before the summit, Kim Dae Jung's "sunshine policy" had led to steady, if unspectacular, growth in North-South economic contacts that were accelerated by the summit.

The June 2000 summit accelerated the upsurge of North-South economic and cultural interchange that Kim Dae Jung had promoted since his election. Apart from the South Koreans who have gone to Kumgang Mountain on Hyundai-sponsored tours, the number of business and other visits sanctioned by both governments increased from 1,105 in 1997 to 3,317 in 1998 and 5,599 in 1999. Two-way North-South trade reached $333 million in 1999, a 50.2 percent increase over 1998, reflecting the growth of production contracts in which North Korean factories make products using equipment and materials supplied by collaborating South Korean companies. The Kim Dae Jung government lifted the previous de facto ceiling of $10 million on investments and loosened red tape by permitting businessmen to make multiple visits to the North on a single permit instead of requiring separate permits as in the past. Still, the Unification Ministry in Seoul must give case-by-case approval to all investments. By the end of 1999, in addition to the initial $100.33 million authorization for Hyundai's investment in the Kumgang project, the government had approved thirty-eight ventures involving investment authorizations totalling $20.96 million, including $11 million for one helping to improve corn production and $6.6 million for the inaugural phase of Pyonghwa Motors, which plans to make 10,000 cars in Nampo by 2003 in collaboration with Fiat, the Italian auto manufacturer.[29]

In a significant gesture to Pyongyang during the critical weeks leading up to agreement on the June 2000 summit, Seoul approved a $727,000 Samsung project to develop computer software jointly with the Korea Computer Center in Pyongyang.[30] However, hardware exports remain carefully controlled in an effort to keep the North from getting high-speed computers with possible military applications.

In the first year after the summit, Samsung Electronics and Lucky Goldstar Electronics started selling television sets assembled in the North, the Hanvit Bank became the first South Korean commercial bank to open a branch in Pyongyang, and a North-South joint venture began to market Hanmaum (One Mind) cigarettes, produced in Pyongyang, with a target of eighty million packs a year in the South and twenty million in the North.[31] A South Korean sports promoter gave North Korea $1 million to stage an auto race in which twenty-three teams of South Korean and foreign racers competed over a forty-two-mile course that started near Seoul and ended in the Kumgang tourist complex, where spectators paid handsomely to witness the windup of the race over twisting mountain roads.[32]

One of the more bemusing examples of the North's changing attitude toward the South was a request in late 1999 from a Pyongyang group close to Kim Jong II for the donation of 30,000 pairs of blue jeans to be distributed to young people in the North for restricted use on weekends only. The Nix Company, a Seoul clothing manufacturer, decided to donate 10,000 pairs as a promotion gambit, with the proviso that the Nix label be kept on the jeans. If the company is satisfied that the labels are not being removed and that the jeans are being worn, not exported to earn foreign exchange, further shipments are promised. Until now, jeans have been banned in the North as a symbol of capitalism.[33] Business contacts were still at an exploratory stage in 2001, hampered primarily by the lack of North-South agreements relating to investment protection, double taxation, and dispute resolution. North Korea unilaterally enacted its own legislation providing for "external economic arbitration," but Seoul was pressing for bilateral agreements to help forestall unsound ventures that might fail, putting a damper on future North-South economic cooperation.

The increased flow of exchanges has included a trickle of cultural, artistic, athletic and journalistic contacts, such as a Pyongyang performance by the South Korean Little Angels choral group in May 1998 and a return Seoul visit by North Korea's Mansudae singers. In most cases, the few journalists who have been allowed to visit the North have been restricted to reporting tourist attractions and historical sites. Two months after the June 2000 summit, however, Kim Jong Il invited forty-six South Korean editors to meet with him in a three-hour luncheon exchange that was notable for its easy, good-humored banter but carefully steered clear of hot-button security and political issues.

The changing atmospherics of North-South relations resulting from the "sunshine policy" were symbolized when North Korean and South Korean athletes marched into the Olympics opening ceremony at Sydney together under a single white flag. But the gap between atmospherics and reality was dramatized soon thereafter when the athletes proceeded to compete separately once the games began.

Another example of the gap between atmospherics and reality is the caution that has marked the South's relaxation of the ban on North Korean television broadcasts. Seoul jammed North Korean broadcasts until October 1998, when South Korean television networks were permitted to receive and broadcast uncensored nonpolitical programs via satellite and it became lawful for individuals with satellite dishes and converters to receive North Korean broadcasts in their homes. In practice, the networks have aired only romantic dramas and historical epics. The Seoul Broadcasting System was chastised by hard-line newspapers for broadcasting a movie about the anti-Japanese struggle of Koreans in Manchuria alleged to contain subtle North Korean propaganda themes.

For all of the changes that Kim Dae Jung has made in the South's posture toward the North, he has not commanded sufficient political strength to change it in the one way that North Korea has consistently emphasized as the litmus test of the South's readiness for an equitable unification process: repeal of the 1961 National Security Law promulgated by the Park Chung Hee military dictatorship. On several occasions when he attempted to amend what he called its most "poisonous" provisions, his own coalition partner, Prime Minister Kim Jong Pil, joined with the opposition party to kill the amendment.

The National Security Law was used by the Park and Chun Doo Hwan regimes, in particular, to justify blanket, arbitrary arrests of its opponents in the name of national security. Article 7 of the law provides for up to seven years of imprisonment and even the death penalty for vaguely defined "anti-state" and "espionage" activities that "praise" and "benefit" North Korea. The police and intelligence agencies automatically consider it a violation of article 7 for South Koreans to organize, join, or aid in any way groups designated as sympathetic to North Korea. Amnesty International reported that about four hundred people were arrested under the law during 1998, mostly under article 7, and that another two hundred were in detention at the end of 1999. "Most of these prisoners had done nothing to deserve arrest and imprisonment," the report said, "and were held solely for the non-violent exercise of their rights to freedom of expression and association. Some had formed study groups, distributed pamphlets or published books with left-wing political ideas; others had held discussions about North Korea or disagreed with government policies on North Korea. There is still an intolerance of left-wing or socialist views which are often regarded as being pro-North Korean. This sits uneasily with the government's new 'sunshine policy' towards North Korea, which actually encouraged more civilian and business links with the North."[34]

As examples of abuses under the law, the report cited the cases of publisher Lee Sang Kwan, who was jailed for publishing books about the lives of long-term political prisoners; Ha Young Joon, a student who posted a socialist text on a computer bulletin board; and a Catholic priest, Moon Kyu Hyun, who was arrested after a visit to North Korea with eight other priests, which had been approved by the government. Moon was charged with violating the National Security Law because he allegedly wrote words praising Kim Il Sung in the visitor's book of the mausoleum where the body of the late North Korean leader is displayed.

Kim Dae Jung has long pledged to amend the law to prevent human rights abuses. But his coalition with Kim Jong Pil and opposition to its revision in the National Assembly, the bureaucracy, the police, and the intelligence agencies have kept the law intact. A review of his first two years in office issued by his Information Ministry reported that the number of individuals prosecuted for violation of the law in 1999 was 12.3 percent lower than in 1997. At the same time, it defended the law, stating that "the Republic of Korea is still locked in an ideological struggle with North Korea. As such, the South needs to enforce public security laws such as the National Security Law to ensure its survival and protect its democratic system, thus shielding itself from the North's violent unification policy."[35]

The revisions of the law that Kim Dae Jung submitted to the National Assembly in 1999 were relatively minor. Instead of the broad language in the existing law, which permits the punishment of South Koreans who "praise" or "benefit" groups designated as "anti-state," the amended legislation would have narrowed punishment to those who actually join such groups or participate in other "organized" praise of North Korea. In another attempt to amend the law following the June 2000 summit, Kim Dae Jung proposed the removal of article 2, which defines North Korea as an illegitimate entity, but was once again rebuffed by the assembly.

In defining what constitutes an "anti-state" organization, the Kim Dae Jung government did not deviate from the policies pursued by its predecessors. Both Pomminryon (National Alliance for the Country's Reunification) and Hanchongryon (the South Korean Federation of University Student Councils), the leading youth groups promoting contacts with the North, are blackballed as "anti-state" because their militant demonstrations often involve slogans regarded as pro–North Korea.

The North has argued for the past five decades that mutually agreed steps toward an equitable form of reunification, such as a confederation, can only be negotiated if all shades of opinion in the South are represented in North-South contacts. While not ruling out government-to-government dialogue, Pyongyang has repeatedly proposed North-South conferences in which South Korean representation would embrace not only government officials but also a wide variety of citizen groups in the South sympathetic or neutral toward the North, including Pomminryon and Hanchongryon. Otherwise, the North contends, the deck will always be stacked against it, and a consensus truly reflective of the Korean people as a whole will be stifled. The South has consistently responded by pointing to the fact that the North's totalitarian system does not permit pro-South voices to be heard at all there, thus precluding their representation in North-South conferences.

In October 2000 the North decided to test whether the summit had changed the South's attitude and invited thirteen South Korean citizen groups to send representatives to the fiftieth anniversary celebrations of the Workers Party, including Pomminryon and Hanchongryon. In contrast to previous South Korean regimes, which had either banned or rigidly screened nongovernment contacts, Kim Dae Jung permitted eleven of the invited organizations to send three representatives each to Pyongyang without government interference in the selection process, ignoring criticism from hard-line newspapers. The North, for its part, also showed a new willingness to compromise when Seoul ruled that Pomminryon and Hanchongryon were illegal organizations and could not participate. In earlier years, Pyongyang would have angrily withdrawn all of the invitations, but this time it remained silent and welcomed the other eleven delegations.

THE COSTS OF ABSORPTION

It is often incorrectly assumed that the South, mindful of the German experience, no longer wants to absorb the North because it would cost too much. West Germany's absorption of East Germany has indeed proved to be much more expensive than anticipated, and absorbing North Korea would be even more costly for the South. But it does not follow that the South is reconciled to the permanent division of Korea and has abandoned hopes of absorption. Rather, the lesson of the German experience, in Seoul's perspective, is simply that a sudden absorption would be much less desirable than a gradual process, during which the South could reduce the costs of reunification by helping the North mitigate its economic problems. The general expectation in the South is still that its overwhelming economic superiority makes eventual absorption inevitable.

This expectation pervades a continuing stream of studies by South Korean and foreign economists analyzing the economics of reunification. What is at issue in these studies is not whether the North will be absorbed but how the South can best minimize the costs and economic dislocations that will result from the absorption process. The authors differ as to whether a sudden absorption is most likely. But all of them assume that the South will be in control of the reunified state and will decide the terms of North-South integration. For example, Bae Jin Young, envisaging a gradual process, called on the South Korean government to cushion the impact of reunification by setting up a special reunification fund in advance. "This is extremely important," he declared, "because it will enable the South Korean government to have flexibility in operating the fiscal budget when reunification actually occurs."[36] Yun Kun Young, by contrast, bases his analysis on "the central assumption that Korea is suddenly reunified and the market-oriented reunified Korea is to carry out the reform of the North Korean economy." Explicitly assigning South Korea the task of managing the economic aftermath of reunification, Yun outlined proposals for a "swift transition to a market system" in which South Korean and foreign investors would join in the privatization of North Korean enterprises. The four-year privatization process would be handled by a holding company patterned after the one that managed privatization in East Germany, the Treuhand, to be known as the National Trust Company. Suggesting how the German model could be applied to Korea, Yun envisages that "the controlling shares of the majority of the large enterprises to be privatized will be given to South Korean and foreign firms that operate similar lines of business." In the case of small and medium enterprises, "if they are privatized through direct sales and cash as the only means of payment, South Koreans and foreigners will dominate the scene," since "it is hard to imagine that North Koreans would have accumulated any significant amount of personal wealth." Therefore, he suggests a system of voucher coupons so that North Koreans can participate in privatization on an equal footing. But he adds that "North Korean entrepreneurs may lack the funds that would be needed to restructure enterprises for participation in a market economy" so that "even if North Koreans somehow take control of state enterprises, it may be difficult for them to raise adequate funds for restructuring."[37]

Estimates of the cost of reunification range from $182.7 billion to $2 trillion depending on assumptions concerning such factors as the timing of reunification, how reunification costs are defined, the level of development in the North and South at the time of integration, and development priorities in the North after reunification. The most important of these factors is the first one. There is general agreement that the cost will steadily rise as the disparity in the growth rates between North and South widens. Thus, in 1996, Marcus Noland estimated that reunification would then cost $500 billion to $750 billion and that the figure would roughly double every five years.[38] In 1999, Yong Sun Lee outlined two scenarios based on differing assumptions concerning the comparative levels of economic development in North and South. One assumes that North Korea will increase its per capita gross development product (GDP) to 60 percent of the South Korean level by 2005. Public and private investment costs incurred by the South would then be $182.7 billion.[39] Another assumes that the North will not reach this level until 2010, in which case the cost would be $683.2 billion.

In 1992, Lawrence Summers, then a World Bank economist and later U.S. Treasury secretary, underlined the time factor, warning a South Korean audience that "as your economy grows, the gap with North Korea will widen and the cost of unification will rise. Any theory of the costs of unification suggests that they are likely to be proportional to the gap between South Korea GNP and North Korean GNP." Summers emphasized that the social costs of reunification in the South would be minimized if reunification comes soon. So long as the labor market in the South remains tight, he argued, South Korean companies can take advantage of low-wage labor in the North without damaging the interests of unskilled workers in the South. But the demand for unskilled labor in the South is likely to decline in future decades, he predicted, and the longer that unification is deferred, the more likely it is that South Korean workers will be competing against low-wage North Korean workers in a reunified Korea.[40]

One of the key issues that South Koreans will confront when and if reunification occurs is whether to adopt a uniform exchange rate beneficial to the North or to retain an exchange rate designed to keep Northern wages down. The principal argument advanced for keeping Northern wages down is that this would encourage South Korean companies to invest in the North, thus stimulating economic growth that would encourage residents of the North to stay there instead of migrating to the South. Critics of this argument point out that perpetuating low wages in the North would have an adverse impact on unskilled workers in the South. But fear of a flood of migrants is a more powerful concern. Moreover, there are strong economic arguments against adopting currency parity as Germany did.

As Gifford Combs has observed, parity between the old East German currency, the ostmark, and the deutsche mark had the effect of driving up inflation in Germany as a whole. The result was that "Germany's inflation was rapidly exported to the rest of Europe in the form of higher interest rates and led, eventually to the collapse of the European Monetary System." Germany's leading economic position "allowed it to socialize and spread the cost of parity across the continent," Combs recalls, but "South Korea lacks the economic clout to socialize the cost and spread it implicitly across the globe through economic policymaking as Germany did. Instead, it will require explicit grants and loans from international sources—large amounts of capital." In order to obtain such large-scale financing and to cope with the problems of absorbing the North, Combs adds, "the South must embark now upon a serious commitment to restructure the economy through deregulation, transparency, competition and banking reform"—making good on the restructuring pledges that were given in return for the 1997 IMF financial bailout but have yet to be adequately implemented.[41]

Former West German chancellor Helmut Schmidt has underlined another economic hurdle that a reunified Korea would have to overcome. "Unlike the case of East Germany," he writes, "reunification of the two Koreas will *not* entail readymade access to new foreign markets for either of the two, given the absence of an Asian common market. Protectionism in the United States and Europe—Korea's main export markets—

threatens to erode Korea's export base and places South Korea in a vulnerable economic position. To assist any reunification process, the international community ideally would have to be more accommodating to Korea in the future. But given the present climate in global trade negotiations, it is unlikely that a reunified Korea would be granted assured access to the European Common Market or the United States."[42]

Over time, reunification would have economic advantages that would strengthen Korea as a whole. During the years when North Korea was economically solvent, South Korean economists focused on these advantages, especially the fact that the North has much more extensive natural resources than the South. But as the North's economic problems have persisted and the South, with its own economic difficulties, has increasingly recognized the economic impact reunification could have on its standard of living, the impatient yearning for quick reunification that marked earlier decades has been replaced by a more cautious mood. Kim Dae Jung epitomized this mood when he said that "unification is only a matter of time. But for now, there are more negatives than positives because we are currently not capable of economically supporting North Korea."[43]

In Psychological Limbo

An authoritative public opinion study in South Korea has shown a marked drop in eagerness for early reunification between September 1996 and February 1999. In 1996, 56 percent of those polled were either "very eager" or "somewhat eager" for reunification soon, but in 1999 this number had dropped to 39 percent, while the number of those who were "somewhat cautious" in 1996 had risen to just under 60 percent.[44]

In a penetrating analysis of South Korean attitudes toward reunification, sociologist Roy R. Grinker has shown that economic factors alone do not explain why the South clings so tenaciously to hopes for absorption on its own terms and is so divided over proposals for a loose confederation or "Korean Commonwealth." Grinker's thesis is that the trauma of the 1945 division, reinforced by the Korean War, has led to the idealization of a lost national homogeneity. "The received view," he writes, "is that national division disrupted Korean cultural and national identity and that reunification will recover them." But in reality, significant social, cultural, linguistic, and economic differences[45] have developed between

North and South during the past five decades, apart from an ideological divide that never previously existed throughout Korean history. Until they come to terms with this fact, he argues, South Koreans will be psychologically paralyzed, unable to mourn their loss of national identity and move on to adopt realistic measures to recover it, such as a confederation. His analysis calls to mind the trauma suffered by many relatives of missing U.S. Vietnam War and Korean War soldiers. Living in psychological limbo, waiting to know for certain whether or not their loved ones are dead, they cannot mourn their loss and face the future afresh. In Grinker's analysis, so long as South Koreans remain fixated on restoring, in one stroke, a homogeneous Korea that no longer exists, their psychological paralysis will persist.

"Unable to mourn," he declares, "South Koreans cannot negotiate with the (idealized) past, reconcile with the North Koreans and begin to construct a pluralistic society. . . . Despite the fact that South Koreans clearly recognize how afraid the North Koreans are of 'unification by absorption,' South Korea has not given any signals to the North that reunification might preserve some of the distinctiveness the North has developed during the division. For many South Koreans, 'reunification' is a euphemism for conquest, the annihilation of North Korea and the total assimilation of North Koreans into South Korea . . . in short, winning the war."[46]

Although the idea sounds grandiose, a confederation would merely formalize the de facto division of the peninsula while avoiding the de jure division that diplomatic recognition of each other by the North and South would entail. In practice, nothing would change without mutual agreement. But in psychological terms, the establishment of a confederation would have great symbolic importance for both sides. For the North, it would reduce fears of absorption by committing the South to the coexistence of differing systems. For the South, a confederation would not only keep alive the dream of eventual reunification but would also provide a rationale for postponing formal integration until congruent economic systems evolve.

Whether a confederation is actually possible will depend primarily on Pyongyang's ability to deal with its economic problems. Economic stability in the North would ease its fears of interchange with the South and make the South less confident that absorption is, in fact, a realistic goal. Whether the North can stabilize its economy will be significantly affected, in turn, by the future role of the United States. Until all nonstrategic U.S. economic sanctions are removed and North Korea, in time, gets the normal trade status accorded to China, South Korean companies will be unable to export products made in North Korea to the American market. Until the United States gives the signal, the World Bank, the Asian Development Bank, and other international aid institutions are not likely to support North Korean reconstruction.

The American interest in an economically stable Korea would clearly be better served by the implicit, long-term pursuit of reform through a confederal framework than by explicit clarion calls for reform. Similarly, the American interest in a militarily stable Korea can only be pursued effectively after coexistence is institutionalized. It is putting the cart before the horse to press the North for arms-control and tension-reduction measures before the issue of confederation versus absorption is resolved. Faced with the threat of absorption, the North will remain in a defensive mode and be reluctant to modify its military posture. In a confederal framework, Pyongyang would be more likely to negotiate balanced force redeployments and other measures to ease tensions. The next chapter will examine how American policy affects the prospects for a confederation and how American interests in Korea would be affected if the South should once again pursue absorption.

CHAPTER 9

The United States and Reunification

IN NORTH KOREA and South Korea alike, it is an article of faith that the United States deserves the principal blame for the division of the peninsula and thus has a special responsibility for helping to restore national unity. This deep-seated sense of grievance is linked with the belief that Washington wanted to keep Korea divided during the cold war in order to pursue U.S. strategic objectives related mainly to Japan. Anti-American nationalism is surprisingly virulent even in the South, where military dependence on the United States has generated strong undercurrents of xenophobia that are sweeping aside the gratitude felt by the older generation for the American role in the Korean War. A representative poll of college students found that 79 percent blamed the United States for the division of Korea and 64 percent considered the United States to be the country most reluctant to see Korea reunified.[1]

The Korean indictment of the United States begins with the Cairo, Yalta, and Potsdam conferences, condemning the casual disposition of the peninsula by the wartime allies that led to the division. Since Russian diplomacy traditionally had sought to divide Korea, argues Cho Soon Sung in a representative statement of the dominant Korean attitude, the United States either was a gullible fool or must have been more than ready to sacrifice Korean interests for the sake of its own, emerging cold war strategic concerns.[2]

Due allowance is made in this view for the confusion marking the last months of the war. In particular, Cho recognizes that the Russians knew of the impending Japanese surrender before the Americans did through a decoded diplomatic cable and were thus able to claim an eleventh-hour role in the war, which gave them their access to North Korea. But it is the very accidental character of the division and the low priority given to Korea by Roosevelt and Truman that has been such a persistent insult. As Cho puts it, American interference regarding Korea and the vagueness of the United States about its occupation plans "amounted to a tacit invitation to the Russians to occupy the peninsula, setting in train the events that led to the division."[3]

THE LOST OPPORTUNITY OF 1945

Given Soviet complicity in the crime, the American role in the creation of the thirty-eighth parallel might have been canceled out in Korean memories had it not been for the subsequent U.S. approach to Korean domestic politics during the critical 1945–46 period. Based on firsthand knowledge, former State Department official Gregory Henderson has recounted the struggle inside the U.S. government between military leaders with a visceral anti-Communist preoccupation and State Department officials who were seeking to work out a trusteeship arrangement that would have kept the peninsula unified.[4] Faced with the Preparatory People's Republic established by Yo Un Hyong on August 12, 1945—a representative coalition of nationalist elements, both non-Communist and Communist—the occupation authorities hurriedly sponsored Syngman Rhee, Kim Ku, and other exiled conservative leaders as a counterforce. This consolidated an internecine political conflict that led inexorably to the collapse of trusteeship efforts in July 1947.

The fateful political drama between the proclamation of the People's Republic on August 12, 1945, and the arrival of Rhee under the aegis of the American military government on October 16 crystallized the Korean image of the United States as a self-interested interloper insensitive to the traumatic meaning of a divided peninsula in nationalist terms. In Yo Un Hyong, Korea put forth a non-Communist nationalist leader who had foreseen the possibility of an internationally imposed partition. Yo had laid the groundwork for an independent Korean regime designed to head off such an eventuality by setting up the secret Alliance for Korean Independence in 1944. He was primed to act in the aftermath of V-J Day, when the Japanese colonial authorities, fearful of anti-Japanese riots and searching for a focus of stability, asked him to set up an interim government.[5] The short-lived republic that he led was clearly a broad-based, spontaneous expression of the Korean nationalist impulses that surfaced in the first flush of independence.

In *The Origins of the Korean War*, Bruce Cumings has presented definitive evidence showing that the People's Republic was not initially Communist controlled.[6] It was only after the U.S. occupation authorities cracked down on the republic, inducing non-Communist nationalists to abandon it, that Communists were able to move into the resulting vacuum gradually during 1946. As Cumings stresses, however, while the republic was not Communist dominated at its inception, it did have a powerful "revolutionary thrust."[7] It would no doubt have pursued radical land-reform measures and would have harshly punished Koreans who had collaborated with the Japanese colonial rulers. This did not disturb some State Department officials, who favored recognizing the republic, but it alarmed Lt. Gen. John R. Hodge, the U.S. commander, who branded Yo as "a well-indoctrinated Comintern Communist."[8]

Yo Un Hyong set out to create a unifying coalition of diverse national-ist elements, deliberately giving what he saw as due importance to vet-erans of the underground but assuring the representation, at the same time, of leading conservatives and moderates.[9] His nomination of Syng-man Rhee as chairman of the September 6 People's Congress, a gather-ing of more than one thousand delegates on the eve of the American landing, reflected his desire for a workable nationalist coalition that could head off the impending partition and his recognition that non-Commu-nist Korean nationalist exiles had great popular standing. Nevertheless, the American response was one of automatic hostility to the republic well before the process of Communist penetration got underway. When a moderate delegation representing the republic went to Hodge's com-mand ship in Inch'on Harbor, he refused to see the group. His first eval-uations of the republic came from a handful of English-speaking Korean advisers, hastily recruited from missionary circles, who were "conservative in instinct"[10] and pinned an undiscriminating Red label on the republic. Yo was unable to see Hodge until late October. For three months, the military government issued a succession of increasingly strident edicts re-pudiating the legitimacy of the republic and displacing "people's com-mittees" that often went right on performing local governmental func-tions until the actual physical arrival of American forces. Hoping for a Korean regime that would function as an arm of the occupation, Wash-ington formally outlawed the assertive republic in December, and South Korean politics splintered into a power struggle among Rhee, Kim Ku, and lesser leaders of more than four hundred political parties and social groups.

Yo was assassinated in 1947, but even today, he enjoys a special place in the Korean nationalist pantheon. Memories of Yo were invoked fre-quently by a powerful protest movement in the South, the National Sal-vation Front, that paralyzed action for more than a year on the U.S.–supported normalization treaty between Seoul and Tokyo. In the eyes of its critics, a South Korean alignment with Japan would polarize the North-South division along cold war lines. Opposition to the treaty was so heated that after it was finally signed in June 1965, the ratification bill had to be pushed through the National Assembly by pro-government forces when the opposition was absent from the chamber. In a detailed account of the protest movement, the *Far Eastern Economic Review* reported a Tokyo gathering of pro-Seoul, pro-Pyongyang, and neutralist Koreans "where they agreed that Korea had enjoyed a fine Korean government right after Liberation Day when the Japanese Governor-General capitulated to Yo Un Hyong and his provisional cabinet of anti-Japanese resisters, but that everything had been spoiled by Korea's false friends, Russia and America, who had insisted on cutting her up and sharing the spoils. Had only the Koreans' own government been allowed to carry on after the landing of the Americans on September 7, 1945, all would have been well. That was the consensus of opinion and the basis of a National Salvation Front aiming, ultimately, at a 'Yo-type' setup."[11]

In South Korea, I have found that the name of Yo Un Hyong touches a raw nerve of emotion, evoking respectful tributes and a note of distress at the lost opportunity he personified. On my first visit to the North, Ch'a Il, a commentator on the government organ *Minju Choson*, appeared moved at mention of Yo, commenting that he "was not a Communist, but he had a national conscience. If he had lived and had stuck to his original attitude, we could have worked together."

"Sacrificed on the Altar of Power Politics"

Having alienated those who sought unification through a coalition with the Communists, the United States later found itself on a collision course with Syngman Rhee, whose anticommunism proved to be inseparable from his own brand of nationalism. Rhee's "March North" slogan reflected a grimly serious desire to use American military power for the achievement of unification, a desire much more integral to Rhee's commitment to Washington than has generally been realized. In a July 1954 meeting with President Dwight Eisenhower recalled by one of the South Koreans present, Rhee wanted assurances that the United States "would stay with us until we could reunify our country." Eisenhower focused instead on getting Rhee to promise that he would negotiate a normalization treaty with Japan, which Rhee angrily refused to do. One of Rhee's prime ministers, Paek Tu Jin, said in an unpublished interview with the Dulles Oral History Project that the American draft of the agreed minutes pledged support for unification by "peaceful means," while Rhee insisted that it read "by all means."[12] This was the reason why Rhee refused to sign the minutes for six months after the 1954 meeting until the U.S. cutoff of civilian oil supplies forced the issue.

South Korean resentment over the Panmunjom armistice is inextricably linked to the perception of the United States as principally responsible for the division. Kim Jong Pil, the architect of Park Chung Hee's military coup, who later served twice as prime minister, declared in 1963 that "American self-interest and convenience dictated our twin national disasters, the thirty-eighth parallel and the 1953 armistice line."[13] One of South Korea's most respected ambassadors to Washington, Hahm Pyong Choon, wrote that the truce made the United States responsible thereafter for supporting Seoul, and South Koreans looked on American aid as "a form of reimbursement to us for carrying a disproportionate share" in the defense of what were "above all, the interests of the United States in the Western Pacific."[14] When the United States pressed Seoul to send troops to South Vietnam, the ensuing debate was infused with a deep sense of grievance. A government spokesman justified the South Korean effort to drive a hard bargain by harking back to the "humiliating truce, in which Korea was sacrificed on the altar of power politics."[15] Escalating economic demands were accompanied by bitter reminders that the "unequal" 1953 mutual security treaty between Seoul and Washington had been "arbitrarily imposed" on the Rhee government. A key provision of the treaty giving the United States operational control over the South Korean armed forces has been consistently perceived in Seoul ever since 1953 as a "leash" intended primarily to restrain any "March North" impulses.

In assessing American motives, Koreans in the South and North alike have been powerfully influenced by a persistent American tendency to treat the peninsula as a subsidiary factor in American relations with Japan. The Taft-Katsura Agreement of 1905 was a transparent trade-off designed to assure American hegemony in the Philippines in exchange for U.S. acquiescence in the Japanese annexation of Korea. Washington then added insult to injury after 1945, showing little or no awareness of what Japanese colonialism had meant. Lieutenant General Hodge, the occupation commander who had outlawed Yo Un Hyong's nascent government, made an often-quoted comment to an American journalist that Koreans and Japanese "are the same breed of cat."[16] This mindset made it natural for the United States to take the path of least resistance by keeping the Japanese colonial bureaucracy and police apparatus intact. Similarly, the United States built its newly created constabulary around Koreans who had served in the Japanese forces, and the twenty Tokyo-trained officers who survived World War II were favored by the United States for the top posts when the armed forces were set up in 1948.[17]

In American eyes, a normalization treaty between Tokyo and Seoul was indispensable for South Korean development and for facilitating Japanese–South Korean military cooperation under U.S. leadership. Rhee's intransigent opposition to the treaty was viewed as irrational emotionalism. In Korean eyes, however, the United States seemed once again to be handing over the peninsula to the Japanese under more dangerous historical circumstances than ever. Not only in Seoul but in Tokyo, too, it was only sustained and determined American pressure that pushed the two treaty signatories to the negotiating table in 1965.

The South Korean perception of the United States as an obstacle to unification did not change when Washington gave its blessing to the 1972 North-South dialogue. Koreans were well aware that this reversal of U.S. hostility toward Pyongyang came largely as an offshoot of the Sino–U.S. détente symbolized by President Nixon's visit to Beijing. In Korean eyes, the U.S. volte-face typified the American tendency to treat Korea as a subsidiary factor in U.S. relations with other powers, not as a factor important to Washington in its own right.

In reality, Park Chung Hee and Kim Il Sung had arranged the secret contacts that led to the 1972 North-South dialogue largely on their own initiative. They were both concerned that a Sino–U.S. accommodation would expose them, once again, to the big power manipulation that had been so disastrous for Korea at the turn of the century. Similarly, during the next decade, as Washington moved toward accommodation with Moscow as well as with Beijing, Park's successors, Chun Doo Hwan and Roh Tae Woo, arranged secret contacts of their own with Pyongyang, often without the knowledge or approval of Washington. On October 17, 1985, Chun's intelligence chief, Chang Se Dong, and a foreign policy confidante, Park Chun Un, met with Kim Il Sung and agreed to an exchange of summit meetings scheduled to begin with a visit by Chun to Pyongyang. But according to a statement by Park in 1998, "pressure from the United States" led to Chun's abrupt cancellation of the summit plans.[18]

Until 1992, the United States was not explicitly committed to reunification as a goal of U.S. policy. It was therefore not surprising that in the South Korean polling study cited earlier, 64 percent of the students interviewed viewed the United States as the country most reluctant to see Korea reunified. In an effort to counter such feeling and to get in step with the conciliatory policy toward the North being pursued by Roh Tae

Woo, President George Bush told the South Korean National Assembly on January 6, 1992, that the American people favored "peaceful unification on terms acceptable to the Korean people." This deliberately vague statement to some extent insulated the United States from criticism as an outright enemy of unification. But it conveyed a sanguine attitude toward the prospect of indefinite division, and in both the North and South, American motives are still suspect. In Pyongyang, it is assumed that the United States favors unification only if it comes through absorption. In Seoul, what makes many South Koreans wary of a U.S. normalization of relations with Pyongyang is the fear that this will freeze a "two-Korea" division of the peninsula. By contrast, collapse scenarios offer the hope of a quicker, albeit costly, route to unification.

RESHAPING THE AMERICAN ROLE

In charting new policies in Korea attuned to post–cold war realities, the starting point for the United States should be an expression of regret for the U.S. role in the division of the peninsula addressed to both the South and the North, accompanied by a declaration of support for peaceful reunification much more explicit and much more positive than the 1992 Bush statement.

Visiting Pyongyang on March 31, 1992, Rev. Billy Graham stopped just short of expressing regret in his airport arrival address but displayed a sensitivity to Korean feelings that should be emulated in U.S. official pronouncements. "Korean unity," he declared, "was a victim of the cold war. Because of the competition which existed then between the United States and the former Soviet Union, decisions and compromises were made which divided Korea at the thirty-eighth parallel. I share the concern of many Americans that my nation was one of those which had a part in those cold war decisions, and I pray that the Korean people will soon be united peacefully."[19]

During the decades since 1945, the polarization of Korea along cold war lines constituted a built-in barrier to reunification. Nevertheless, the division of the peninsula, while a tragedy for the Korean people, did not destabilize Northeast Asia. In the post–cold war environment, however, a divided Korea is increasingly likely to become a focus of rivalry involving not only the neighboring powers but also the United States. The American interest in a stable Northeast Asia would thus be served by the emergence of a reunified Korean buffer state, leading to the neutralization of the peninsula as an arena of major power conflict.

To pursue this interest, the United States would have to reshape its policies in the peninsula so that it does not stand in the way of movement toward a loose confederation, as it does now, while at the same time doing what it can to promote such movement. This would require, above all, a basic redefinition of the role of U.S. forces in Korea that would induce the South to think in terms of accommodation with the North. In its present form, the U.S. military presence sustains a climate of indefinite confrontation. The United States has an open-ended commitment to one side in a civil war. It is providing a massive economic subsidy that enables its ally to minimize the sacrifices that would otherwise be necessary for the maintenance of the conflict. The South's upper- and middle-income minority, in particular, has acquired a vested interest in the status quo. Without its U.S. subsidy, Seoul, which now spends an average of $13 billion per year for defense, would have to double or triple its military budget to replace the conventional forces deployed for its defense by the United States, not to mention the much higher outlays that independent nuclear forces would require. In addition to the direct cost of its forces in Korea, averaging $2 billion per year, the United States spends more than $40 billion annually to maintain the overall U.S. force structure in East Asia and the western Pacific on which its capability to intervene in Korea depends. So long as the South regards this U.S. economic cushion as an entitlement, it will be under no compulsion to pursue a modus vivendi with the North.

Some observers argue that the South might respond to U.S. force withdrawals by upgrading its own military capabilities, not by adopting a more conciliatory posture toward the North. These observers cite Park Chung Hee's efforts to acquire a nuclear weapons capability after the U.S. made unilateral withdrawals under the Nixon Doctrine. But there is a basic difference between the environment of unremitting North-South hostility that Park faced during the cold war and the post–cold war climate of accommodation that opened up after the June 2000 summit. Similarly, there is a basic difference between unilateral U.S. withdrawals, such as those that Nixon made, and the U.S. withdrawals envisaged in part 3 as part of arms-control trade-offs in which North Korea, too, would be required to make concessions. In this new context, with South Korea polarized between supporters and opponents of the "sunshine policy," the prospect of an indefinite U.S. presence, with its comfortable economic cushion, would help the opposition perpetuate the status quo and block arms-control compromises. By the same token, a U.S. shift to the role of honest broker discussed in part 3, accompanied by the prospect of a declining U.S. presence, would compel the South to make hard choices between military and civilian budgetary priorities that can now be postponed.

Despite the end of the cold war, the role of U.S. forces in Korea has not changed to keep pace with geopolitical realignments in Korea. The U.S. military presence in the South was a response to the projection of Soviet and Chinese military power on the side of the North. Now Russia no longer has a security commitment to the North. While retaining a nominal security commitment to Pyongyang and keeping up economic aid, China has in reality moved steadily closer to Seoul. Both Moscow and Beijing are increasingly attempting to play the role of honest broker between the North and South. That is what they want the United States to do, and that is what the North also wants the United States to do.

What a redefinition of the U.S. military role would mean in concrete terms is explored at length in the chapters that follow. In essence, the mission of U.S. forces would no longer be limited to the defense of the South but would be broadened to embrace the deterrence of aggression by either the North or the South against the other. In its new role as a stabilizer and balancer in Korea, the United States would provide the security umbrella necessary for stable progress toward a loose confederation, helping promote a climate of mutual trust. Conceivably, U.S. forces could remain for a limited period following the establishment of a confederation. North Korea, for its part, has left such a possibility open. Kim Byong Hong, policy-planning chief in the Foreign Ministry, told me on May 7, 1998, that "Korea is surrounded by big powers—Russia, China, and Japan. We must think of the impact of the withdrawal of U.S. troops on the balance of power in the region. It is possible that if U.S. troops pull out of Korea, Japan will rearm immediately." A day earlier, Kim Yong Nam, then foreign minister and now chairman of the Supreme People's Assembly, said more obliquely that "the United States is standing in the way of a confederation, but it would be in your interests to help us work for one because it would enhance stability in the region, and the United States can advance its interests in both halves of Korea if we are confederated." Han Song Ryol, former North Korean deputy representative at the United Nations, went still further over dinner on May 10, 1997. "Under certain circumstances," he said, "depending on your policy, I can imagine U.S. forces stationed in North as well as South Korea."

PART III

Toward U.S. Disengagement

CHAPTER 10

Tripwire

> While they have many reasons for wanting this missile
> program, their primary reason is security, is deterrence. Whom
> would they be deterring? They would be deterring the United
> States. We do not think of ourselves as a threat to North Korea,
> but I fully believe that they consider us a threat to them.
>
> —Former secretary of defense William Perry, interviewed on
> *The News Hour with Jim Lehrer*, Public Broadcasting
> System, September 17, 1999

OF ALL THE pronouncements made by Perry following his mission to Pyongyang on behalf of President Clinton, this was the most far-reaching in its implications, underlining as it did the integral connection between the U.S. military presence in Korea and North Korean missile ambitions. Yet despite this unambiguous recognition of North Korean motivations, Perry ignored North Korean security concerns in his policy recommendations to the White House. Focusing solely on U.S. security priorities, he said that Washington should condition the normalization of relations on two key North Korean concessions. First, Pyongyang should agree to limit the range of its missiles to 380 kilometers (180 miles). Second, it should give up its nuclear weapons option once and for all, going beyond the suspension of its nuclear program negotiated with Washington in 1994.

The underlying assumption of the Perry approach—that economic incentives and political recognition would be sufficient to bring about an accommodation with Pyongyang—has proved to be questionable. In bargaining for economic help, North Korea has offered to negotiate restraints on its missile program similar to the 1994 nuclear freeze. But giving up its missile option altogether is another matter. The military-dominated regime in Pyongyang may be ready to discontinue the development, production, and deployment of all missiles with a range over 180 miles, but how far it will go in this direction will depend, first, on whether hostile relations with the United States are ended through the normalization of relations and a peace treaty terminating the Korean War, and second, whether the United States is prepared to make changes in the nature of its military role in Korea that address North Korean security concerns.

In a formal proposal on June 16, 1998, Pyongyang did express its readiness to discuss the "discontinuation" of its missile development in conjunction with a formal end to the Korean War, followed by the removal of the U.S. military "threat."[1] Carefully avoiding a demand for the withdrawal of the U.S. military "presence," Pyongyang envisaged a transitional phase during which the role of U.S. forces would change. The United States would shift from its present adversarial role, limited to the defense of the South, to a new, broader role as a stabilizer and balancer, dedicated to deterrence of an attack by either the South against the North or the North against the South. This shift would set the stage for a trilateral (the United States, South Korea, and North Korea) arms-control and tension-reduction process in which the security concerns of all parties would be addressed. The long-term future of the U.S. military presence in Korea, the threat posed to the South by the forward deployment of North Korean conventional forces, and North Korean nuclear and missile capabilities would all be on the table.

The new North Korean posture was formally reflected in the four-power (the United States, China, North Korea, and South Korea) Geneva talks on March 18, 1998, when the North Korean delegate offered to replace a proposed agenda item, "the withdrawal of U.S. forces," with another one referring to the "status of U.S. forces."[2] Washington and Seoul rejected this offer, insisting that discussions relating to U.S. forces can take place only *after* confidence-building and tension-reduction measures at the thirty-eighth parallel have been negotiated. North Korea responded that this is putting the cart before the horse, since military adversaries still formally at war cannot risk the concessions necessary for a reduction of tensions.

The five chapters that follow focus on how this impasse can be broken. I begin by assessing the North-South military balance that existed in 2000 and the impact of the U.S. military presence on this balance. Next, in chapter 12, I suggest specific arms-control trade-offs, drawing on the formal proposals put forward in the past by Seoul and Pyongyang and on informal discussions with generals and diplomats in the North and South that began in 1968 and have continued through 2000.[3] The gradual redeployment, reduction, and eventual withdrawal of U.S. forces would be part of such trade-offs if North Korea is prepared for adequate reciprocal concessions. In return for a complete U.S. withdrawal, Pyongyang would have to end not only the existing threat posed to the South by the forward deployment of its conventional forces but also the potential threat that would be posed to the United States if Pyongyang should develop long-range missiles capable of reaching U.S. territory.

After exploring the nature of possible tension-reduction scenarios in Korea, I turn in chapter 13 to a discussion of the procedural deadlock that has until now obstructed the consideration of such scenarios. My conclusion is that the first step toward breaking this deadlock should be a formal end to the Korean War and the replacement of its vestigial symbols, the Military Armistice Commission and the United Nations Command, with a new trilateral Mutual Security Commission in which the United States would play the role of stabilizer and balancer proposed by the North.

Significantly, if the United States does end its adversarial role, Pyongyang would not object to the continuation of a modified U.S. force presence for an indefinite transition period while arms-control trade-offs are explored. During this period, the United States could retain its security treaty with South Korea, Pyongyang says, and North Korea would retain its security link with China. But the ultimate goal of the United States, my analysis suggests, should be a neutralization agreement with China, Russia, and Japan in which all four powers would agree not to introduce military forces into Korea.

In chapter 14 I explain why the U.S. military presence in Korea has retained political support in Washington for five decades despite the end of the cold war and the shift of Russia and China to the role of honest broker between North and South. At the same time, I underline the increasing nationalistic opposition in South Korea to the U.S. presence, especially since the North-South summit of June 2000, warning that the United States could ultimately be forced to withdraw militarily from the peninsula without obtaining arms-control concessions in return.

Finally, in chapter 15 I consider what the United States should do if arms-control negotiations are sabotaged by hard-liners in either the North or the South. My conclusion is that the North, for economic reasons, needs to reduce military spending more than the South does, and that the South could well prove to be a greater obstacle to a settlement. The United States would face a difficult dilemma, I point out, if Pyongyang should prove to be ready for the asymmetrical pullback zone discussed in chapter 12, but Seoul opposes the U.S. force redeployments and withdrawals necessary to conclude an agreement. In such a situation, I suggest, the United States should not become a hostage to South Korea and should be prepared to negotiate a bilateral arms-control agreement with the North involving changes in the U.S. force posture.

The Danger of a New Korean War

The basic premise of my proposal for eventual disengagement is that the danger of another Korean war with U.S. involvement continues to be grave. Indeed, if there should be another Korean war, American forces would, by design, become involved at the very outset under the "tripwire" strategy now in force. Some 15,000 soldiers, nearly half of the total U.S. military presence in the South, are deployed in the Munsan and Chorwan invasion corridors leading to Seoul. This reflects a belief on the part of the United States and South Korea alike that North Korea will be deterred from an attack only if it regards U.S. involvement as a certainty.

South Korea, for its part, fears that the United States might seek in the end to avoid or minimize its involvement. Seoul points to article 3 of the U.S.–South Korean mutual security treaty, which stipulates that the involvement of the United States would be subject to its "constitutional processes." It is this anxiety concerning the reliability of the U.S. commitment that explains why the South wants U.S. combat forces stationed directly in the most likely path of a North Korean advance, where they would suffer heavy casualties, thus enhancing the likelihood that U.S. reinforcements would be rushed to Korea. This anxiety also explains why most South Korean military planners are wary of any change in the status quo at the thirty-eighth parallel, such as replacing the 1953 armistice machinery or terminating the United Nations Command.

South Korean military planners are particularly wary of proposals to shift wartime operational control over South Korean forces from the U.S. general who heads both the U.N. Command and the Combined Forces Command to his South Korean counterpart in the Combined Forces Command. By the same token, some influential advocates of accommodation with the North favor a shift in wartime operational control precisely because they believe that the status quo enables Pyongyang to depict the South as a U.S. "puppet" and blocks meaningful North-South dialogue on tension reduction.

Maj. Gen. (Ret.) Lim Dong Won, who served as national security adviser to President Kim Dae Jung and later as director of the National Intelligence Service, declared in 1996 that "only with the reversion of operational control will North Korea respect and fear the South. Unless operational control is returned to us, the North will continue to confine its approaches to the United States alone and sidestep or bypass the South."[4] Lim's position implicitly recognizes that the U.S. military presence in the South is likely to become an agenda item in tension-reduction negotiations with Pyongyang. But this is a minority view in the South Korean military leadership. The dominant view in Seoul is that the U.S. surrender of operational control might presage a U.S. withdrawal; and in Washington, American policy is guided by a very different concern that the South might drag the United States into needless conflict unless it is kept on a tight leash.

The danger of a quick slide into war was dramatically demonstrated during the tense showdown with Pyongyang in May and June 1994. When North Korea removed the spent fuel rods from its Yongbyon reactor on May 8, many North Korea specialists argued that Pyongyang was simply stepping up the pace of its effort to engage the United States in negotiations on a "package" deal to resolve the nuclear crisis. But the majority view in Washington was that Pyongyang had crossed the Rubicon, signaling its determination to develop nuclear weapons, and that military pressure was the only answer.

On May 18, Gen. John Shalikashvili, chairman of the Joint Chiefs of Staff, called in four-star generals and admirals from all over the world to consider how other commands would support Gen. Gary Luck, commander of U.S. forces in Korea, if a conflict should break out. The resulting contingency plans envisaged the hypothetical deployment in Korea of roughly half of all U.S. combat forces.[5]

On May 24, Senator John McCain made a Senate speech calling for "air or cruise missile strikes" against the reprocessing facility at Yongbyon. "Precision targeting," he said, "could effectively damage its capabilities with little or no radiation release."

On June 2, with tensions mounting, President Clinton announced that he would seek U.N. Security Council sanctions against North Korea, provoking a response from the Foreign Ministry in Pyongyang on June 13 that "U.N. sanctions will be regarded immediately as a declaration of war."

To Ambassador James Laney and General Luck in Seoul, the situation seemed so dangerous that on June 15, without waiting for formal orders from Washington, they met to map emergency evacuation plans. Laney ordered his daughter and three grandchildren, then in South Korea on a visit, to leave for the United States two days later.

On the following day, U.S. preparations for war came to a climax when

President Clinton and his top national security advisers met in the White House to finalize an "Action Plan" for a major expansion of American military forces in and near Korea. The plan called for immediately sending 10,000 combat-ready infantrymen, 40 fighter planes, several Stealth bombers, and an aircraft carrier battle group to augment U.S. forces already in Korea—plus 13,000 noncombat troops to prepare for the massive influx of 400,000 more troops that would be dispatched if U.N. sanctions triggered a military confrontation with Pyongyang.

General Shalikashvili had just explained the Pentagon's scenario for a military buildup when a National Security Council aide rushed into the Cabinet Room with the news that former President Jimmy Carter was on the telephone from Pyongyang. Carter, who had just met with Kim Il Sung, stunned the White House with the news that the North Korean leader had agreed to freeze his nuclear program. By announcing the North Korean offer on the Cable News Network several minutes later, Carter stole the diplomatic initiative from the Clinton administration, which suspended its military preparations and began to pursue a negotiated solution to the nuclear crisis.

Ambassador Robert Gallucci, who negotiated the October nuclear agreement with Pyongyang, told Don Oberdorfer that the spring of 1994 was reminiscent of the summer of 1914, described by Barbara Tuchman in *The Guns of August*, "when World War I began in cross-purposes, misunderstanding and inadvertence." Gen. Howell Estes, the senior U.S. Air Force commander in Korea at the time, recalled that "although neither he nor other commanders said so out loud, not even in private conversations with one another, 'inside we all thought we were going to war.'"[6]

FLIRTING WITH A PREEMPTIVE STRIKE

The danger of a war triggered by "misunderstanding and inadvertence" has been magnified by a basic transformation that has taken place in Operations Plan 5027, the Pentagon's official scenario for the conduct of any new conflict in Korea.

During the first decades after the 1953 armistice, Op Plan 5027 envisaged a replay of the Korean War. The United States and South Korea had a limited objective: repelling a North Korean invasion and reestablishing the DMZ at the thirty-eighth parallel. In this defensive strategy, Seoul was to be evacuated. American and South Korean forces would pull back in phases to the Han River, which bisects the capital. In 1973, however, the United States proclaimed a new "Forward Defense" concept in which U.S. forces would seize Kaesong, a key North Korean city close to the DMZ, while round-the-clock B-52 strikes would stop a North Korean advance north of Seoul, ending the war in nine days. In response to this new strategy and the accompanying forward deployment of U.S. and South Korean artillery along the southern edge of the DMZ, North Korea moved its own artillery forward, where it has remained ever since.

The 1973 shift to a strategy that called for the occupation of a key North Korean city opened the way for a more dramatic strategic shift in October 1992. In the 1992 update of Op Plan 5027, the U.S. Third Marine Division and the South Korean First Marine Division would land at Wonsan on the east coast of North Korea and march west to capture Pyongyang, supported by U.S. and South Korean infantry units that would simultaneously march north across the DMZ to the capital. After occupying Pyongyang and unseating the North Korean regime, U.S. and South Korean forces would proceed to nearby Yongbyon, where they would destroy North Korean nuclear facilities. A key feature of the 1992 update was that it provided for moving U.S. and South Korean forces into battle-ready forward positions during the "pre-hostility" phase, prior to the actual outbreak of conflict, in response to intelligence indicating that North Korea was preparing for an attack.

Although the details of Op Plan 5027 are supposed to be a closely guarded secret, many aspects of the 1992 update were revealed by South Korean Defense Minister Lee Pyong Tae in the South Korean National Assembly on March 23, 1993, without consulting his U.S. counterparts. Lee explained later that he felt a "deterrent" was necessary in response to the provocative statements then emanating from Pyongyang. A similar incident occurred on October 9, 1998, when Marine Lt. Gen. Raymond P. Ayres, then assistant chief of staff for plans (J-5) of U.S. forces in Korea, gave a not-for-attribution briefing in Seoul to a delegation of leading Asian journalists sponsored by the U.S. Information Agency.

Ayres spelled out a scenario for carrying the battle to the North that was similar in many respects to the one that had emerged in the Lee Pyong Tae disclosures and subsequent leaks. But Ayres added two sensitive new themes: the explicit goal of installing a South Korean occupation government, and "the possibility of preemptive strikes" in the event of "unambiguous signs that North Korea is preparing to attack."

The Ayres briefing, attributed to "senior U.S. officials," was reported in detail by former *New York Times* correspondent Richard Halloran in the *Washington Times,* the *Far Eastern Economic Review,* and on the Internet.[7] When the thirteen other journalists who had been present were asked what Ayres had said, the ten who replied all endorsed Halloran's account.

The key to the success of the war plan, Halloran quoted Ayres as saying, "would be a strategic warning in which the United States and South Korea pick up unambiguous signs that North Korea is preparing to attack, such as massive movements of tanks or artillery emerging from protective shelter." In the event of such unambiguous warning, he wrote, the plan "provides for the possibility of preemptive strikes that would seek to stun key North Korean units, particularly long-range artillery and bombers, before they can go into action." Like the 1992 update, which referred to a "pre-hostility" phase in which U.S. and South Korean forces would make preliminary military moves in preparation for the actual outbreak of hostilities, the 1998 version as presented by Ayres called for four stages of U.S. and South Korean operations: "pre-North Korean attack, stopping the initial assault, regrouping for a counter-attack and the full-scale invasion of the North." In the final stage, "the entire resources of the U.S. Marine Corps would flow there." Once North Korean resistance had been crushed, U.S. and South Korean forces would "abolish North Korea as a functioning state and reorganize the country under South Korean control." When it is all over, "they won't be able to mount military activity of any kind. We'll kill 'em all."

Plans for a Combined Psychological Operations Task Force, announced on January 14, 1999, envisaged U.S.–South Korean cooperation to win North Korean popular support for an occupation force, spearheaded by "a 'Command Solo' flying broadcasting system that can neutralize completely North Korea's broadcasting system, while at the same time transmitting its own signals." The task force would be headed by a South Korean general under the overall control of the Combined Forces Command. It would be activated "when both countries' forces detect signs of an imminent invasion of North Korean troops."[8]

When I discussed the Ayres incident with Gen. John Tileli, then commander of U.S. forces in Korea, he firmly denied that Op Plan 5027 provides in any way for a preemptive strike but did not question other aspects of the Halloran report or of my own analysis of the briefing in the South Korean newspaper *Hankyoreh Shinmun.* Shortly before my meeting with Tileli on May 3, 1999, Ayres was transferred to Washington, where he now serves as deputy chief of staff for plans, policies, and operations at Marine Corps headquarters. In a conversation on May 26, 2000, he said that "I was no part of talking about preemptive strikes." Halloran's story drew on "multiple sources." In any case, "'unambiguous warning' doesn't mean you take preemptive action. It means you go on a war footing, you start defensive action. That's not the same as deciding to attack. The United States has no intention of attacking North Korea."

Pausing to reflect, he added that "of course, at some point you have the right to defend yourself. At the point you're convinced you're about to be attacked, you take action. It's not inconceivable that a military leadership could come to the conclusion that they have definitive information and have the right to defend themselves."

Whatever the precise contents of Op Plan 5027, discussions with a variety of military sources, including Ayres, suggest that the briefing was not an accident but a deliberate exercise in psychological warfare. Like Lee Pyong Tae in 1993, Ayres and at least some of his military superiors in Seoul and Washington thought that a stern warning was needed to head off a possible North Korean invasion. "I'm perfectly happy," Ayres said at one point, "if the North Koreans took it as threatening." Then and now, the dominant thinking in the Pentagon has been that since North Korea is stagnating economically, its armed forces are a wasting asset, and a "use it or lose it" mentality could lead Pyongyang to lash out in a surprise attack. But if the purpose was to induce sobriety in North Korea, this was precisely the wrong way to go about it. Most North Korean leaders genuinely suspect that the United States would like to see their regime collapse. They genuinely suspect that the Pentagon is seeking an excuse to attack by magnifying the threat posed by their missile and nuclear programs. The effect of the Ayres briefing was clearly to strengthen hard-liners in the North Korean armed forces. It provoked a barrage of more than ordinarily bellicose North Korean saber rattling throughout December 1998. Day after day, the General Staff in Pyongyang warned in almost identical words that "the right to a preemptive strike does not rest exclusively with the United States. We have our own operation plan, and if we are forced to carry it out, there will be no room on this planet to escape our striking power."[9]

The Ayres incident was a reminder that either North Korea or the Combined Forces Command could easily misread moves by the other side, jumping erroneously to the conclusion that preparations for a surprise attack were underway. It is the risk of inadvertent war that makes the mutual steps to defuse tensions discussed in the following chapters imperative. Clearly, no military commander would rule out the possibility of a first strike if faced by an imminent attack. But what are "unambiguous signals'? Even if "massive movements of tanks or artillery emerging from protective shelter" were discovered, would that necessarily mean that an attack is imminent? Suppose that North Korea sees what *it* considers to be "unambiguous signs" of an American–South Korean intention to attack? Could moving tanks and artillery represent a defensive contingency measure rather than the prelude to an invasion?

Asked about the Ayres incident, Lt. Gen. (Ret.) John H. Cushman, former commanding general of the U.S.–ROK First Corps Group from 1976 to 1978, who was responsible for the defense of the western sector of the DMZ and the approaches to Seoul, commented that "if the possibility of a preemptive strike is in the Op Plan, it would be very dangerous and would represent a fundamental departure from the past. No commander wants to wait for the other side to strike first if he can see it coming. But there is a very delicate calculation on both sides and it's very important to give North Korea assurance that we will not be the first to attack."[10]

The possibility that one side could misread the intentions of the other would be greatly enhanced if provisions were indeed added to Op Plan 5027 in 1992 and 1998 for initiating "pre-hostility" and "pre–North Korean attack" military moves, as the Lee Pyong Tae and Ayres incidents suggest.

Whether or not Op Plan 5027 allows for a preemptive strike against North Korean conventional forces, there is increasingly overt support for preemptive action against Pyongyang in the event that it has acquired, or is about to acquire, nuclear warheads for its missiles. On March 3, 1999, Hosei Norota, director of the Defense Agency in Japan, responding to a question in the Diet concerning North Korean missile capabilities, said that Japan has "a constitutional right to conduct a preemptive strike if circumstances so warrant."[11] This prompted a response from South Korean Defense Minister Chun Yong Taek on March 5 criticizing Norota for "such a dangerous idea."[12] General Tileli, asked during testimony before a House committee whether the United States should take preemptive action against suspected North Korean nuclear facilities, replied that "I would not use the term 'preemptive,' but I do not believe that we should allow North Korea's nuclear program to come to fruition."[13]

During the 1994 nuclear crisis, when Senator John McCain and former national security adviser Brent Scowcroft were calling for preemptive strikes against the Yongbyon nuclear facilities, Defense Secretary William Perry ordered the Air Force to prepare a detailed contingency plan for destroying Yongbyon. Perry decided not to act on the plan, however, he told me, because he believed that such a strike "was highly likely to start a general war" on the peninsula.[14] Five years later, amid suspicions that North Korea might be violating the 1994 freeze agreement, the *Wall Street Journal* suggested that a preemptive strike, accompanied by a U.S. troop withdrawal, might be better than submitting indefinitely to what it considered "nuclear blackmail." Ridiculing Kim Dae Jung's "sunshine policy" as "moonshine" and berating the Clinton administration for its own engagement policy, the *Journal* declared that "administrations do change in the U.S., and a future one might come under compelling pressure from Congress and the American public to back off, get the troops out of harm's way and do what it takes to remove any threat of North Korean missiles or nukes ever reaching American shores."[15]

CHAPTER 11

The United States and the Military Balance

IN SEPTEMBER 2000, the United States maintained conventional forces in South Korea totaling 36,388 Army, Air Force, Navy, and Marine personnel. This military presence consisted primarily of ground forces and their logistical support, including the combat infantry force of 15,000 deployed in forward positions as a "tripwire." President Bush removed U.S. tactical nuclear weapons from South Korea and from Pacific aircraft carriers in 1991. But the United States has not ruled out their reintroduction and the use of both tactical and strategic nuclear weapons against North Korean conventional forces. Successive U.S. administrations have pledged to maintain a U.S. "nuclear umbrella" over the South and have threatened to use nuclear weapons in Korea first, if necessary, a threat that was made most explicitly during the cold war but has never been withdrawn. Article 3 of the 1994 nuclear freeze agreement between Washington and Pyongyang provides that the United States will make a formal pledge not to use nuclear weapons against North Korea, but the two sides have yet to agree on the language of such a pledge.

The policy choices confronting the United States with respect to the future of its "nuclear umbrella" over the South will be examined separately in part 4. This chapter will focus specifically on the conventional military balance between the North and South and the impact of the U.S. force presence on the balance. At the same time, in my analysis of the conventional balance, I will take into account the changes in North Korean military strategy resulting from the erosion of its conventional forces and the growth of its nuclear, chemical, and biological warfare capabilities. Based on my assessment of the impact of the U.S. presence on the conventional balance, I will consider the future of the U.S. presence in the broader context of arms control and tension reduction in Korea.

To be sure, much of this book shows that another North Korean invasion of the South is unlikely. Parts 1 and 2 present evidence that North Korea is preoccupied with its economic survival, fears a U.S.–South Korean invasion, and has lost confidence in its ability to "liberate" the South militarily. Part 5 emphasizes that Moscow has severed its security treaty commitment to North Korea and that Pyongyang cannot count on military support in any new war even from Beijing, which has kept its security commitment operative. Nevertheless, military planners must operate on the basis of worst-case scenarios. Thus, before evaluating other factors relevant to the future of the U.S. presence, it is necessary to assess North Korean, South Korean, and U.S. military capabilities.

COMPARING THE NORTH AND SOUTH

American policy throughout the cold war decades was based on the assumption that dedicated, numerically superior North Korean conventional forces would be able to subdue South Korea in the absence of U.S. military support. It was the specter of "human wave" attacks by North Korean "hordes" that was invoked to justify the deployment of tactical nuclear weapons. In contrast to this image of invincible North Korean conventional forces, U.S. intelligence officials have radically altered their assessment in recent years. Testifying before the Senate Intelligence Committee on January 28, 1998, Lt. Gen. Patrick M. Hughes, director of the Defense Intelligence Agency, declared that "North Korea's overall military readiness continues to erode in line with its worsening economic situation. However, because the North retains significant forward-deployed strike systems—artillery, missiles, rocket launchers and aircraft—it will maintain its ability to inflict enormous damage on heavily populated areas of South Korea with little or no warning." Similarly, citing a "steady erosion in the readiness and capability of North Korea's military forces in recent years," CIA director George Tenet told the committee on July 9 that "they have had to endure shortages of food and fuel, increased susceptibility to illness, declining morale, often sporadic training and a lack of new equipment." Two years later, the U.S. Eighth Army in Korea reported that even though Kim Jong Il gives priority to keeping his "core" forward-deployed troops well fed, "at times even the 'core' units have experienced food shortages, and troops in the rear areas are forced to find food on their own." Supply shortages, the report added, have forced some units "to occupy themselves with activities that have nothing to do with their military duties."[1] In March 2001, however, Gen. Thomas Schwartz, commander of U.S. forces in Korea, openly differing with less alarmist South Korean assessments following the June 2001 North-South summit, told a Senate committee that "when I look North, I see an enemy that is bigger, better closer and deadlier."[2]

Brig. Gen. Young Koo Cha, policy planning director in the South Korean Defense Ministry, echoed these assessments in a discussion on February 28, 2000. "Their overall readiness is degrading," he said, "but even though their capabilities have weakened, and they can't win, they can still inflict critical damage on us." Ra Jong Il, who served as deputy director of the National Intelligence Service during 1998 and 1999, told me after his return to academic life that "70 to 80 percent" of the North Korean armed forces suffered from malnutrition, which made them disgruntled and thus accessible to the penetration of South Korean intelligence.

Numerically, North Korea's conventional forces are still much larger than those of South Korea not only in manpower (regular, as distinct from reserve, combat, and noncombat forces totaling 1.08 million, as against 672,000 in the South) but also in many important categories of weaponry and equipment. Among the most striking examples of this numerical advantage are tanks, 3,800 to 2,250; field artillery, 12,000 to 5,200; surface ships, 430 to 170; submarines, 90 to 10; jet fighter aircraft, 760 to 520; and transport aircraft, 300 to 25.[3] But this numerical advantage is offset in most categories by South Korean and U.S. technological superiority.

Nearly half of the South's tanks are equipped with late-model U.S. engines and transmission systems. These cutting-edge K-1 tanks are much faster and have much more firepower than North Korea's T-62 tanks, which are equipped with the type of 1970s technology used by Iraq in the Gulf War. All 150 of the tanks deployed by the U.S. Army in Korea are the most advanced model in the U.S. armory, the Abrams M-1A1. Similarly, North Korea's fighter jets include only 60 advanced models (Mig-23s, Mig-29s, and SU-25s). Most of its mainstay fighters are Mig-19s, Mig-21s, Il-28s, and SU-7s. Some 320 are outmoded Mig-15s and Mig-17s. By contrast, the South has 520 advanced fighters, including 162 F-16s, plus 180 F-5s and 60 F-15 Phantoms. The U.S. Air Force bases 100 planes in Korea, including 70 F-16s, most armed with "smart" bombs.[4]

This air superiority is enhanced by sophisticated U.S. satellite intelligence capabilities, augmented by U-2 spy planes for closer-range radar and photographic imagery and by RC-7B photo reconnaissance and signals intelligence aircraft that the United States has supplied to the South. At present, the South depends on U.S. forces for electronic and satellite intelligence, but this dependence will be reduced after it receives eight U.S. Hawker 800XP spy planes in 2001. The Hawker 800XP will be able to eavesdrop on North Korean communications, take pictures of basketball-sized objects on the ground, and detect moving targets at night

while staying south of the DMZ. Seoul also hopes to develop a reconnaissance satellite of its own by 2005.[5]

Countless scenarios, official and unofficial, published and unpublished,
have projected what might happen in the event of a North Korean attack.[6]
In all of these, the superiority of U.S. and South Korean air power, intelligence, and command and control emerge as critical factors that would
make it virtually impossible for North Korea to conquer and absorb the
South. The North's inability to sustain a protracted conflict, resulting
from its economic problems, is another widely cited factor. However,
there is no consensus concerning how long the war might last or how
much damage the North could inflict, and it is assumed in some scenarios
that Pyongyang might use nuclear or chemical weapons, or threaten to
use them, to deter the occupation of the North envisaged in Op Plan
5027.

If North Korea Attacks

The predominant assessment in most of these projections is that North
Korean forces might reach the northern suburbs of Seoul but would be
stopped at the Han River before they could get to the heart of the city.
In a characteristic scenario, the war starts with a North Korean artillery
barrage targeted on Seoul, with its 10.8 million people; on U.S. and
South Korean "tripwire" forces in the Munsan and Chorwan invasion
corridors; and on airfields and air defense installations in the South. Casualties are horrendous, numbering in the tens of thousands. At the same
time, under artillery cover, some 300,000 forward-deployed North Korean foot soldiers pour across the DMZ, backed by tanks and armored
personnel carriers. Meanwhile, thousands of commandos in special forces
units that have previously infiltrated the South start attacking command
and communication centers, supply depots, and, above all, airfields and
air defense systems.

The commandos come partly through tunnels running under the
DMZ but are mostly airdropped or brought by sea, which explains why
the North has such a large number of transport aircraft and submarines.
North Korean fighters and bombers attempt to hit key airfields before
U.S. and South Korean planes can get off the ground. But within a few
days, U.S. and South Korean aircraft have achieved air superiority in the
South and have launched an offensive in the North, systematically deci-
mating the North Korean military infrastructure. Having lost control of

the air, the North can damage the military infrastructure in the South only through artillery fire and commando attacks.

How long the war lasts would be determined by whether the North is able to follow up the initial phase of its infantry offensive quickly with a successful push across the DMZ by second-echelon armored and truck-mounted infantry units, totaling 75,000 men, some of which have been deployed as far back as thirty miles from the DMZ, and by third-echelon mechanized forces deployed still further to the north. The predominant assessment is that air power will cripple second- and third-echelon forces before they can get as far as Seoul. But there are some scenarios in which the war goes beyond two weeks and the second wave of the North Korean invasion force, bypassing Seoul, drives southward to Pusan in a repetition of the early days of the Korean War. This time, U.S. reinforcements land at Pusan before the North Koreans get there, which was not the case in 1950. While the fighting continues in the South, U.S. and South Korean forces are penetrating deeply into the North, and North Korea eventually surrenders. However, the assumption in these scenarios that North Korea could be easily defeated on its home ground is questioned by some observers, myself included, who point out that highly motivated civilian and military supporters of the Kim Jong Il regime would be likely to wage prolonged guerrilla warfare even if regular North Korean forces did surrender.

The most categorical judgment that the chances of an initial North Korean breakthrough and approach to Seoul are slim has come in a study by Michael O'Hanlon of the Brookings Institution. Military history shows that attackers can rarely achieve rapid breakthroughs when attacking prepared defenses with a strength comparable to their own, he argued, and the South's defenses "are not only prepared, and comparable in fire power to North Korea's military, but they are dense." Rivers, marshes, and difficult terrain in the DMZ region would obstruct a North Korean advance. Although the anticipated North Korean artillery assault would inflict great damage, the North's forces would themselves be highly exposed to artillery fire. Above all, he emphasizes the technological superiority that U.S. and South Korean forces have in weaponry and in their all-weather, day-night reconnaissance capabilities.

O'Hanlon's analysis assumes that U.S. and South Korean forces "would quickly establish air superiority," with a combined force of at least five hundred planes and attack helicopters available for ground attack operations. He predicts that North Korean commando forces would have "limited effectiveness." Tunnels would be more effective than airplanes and submarines for getting commandos into the South, but "given the limited length of the tunnels, troops arriving via underground passageways would be unable to penetrate deeply." Finally, citing North Korean economic difficulties, he concludes that "major question marks over the availability of fuel, spare parts and other supplies are the *coup de grace* that would almost certainly doom any attack to devastating failure."[7]

The potential effectiveness of commando operations is the central theme of several worst-case scenarios that contrast markedly with O'Hanlon's analysis, such as a 1991 study by the Pentagon's Office of Net Assessments directed by Col. Robert Gaskin of the Air Force.[8] The Gaskin study argues that U.S. defense planners have underestimated the threat posed by commandos in North Korean Special Forces units and of Scud missile attacks in disabling U.S. and South Korean airfields and air defenses in the initial days of a conflict. The study also emphasizes that the opening North Korean artillery barrage, involving up to twenty million rounds of high explosives per day, could drive big gaps into U.S. and South Korean defenses, opening the way for a rapid drive southward to Pusan before U.S. reinforcements arrive. It was the Gaskin study that prompted the 1992 update of Op Plan 5027, which provided for a much more aggressive U.S. military campaign in the North than previous contingency plans had envisaged.

In another published worst-case scenario with a distinctive denouement, the North starts the war in the western sector of the DMZ, north of Seoul, only as a diversionary action while the main thrust of its offensive gets underway in the east. After North Korean forces penetrate far into the South and U.S. and South Korean troops have moved far into the North, a military coup in North Korea overthrows Kim Jong Il and the new government sues for peace with Seoul.[9]

Publicly declared U.S. and South Korean assessments of the military balance in Korea emphasize two themes. On the one hand, they acknowledge that North Korea's conventional capabilities have eroded and that it is unlikely to prevail in a protracted war. On the other hand, they warn that precisely because its conventional forces lack staying power Pyongyang is likely to resort to nuclear, chemical, and biological warfare. The 1999 South Korean *Defense White Paper* concludes that "the North is expected to deviate from normal attack strategies and conduct preemptive surprise attacks using massive amounts of chemical and biological weapons from the beginning of the war." This conclusion was linked to intelligence findings that the North has accumulated at least 2,500 tons of chemical agents suitable for weapons and maintains eight facilities capable of mass-producing such agents. Pyongyang already deploys missiles with a fifteen-hundred-kilometer range, the *White Paper* says, "and if these missiles carry chemical or biological agents, these weapons of mass destruction will pose a devastating threat to the South."[10]

Lt. Gen. Raymond P. Ayres, deputy chief of staff of the Marine Corps, who served in Korea, told me that Iran and Iraq had clearly demonstrated the efficacy of "putting chemicals in artillery." How much damage chemicals could inflict in missile warheads is less certain, he said, because chemicals become diffused once the missile is fired and it is more difficult to hit a target with them accurately. Although U.S. intelligence shows that North Korea has chemical warheads on some of its Scud missiles, Ayres says "it is not clear how effective they would be."

A leading South Korean military analyst, Kim Tae Woo, has envisaged the North's selective use of chemical weapons at the outset of an invasion "to create a panic situation" in a scenario for what he calls a "surprise limited war." Chemical attacks would be targeted against the South's major air bases and ports and would be synchronized with the release of poison gas during rush hour in the Seoul subway. This onslaught would be immediately followed by artillery and missile attacks against Seoul and other major cities and the occupation of the capital. Hostages would be taken. Pyongyang would threaten nuclear retaliation if the United States and the South carry out their threat to counterattack in the North. In this scenario, instead of driving southward, the North would offer to negotiate a peace agreement based on the status quo ante, with the DMZ restored as the North-South boundary. "This 'surprise limited war' is highly plausible," Kim declares, "if Pyongyang's purpose is limited to eliminating the possibility of absorption, and if it decides to act sooner rather than later, before its economic and technological inferiority become more treacherous."[11]

The assumption in the *Defense White Paper* that the North is likely to resort to chemical weapons is not universally accepted in the South Korean government. In internal debates, the most vocal dissenter on this issue, as in the controversy over operational control cited earlier, has been Kim Dae Jung adviser Lim Dong Won. Lim questions, in particular, whether North Korea is likely to put chemical warheads on its missiles. "Where in the world, anywhere, have chemical warheads ever been used with missiles?" he asked in a conversation on February 28, 2000.

The dissenters do not dispute the technical feasibility and possible political utility of using chemical agents in terrorist attacks but downgrade their potential effectiveness in military operations and thus the likelihood of their use. Michael O'Hanlon concludes that Pyongyang might conceivably use the "non-persistent" type of chemical weapons but that "they would be unlikely to change the military situation appreciably. On the whole, the chemical threat against front-line, dug-in troops appears modest in magnitude." The use of the more dangerous "persistent" chemicals would pose daunting problems of protection and decontamination for North Korean as well as U.S. and South Korean forces. He cited a study by the U.S. Office of Technology Assessment showing that "developing missile systems to disperse chemical or biological agents is technically challenging." The more likely and more effective way to deliver chemical munitions for maximum effect would be by aerial attacks, and the aircraft involved "would run a high risk of being shot down." As for attacks on South Korean ports, airfields, and other fixed assets, their chief effect "would be to slow operations, necessitating that allied forces wear chemical gear. For air power, the tempo of operations might be cut in half by the enemy use of chemical weapons (or even the threat of use). But a robust pace of aerial attack could continue nonetheless."[12]

The emphasis on a chemical weapons threat in U.S. and South Korean pronouncements has been questioned by an Australian analyst in *Jane's International Defense Review*, Brian Cloughley, who writes that "the use of chemical weapons or biological agents in Korea is highly unlikely as they are too much of a double-edged weapon." If North Korea ever does use chemical weapons, writes Cloughley, it will be because "they appear convinced of the intention of the United States to employ them."[13]

The chemical weapons issue is analyzed at length in part 4 in the context of U.S. nonproliferation policy. Although the possible use of chemicals in artillery must be considered in assessing the conventional military balance between North and South, I show in part 4 that it would be self-defeating for the United States to complicate its pursuit of a nuclear-free Korea by exaggerating the threat of chemical weapons.

After the Cold War: Reassessing North Korean Goals

As former defense secretary Perry observed, North Korea wants missile capabilities to deter a perceived U.S. threat to its security. Similarly, if the North is, in fact, seeking to develop nuclear, chemical, and biological weapons, the explanation would lie in its embattled, defensive psychology, not in a mindless desire to inflict wanton destruction.

Gen. Schwartz declared in Senate Armed Services Committee testimony on March 3, 2000, that "North Korea's military goal is to reunify the peninsula by force." This statement stands in conspicuous contrast not only to Perry's assessment but also to the views of prominent retired U.S. military intelligence officers with experience in Korea who are no longer constrained by their official position. For example, when asked what goals motivate the North in maintaining such large and costly armed forces, Brig. Gen. (Ret.) James F. Grant, who served as director of intelligence of U.S. forces in Korea from 1989 to 1992, listed four: "regime and state survival and continuity; external respect and independence of action; controlling the nature and pace of internal change; and the eventual peaceful unification of the Korean peninsula under terms acceptable to North Korea." North Korea sees nuclear and chemical weapons and ballistic missiles as "essential instruments of survival," Grant said, since "it is their only current asset that makes them a serious player at the negotiating table. In their minds, it is the ultimate poison pill that will forestall military actions against them, or prevent significant escalation of any CFC military operations that might begin at the DMZ."[14]

It is not surprising that in his role as the principal U.S. military spokesman in Korea General Schwartz feels compelled to uphold cold war theology in his official pronouncements in order to make the most unambiguous case possible for political and budgetary support of the U.S. presence. In practical terms, however, this theology is dead. The picture that emerges from the official and unofficial projections of a new war presented earlier is one of a military environment radically different from that of the cold war decades. The United States and South Korea do not, in fact, base their military strategy on the premise that North Korea is still dedicated to unifying the peninsula by force. Rather, their mission is to limit the damage that the North's forward-deployed forces might inflict before their defeat if a war should occur through miscalculation by one side or the other, or if the North should stage a surprise attack to pursue objectives short of forcible unification. One such objective, envisaged in Kim Tae Woo's scenario, would be the complete opposite of forcible unification: to forestall absorption by the South and assure the survival of the regime in Pyongyang. A variation on this theme, heard often in the Pentagon, is that an insecure leadership in Pyongyang perceived as irrational might decide to use its eroding military assets to enforce a modus vivendi with the South before it is too late.

Much of this book seeks to show that the North's leadership is not irrational. Indeed, it was eminently rational when, as early as 1980, the North recognized that it could neither communize the South nor conquer it militarily and started, accordingly, to pursue a confederation that would assure its survival pending a peaceful, long-term unification process. If the North should now conclude that it faces imminent absorption by the South, there would no doubt be those in Pyongyang who would support the "limited surprise attack" option, but the high costs and risks of such an adventure would be so obvious that it is no more than a remote possibility.

South Korea under Kim Dae Jung has, in fact, begun to move toward a modus vivendi. However, a necessary element of such an accommodation would be a U.S. shift to the role of an honest broker in Korea, for the reasons explained in chapter 13—a shift accompanied by a redefinition of the role of U.S. forces and their redeployment and eventual withdrawal in conjunction with North Korean and South Korean pullbacks from the DMZ.

The Impact of a U.S. Withdrawal

The key issue in considering the future of the American presence is whether U.S. forces make a decisive difference in the military balance. As the scenarios presented earlier show, the role of U.S. air power, together with concomitant intelligence and command and control capabilities, does indeed make a difference. The importance of U.S. ground forces is more debatable, especially the need to deploy these forces in forward positions. The principal reasons for the deployment of 15,000 U.S. combat infantrymen in the Munsan and Chorwan invasion corridors, where they are sure to suffer heavy casualties, are not military but political. Indeed, Brig. Gen. (Ret.) John C. Bahnsen, chief of staff of the South Korea–U.S. Combined Field Army from 1982 to 1985, wrote that "the wisdom of maintaining any U.S. infantry in a country so rich in manpower is purely political."[15]

The South Korean forces now deployed side by side with these U.S. forces could be expanded to fill the gap left by a pullback of American troops to less exposed positions. But the South has resisted such a pullback precisely because Seoul believes that heavy U.S. casualties at the outset of any fighting would be necessary to assure immediate, large-scale U.S. intervention.

In 1990, Gen. Robert Riscassi, then commander of U.S. forces, proposed a joint pullback of U.S. and South Korean forces to the Han River, where they would be less vulnerable to North Korean artillery fire. South Korean generals were amenable, but their civilian superiors balked. Their stated reason was that the South Korean people, especially residents of Seoul, would be demoralized by the prospect of an unimpeded North Korean advance to the outskirts of the capital, even if this made military sense. But another, decisive consideration in South Korean resistance to any change in the present forward strategy is the belief that a U.S. "tripwire" is essential to assure U.S. intervention and that even a limited pullback could lead to more pullbacks as part of a negotiated tension-reduction scenario culminating in complete U.S. disengagement.

In the event that negotiations on tension reduction should at some point get underway in Korea, the United States would have to consider not only how pullbacks of forces from the DMZ would affect the military balance but also the impact of a partial or complete withdrawal from the peninsula on the balance. In 1987, the North proposed a U.S. pullback to Pusan as the first step in a parallel process of U.S. disengagement and mutual North-South force reductions leading to the complete withdrawal within five years of U.S. ground, air, and naval forces, in that order. Pyongyang has now indicated that it would not seek a complete withdrawal within any specified time period if the United States shifts to the role of an honest broker and redefines its military role accordingly, provided that Washington acknowledges the "principle" that foreign forces will eventually be withdrawn.

In considering the possible effects of a U.S. withdrawal, it is important to distinguish between the value of the U.S. presence as a deterrent to adventurism by the North and the impact of a U.S. withdrawal in operational military terms. Assessments of the operational impact of a withdrawal vary among military men with experience in Korea, often reflecting interservice differences.

For example, I asked Gen. (Ret.) Robert W. Sennewald, who served as commander in chief of U.S. forces in Korea from 1982 to 1984, how a complete withdrawal of U.S. ground forces would affect the ability of the South to prevail in any new war. "What do you mean by 'prevailing'?" replied Sennewald, an Army man. "A complete withdrawal of our ground forces would increase the risk that the North Koreans could not be stopped short of Seoul. The United States might then have to come back to help retake Seoul. Ultimately, the South would prevail, with or without U.S. ground forces, but at what cost?"[16] Asked what difference a ground force withdrawal would make, Brigadier General Grant, replied that the difference would be relatively marginal, measurable in the additional "miles and centimeters" that the North might be able to advance in the South before being repulsed. Pressed further about a withdrawal of the U.S. Air Force units based in Korea to bases in Japan, General Grant, an Air Force officer, said that the South would still prevail if U.S. planes could join in the fighting from bases in Japan. The key issue, he added, would be whether U.S. intelligence, targeting, and command and control support would still be available to South Korean forces. The absence of such support or the refusal of Japan to permit U.S. planes to operate from its territory would indeed make a fundamental difference in South Korean war-fighting capabilities, he said, prolonging any conflict and rendering its outcome less certain.

CAN SOUTH KOREA BE SELF-SUFFICIENT?

Until recently, the South Korean Defense Ministry never publicly acknowledged that it is planning for the possibility of a U.S. force withdrawal. In March 2000, however, the ministry pointed to the danger of U.S. disengagement as a justification for increased defense spending. "In order to prepare for a possible withdrawal of U.S. forces or a change in their mission," said a study forecasting future defense needs, "we should allocate the resources necessary to develop forces of our own that can substitute for the U.S. forces if necessary."[17] The ministry called for a five-year buildup from 2002 through 2006 totaling $70.6 billion, starting with $12.7 billion in 2002, a 7.6 percent increase over 2001.[18]

Whatever the immediate impact of a U.S. withdrawal on the existing military balance in the peninsula, it is clear that South Korea, with its overwhelming economic superiority, could achieve military dominance over the North on its own in those aspects of its defense posture where it does not already have the edge. How long this would take and whether the United States should help in this process with targeted military aid are debatable issues. That is why an abrupt U.S. withdrawal would be undesirable and why a transitional peace process of the type envisaged in subsequent chapters should be pursued. Such a peace process would make it possible for the South to reduce and downgrade rather than increase and upgrade its forces. But whether or not this occurs, the capacity of the South to cope with its own security is indisputable.

The South had 8.1 million males fit for military service in 1997, more than double the number in the North. Demographic data show that roughly 456,000 men turn eighteen every year in the South, compared to 247,000 in the North, and that the ratio of sixteen- to twenty-eight-year-olds to the total population is steadily dropping in the North.[19] More important, the South has developed an extensive indigenous military-industrial complex, aided by a conscious U.S. effort to transfer defense production technology to South Korean companies as an incentive for them to purchase defense equipment in the United States rather than elsewhere.

The South Korean effort to maximize self-reliance in defense production started with the creation of the Agency for Defense Development in 1970 and has been accelerated by subsequent government encouragement of the defense-related petrochemical, chemical, iron, steel, and machine-building industries. By 1979, when the United States agreed to provide F-5 fighter planes to the South, Seoul began to push for "direct offset" arrangements comparable to those that had already routinely accompanied U.S. defense sales to European allies. Under these arrangements, the U.S. manufacturer sweetens the deal by agreeing to transfer technology without increasing the price and to permit the local assembly of the equipment being sold.

Assessing the rapid growth of these arrangements, a U.S. analyst concluded in 1987 that the South's offset program "is more demanding, more focused and more precise than any other offset program now being executed. The technology already transferred to the ROK runs the full gamut of medium to high technology defense equipment. It is a successful program that has actually forced the transfer of technology and has created an independent defense industry for the South that might otherwise not have existed."[20] General Sennewald recalled that "every large defense transaction between South Korea and the United States has had an offset component. It isn't called offset any more, but it's alive and well." By 1999, more than eight hundred free technical data packages had been given to South Korean defense industries as part of licensing and co-production agreements linked to U.S. commercial defense sales with a cumulative total value of at least $13 billion.[21]

Nearly one-third of all defense spending in the South from 1970 to 1990 was channeled into defense production. By design, some of this spending was tied in with the establishment of civilian automobile and shipbuilding industries. There were 83 defense contractors in South Korea in 1999 producing 319 categories of defense equipment in 130 factories.[22] In some items, such as small arms, ammunition, mortars, tanks, artillery, and patrol boats, the South is now largely self-sufficient. The companies producing sophisticated aerospace, communications, and electronic systems are still dependent in varying degree on imported components and subsystems. Surveying South Korean defense industries in their totality, a 1999 Chinese study said that the South "is transforming its military strategy from one of dependence on advanced foreign weapons purchases to one of self-reliance based on licensed production, co-production and imports of technology."[23]

The close defense production cooperation between South Korea and U.S. companies has led to continuing frictions resulting from the terms of offset arrangements, which prohibit South Korean exports to third countries of defense equipment produced under these arrangements. The U.S. companies concerned must grant permission for such third-country exports, and they have done so in no more than one out of seven cases, a South Korean study has charged.[24] Many of these U.S. companies fear that South Korean defense manufacturers will eventually be their competitors. But another, much more profound dilemma has resulted from the U.S. policy of building up a South Korean military-industrial complex. There is now a powerful, deeply entrenched lobby in Seoul that works hand in glove with the South Korean military establishment and its allies in Washington to block any arms-control agreements with North Korea that would reduce the South Korean defense budget and lead to a mutual reduction of North and South Korean forces.

CHAPTER 12

New Opportunities for Arms Control

THE POSSIBILITY of negotiating verifiable conventional arms-control agreements with North Korea has never been seriously tested. In responding to a series of proposals from Pyongyang for defusing the military confrontation in Korea, South Korea and the United States have ignored the central element in these proposals: the redeployment and eventual withdrawal of U.S. forces. Seoul and Washington have argued that both the future of U.S. forces and North Korean proposals for parallel North-South force reductions can only be addressed after tensions have been reduced through more modest confidence-building measures. Pyongyang's response has been that confidence-building measures presuppose a climate of trust—a climate that will not exist until there is a formal end to the Korean War, accompanied by a normalization of relations with the United States, replacement of the Military Armistice Commission with a permanent peace structure, and the termination of the United Nations Command.

This stalemate appeared intractable until North Korea introduced a fundamental change into the bargaining equation with its acquisition of a nuclear weapons option and its progress in developing missiles capable of reaching the United States. Now it is clear that the United States can get North Korea to make definitive concessions relating to the termination of its missile and nuclear programs only in return for steps to end the Korean War and to modify or phase out the U.S. military presence. If the United States normalizes its relations with Pyongyang and shifts to the role of an honest broker between North and South, Pyongyang has signaled that it would not object to the continuance of a reduced U.S. military presence for a protracted transition period of a decade or longer.

NORTH KOREA AND CONVENTIONAL ARMS CONTROL

With a population less than half as large as that of the South, the North has nonetheless attempted to maintain armed forces comparable or superior in size and sophistication to those of the South. Pyongyang has consistently devoted much more of its gross national product to defense than has Seoul. In 1993, the North's defense spending ($5.62 billion) was 27.4 percent of its GNP, compared to 3.5 percent in the South, which spent $11.5 billion. Although its military spending has dropped since then, the North has continued to devote a greater share of a declining GNP to defense than the share allocated by the South with its skyrocketing GNP.[1] This disproportionate defense burden imposed grave strains on the North's economy even before the economic crisis resulting from the end of cold war Soviet and Chinese aid subsidies. For this reason, the North has focused from the start on mutual North-South force reductions so that it can redirect resources and labor from military to civilian needs.

Nicholas Eberstadt and Judith Bannister have presented demographic data showing that the size of the North Korean Army "is now an insuperable burden for the economy that must support it. . . . Though North Korea's soldiers episodically engage in farming, construction and the like, they are basically non-productive workers who must draw sustenance and materiel from other sectors to perform their assigned task . . . to satisfy its thirst for ever more inductees, the Army must deprive state enterprises or universities of their recruits. In this institutional competition, the Army's success in amassing its troop base undercuts training and productivity for the workforce as a whole."[2]

Starting with my first visit to Pyongyang in May 1972, North Korean leaders have emphasized the economic rationale for force reductions. At the same time, they have insisted that the military balance resulting from North-South reductions would not be equitable unless such reductions are accompanied by U.S. force withdrawals, since the threat faced by the North encompasses both U.S. and South Korean forces.

On June 26, 1972, in the first of my two meetings with Kim Il Sung, I was struck by the intensity and animation with which he spoke of force reductions. This was one of the few subjects on which his comments did not sound like a canned propaganda recording. After the formal interview, he took me aside and said amid toasts of Korean champagne that it was time for Seoul and Washington to take him more seriously when he put forward proposals for better relations, especially his proposals for force reductions. "We can see where the world is going," he said, "when your country begins to talk of 'détente' with Russia and China. Where will that leave us? We are stifled by the burden of armaments." Several weeks later, I related this exchange to John Holdridge, then director for Asian affairs in the White House National Security Council, who sat next to me at a Tokyo dinner hosted by Ambassador Robert Ingersoll. "Tell it to the South Koreans," he responded. "We don't do anything regarding North Korea unless the South Koreans want us to."

Kim made a significant concession in this interview concerning the terms for force reductions. In its standard position before and since, Pyongyang has argued for reductions *to* a level of 100,000 troops on both sides. But in this interview, he suggested that the forces on both sides should initially be reduced *by* 150,000 to 200,000 men.

An aide later explained that this change was intended to make force-reduction negotiations easier for the South to accept, since Seoul would not have to commit itself to a final level of reductions and the existing North-South balance would be left undisturbed.[3]

This change in the North's position came as the climax of several weeks of negotiations concerning the questions that Kim would discuss during the interview. In the first written list of proposed questions submitted at the request of my hosts, I asked for amplification concerning how any force-reduction plans would work, including how reductions would be verified and whether they would have to be linked with U.S. force withdrawals, as previous North Korean statements had suggested. My handlers told me that Kim had not been previously asked such detailed questions and that these were quite unreasonable. I had to submit two more drafts before we arrived at a mutually agreed agenda. In our meeting, however, Kim began by saying that he wanted to give me "something new" and that he wanted to dispel my apparent suspicions that the North did not really have a serious plan for force reductions. He then made his suggestion for first-stage reductions of 150,000 to 200,000 men, together with another new proposal for demilitarization of the demilitarized zone. This modification in Pyongyang's standard position on force reductions was officially chronicled in a 1975 review of important statements by Kim.[4]

Seoul dismissed Kim's overture as propaganda and refused to discuss force reductions in the abortive North-South Coordinating Committee set up one month later. The committee was intended to facilitate structured North-South interchange through a variety of subcommittees. After initially agreeing to establish a military subcommittee, the South reversed itself, arguing that confidence-building measures should come before discussions on the North's proposals for force reductions. According to Kim, Lee Hu Rak, then director of the KCIA, who represented the South in the Coordinating Committee, told him that "I couldn't persuade our Army to discuss any reductions, despite many efforts."[5] This reversal led to a collapse of the committee and a rupture in formal North-

South contacts until a series of arms-control exchanges began in late 1990 after a three-year North Korean diplomatic effort.

In successive arms-control proposals made in 1987, 1988, and 1990,[6] North Korea proposed a mutual reduction of forces by the North and South over a three- or four-year period, accompanied by a phased withdrawal of American forces. By the end of the first stage the armed forces of North and South would be cut to 400,000. The United States would pull back its ground forces and their command headquarters during this first stage to a line running between Pusan and Chinhae (35 degrees, 30 minutes north latitude). By the end of the second stage, North-South force reductions would reach a level of 250,000 and American ground forces and nuclear weapons would be completely out of Korean territory. By the end of the final stage, with force levels down to the 100,000 goal, American air and naval forces would also be gone.

These proposals envisaged a verification role for the now defunct Neutral Nations Supervisory Commission at Panmunjom. The most detailed of these proposals (November 10, 1988) specified that the North and South would cut military equipment as well as force levels "stage by stage, commensurate with the reduction of military personnel." It emphasized that peace could be lasting "only when a balanced disarmament between North and South is realized together with the withdrawal of the foreign armed forces."

The strongest impression that emerges from arms-control discussions with North Korean leaders over the past three decades is that they view their formal proposals only as a starting point for negotiations in which they are prepared to strike the best bargain available. For example, Kim Yong Nam, then foreign minister, said on October 15, 1987, that the proposed four-year time frame for the completion of U.S. withdrawals and for North-South force reductions was negotiable. Pressed, he said that it could even be ten years for ground forces, with U.S. air and naval forces remaining longer. If the Neutral Nations Supervisory Commission could not handle verification adequately, he said, another structure could be created involving personnel from countries other than the four commission members (Poland, Czechoslovakia, Sweden, and Switzerland). He acknowledged that its first task would be to investigate the size of the existing forces on both sides and seek to reconcile the contending claims made by the North and South.

In its formal proposals, Pyongyang made no mention of the redeployment of its own forces in conjunction with U.S. pullbacks. However, pressed on this issue at a 1989 Carnegie Endowment seminar in Washington, North Korean delegates left the door open for negotiations. Discussing the North's proposal for a U.S. withdrawal linked with force reductions, American participants said that it was a promising initiative but that no U.S. administration could consider it seriously unless it also included a pullback of forward-deployed North Korean forces. "I'm not a military commander," replied the leader of the North Korean delegation, Kim Jong Su, who later became Pyongyang's deputy ambassador to the United Nations. "But the principle is that we should move together. When we say to you continuously that American forces should move from there, we should also be ready to move at the same time, perhaps. When your side shows a positive attitude, we would, I hope, see it from that angle."[7] At another Carnegie seminar on June 5, 1991, former North Korean U.N. ambassador Han Si Hae was more categorical in responding to a similar question. "If U.S. and South Korean forces can be redeployed," he said, "our forces can also be redeployed. We are ready to readjust on the basis of a mutual agreement. This is no problem for us if the principle is one of mutuality."[8]

The food crisis in the North was becoming increasingly serious in early 1997 when I had a three-hour conversation over dinner on April 5 with Han Song Ryol, the political counselor of the North Korean U.N. Mission. In earlier exchanges with Han, I had frequently emphasized the need for North Korean pullbacks from the DMZ as part of any arms-control package. On this occasion, he made no secret of his alarm over the food shortage in the North and said that "we have to do something. We could do what you always ask for, redeploy our forward forces, if you would give us enough food for this year and next year. Of course, it would have to be negotiated, it would have to be a mutual pullback, but it's possible, a 'food for peace' negotiation. If 'land for peace' is possible, why not 'food for peace'? Why doesn't your side propose it?"

I knew that Han is a protégé of First Deputy Foreign Minister Kang Sok Ju, who is close to Kim Jong Il. As the evening wore on, I gathered that Han was not speaking for himself alone and that he was serious. A two-year, three-million-ton U.S. food aid offer would give Kim Jong Il the leverage needed to push his military commanders into negotiations on mutual pullbacks. It was necessary for the United States to make the first move so that North Korea would not appear to be "bowing down before the mighty superpower." Told about this feeler, the State Department official handling negotiations with North Korea, Charles Kartman, replied, "Let them come to us." Once it became clear that the U.S. government did not intend to pursue the idea, I wrote about it in the

International Herald Tribune,[9] and Han told *Hankyoreh Shinmun* of Seoul that "it would be possible to pull back the military forces of North and South from the DMZ on a mutual basis if adequate food aid can be fully guaranteed."[10]

North Korea's arms-control policy is a work in progress, periodically subject to revision in response to its changing economic and political circumstances. Thus the North's 1988 proposal, which made mutual North-South pullbacks and force reductions contingent on a complete U.S. withdrawal within five years, conflicted with the more relaxed approach to the future of U.S. forces that followed the 1994 nuclear freeze agreement with Washington. At first, in a meeting on May 9, 1996, Foreign Ministry Policy Planning Director Kim Byong Hong denied that any such proposal had ever been made. Finally, as I pulled out a copy and cited chapter and verse, he "recalled" the proposal but said that times had changed and that the North would be "more realistic" about the future of U.S. forces if the United States would do its part to end the adversarial relationship between the two countries.

SOUTH KOREA AND CONVENTIONAL ARMS CONTROL

South Korea did not even acknowledge North Korea's arms-control offers until military rule ended, President Roh Tae Woo initiated his Nordpolitik policy, and the prime ministers of North and South held a series of meetings in Seoul starting in September 1990. Thus, it was a breakthrough when South Korean Premier Kang Young Hoon responded to the North's proposals with a five-point counterproposal:

1. "The withdrawal of forward-deployed offensive arms and troops to the rear area and the reduction of offensive arms and troops to prevent surprise attack and a recurrence of war."
2. Arms and force reductions based on the principle of parity, with "the superior side reducing its arms and troops to the level of the inferior side."
3. Reductions in paramilitary and reserve forces as well as regular forces.
4. On-the-spot verification and monitoring of arms and force reductions by joint verification and monitoring teams.
5. Mutual consultations to determine the "final military strength level appropriate to the unified nation."[11]

By accepting the principle of reductions, Kang went beyond Seoul's 1972 position. However, he refused to put reductions on the negotiating agenda, declaring in an echo of 1972 that this issue should "be pursued only after political and military confidence-building and a declaration of non-aggression have been realized." North Korean premier Yon Hyong Mok declared that force reductions should be discussed together with discussions on confidence-building measures. Indeed, he argued, the South's effort to put off talks on reductions is "confidence-destroying," since it suggests that Seoul is simply seeking to make the status quo safer rather than to end the military confrontation.

The 1990 dialogue underlined the significant differences between Seoul and Pyongyang over the terms for conventional arms control. To carry out force reductions on the basis of parity, as Kang suggested, would require that the two sides first agree on the size of their respective forces. But the North disputes the South's estimates of both the magnitude and makeup of its forces. Pyongyang argues that its concept of equal force reductions could be easily monitored and could lead to rapid progress in easing tensions, while insistence on parity could result in endless bickering. Equally important, while Seoul envisaged equal ceilings on troops and weapons, Pyongyang wanted weapons cuts to be proportional to the troops reduced.

The culmination of the 1990–91 North-South arms-control dialogue was an agreement to establish a Joint Military Commission that would provide a forum for carrying the dialogue further. Article 12 of the North-South Reconciliation Agreement concluded in December 1991 said that the commission "shall discuss and carry out steps to build military confidence and realize arms reduction, including the mutual notification and control of major movements of military units and major military exercises, the peaceful utilization of the Demilitarized Zone, exchanges of military personnel and information, phased reductions in armaments including the elimination of weapons of mass destruction and attack capabilities, and verification thereof." A special codicil stipulates that the commission would have seven members and a co-chairman from each side and would meet every three months, starting on May 7, 1992. By the end of 2000, however, the commission had not, in fact, ever met. In refusing to meet on May 7, Pyongyang accused Seoul of bad faith for having gone ahead with planned South Korean–U.S. "Team Spirit" military exercises even though the control of "major military exercises" was specifically mentioned in article 12 as a topic for consideration by the commission.

"Team Spirit" provided a convenient excuse for Pyongyang. In reality, however, North Korea's refusal to activate the commission and its failure to honor other provisions of the Reconciliation Agreement resulted from the confrontation over its nuclear program with the United States that erupted in early 1992. Pyongyang had entered into the Reconciliation Agreement in the belief that this would hasten the process of normalization with the United States. When Washington responded with stepped-up pressure, North Korea put the agreement on the back burner. Significantly, however, in a conversation on September 28, 1995, Gen. Ri Chan Bok, North Korean representative at Panmunjom, volunteered that the commission should be put into operation concurrently with the establishment of the trilateral peace structure (the United States, North Korea, and South Korea), which is discussed in a later chapter.

Given its insistence that confidence-building measures (CBMs) must come first, South Korea has limited its explicitly announced tension-reduction proposals to CBMs. At the August 1999 meeting of the Geneva four-power talks (China, the United States, North and South Korea), the South Korean delegate mentioned three specific CBMs: "the installation and operation of a direct military hotline between the military authorities of the two Koreas; notification of major military exercises and permission for on-site observers with certain restrictions; and the exchange of military officers."[12] However, in addition to official pronouncements, there has been extensive public discussion of arms control. This discussion suggests the type of scenarios that Seoul and Washington might put forward when and if substantive negotiations with the North take place.

For example, Lim Dong Won, who later became Kim Dae Jung's national security adviser, made a detailed proposal in 1989 for a sixty-two-mile "Offensive Weapon-Free Zone" or "Limited Deployment Zone." Tanks, mechanized infantry, armored troop carriers, and self-propelled artillery would be barred completely from this zone, and the number of infantry divisions would be subject to agreed limits. Lim emphasized that equipment is easier to quantify—and verify—than personnel.[13] Elaborating on this proposal in 1994, he stated that "in light of Seoul's relative proximity to the DMZ, the Limited Deployment Zone should be asymmetrically placed with respect to the Military Demarcation Line. That is, since Pyongyang is much further away from the Demarcation Line than is Seoul, the Zone should be framed in terms of promoting equal security rather than geometric symmetry." Contending that there were imbalances favorable to the North in both the number of troops and major categories of equipment, he emphasized that "in the first phase of reductions, the South and North should eliminate imbalances and asymmetries as regards both main armament and troop numbers. Given the difficulty of verifying troop numbers, it seems important that cuts in major items of equipment proceed in parallel with less verifiable troop reductions."[14]

In a more modest variant of Lim's proposal for a Limited Deployment Zone, Yong Sup Han has proposed an asymmetrical widening of the DMZ in which the North pulls its forces back twenty-six miles to the north and Seoul pulls back thirteen miles. Under this plan, he argued, it would take a day for North Korean infantry units to reach the military demarcation line, "and they will not have the advantage of surprise."[15]

Entrenched interests, centered in the armed forces and a politically powerful military-industrial complex, have spearheaded opposition in the South to a serious dialogue on force reduction. To be sure, there is also a military-industrial complex in the North, allied with hard-liners in the Workers Party, that has grown much stronger under Kim Jong Il. Force reductions are not popular with this hard-line faction in Pyongyang. In the case of the North, however, economic factors have made such reductions imperative and have tipped the scales in the internal debate. By contrast, since the South spends so much less of its GNP on defense, the pressures for reductions are not as great as in the North. The South's rapid economic growth has enabled successive regimes to avoid increasing the proportion of GNP allocated to defense while, at the same time, steadily raising the actual level of defense expenditures. Another factor making force reductions less urgent than in the North is the economic subsidy provided by the American military presence. It should be emphasized, however, that the middle- and low-income majority of the populace in the South would benefit greatly from any diversion to civilian welfare needs of resources now going into military spending.

Prof. Lee Chang of Seoul National University has pointed to the urgent need for increased expenditures on health, welfare, and social security, comparing what South Korea spends on these programs (2.6 percent of GNP) with comparable outlays in Sweden (33.3 percent), the United States (13.8 percent), and Japan (12 percent). Fewer than 2 percent of the elderly receive any form of social security. According to Lee, the government spends only $390 million per year on all forms of welfare and would have to spend $1.3 billion "for every citizen to have a minimally adequate income" (defined as $32 per month).[16] In its annual Human Development Report for 1996, the U.N. Development Program revealed that the amount spent by the South on defense in 1994 was equal to 60 percent of its combined spending on education and health in that year.

The comparable figure for Japan was 12 percent; Canada, 15 percent; and Australia, 24 percent.

Pressures for reduced defense spending have come in recent years from a variety of sources ranging from the Federation of Korean Industries on the right to the Citizens Coalition for Economic Justice on the left. Significantly, the resistance to force reductions does not come primarily from government technocrats concerned about its economic impact. Rather, it comes from defense contractors whose profits would be reduced; from a military elite fearful of losing jobs and perquisites; and from hawkish strategists who believe that both North and South should keep their military forces at high levels so that a unified Korea can confront Japan and China from a position of strength.

THE KEY ISSUES

As Yong Sup Han observed, South Korea's expectation that CBMs "would lead the two sides to sign reduction measures later is not well founded. In Europe, CBMs were agreed upon ahead of reduction measures, but there is no causal relationship proving that CBMs brought about success in the European case. Rather, the agreement on reduction measures in Europe was accelerated by political changes in Eastern Europe and the Soviet Union."[17]

Even if the South would agree to negotiate on force reductions in parallel with discussions on CBMs, the North and South would have to agree on the size of their respective forces before meaningful negotiations could begin. For this reason, while preparations for negotiations on force reductions are proceeding, a North-South arms-control process should begin to address cuts in major categories of weaponry and, above all, the mutual pullback of forward-deployed forces.

In one of the more ambitious and more realistic of the many proposals focused on cuts in weaponry, Michael O'Hanlon of the Brookings Institution has proposed reductions of 50 percent in all major types of heavy weaponry on both sides of the DMZ. This is a realistic approach because such across-the-board cuts would not alter the existing balance in major categories of equipment and would thus allow North Korea to retain its numerical advantage in tanks and artillery. Another attractive feature of this proposal for the financially hard-pressed North is that it would reduce the cost of maintaining its heavy weaponry. The resulting savings could be used either to meet civilian needs or to improve military readiness by devoting increased resources to a smaller number of units. At the same time, O'Hanlon argues, even an agreement so "generous" to North Korea "would not harm the net military position of the combined U.S./ South Korean forces." South Korea would still have its qualitative superiority over the North, he says, and "allied reconnaissance capabilities, communications systems, precision-guided munitions and other asymmetric capabilities would also be unchecked."[18]

What is missing from this proposal is a recognition that North Korea feels threatened by the U.S. presence. William Perry, who visited the North, reported on national television how the North does, in fact, feel. O'Hanlon, from his Washington perspective, explained how he thinks the North *should* feel. Pointing to Pyongyang's missiles, long-range artillery, chemical weapons, and special forces, he contends that "these capabilities should give North Korea a strong assurance that, even if it cuts its forces substantially, Seoul and Washington would not contemplate an offensive military thrust northward under any but the most extreme circumstances." At the same time, he acknowledges the limitations in its own striking power that lead Pyongyang to feel threatened. "North Korea's forces do not amount to a plausible invasion capability against South Korea," he writes, even though they do pose a "terrorist threat" to the South, especially to Seoul. Yet despite this important assumption, the proposed agreement would not require any cuts in the U.S. weaponry deployed in South Korea. Seoul and Washington could count U.S. equipment in Korea against South Korean allotments and would be free to decide on their own how to apportion their respective holdings.

Even though Perry explicitly recognized that North Korea feels threatened militarily by the United States, he did not recommend a security dialogue with Pyongyang in his report to the president. On the contrary, his report rested on the premise that economic and political incentives alone should be sufficient to induce Pyongyang to abandon any nuclear and missile ambitions. O'Hanlon, too, assumes that economic and political incentives can help obtain security concessions. The keystone of his proposal is that the United States would offer a normalization of relations and a five-year economic aid program. But he does not rely on economic and political incentives alone. His proposal offers specific security benefits to Pyongyang.

The "food for peace" feeler related earlier and the overtures for a missile deal made to Secretary of State Madeleine Albright in October 2000 showed that North Korea is ready for significant security concessions in response to economic and political incentives. But the United States is seeking a complete termination of the North Korean missile and nuclear programs, and Pyongyang would be likely to make this ultimate security concession only in the context of balanced arms-control arrangements. To be balanced, in the North Korean perspective, such arrangements would have to take into account its perception of the U.S. military presence as a threat to its security. The critical issue confronting the United States and South Korea is what their priorities should be in pursuing balanced arms-control arrangements. Cuts in weaponry, as O'Hanlon suggests? Mutual force reductions linked with U.S. force withdrawals, as the North urges? Or the pullbacks of the North Korean forward-deployed forces and artillery that threaten Seoul, which the South emphasizes?

The most compelling priority is clearly to relieve South Korean fears of a surprise attack on Seoul. North Korean pullbacks from the DMZ would have an immediate and profound political payoff, greatly reducing North-South tensions. The operative questions for Washington and Seoul in approaching arms control in Korea, therefore, are what concessions would be required to get differing degrees of redeployment on the part of Pyongyang, and what changes in the U.S. and South Korean force posture would be acceptable in order to get North Korean redeployment.

The major bone of contention in any discussions with the North on mutual force pullbacks is likely to be the principle of asymmetry emphasized in the South Korean proposals cited earlier. Since Seoul is so close to the DMZ, symmetrical pullbacks equal in distance could place South Korean and U.S. forces at a disadvantage. For example, suppose that both sides pull back twenty-five miles. South Korean and U.S. forces would then be on the northern outskirts of Seoul. In a surprise attack, North Korean forces could be well on their way to the DMZ before South Korean and U.S. forces could get their counteroffensive started. More important, North Korean artillery fire would impede their advance. South Korean and U.S. generals argue that they would have more warning time if the opposing forces remain in their existing forward positions than if both sides pull back an equal distance. In short, the location of Seoul would make pullbacks unacceptable to Seoul and Washington unless North Korea pulls back further than the South. How much further would be the pivotal issue.

Significantly, Kim Il Sung, in his June 17, 1994, meeting with Jimmy Carter, acknowledged that pullbacks would have to be asymmetrical. Recalling his meeting with Kim, Carter told me that he had emphasized the South's fears of a surprise attack, whereupon Kim had said: "I am ready to discuss a withdrawal of both sides back from the DMZ, and I recognize that we would have to withdraw a further distance than the South, given the realities of geography and the location of Seoul."[19]

Kim also took a relaxed attitude toward the U.S. presence, Carter said, linking the pace of U.S. withdrawals with the extent of North-South mutual force reductions. Thus, if the North and South agreed to cut their forces in half, half of the U.S. forces would leave. This contrasted sharply with the North's 1988 arms-control proposal, which called for a phased U.S. pullout within four years.

Pyongyang might well expect concessions on other issues in return for accepting asymmetrical pullbacks. For example, the United States sold the South 120 Apache attack helicopters during the nuclear crisis of 1994 and maintains some of its own in the South. The Apaches and other weapons systems perceived by the North to be offensive in character could be removed from Korea in order to get a pullback agreement.

In 1982, when General Riscassi proposed a unilateral pullback of U.S. and South Korean forces, South Korean leaders bitterly resisted, arguing that forward deployments were a symbol of South Korean and American resolve. The United States backed off, and 15,000 American soldiers in forward positions are still cannon fodder, not for overriding military reasons but in deference to Seoul. Such deference to an ally was understandable when the argument was over a unilateral pullback. But if North Korea should agree to mutual asymmetrical pullbacks and the South should say no, the United States should be prepared for a showdown with Seoul no less fateful than its 1953 confrontation with Rhee over the armistice. This time, instead of buying Seoul off once again with open-ended military aid commitments, Washington should bar all U.S. sales of military hardware and technology until Seoul cooperates.

Throwing cold water on the idea of mutual pullbacks, Brig. Gen. Young Koo Cha, director of policy planning in the Defense Ministry, said that "it would simply be too expensive. Relocating forces would be a very expensive business for all concerned." But if the United States is willing to spend so much on maintaining its forces in Korea, it should be willing to help pay for arms-control arrangements that reduce tensions and make its force presence in Korea progressively less necessary. The possibility of such an American role was suggested obliquely in the 1991 report of a South Korean–U.S. conference in which I participated together with General Cha, then director of a South Korean military think tank. The conference report observed that "in early negotiations with North Korea, the South might wish to avoid requesting reciprocal measures from Pyongyang that are very expensive and time-consuming. Major redeployments of troops, for example, can take some time and require the construction of new bases and housing." Referring specifically to Lim Dong Won's proposal for a Limited Deployment Zone, the report added that "such a move would be expensive—unless an outside sponsor offered to make up the costs."[20] A 1998 working group on Korea sponsored by the U.S. Institute of Peace concluded more categorically that "international financial support will be necessary to cover certain costs associated with a Korean arms reduction process, including mutual troop and equipment reductions and repositioning." Such support, the report said, would have a precedent in the U.S. support provided for strategic arms reductions with Russia under the program initiated by Senators Sam Nunn and Richard Lugar.[21]

What concessions would North Korea seek as the price for asymmetrical pullbacks? A categorical answer to this question quickly emerged when a Carnegie Endowment delegation met with a leading North Korean military spokesman in May 1992. One of our members was Gen. Edward C. Meyer, former U.S. Army chief of staff. General Meyer's presence led to an hour-long meeting on May 2 with Lt. Gen. Kwon Jung Yong, then deputy army chief of staff for strategy, disarmament, and foreign affairs. When we raised the issue of mutual pullbacks, General Kwon smiled indulgently. Pointing to a map showing U.S. air bases in South Korea and Japan, he spoke slowly, as if explaining something to children. "Look where you are," he said. "You can leapfrog over us, deep into our territory. That is why we must keep our forces far forward, to deter you, to make it too costly for you to do that. You talk of equitable redeployments but they wouldn't be equitable unless we are no longer threatened by your air forces as well as your ground forces." Much the same argument has been repeated in my 1994, 1995, and 1998 meetings with General Kwon, Gen. Ri Chan Bok, North Korean delegate at Panmunjom, First Deputy Foreign Minister Kang Sok Ju, and other officials in Pyongyang. When I emphasized the importance of pullbacks from the DMZ several times in a one-on-one dinner with Kang on September 29, 1995, he held up a knife, drew it across his throat, and said that "my military friends will do this to me if I even mention such a thing. Unless, of course, you are prepared to withdraw your forces, especially your air forces."

Brig. Gen. James Grant, the former director of intelligence of U.S. forces in Korea, expressed doubt that North Korea would ever negotiate pullbacks. Pyongyang wants to keep its own forces forward, he said, because it knows that the forward-deployed U.S. forces are in a vulnerable position. "They don't want us to pull back," he said. "They're not really afraid of an American attack, and they're happy to have us right where we are if there ever is a war." As in other U.S. military analyses, Grant pointed out that North Korean forward deployments are not, strictly speaking, defensive, since key logistics dumps and artillery are deployed in front of their major infantry forces. "They're too exposed," he explained. "It wouldn't make sense to do that if they expect the United States to attack first."

The answer to this argument is that North Korean fears of a surprise attack appear to be focused not on U.S. ground forces but on U.S. air capabilities. The reason for deploying its forces so far forward and for seeking to develop nuclear, missile, and chemical warfare capabilities is to make sure that North Korea never again suffers an air onslaught like the one during the Korean War described in part 2. Thus, to get Pyongyang to negotiate the Limited Deployment Zone proposed by Lim Dong Won and to end its nuclear and missile programs, the United States would have to make concessions relating to its air forces as well as its ground forces. The trump card in the U.S. hand would be a readiness to transfer the U.S. combat aircraft now based in Korea to bases in Japan or Hawaii. Most experts agree that the South Korean Air Force could prevail in a war with the North, even after a withdrawal of U.S. combat aircraft, if the United States continued to provide command and control, targeting, and intelligence support.

Just as the North points to U.S. and South Korean airpower to justify its forward deployments, so many South Korean analysts who oppose mutual pullbacks point to the North's missile capabilities. The South will have to maintain its forward deployments, they argue, even if the North is ready for pullbacks, until the South is able to target all of North Korea with its own missiles. Thus, conventional arms-control negotiations in Korea are not likely to succeed unless they are accompanied by the flexible U.S. posture in negotiations on ending North Korean nuclear and missile programs discussed in part 4.

Until the United States, South Korea, and North Korea begin a security dialogue, North Korean intentions concerning the pace and extent of U.S. ground force withdrawals will remain unclear. In my meetings with General Kwon, Gen. Ri Chan Bok, and Foreign Ministry arms-control officials, they have consistently reaffirmed the linkage between U.S. withdrawals and North-South force reductions that was central in past North Korean arms-control proposals. At the same time, they have indicated a new flexibility concerning how fast the disengagement of U.S. forces would have to be. As the next chapter will elaborate, the North Korean attitude toward arms control and the future of the U.S. presence will be decisively shaped by whether Washington is ready to bring a formal end to the Korean War; end the adversarial relationship symbolized by the Military Armistice Commission and the United Nations Command; and shift to a new role as an honest broker between the North and South.

The principal stumbling block to successful arms-control negotiations with North Korea is likely to be the desire of the United States to keep forces in Korea for larger Asian strategic reasons—regardless of what Pyongyang is willing to do to reduce North-South tensions or ease U.S. concerns regarding its missile and nuclear capabilities. This was the bottom line of a discussion I had with William Perry about arms-control scenarios.

The United States could agree to a pullback of its forward-deployed forces in return for North Korean pullbacks, he said, "but even if we could get satisfactory terms for that, we will probably want to keep our forces in Korea for the foreseeable future to promote stability in the region, if the South Koreans will let us, so that is as far as we could go." He dismissed a suggestion that ground forces alone might be withdrawn, with air forces remaining and the U.S–South Korean Security Treaty intact. "If we didn't have ground forces there," he replied, "would it be politically sustainable in the United States to remain committed to defend South Korea? Would we keep air forces there if we had pulled out our ground forces?" In any case, he added, "Why are you so fixated on those 37,000 ground troops? That's not what worries them—it's our airpower. They're afraid of a preemptive strike."

I reminded Perry of his statement after returning from North Korea that Pyongyang wants missile capabilities to deter what it considers a U.S. threat to its security. How can the United States get North Korea to limit or end its missile program, I asked, if we are unwilling to reciprocate by limiting or ending our military presence in Korea? "I haven't seen that as a stumbling block," he said, "if we are on a path to normalization. I don't expect a stalemate to occur on the missile issue because of the U.S. presence. If it does, we'll have to see. I don't know what we'll do."[22]

CHAPTER 13

Ending the Korean War

Is NORTH KOREA serious about arms control?

Would Pyongyang agree to tension-reduction measures and the termination of its nuclear and long-range missile programs in conjunction with a phased U.S. withdrawal?

The only way to find out is to bring the Korean War to a formal end, normalize relations with Pyongyang, and replace the anachronistic 1953 armistice machinery with a new peace structure. The Military Armistice Commission set up in 1953 was a temporary expedient to oversee the cease-fire. But it still lingers on. Similarly, the United Nations Command, which provided a genuinely multilateral umbrella for U.S. intervention in the conflict, is now only a fig leaf for what is a unilateral U.S. security commitment to South Korea. Pyongyang points to the commission and the U.N. Command as symbols of an adversarial relationship that should properly have ended (but did not) when the North agreed to freeze its nuclear program in 1994. "We are in a halfway house, neither peace nor war," observed Gen. Ri Chan Bok, North Korean representative at the DMZ. "How can we let our guard down and talk of arms control in such an uncertain situation?"[1]

For North Korea, as this chapter will show, the replacement of the Military Armistice Commission and the U.N. Command with a new peace structure is a precondition for arms-control and confidence-building measures. During most of the cold war, Pyongyang also insisted on the complete withdrawal of U.S. forces as a prerequisite for steps to reduce tensions. As the cold war drew to an end, however, the North accepted the principle that a U.S. withdrawal could be linked to tension reduction. The 1988 arms-control proposal discussed earlier stipulated that each step in a phased U.S. withdrawal would be contingent on parallel North-South force reductions. More recently, while continuing to call for an eventual withdrawal, Pyongyang has further softened its position. American forces could stay for an indefinite transition period, the North now says, if the United States would broaden its mission in Korea from one limited to the defense of the South to a new role designed to deter aggression by either side against the other. During this transition period, the U.S.–South Korean Security Treaty could remain in force.

This shift in position concerning the purpose and duration of the U.S. presence has been signaled both in formal diplomatic overtures and in unofficial exchanges with U.S. visitors that will be spelled out in this chapter. More important, in a key arms-control offer on June 16, 1998, outlining the terms for ending its missile program, Pyongyang pointedly distinguished between removal of the American military "presence" and removal of the American military "threat." "The United States, which is technically at war with the D.P.R.K., has the largest quantities of nuclear weapons and ICBMs in the world," the 1998 statement said. "With U.S. missiles aiming at our territory, we find no reason to refrain from developing our own to counter them. The discontinuation of our missile development is a matter which can be discussed after a peace agreement is signed between the D.P.R.K. and the United States and the U.S. military threat completely removed."[2]

The U.S. military threat arises not from the U.S. force presence, as such, General Ri and others in Pyongyang emphasize, but from the adversarial posture of the United States toward the North and from a one-sided U.S. military alignment with Seoul. The threat would be reduced, they say, to the extent that Washington shifts to a more symmetrical role.

By referring to a peace "agreement" with the United States and, on other occasions, to an "interim peace agreement," North Korea has attempted to circumvent the long-standing stalemate over who should sign a formal treaty replacing the armistice. The signatories to the 1953 agreement were North Korea, China, and a U.S. general acting on behalf of the U.N. Command. The United States and South Korea now want a peace treaty limited to North Korea and South Korea.[3] But this is an untenable position, since the South refused to sign the armistice. Syngman Rhee wanted to continue fighting and reluctantly agreed to observe the provisions of the armistice only after the United States bought him off with a mutual security treaty and a cornucopia of economic and military aid. A solution to the legal snarl over how to end the Korean War will clearly require a more flexible formula.

North Korea wants the armistice commission to be replaced by a trilateral "mutual security assurance commission" in which North Korean, South Korean, and U.S. generals would have equal status. The trilateral body would not only monitor provocations by either side at the DMZ, as the armistice commission does, but would also have a broader mandate to negotiate arms-control agreements and supervise their implementation. At the same time, the Joint Military Commission agreed upon in 1991 would be put into operation. Pyongyang has carefully avoided making detailed proposals concerning the allocation of functions between the proposed trilateral body and the North-South commission, leaving the door open for a flexible response to U.S. and South Korean counter-proposals. But Washington and Seoul have refused to negotiate any change in the status quo. Their position continues to be that negotiations on a new peace structure should be limited to the North and South and should come only after tension reduction has already been achieved.

A formal end to the Korean War leading to the replacement of the armistice commission and the U.N. Command is resisted by a U.S. military establishment reluctant to surrender its quasi-imperial power and perquisites in South Korea. The extent of this power is symbolized by the fact that a four-star U.S. general not only presides over the U.S.–South Korean Combined Forces Command but would also exercise operational control over South Korean forces in wartime. The United States acquired operational control in July 1950 during the dark early days of the Korean War, just two weeks after the South Korean Army abandoned Seoul to the North Korean forces. After the fighting ended, American generals continued to exercise this authority until 1994, when South Korean nationalist pressures forced Washington to relinquish peacetime operational control to Seoul. In the event of war, however, the United States would automatically regain it. This is the key reason why North Korea regards the United States as its main adversary and why some form of direct peace agreement between Washington and Pyongyang is likely to be unavoidable when and if the armistice is replaced.

The South and the Armistice

The United States has properly resisted North Korean demands for a bilateral peace treaty excluding South Korea as the only legal instrument needed to end the Korean War. But the U.S. counterproposal for a North-South treaty excluding the United States is equally unrealistic. So long as the United States retains wartime operational control over South Korean forces, North Korea can logically insist on some form of U.S. participation in the agreement or agreements that replace the armistice accord.

By the same token, a stable peace in Korea must necessarily include some form of separate North-South peace agreement. Washington and Seoul argue that the South was, in fact, a party to the armistice because it fought under the U.N. Command. In this argument, the United States was not a party to the truce because Gen. Mark W. Clark, although a U.S. general, signed the agreement on behalf of the U.N. Command, not the United States. Above all, it is said, although Rhee did not sign, his eleventh-hour public commitment to honor its provisions amounted to the same thing as signing.

These arguments contain substantial elements of historical revisionism. From the very outset of negotiations on a cease-fire in June 1951, the Rhee government insisted that it would fight on alone rather than accept a truce that did not provide for the reunification of Korea under the South. On April 21, 1953, the South Korean National Assembly formally opposed the impending armistice, and Rhee ordered the South Korean representative in the negotiations to withdraw.[4] The possibility of getting Seoul to sign was not even considered by the United States. All that mattered was making sure that Rhee did not obstruct the operation of the agreement, even if this meant submitting to his blackmail. On May 12, Rhee made his first demand, a bilateral mutual security agreement that would commit the United States indefinitely to the defense of the South in the event of a new attack. President Eisenhower resisted, offering instead to seek a pledge by the sixteen U.N. member states represented in the U.N. Command to renew their intervention if necessary.[5] As tensions between Seoul and Washington mounted, General Clark prepared a series of contingency plans known as "Operation Everready" to deal with the possible obstruction of the impending armistice by South Korean forces. These included disarming "disloyal" South Korean units, restricting both civilian and military movements in the South, and if necessary, sponsoring a military coup by cooperative South Korean generals, accompanied by the arrest of Rhee and a proclamation of martial law.[6]

When agreement was reached on a final demarcation line on June 17 and the prospect of a truce seemed imminent, Rhee made a determined effort to wreck the armistice. On the night of June 18, South Korean Army units organized a mass breakout of more than 27,000 North Korean prisoners of war, imprisoning and intimidating U.S. guards.[7] This was just four days before a scheduled visit by Walter S. Robertson, the U.S. assistant secretary of state for Far Eastern affairs. Robertson's mission was to get a firm South Korean commitment not to interfere with the operation of the armistice. On July 12, after two weeks of intense discussions, Rhee gave Robertson a letter for President Eisenhower saying that he had "decided not to obstruct, in any manner," the implementation of the armistice.[8]

Robertson thought he had an agreement and left. The United States had agreed to conclude a mutual security treaty and to provide both massive economic assistance and enough military aid to build a twenty-division South Korean Army. On July 24, however, Rhee upped the ante, demanding a U.S. commitment to join in a new military offensive against the North if the projected post-armistice political conference failed to agree on plans for reunification within ninety days. Secretary of State Dulles openly criticized Rhee's "uncertain" position, complaining that "we had believed that your attitude toward a truce was already decided." At this point, the White House decided to go ahead with the armistice regardless of what Rhee did and, if unavoidable, to invoke a toughened version of "Operation Everready" to deal with him. In addition to its original provisions, the new version envisaged withdrawing recognition of the Rhee government, blocking South Korean dollar and sterling accounts, and, as a last resort, a naval blockade.[9]

On July 27, 1953, the armistice agreement was finally concluded, providing for a cease-fire, a demilitarized zone 4,000 meters wide between the opposing forces, a military demarcation line roughly parallel to and 25 miles north of the thirty-eighth parallel, and the creation of a Military Armistice Commission to deal with violations of the accord. The South Korean Army refused to join in the honor guard at the signing ceremonies along with troops from the fifteen other countries that had fought in the war.[10] On August 27, the United States signed the mutual security agreement with Seoul that remains in force today.

Article 4 of the armistice agreement envisaged negotiations "to settle the questions of the withdrawal of all foreign forces from Korea, the peaceful settlement of the Korean question, etc." Having failed to block conclusion of the armistice, however, Rhee did his best to block implementation of article 4 at the Geneva conference on Korea from April through June 1954. Evelyn Shuckburgh, private secretary to British foreign minister Anthony Eden, wrote in his diary on May 4 that "the Americans have not yet induced Syngman Rhee to agree to any plan remotely acceptable to the rest of us."[11] The North proposed a simultaneous and proportional withdrawal of all foreign forces as a prelude to elections. The elections would be conducted on a nationwide basis by a North-South electoral commission under the control of a neutral supervisory commission. South Korea and the United States countered with a plan certain to be rejected. They called for elections to be held in North Korea alone under the authority of an election commission set up by the U.N. Security Council. Since the U.N. Command had been its adversary in the war, Pyongyang spurned the proposal. Many of the governments that had contributed forces to the U.N. Command were critical of the U.S.–South Korean stand. The chief Canadian delegate, Chester Ronning, declared later that the North Korean plan "could have been accepted as a basis for a settlement by most of the sixteen states that fought under the U.N. flag."[12]

With tensions between Seoul and Washington continuing to simmer a year after the armistice, President Eisenhower invited Rhee to Washington in July 1954. But their encounter only made matters worse. Rhee insisted on language in the minutes of the White House talks that pledged U.S. support for unification "by all means." A U.S. draft of the minutes specified "peaceful means." Rhee's prime minister, Paik Too Chin, said in an unpublished interview for the Dulles Oral History Project that Rhee had come to Washington with a plan for a 1955 offensive against the North that he never presented because "the atmosphere at that time didn't allow him to do so." For six months Rhee refused to sign the minutes, which led to a virtual paralysis in Seoul-Washington relations and a U.S. cutoff of civilian oil supplies. He finally agreed to abandon his language on unification only under pressure from South Korean military leaders eager to complete a major arms aid agreement.[13] Nevertheless, during 1955, Rhee secretly ordered preparations for recapturing the Kaesong and Ongjin areas of North Korea. As late as 1957, according to National Security Council records, Dulles frequently expressed concern that Rhee might "start a war." On one occasion, Dulles declared that "if war were to start in Korea, it would be very hard indeed to determine which side had begun it."[14]

REPLACING THE ARMISTICE

Against this background, South Korea clearly has no legal status as a signatory to the armistice agreement. Rhee's undertaking not to disrupt the truce was made in a letter to President Eisenhower, not to North Korea. Thus, it does not amount to the same thing as having signed the agreement, as some argue. The contention that General Clark signed on behalf of all of the forces under his command is irrelevant in the context of Seoul's opposition to the agreement itself. In any case, the South was only one of sixteen countries that fought under the U.N. banner, and all of them cannot be treated as signatories in replacing the armistice agreement. But to say that the South was not a signatory does not alter the fact that it must be a central part of a peace settlement. A distinction should be made between the replacement of the armistice accord per se and the broader challenge of establishing a stable peace structure.

The 1953 agreement should be replaced by one or more legal instrumentalities involving the three states that did, in fact, sign the agreement—the United States, China, and North Korea. At the same time, in order to create a stable peace regime, North Korea and South Korea, as the principal antagonists in the war, would either have to conclude a separate, new peace agreement of their own or take the steps needed to upgrade their 1991 "Basic Agreement" into a credible peace accord that explicitly writes finis to the war.

In technical legal terms, the United States is on solid ground in stating that General Clark signed the armistice in his capacity as commander of the U.N. Command. As a practical matter, however, the command has been multilateral in name only since its inception. This has been conclusively demonstrated by John Barry Kotch in his definitive study of its origins.[15] In giving the United States the right to act on behalf of the United Nations, the Security Council merely authorized it to enlist the help of other U.N. members. It did nothing to establish multilateral control over the U.N. Command. The United States rejected as "impractical" a proposal by U.N. Secretary General Trygvie Lie to create U.N. machinery that would "coordinate offers of military assistance and take other action in implementing the Council's decision." In his memoirs, Lie bitterly recalled that his plan was stillborn because the United States was "unwilling, in those early days when the pattern of the police action was being set, to accord the U.N. a larger measure of direction and thereby participation." Many U.S. allies such as Britain, France, and Norway liked the idea of a U.N. coordinating role, he said, but U.S. representatives at the U.N. "promptly turned thumbs down," blaming "Pentagon opposition."[16]

During the war, successive American commanders of the U.N. Command insisted on unfettered U.S. control over military operations, and in subsequent years even the cosmetic trappings of multilateral control have been progressively reduced. The headquarters of the command in Seoul is staffed solely by Americans. Half of the sixteen countries that fought under it had severed their connections by 1992. The rest do not have full-time representation in the command but give their defense attachés in Seoul nominal accreditation to it for ceremonial occasions, such as meetings of the armistice commission, where British and Thai officers occasionally flank the U.S. delegate. Unlike the officers commanding U.N. peacekeeping forces, such as the one in Cyprus, the head of the

U.N. Command in Korea has never reported to the U.N. secretary general. When Kofi Annan visited Seoul in 1998, he did not meet Gen. John Tileli, who was then titular head of the U.N. Command.

For more than two decades, the U.N. Command has had no military functions. In 1978, when the United States and South Korea created their Combined Forces Command, the U.N. Command formally transferred its authority to the new command. The same U.S. general who headed the new command continued to retain the title of commander in chief, United Nations Command, but he has worn his U.N. hat only when participating in meetings of the Military Armistice Commission. Although its military functions have ceased, the U.N. Command provides useful diplomatic cover for the United States within the armistice commission. Wearing his U.N. hat, the U.S. representative can deal with North Korea without giving it implicit diplomatic recognition.

The insistence of the United States that it was not a party to the armistice is governed by political, not legal, considerations. At bottom, it reflects a fear that normalization of relations with North Korea and the replacement of the armistice could threaten the future of the U.S. military presence in Korea. When and if the United States decides to normalize relations with Pyongyang, the fact that General Clark signed as U.N. commander need not be an insuperable legal obstacle to replacing the armistice.

In a detailed analysis of the many legal scenarios that have been proposed for ending the Korean War, Patrick M. Norton, former legal counsel to the State Department's Bureau of East Asian and Pacific Affairs, has suggested a flexible approach that could include direct U.S. participation. "Legally," he argues, "a direct U.S. role would clearly be appropriate in light of Security Council Resolution 84V," which refers to the role of the United States as the "unified command" in Korea, in light of its "direct command role in the fighting itself, and in light of its intimate political and military involvement in the maintenance of the Armistice over more than four decades."

Although it is often assumed that the armistice must be replaced by a single "peace treaty," Norton says, "form should not dictate policy, and there is no compelling reason why the Korean Armistice could not be superseded by an agreement, or agreements, not expressly entitled 'treaty.' The legal tail should not wag the policy dog." Such an agreement, or agreements, could be submitted to the U.N. Security Council, which would pass a resolution confirming that they bring the Korean War to an end.[17]

Norton envisages a North-South agreement as an integral part of such a package of agreements. In my own view, since South Korea cannot be considered a signatory to the armistice and Pyongyang is likely to be unshakable on this point, the agreements explicitly designated as replacing the armistice could be between the United States and North Korea and the United States and China. As suggested earlier, South Korea and North Korea could conclude a separate companion agreement not linked to the armistice. The fact that the North and South do not formally recognize each other as sovereign need not be an obstacle to this formula. Since the U.N. recognized them as sovereign states when it admitted them, the Security Council could confirm a North-South agreement as part of its resolution without legal difficulty. Seoul and Pyongyang could then finesse the issue of sovereignty in the language of their agreement as they did in the 1991 "Basic Agreement." Other possible legal complications could be resolved if there is a political will to do so. For example, the fact that the signatories to the armistice signed as military commanders, not as heads of government, could be untangled through diplomatic exchanges between the governments concerned that could then be appended to the Security Council resolution.

The key element in this formula is that the United States would sign a direct bilateral agreement with North Korea. Until now, Pyongyang has rejected a direct North-South agreement, but its position would become more flexible if Washington agreed to sign a bilateral accord with the North. When I emphasized the need for South Korean participation in a peace agreement, or agreements, during my June 8, 1994, meeting with Kim Il Sung, he smiled and said, "Don't worry, the diplomats have ways of dealing with these things."

THE U.N. FIG LEAF

The possibility of dissolving the U.N. Command while retaining the Military Armistice Commission was considered by the United States in 1974. Henry A. Kissinger, as secretary of state, formulated this concept in response to abortive diplomatic moves in the U.N. General Assembly to end the U.N. role in Korea. In a recently declassified National Security Council Decision Memorandum (no. 251, dated March 29, 1974), titled "Termination of the U.N. Command in Korea," Kissinger said that the president had decided to seek substitution of the U.S. and South Korean military commanders for the commander of the U.N. Command as "our side's signatories to the 1953 Korean Armistice agreement." The South Korean and North Korean representatives "should then become the principal members of the Military Armistice Commission," and the U.N. Command could be terminated. This change would have been contingent on "tacit acceptance by the other side of a continued U.S. force presence in South Korea for at least the short term, in return for a Shanghai-type communiqué committing ourselves to reduce and ultimately withdraw U.S. forces as the security situation on the Peninsula is stabilized." The "minimum objective" of this negotiating approach, Kissinger said, "is to place ourselves by early summer in a defensible position for possible debate of the Korean issue in the U.N. General Assembly this coming fall."[18]

Kissinger's concept of a "Shanghai-type communiqué" linking the reduction and withdrawal of U.S. forces to the stabilization of the security situation in Korea could well prove useful in formulating a way to deal with the future of U.S. forces today. However, his proposal for changing the signatures on the armistice agreement and keeping the armistice commission intact would accomplish little, even in the very unlikely event that it proved acceptable to North Korea. Pyongyang would continue to seek a bilateral peace treaty with the United States and the replacement of the armistice commission as prerequisites for arms-control and tension-reduction negotiations. A U.N.–blessed peace settlement that replaces the armistice agreement should logically be accompanied or followed by the dissolution of the U.N. Command, the replacement of the armistice commission with new machinery to stabilize the peace, and the normalization of relations between Washington and Pyongyang.

On May 28, 1994, North Korea formally asked U.N. Secretary General Boutros Boutros-Ghali to initiate steps that would lead to the replacement of the armistice agreement and the termination of the U.N. Command. Boutros-Ghali replied categorically on June 24 that the United States alone has the authority to "decide on the continued existence or the dissolution of the United Nations Command." He recalled that Security Council Resolution 84 of July 7, 1950, "limited itself to recommending that all Members providing military forces and other assistance to the Republic of Korea 'make such forces and other assistance available to a unified command under the United States of America.' It follows, accordingly, that the Security Council did not establish the unified command as a subsidiary organ under its control, but merely recommended the creation of such a command, specifying that it be under the authority of the United States. Therefore, the dissolution of the unified command does not fall within the responsibility of any United Nations organ but is a matter within the competence of the Government of the United States."

Apart from the utility of the U.N. Command as diplomatic cover for U.S. representatives to the Military Armistice Commission, the United States has three other reasons for wanting to retain the U.N. Command indefinitely. One is a desire to avoid the need for renewed U.N. Security Council approval of U.S. intervention in the event of a new war. American and South Korean forces could once again fight in the name of the U.N. Command without seeking U.N. approval as the United States did in the case of Desert Storm. A more substantial reason relates to the U.S. use of bases in Japan in connection with military operations in Korea. An agreement with Japan during the Korean War gave seven U.S. bases in Japan dual legal status as U.N. Command bases. The U.N. Command has explicit authority to use these bases to refuel and service U.S. aircraft en route to Korea in the event of hostilities.

Lim Dong Won, who conducted the 1991 South Korean talks with North Korea that led to the "Basic Agreement," raised the subject of the U.N. Command in discussions with U.S. officials prior to his negotiations with the North. He wanted to know how Washington would feel about a possible offer to dissolve the U.N. Command as a bargaining chip with Pyongyang. "The United States took the position that the dissolution of the U.N. Command was premature and undesirable," he said, "because it is a matter that is directly related to the continued use of military bases in Japan and to the return of 'operational control' of the South Korean armed forces to the Republic of Korea."[19] Lim pointedly noted that the United States and Japan had adopted a new defense guidelines agreement in April 1996 providing for "the continued use of the bases in Japan by the United States." Since 1996, however, the final detailed guidelines have emerged. While they do indeed envisage continued and even strengthened Japanese logistical support for U.S. forces in unspecified "regional" crises, the use of U.S. bases in Japan for combat operations in Korea would still be governed by the "prior consultation" requirement of the 1961 U.S.–Japan Security Treaty. The U.S. use of U.N. Command bases in Japan for logistical support of combat operations and refueling aircraft en route to Korea would not require Japanese approval.

As Lim observed, in addition to the issue of Japanese bases, the United States is also concerned that the dissolution of the U.N. Command would undermine the legal and political foundations of U.S. operational control over South Korean forces. This concern arises from the fact that when Rhee originally transferred operational control in 1950, it was to the U.N. Command.

THE "OP CON" ISSUE

In the U.S. view, the termination of the U.N. Command would intensify what is already a growing debate in South Korea over the return of operational control to Seoul. Even a U.S. general, the late Richard G. Stilwell, once commented that the degree of operational control enjoyed by the United States in Korea is "the most remarkable concession of sovereignty in the entire world." Stilwell pointed in particular to the fact that the U.S. commander of the U.S.–South Korean Combined Forces Command "reports only to U.S. higher authority" and would have the technical legal freedom to do so even with respect to the use of nuclear weapons, in contrast to the dual authority over the nuclear trigger in Germany.[20]

For Lim Dong Won, like many other leading South Koreans, the continuance of U.S. operational control so many years after the Korean War is not only an affront to sovereignty but also an impediment to meaningful dialogue with the North. "South Korea must recover its independent identity as the main player in negotiations with North Korea," Lim declared in 1996. "This issue is intrinsically related to the question of recovering the operational control of its military forces from the Commanding General of the U.N. Command. Only with the reversion of operational control will North Korea respect and fear the South. Only then will North Korea genuinely respect South Korea's authority and capability. Unless operational control is returned to us, North Korea will continue to confine its approaches to the United States alone and to exclude South Korea as its natural negotiating partner." Urging on another occasion that wartime operational control "must be returned as soon as possible," Lim said that this would necessarily entail the restructuring of the existing U.S.–South Korean Combined Forces Command along the lines of the U.S.–Japan military arrangements, "linking two separate operational structures on a cooperative basis." A continued U.S. force presence in Korea is desirable, he added, emphasizing that the U.S. presence is "primarily based on the R.O.K.–U.S. Mutual Security Treaty of 1953 and is totally unrelated to the existence or dissolution of the U.N. Command."[21]

Similar sentiments have been expressed by another retired major general, Hwang Won Tak, who succeeded Lim as national security adviser to Kim Dae Jung, and by Gen. Kim Yoon Ho, a former chairman of the Joint Chiefs of Staff. General Kim has told me on repeated occasions that U.S. operational control leads to a "dependent psychology" and that South Korean forces would develop "greater confidence in facing the North" if Washington turned over wartime operational control to a South Korean general.

The South Korean government position is that operational control can be safely returned only "as the North Korean threat declines." So long as the United States retains operational control, officials say, the United States will be automatically involved in the event of hostilities, and "we will have a guarantee of U.S. commitment and reinforcement on the basis of which we can make operational plans." Conversely, it is argued, the United States would be free to delay and limit its involvement if South Korea has operational control.

From the perspective of most U.S. officials and military officers, it would be dangerous and unworkable for the United States to keep forces in Korea without retaining operational control—dangerous because South Korea might overreact to North Korean provocations and drag the United States into a needless conflict, and unworkable because it would be difficult to coordinate U.S. and South Korean forces without a single unified chain of command. Logically, U.S. officials say, a South Korean general could head the existing Combined Forces Command, but Congress would balk at the idea of American troops fighting under a foreign command, anywhere, and might not be willing to keep any U.S. forces in Korea at all without U.S. operational control.

Those in the South who call for the return of operational control believe that a coordinated command structure patterned after the U.S.–Japan model would work effectively. Asked about this concept, Lt. Gen. John H. Cushman, who commanded the U.S.–South Korean First Corps Group from 1976 to 1978, expressed concern that such an arrangement "would fall apart under pressure." It would be especially difficult under such circumstances, he said, for U.S. forces to provide the efficient intelligence, command and control, and targeting on which the South now depends. Reminded that there is no provision for U.S. wartime control over Japanese forces in U.S.–Japan security arrangements, General Cushman replied that U.S. and Japanese forces only have a loose liaison structure, not a truly unified command, since there is no clear and present danger that they will have to fight an actual war together.[22]

Objections such as these to coordinated command arrangements in

Korea similar to or stronger than those in Japan rest on the assumption that the two Koreas will remain poised on the brink of war indefinitely. But some version of the Japan model would be appropriate for Korea during a transitional peace process when tensions are gradually subsiding and arms-control efforts are proceeding under the aegis of a new post-armistice peace structure.

To be sure, operational control does give the United States a leash that can be used to restrain South Korea. It should be surrendered only in the context of a meaningful peace process in which Washington is prepared for the compromises necessary to reduce tensions. However, it also adds to the danger of U.S. involvement in low-level encounters such as the June 15, 1999, North-South boundary clash in the Yellow Sea. The fighting took place on the South Korean side of a demarcation line defined by the U.N. Command in 1953 as the North-South maritime border but disputed by Pyongyang. In such a conflict, the line between peace and war can quickly become blurred. If the North Korean naval craft involved had not proved so impotent and the initial ten-minute exchange of gunfire had escalated, General Tileli, then the commander of the Combined Forces Command, might have felt compelled to take over operational control. This could well have triggered action requiring U.S. participation. American fighter planes, reconnaissance ships, and an aircraft carrier were on their way to the Yellow Sea when the conflict sputtered out.

Although the U.S. military in Korea wants to retain operational control, many U.S. diplomats who have served there express grave doubts about it. One of the most outspoken was the late Francis Underhill, who served as deputy chief of mission in Seoul from 1971 to 1974 and later as ambassador to Malaysia. Underhill waged a lonely battle during his years in Seoul for a reevaluation of U.S. diplomatic and military goals in the peninsula. In a memorandum to Ambassador William Porter on February 19, 1971, Underhill wrote that "we seem to put great stock in the U.N. fig leaf for Op Con, but are we being realistic? They give us Op Con because it helps to keep us here and because it makes us happy. . . . They can tell themselves that when the crunch really comes we'll see who has Op Con over whom. All it would take would be a twenty-four hour breakdown to commit us."[23]

NORTH KOREA'S PEACE PROPOSAL

Since the United States and South Korea are reluctant to take the risks that would be involved in replacing the existing armistice machinery, they have brushed aside a series of increasingly conciliatory North Korean scenarios for a reduction of tensions marked by a softened attitude toward the size and duration of the American presence.

When Kim Il Sung met Jimmy Carter on June 16, 1994, he told him that North Korea was "not too concerned" about a continued U.S. military presence but would like to see it gradually reduced to about 4,000 from the present level of 37,000.[24] Two months later, Ambassador Robert Gallucci was surprised when First Deputy Foreign Minister Kang Sok Ju expressed a tolerant attitude toward U.S. forces over the dinner table during their Geneva negotiations on the nuclear freeze agreement. "He seemed to say that if the United States and North Korea normalized their relations and became friendly, they wouldn't care much about U.S. forces."[25]

The conclusion of the nuclear freeze agreement in October led to a series of North Korean proposals for an undefined "new peace mechanism" to replace the Military Armistice Commission and the U.N. Command. The U.S. government ignored these proposals and made no effort to explore them with North Korea during the ensuing six years. For this reason, my own discussions with senior North Korean officials concerning these proposals merit a detailed review, showing as they do that Pyongyang has been flexible during this period on two key issues: the future of U.S. forces and the nature of South Korean participation in the proposed peace structure.

In a meeting with Gen. Ri Chan Bok, the North Korean representative at Panmunjom, on September 28, 1995, I pressed him to explain what sort of "new mechanism" North Korea had in mind. First, he said, the armed forces of the United States and North Korea would set up what might be called a North Korea–United States "mutual security assurance commission." It would consist solely of military officers. Immediately following establishment of the commission, the North Korea–South Korea Joint Military Commission negotiated in 1992 but never instituted would begin to operate in parallel with the North Korea–United States commission.

The functional role of both commissions would be to prevent incidents in the DMZ that could threaten the peace and to develop arms-control and confidence-building arrangements. General Ri said explicitly that the North would not object to the presence of U.S. forces in Korea if the armistice and the U.N. Command were replaced: "The Americans think that if they join in establishing the new peace mechanism that we will raise the question of withdrawing troops from the Korean peninsula. But it's clear from the Asian strategy of the United States that the U.S. army will not pull out tomorrow. It will take a long time. Accordingly, we will set up a new peace mechanism on the basis of a mutual understanding that U.S. forces will continue to be stationed in Korea."

The purpose of the "new peace arrangements," First Deputy Foreign Minister Kang Sok Ju told me a day later, would be to stabilize the North-South status quo militarily. "The armistice was concluded between two hostile parties," Kang said. "The purpose of the new peace arrangements will be to end adversarial relations and prevent any threat to the peace, whether from the South against the North or the North against the South."

Kim Byong Hong, policy planning director in the Foreign Ministry, observed during my 1995 visit that "Korea is surrounded by big powers—Russia, China, and Japan. We must think of the impact of the withdrawal of U.S. troops on the balance of power in the region." Another said that "if U.S. troops pull out of Korea, Japan will rearm immediately. We will formally ask you to withdraw your troops, but there is room for discussion about this matter."

I told General Ri and Foreign Minister Kim Yong Nam that in order to be acceptable at some point to the United States, the new mutual security commission should be a trilateral one involving South Korea, or at the very least, the Joint Military Commission should go into effect simultaneously with the proposed United States–North Korea commission. Since the United States could not speak for South Korea, I said, the U.S.–North Korea commission should not deal with North-South issues and should confine itself to issues involving U.S. forces. Their answer was that the North is willing to negotiate a compromise on the modalities of a new structure and to consider arms-control measures. But both insisted on a bilateral mutual security commission consisting only of U.S. and North Korean generals.

Within six months, the party line had changed on the issue of South Korean participation. General Ri told visiting State Department official Kenneth Quinones on July 18, 1996, that the United States and North Korea should first meet separately to set up the new peace structure, since the South had not signed the armistice, but should then immediately invite the South to join it as a full partner. Quinones, a Korean-speaking former director of the North Korea desk, was visiting Pyongyang as an adviser to a U.S. Army delegation seeking the return of the remains of U.S. servicemen missing during the Korean War. He was not authorized to respond to General Ri but formally reported this significant change in North Korean policy to his superiors in Washington in a memorandum that was promptly pigeonholed.

In a conversation with Ri on May 6, 1998, I emphasized that any new peace structure would have to be trilateral from the outset in order to be seriously considered by the United States. He replied that "if your side comes to the talks without the U.N. hat, they can come with the South Koreans. If there is an official proposal to this effect from your side, we will consider it affirmatively." General Ri made clear that the South could be a full member of the commission, not an observer. Why, I asked, didn't the North itself propose a trilateral structure? "It's not for us to bow down to you, pleading for your cooperation," he said. However, a U.S. spokesman told me, General Ri did formally propose to U.S., South Korean, and U.N. Command representatives at Panmunjom on October 9, 1998, that to replace the armistice, "both sides should establish a military security assurance commission as a joint military mechanism to be composed of the Korean People's Army, the U.S. military and South Korean officers."[26]

Asked whether the U.S.–South Korean Security Treaty could remain in force under the proposed "new peace arrangements," he replied, "Definitely yes." I observed that "this is possible because you don't want the issue of your mutual security treaty with China to be raised, isn't that right?" He smiled, commenting that "these are longer-range issues that can be considered in time at the political level."

I asked Ri whether establishment of a "new peace mechanism" would make it unnecessary to conclude a peace treaty formally ending the war. His answer was that a treaty would still be necessary. However, a Foreign Ministry statement soon afterward on June 16 offered to discuss "the discontinuation of our missile development after a peace agreement with the United States is signed and the U.S. military threat completely removed."

North Korean diplomats have subsequently made clear that the use of the phrase "peace agreement" rather than "peace treaty" was calculated. In a conversation on May 16, 2001, Li Hyong Chol, North Korean U.N. representative, said that "our concern is to end hostilities and formalize relations between us in a mutually agreeable way. But the United States must deal with us directly. A peace agreement would end the Korean War and a treaty might not be necessary, certainly not any time soon. After all, Japan and Russia have diplomatic relations without a formal peace treaty." The replacement of the armistice could either accompany or follow conclusion of the peace agreement, he added, leading to the creation of the mutual security commission and negotiations on arms-control measures. However, he cautioned that North Korean force pullbacks from the thirty-eighth parallel would depend not only on U.S. force redeployments and pullbacks as part of arms-control agreements but also on U.S.–supported progress toward a North-South confederation that would defuse the military threat from the South.[27]

It was to counter North Korean pressures for direct talks with the United States on replacing the armistice that South Korea began to float trial balloons in mid-1995 suggesting a four-power peace process including China. North Korea initially resisted Chinese participation in the Geneva four-power talks held from 1997 through 1999. This reflected an overall strategy designed to offset the power of neighboring China, Japan, and Russia with a U.S.–focused diplomacy. Although ready to accept China as a signatory to an eventual peace treaty, North Korea does not want its giant neighbor to be involved in the proposed trilateral commission. Beijing does not belong in the commission, Pyongyang argues, because it has not had forces in Korea since 1958, in contrast to the United States, which still has troops in the South and retains wartime operational control.

North Korea never wanted the Geneva talks in the first place but has used them to signal its readiness for a flexible approach to tension reduction. On March 17, 1998, the North Korean delegate offered to replace a proposed agenda item referring to the "withdrawal of foreign forces" with another one referring to "the status of foreign forces." Washington and Seoul rejected this offer, but Kim Dae Jung, who had just been elected, expressed curiosity about the idea to his aides, and a meeting of the National Security Council in Seoul discussed it "in depth" in early April, according to Ra Jong Il, then the deputy director of the South's National Intelligence Service.

In rejecting the North Korean offer at the Geneva talks, the U.S. delegate objected to singling out U.S. forces. The United States, he said, would discuss its force presence only as part of a broad discussion of the overall structure of forces in Korea embracing North Korean as well as South Korean and U.S. forces. Ironically, it is precisely such a wide-ranging approach that North Korea has invited in its proposal for a new peace structure. What is at issue is whether such a discussion should take place before or after the armistice machinery has been replaced.

Reporting on his visit to North Korea as an emissary of President Clinton in May 1999, William Perry ruled out the idea of a "package deal" in which both sides would put their concerns on the table and negotiate trade-offs. Instead, Perry recommended to Clinton that the United States seek to keep control of the negotiating process by laying down what he called a "two-path" ultimatum. North Korea would have to decide whether or not to accept path one, "complete and verifiable assurances that it does not have a nuclear weapons program, and the complete and verifiable cessation of the testing, production and deployment" of missiles with a range over 180 miles. "If North Korea moved to eliminate its nuclear and long-range missile threats," Perry said, "the United States would normalize relations, relax sanctions, and take other positive steps that would provide opportunities for the DPRK." On the other hand, "If North Korea rejects the first path," the report says, "it will not be possible for the United States to pursue a new relationship."[28]

Discussing the Perry report, the U.S. ambassador to South Korea, Stephen Bosworth, made no secret of the reason for avoiding a package deal. "There was a fear," he said, "that if we were to engage in discussions on a package deal, such a deal would have to include a change in the status of U.S. forces."[29]

Kim Jong Il made clear during his June 2000 summit meeting with Kim Dae Jung that he does not want the issue of U.S. forces to get in the way of obtaining quick economic help from the United States and South Korea. But precisely what he said concerning U.S. forces is a subject of some confusion.

Kim Dae Jung raised the issue, saying that "U.S. forces will be needed in Korea even after unification to preserve a regional balance of power." On one occasion, Kim Dae Jung said that Kim Jong Il replied, "I totally agree with you."[30] On another occasion, Kim Dae Jung said that the North Korean leader "showed substantial understanding of my position on the need for U.S. troops."[31] An adviser to Kim Dae Jung who briefed Secretary of State Madeleine Albright had a different version: Kim Jong Il had responded that he was "not totally opposed" to what Kim Dae Jung had said.[32] Another South Korean official who participated in the summit said that North Korea "wants to retain some strategic ambiguity on this matter."[33] China's official *Beijing Review* offered its own clarification of North Korean policy. One option acceptable to Pyongyang, the *Review* said, would be for the United States to "return operational control over South Korean forces to the South, change the adversarial role of U.S. forces into a peacekeeping role and transform the Demilitarized Zone into a zone of peace." Indirectly suggesting a Chinese role that North Korea itself had not proposed, the *Review* added that "another option acceptable to North Korea would be to replace U.S. forces with a peacekeeping force made up of Northeast Asian countries and the U.S. work-ing together."[34]

Twenty-five years after Henry Kissinger made his proposal for a "Shanghai-type communiqué" linking a U.S. withdrawal with the reduc-tion of tensions in Korea, the United States is more reluctant than ever to move in this direction. Yet for its part, North Korea, which was not ready for the Kissinger approach in 1975, is now in tune with it. In his address to the Council on Foreign Relations in New York on September 27, 1999, Foreign Minister Paek Nam Sun declared that the United States need only announce a "political decision" accepting the principle of an eventual withdrawal as part of a negotiated tension-reduction process that could extend over an indefinite period. Should the United States decide to play a transitional role as an honest broker or peacekeeper in such a process, Kenneth Quinones foresees open-ended possibilities. "The implementation of a new peace arrangement," he writes," must determine whether U.S. forces are to remain, depart or be posted in both Koreas."[35]

CHAPTER 14

The Tar Baby Syndrome

"THEY HAVE attached themselves to the big fat udder of Uncle Sam, and naturally they don't want to let go."

I was not too surprised to hear this irreverent comment about South Korea from the plain-talking U.S. ambassador in Seoul, the late William J. Porter, during an off-the-record discussion in his residence in early 1971.[1] Porter was engaged at the time in bitter negotiations with the Park Chung Hee military regime over the size of the U.S. military presence in the South. He had successfully pushed the Nixon administration to cut the U.S. presence from 60,000 to 40,000 troops, prompting apocalyptic warnings of imminent disaster from Park, demands for compensatory U.S. military aid, and counterdemands from Washington for South Korean help in paying for the costs of the U.S. presence.

Our conversation took place shortly after the visit of Vice President Spiro Agnew, who had come to inform Seoul of the impending troop cuts. To illustrate the South's tenacious bargaining tactics, Porter told a revealing anecdote. Park and his fellow generals were determined to outlast their U.S. opposite numbers at the negotiating table, without interruptions for trips to the rest room. "They were equipped with catheters connected to plastic bottles strapped to their legs under their trousers," he recalled. "But Agnew's bladder was stronger than theirs."

There were stirrings of ferment and reappraisal concerning Korea among many U.S. policymakers in 1971, stimulated by growing disenchantment with the Vietnam War and the movement toward détente with Russia and China that culminated in Nixon's 1972 visit to Beijing. Porter's Deputy Chief of Mission Francis Underhill reflected this mood in a memorandum to the ambassador that he shared with me. "I understand, in historical perspective," he wrote, "why the cost and risk of our present position in Korea was justified twenty years ago: containment of Stalinist expansion and protection of a prostrate Japan. North Korea is still nasty, belligerent and dangerous, but like the stonefish, only if you get too close. It is no longer the instrument of global communist military expansion. . . . Who beside ourselves would be ready to put their own men and resources back into Korea today?" He urged that a timetable be fixed for a pullout of all U.S. ground troops by 1975, together with a termination of the U.N. Command.[2]

Underhill used imagery to describe the U.S.–South Korean relationship that was even more graphic than Porter's. Recalling the *Tales of Uncle Remus*,[3] he mused that "we seem to be stuck to South Korea like Brer Rabbit was to the Tar Baby."[4]

Told of this conversation with Underhill, James Laney, who served as U.S. ambassador in Seoul from 1992 to 1996, said he thought the analogy is inappropriate. "Casting South Korea as the Tar Baby isn't very flattering," he said, "and the idea isn't quite right, because it suggests that we would like to become unstuck. The problem is that many in our military would like the status quo to go on indefinitely. We need a new approach to security in Northeast Asia in which the regional powers would play a bigger role, a cooperative role, and our presence could be gradually reduced."

Reflecting on "how difficult it would be to become unstuck," Laney used the imagery of Siamese twins. "When you're involved like this, like Siamese twins, what one does affects the other, and it won't be easy. I don't think Siamese twins are healthy. It's not a healthy relationship. We're keeping them childishly dependent, and we're aggravating tensions."[5]

Nixon's withdrawal of 20,000 troops from South Korea was one of the more enduring legacies of his "Guam Doctrine," which sought to promote a gradual transition to greater self-reliance on the part of U.S. allies in Asia. Since the Nixon administration, the level of U.S. deployments in Korea has remained substantially unchanged despite the intermittent congressional pressures for further reductions described in this chapter and President Carter's abortive initiative in 1977 to pull out all U.S. ground combat forces. Each time pressures for U.S. disengagement have grown serious, South Korean and U.S. advocates of an indefinite U.S. presence have urged delay, pleading that the South is on the verge of self-reliance. The United States can honorably disengage, they have argued, only when self-reliance has actually been achieved. But now their argument has fundamentally changed, even though the South is steadily widening its margin of economic superiority over the North and possesses much more sophisticated weaponry in most military categories than Pyongyang. Whether or not the threat from the North subsides, they say, the United States would have to keep its forces in Korea for larger Asian strategic reasons, especially now that the North may be developing nuclear and missile capabilities.

The underlying premise of the case for disengagement is that the South could, and would, do what is necessary to defend itself in the absence of a U.S. force presence—but that it would not necessarily seek to match the level of military security provided by the United States with a costly compensating buildup of its own. Instead, in this view, the loss of its U.S. defense subsidy would increase economic and political pressures in the South for mutual force reductions and other arms-control agreements with Pyongyang, which is eager for such agreements to help resolve its economic problems. Even in the event that arms-control efforts fail, war erupts, and the South is unable to stop a Northern advance, advocates of disengagement argue, the United States, with its growing airlift and sealift capabilities, could get back to Korea quickly enough to save the situation.

Proponents of disengagement are polarized between those who favor an unconditional, rapid withdrawal and others who would support U.S. disengagement only when and if North Korea agrees to a clearly defined set of arms-control concessions. In this chapter I seek to make the case for another view falling between these two extremes. The view presented here envisages a continuing U.S. presence for a finite transition period, linked to U.S. support of arms-control efforts as an honest broker between the North and South. At the same time, it emphasizes that the United States should not permit itself to become a hostage to hard-line elements in the North and South opposed to the arms-control compromises necessary for a reduction of tensions.

It is often assumed that the South is united in support of an indefinite U.S. force presence. But the reality is more complex and uncertain. As fears of the North decline, there is a growing nationalist restiveness in the South over the continued presence of foreign forces that cuts across ideological divisions and could well force the pace of U.S. disengagement.

The Unending Debate

Looking back on the debates over Korea that have intermittently exploded in Washington during the past three decades is instructive. Many of the arguments of yesteryear are still relevant to a debate that has not changed in its fundamentals during this period.

When Ambassador Porter faced a hostile Senate Foreign Relations Committee in late 1970 just before Nixon's troop reduction, Chairman William Fulbright told him that "there is something wrong with a situation in which we have spent over $7 billion in South Korea and then are told that South Korea is threatened by North Korea, which is far smaller in population and should be weaker in every other way. We have put the money in. We have given them planes. What do they do with the money?" Senator Stuart Symington struck a similar note, asking, "Why can't they defend themselves with all this money and supplies? Why do we also have to keep 60,000 troops there for 20 years? The South Koreans have the North Koreans licked in every category, except they don't tax their people as much."

At this point, Porter defended the U.S. presence by suggesting that the South might attack the North without a U.S. presence. "What would be wrong with that, if it is their country?" replied Symington. "Do we restrain them from trying to get their country back? What would have been the reaction in this country if the French or the British had told either side in our Civil War not to move into Maryland or Pennsylvania? What do we do, tell these people they cannot try to get their country back and then pay them not to try? Are you saying that if they attacked North Korea like the North attacked them, that would be bad?" "What I am saying," Porter shot back, "is that this would immediately arouse the attention and perhaps the action of the two major Communist states, especially if the Southerners seem to be succeeding."[6]

Just eighteen months after Nixon's troop reduction, his defense secretary, Melvin R. Laird, drafted a plan for a further cutback to one combat brigade of five thousand. Nixon rejected it as a needless irritant to far-right elements in Washington already upset by his opening to China. But the mere fact that Laird, himself a conservative, had sponsored the move was a measure of the skepticism generated in Washington by the Vietnam War concerning U.S. troop commitments in Asia.

Returning from a 1972 mission to Korea, a Senate Foreign Relations Committee delegation warned that the U.S. commitment to Seoul "carries with it the danger of automatic U.S. involvement in another Asian war." A committee staff report asked: "Why does the United States have troops and advisers in the South while the Russians and Chinese have none in the North? Why must American ground forces be retained if they are no longer necessary to maintain the military balance? Are the existing interlocking U.S.-U.N.-Korean Command arrangements still desirable?" The arguments for continued military aid to Seoul would be "far more appealing," the report concluded, "if there were some assurance that by a date certain there would be no further need for . . . automatic U.S. involvement in Korea's defense."[7]

Three years later, the House Appropriations Committee, in its report on the 1975 Defense Appropriations Bill, recommended "prompt and decisive action to reduce the risks of automatic combat involvement." The operational control over South Korean forces exercised by the United States "makes some degree of U.S. involvement automatic in the event of even minor clashes between North and South Korea," and "elements of the Second Infantry Division are deployed so as to make U.S. combat involvement almost inevitable in the event of a major enemy offensive." The committee urged the Pentagon to move all of the division south of Seoul and to make South Korea responsible for constructing new cantonment facilities. If this is not done within six to twelve months, the committee declared, "then a gradual withdrawal of the Second Infantry Division from Korea should begin in fiscal year 1976."[8]

The Ford administration ignored this recommendation and several like it made by nongovernment specialists.[9] However, Jimmy Carter, then eyeing the Democratic presidential nomination, was following the debate on Korea closely because he intended to make the pullout of U.S. troops one of his campaign issues. Soon after taking office in 1977, Carter announced his plan to cut the size of the U.S. presence down to 12,000 Air Force, Navy, and Army logistics personnel by 1981, withdrawing all of the 26,000 remaining ground combat troops, together with their tactical nuclear weapons units.

Carter's decision was rooted in three factors. As a naval officer, he shared the belief of Navy strategic thinkers like Alfred Thayer Mahan that the United States should avoid tying down its ground forces in exposed forward positions on the Asian mainland. As a former nuclear engineer, he was particularly alarmed by the U.S. deployment of tactical nuclear weapons in Korea near the front line. As a human rights advocate, he found the Park military dictatorship in South Korea abhorrent.

Carter announced his plan without first putting forward a clear rationale that would have helped him to combat predictable opposition in the U.S. national security bureaucracy and among conservatives in Congress. More important, he failed to consult Japan in advance to make clear that he did not intend to go beyond the withdrawal of ground combat forces and that the U.S. security commitment to Japan would not be affected. He immediately became embroiled in a losing struggle within his administration in which opponents of the withdrawal enlisted the help of sympathizers in the intelligence community. Carter's premise was that the pullout would not alter a North-South military balance favorable to the South. The Defense Intelligence Agency (DIA) produced a revised estimate of North Korean capabilities showing that its tank forces were 80 percent larger than previously estimated and that Pyongyang had 200,000 more men under arms than previously believed. As the intra-administration struggle over the plan neared a climax, the DIA leaked these findings. "Suddenly," Carter told me, "the estimate of North Korean capabilities was almost doubled. I have always felt that the intelligence community played fast and loose with the facts, but I couldn't prove it."[10] By the end of his term, Carter had succeeded in reducing the number of U.S. forces in Korea by only 3,000, including 700 ground troops.

The underlying weakness of the Carter approach to disengagement was that it was not accompanied by a broader effort to reduce U.S. and South Korean tensions with North Korea. Carter himself revealed an awareness of this basic flaw when he conceived the idea of inviting South Korean President Park and North Korean leader Kim Il Sung to meet with him in the demilitarized zone in the spring of 1979. But he eventually dropped this idea after his advisers persuaded him that it had little prospect of success and would only succeed in aggravating what were already tense relations with Seoul.

In the end, the Carter presidency locked the United States into its military alliance with South Korea more tightly than ever and escalated the North-South arms race. To ease Seoul's anxieties about the reliability of the U.S. security commitment, the United States agreed to establish the U.S.–South Korean Combined Forces Command, and Carter pledged an additional $1.9 billion in military aid. Most important, he upgraded the level of U.S. military aircraft provided to Seoul. In place of the F-4, he promised the faster and more powerful F-16, the latest-model fighter-bomber in the U.S. armory, which gave North Korea a justification for getting advanced-model Migs from the Soviet Union.

The debate over disengagement remained quiescent after Carter's departure until improved U.S. relations with Moscow and Beijing, coupled with Seoul's dramatic economic upsurge, once again prompted questions about the U.S. presence. *Business Week*, citing South Korea's "newfound economic strength, in a time of easing superpower tensions," said in 1988 that the United States "should start planning a phased withdrawal of most of its 43,000 troops from Korean soil. With a population more than double the North's, an economy six times as large, and a thriving domestic arms industry, South Korea is clearly in a position to resist an invasion and to pay most of its defense costs."[11] Returning from a visit to South Korea in 1989, Carl Levin, chairman of the Subcommittee on

Conventional Forces of the Senate Armed Services Committee, proposed a phased reduction of U.S. forces in Korea down to the level of one brigade, with the pace of reductions keyed to "concrete military steps by North Korea that lessen the prospect of surprise attack."[12] Kim Dae Jung, then the principal opposition leader in the South, endorsed the proposal, describing the continued U.S. troop presence in the South as "a stumbling block to inter-Korean dialogue."[13] Levin never pushed his ideas in the Senate, but in the House, Congressman Robert Mrazek of New York twice attempted unsuccessfully to get support for legislation relating to U.S. forces in Korea. In 1987, Mrazek got 64 votes for a bill urging the withdrawal of all ground forces within five years. In 1990, he made a more modest proposal for a reduction of U.S. forces from 43,000 to 30,000, for which he received support from 157 members.

"Because of improved South Korean military capabilities and overall force reductions," the Bush administration said in 1991, the United States would "decrease the number of U.S. forces stationed in South Korea," starting with an "initial" cut of 7,000 by the end of 1992.[14] This cut was made, but the Clinton administration did not go further, pointing to the emergence of the North Korean nuclear threat. Indeed, President Clinton made an unprecedented pledge during the 1994 nuclear crisis with the North to keep U.S. forces in the South "as long as they are needed and the Korean people want them to remain."[15] This open-ended commitment prompted an outraged rebuttal from the editor of *Foreign Policy*, Charles William Maynes. "Once the current crisis is over," he told the Aspen Strategy Group, "the United States should step back from this foolish presidential statement, which places too much of the initiative in Seoul's hands, and press South Korea to assume progressively full responsibility for its land defense, with the United States progressively fulfilling its treaty obligation through air and sea power. It is preposterous that the United States should have to assist in the land defense of a country that is twice as populous and by some accounts 15 times as rich as its northern brother."[16]

THE U.S. SUBSIDY AND NORTH-SOUTH TENSIONS

Why has the presence of U.S. ground forces in South Korea remained politically inviolate in Washington for nearly five decades?

Part of the answer lies in the searing psychological legacy of the Korean War and the resulting imagery of North Korea as irrational and threatening, a new "Yellow Peril," an imagery inflated by fears that it will develop long-range missiles. This imagery has persisted despite the North-South summit meeting of June 2000 and the subsequent visits of North Korea's second-ranking leader, Vice-Marshal Jo Myong Rok, to Washington, and of Secretary of State Madeleine Albright to Pyongyang. Indeed, Albright was widely criticized for legitimizing a brutal dictatorship.

Some of the answer lies in the superficial appeal of the strategic arguments examined in part 5: that the U.S. presence helps stabilize a volatile part of the world and that any change in the U.S. posture would be seen as a "retreat" from Asia. But the key reason why the United States is stuck to South Korea "like Brer Rabbit was to the Tar Baby" is that Seoul has shown remarkable skill and determination in resisting any change. The impact of the negative images and the positive strategic arguments has been maximized over the years by sustained and effective South Korean lobbying efforts, aided by sympathizers in the Pentagon and in defense industries with a stake in Korea.

The payoffs to members of Congress exposed in the 1976 "Koreagate" scandal were not isolated cases. A former Washington station chief of the South Korean CIA, Gen. Kim Yoon Ho, has told of how he arranged support for legislation relating to U.S. military aid and the U.S. force presence by channeling big export contracts to states with cooperative representatives in Congress, especially exports subsidized under a variety of U.S. economic and military aid programs. The manipulation of pricing in such contracts offered easy opportunities for rake-offs to middlemen. In South Korean eyes, anything that will keep the United States in South Korea is morally justified because Washington was largely to blame for the division of the peninsula and remains obligated to stay until reunification is achieved.

"The South Korean Embassy swings a lot of weight in Washington," observed David E. Brown, former director of Korean affairs in the State Department, in 1997. "Long-tended friendships between conservatives in both capitals give extra potency to the political clout they wield."[17]

South Korean influence in Washington has been reinforced by the support of legions of U.S. military officers with fond memories of their years in Korea. The semi-imperial trappings of U.S. military life there are epitomized by three eighteen-hole golf courses, one of which occupied some of the most valuable real estate in Seoul until former Ambassador James Lilley persuaded the U.S. Army to relocate it. "The pain it took to do this," Lilley recalled, "is symptomatic of the military's resistance to giving up its perks. They told me about how they have to keep up morale to retain personnel, but you can't do this at the expense of your relations with the host country."[18] For officers with their families, the nine U.S. military installations in the South are self-sufficient enclaves equipped with most of the comforts of home and largely insulated from the local society. For the footloose, there are *kiesang* hostesses, the Korean equivalent of Japanese geisha. Most important, for the top brass of the U.S. Army, Korea is the last and only place left in the world where a four-star general can be a "commander in chief" presiding over an operational command in a foreign country. All of the nine other "CinCs" with regional and functional commands have their headquarters in the United States.

As a *Washington Post* series, "The Proconsuls," observed, "the CinCs (pronounced "sinks") have evolved into the modern-day equivalent of the Roman Empire's proconsuls—well-funded, semi-autonomous, unconventional centers of U.S. foreign policy. . . . The CinC's jobs have always been loaded with perks. They live in well-appointed homes, draw $135,000 salaries for terms that usually run three years and have lavish entertainment and travel budgets."[19] Any change in the 1953 armistice machinery involving an end to U.S. operational control and the breakup of the U.S.–South Korean Combined Forces Command would destroy the rationale for maintaining a four-star general in Seoul.

Although the South Korean populace resents the U.S. use of prime real estate for golf courses and for bases that are oases of foreign culture and affluence, the South Korean and U.S. military elites have a cozy camaraderie. Retired South Korean officers are permitted to use the golf courses and shop in the duty-free base commissaries for U.S. luxury goods not available at comparable prices on the Korean market.

Covering South Korea since 1967, I have often felt as if I am in a revolving door. Year after year, South Korean leaders and their Pentagon allies have sought to fend off cutbacks in U.S. military aid and force levels by setting target dates for achieving South Korean self-reliance. Year after year, these target dates have been extended. To forestall further reductions after Nixon announced his troop cut, President Park declared that the South would achieve self-reliance by 1975, only to say then that further cuts would still be premature "until we have the capability to defend ourselves, and that will take four or five more years."[20] In 1983, South Korean leaders spoke confidently of reaching military parity with the North in three years, but in 1985, Gen. William Livsey, the U.S. commander in Korea, said that parity would not be achieved until "the early 1990's."[21] General Livsey's successor, Gen. Louis Menetry, announced in 1989 that thanks to U.S. military aid, "there should be stability on the peninsula without the United States being part of the equation in the mid-1990s."[22] Soon afterward, a South Korean *Defense White Paper* said that "by 1996, the armed forces of the South would be able to defend the country alone."[23] The latest target date was more cautious. Announcing a five-year defense modernization plan in 1999, a Defense Ministry spokesman said that the new plan would enable the South to reach parity with the North by 2010.[24]

As Doug Bandow has observed, referring to unfulfilled self-reliance targets, the South "never quite seems to get there, and it almost certainly will not so long as it believes it can count on American military support."[25] In a similar vein, Ted Galen Carpenter ridiculed a statement by Pentagon official Walter Slocombe that the United States would like to see South Korea "do more" militarily and that "we have made that clear to them." "Why would the R.O.K. volunteer to incur the economic burden of spending substantially more on defense," he asked, "if the United States is willing to continue providing a security shield at its own expense?"[26]

Estimates vary concerning how much it would cost Seoul to compensate for the loss of the U.S. force presence. Carpenter has suggested a figure of $10 billion to $12 billion annually.[27] Former ambassador James Laney has offered a similar estimate, commenting in 1994 when the South Korean defense budget was $13 billion, that "they would have to double their defense budget if we weren't there."[28] Former South Korean defense minister Lee Sang Hoon has speculated that the military share of South Korean gross domestic product would have to go up by 5 to 8 percent.[29]

Such estimates are probably on the low side. The costs incurred by the United States in maintaining its readiness for a possible Korean War involve not only the direct costs of the U.S. presence in Korea itself but also the much larger indirect costs of its bases and force deployments in adjacent areas of Asia.

The direct local costs for the operation and maintenance of U.S. forces has averaged $2 billion annually, but this estimate goes over $5 billion if the cost of training and equipping these forces is added. Moreover, it does not take into account the costs of continually upgrading obsolete military equipment such as the $3.7 billion spent since 1991 to replace the entire fleet of U.S. helicopters in Korea. Nor does it reflect the fact that it costs more to station forces in other countries than in the continental United States—in the case of Korea, about $900 million more per year—or the millions continually spent on new construction. Military construction in Korea is projected to cost $4.2 billion ($234 million annually) from 2002 to 2020.[30]

Estimates of the indirect costs involved in maintaining Korea-related U.S. forces in Asia vary in accordance with the methodology used. The largest figure—$42 billion per year—has come from the Center for Defense Information.[31] This number includes an estimate of the costs of weapons acquisition, overhead, and logistical support for the U.S. forces deployed in Asia. Earl Ravenal, using similar criteria, has suggested $39 billion.[32] Michael O'Hanlon, examining the overall impact of the U.S. commitment to Korea on Pentagon planning, calculated that the United States could save $20 to $30 billion per year if it was no longer responsible for the defense of South Korea.[33] William W. Kaufmann and John D. Steinbruner, using different criteria, came up with $17 billion.[34]

South Korea, on its own, clearly could not match the level of military security provided by the United States without bankrupting its national economy. For this reason, a U.S. disengagement would not be likely to aggravate the arms race between North and South but rather to strengthen those in the South who have long advocated arms-control and tension-reduction agreements with Pyongyang that would make possible a "peace dividend" in the form of increased social welfare spending. "The burden of armaments and the pressure for consumer goods and public services is one of the important stimulants to détente," Francis Underhill wrote in his 1971 memorandum to Ambassador Porter. "As long as we are ready to pick up the tab for a rigid military confrontation, we divert domestic pressure for accommodation and strengthen those who have a vested interest in tension."

Far from promoting stability in Northeast Asia, as its proponents argue, the U.S. force presence enables the South to channel its defense spending into weapons systems that fuel a Northeast Asian arms race. Ambassador Laney asked me rhetorically, "Why are they buying submarines for use against Japan instead of a stronger defense against the North?" "Comforted by the American security blanket," wrote *Wall Street Journal* correspondent Steve Glain, the South has "spent billions of dollars on weapons systems that are in fact peripheral to repelling a North Korean invasion. They want to bolster South Korea's ability to fend off potential enemies other than North Korea." Military planners in the South "have started whispering about a 360-degree defense," Glain added, which means "defense against Japan."[35]

Strategic Mobility and Disengagement

The case for disengagement has been greatly strengthened by improvements in the technological capabilities of North Korea and the United States alike. As I will elaborate in part 4, if Pyongyang is able to deploy long-range missiles with accurate targeting, U.S. bases in Northeast Asia will be increasingly vulnerable. Equally important, the growing sophistication of U.S. strategic mobility capabilities is progressively reducing the risks of disengagement.

The massive emergency movement of U.S. forces to Saudi Arabia and Kuwait during the Gulf War and to Afghanistan in 2001 have provided a dramatic demonstration of American airlift and sealift capabilities. Drawing on its experiences in Desert Shield and Desert Storm, the United States has subsequently stepped up its strategic mobility buildup, focusing on Korea and the Gulf as the most likely theaters of future crisis.

The centerpiece of this ongoing expansion is the augmentation and eventual replacement of 214 C-141 and 109 C-5 transport aircraft with 120 C-17s capable of carrying much bigger loads. Forty-eight of the C-17s were already in service by 1997. This substantial airlift capacity operates in close coordination with a sealift capability now consisting of 197 ships, including 58 giant "roll-on, roll-off" container ships of varying sizes, most of them laden with prepositioned equipment and supplies for the Army, Navy, and Marine Corps. Significantly, 33 of these ships are based in Diego Garcia (19) and Guam (14), relatively close to potential crisis areas in Asia. Thirteen of these 33, assigned to the Army, carry enough equipment, food, water, and other supplies to support elements of two Army heavy divisions numbering some 34,000 personnel for up to thirty days.[36]

New strategic mobility capabilities now on the drawing board have a science fiction flavor, such as the huge "quad tilt-rotor," as big as a C-130 transport plane, which will be able to carry 100 troops more than 2,000 miles and land without a runway like a helicopter.[37]

Even in 1978, when airlift capabilities were limited to C-141s and C-5s, and when "roll-on, roll-off" ships did not yet exist, a Brookings Institution analyst cited Pentagon data showing that an airborne division and its equipment could be deployed to Korea from Guam and continental U.S. bases in 1.4 days and that two Guam-based infantry divisions could be deployed there in 3.7 days. With equipment prepositioned in

Korea, an infantry brigade could be deployed there in 24 hours and an airborne brigade in 17 hours.[38]

A Congressional Budget Office (CBO) study, *Moving United States Forces: Options for Strategic Mobility*, reveals that since 1996, the Army has prepositioned 120 M-1 tanks and 68 Bradley armored fighting vehicles in Korea—enough to equip one heavy brigade—over and above the 37,000 troops stationed there. This could be rapidly augmented by airlift and by the equipment and supplies prepositioned aboard ships at Guam and Diego Garcia. The CBO study estimated that the volume of airlift deliveries to Korea in any future crisis would nearly triple the average of 1,700 tons per day achieved during the first months of Desert Shield. Moreover, as C-17s (with their greater load capacity) are put into operation, airlift operations to Korea would become progressively easier, since a smaller number of planes would be required, relieving airport congestion. The use of large "roll-on, roll-off" ships would be easier in South Korea than in many less developed Asian countries, the study points out, since it has modern port facilities with berthing areas long enough and deep enough to accommodate these large vessels.[39]

Some of the U.S. military units most readily available for use in a Korean conflict are relatively light and thus well suited for transport by air. As examples, William J. Taylor and Michael J. Mazarr cite the Marine division based in Okinawa; the Seventh, Twenty-Fifth, and Sixth Light Infantry Divisions; and motorized brigades in other divisions. "Such units would be too light to take on heavy, Soviet-style North Korean divisions," they said, "if they comprise the core of the ground force elements. But if the U.S. role were merely to complement South Korean ground units, lighter divisions could be used profitably."[40]

Ironically, many of the same members of Congress who have resisted the $54.2 billion that would be needed for the full implementation of the Pentagon's strategic mobility plans give uncritical support to existing forward deployments that cost almost as much in Northeast Asia alone every year. The armed forces want strategic mobility in addition to their existing force levels, and they seek to justify these levels by hyping up exaggerated Chinese and North Korean threats. North Korea alone has provided the rationale for at least four of the twelve carrier battle groups maintained by the Navy. Similarly, the case for a ten-division Army is buttressed by the purported need to station two combat infantry brigades in Korea and to maintain another five active Army divisions to be sent there as reinforcements in the event of war.[41]

In April 1991, following the Gulf War, Gen. Colin Powell came close to acknowledging the importance of Korea to the Army's budget when he commented wryly, "Now that the Cold War is over, I'm running out of villains. I'm down to Castro and Kim Il Sung."[42]

NATIONALISM AND THE U.S. PRESENCE

The presence of foreign troops in any country is a prescription for tension, and in South Korea American forces have increasingly become a target of nationalistic animosity as memories of U.S. Korean War sacrifices have faded. During the Park Chung Hee and Chun Doo Hwan years, the United States was blamed for supporting military repression, especially when it did nothing to restrain Chun from slaughtering dissidents at Kwangju. On the day that Chun was overthrown, the *New York Times* reported, demonstrators pulled down the American flag and burned it on the balcony of a leading Seoul hotel amid "wild applause" and "a roar of approval among the hundreds of thousands of protesters."[43] The advent of civilian democratic rule, accompanied by the South's growing economic success, has produced a mood of proud self-confidence in which the presence of American troops is increasingly seen as anomalous and an insult to national sovereignty.

Hyun Hong Choo, a former South Korean ambassador to Washington, has pointed to a succession of changes in the South Korean perception of the United States. At first it was the "liberator" who freed Korea from Japanese colonialism. Then it was the "benefactor" who helped fight the Korean War and generously supported postwar reconstruction. Finally, Hyun writes, "as Korea's economic might has grown and its exports to the U.S. have expanded rapidly, a different side of the U.S. emerged in the form of trade pressure. Koreans then discovered 'America the peddler.'"[44]

Three specific, emotionally supercharged issues dominate South Korean agitation against the U.S. military presence.

One is prostitution. Korean women's groups charge that all of the nine U.S. military installations in Korea are surrounded by "prostitution towns" that breed disease and disrupt Korean families. "Brothels are as integral to Kunsan Air base as its aircraft bombs," said a report by Korean Women's Organizations United, and at Tongduchun, where part of the Second Infantry Division is based, there are more than five thousand prostitutes and seven hundred pimps.[45]

Second, an equally important focus of anti–U.S. sentiment is the extra-territorial immunity enjoyed by U.S. servicemen for crimes committed while in Korea. A Status of Forces Agreement (SOFA) signed in 1966 gave South Korea less control over the handling of such crimes than similar agreements do in the NATO countries and Japan. In an attempt to placate South Korean critics, the United States agreed to a revision of the accord in 1991, but the compromise did not go far enough. The issue continued to simmer until a series of widely publicized offenses by U.S. servicemen brought it to a boil. Reporting "a surge of anti-American demonstrations in the streets of Seoul" in April 2000, the *Financial Times* noted that demands for further revisions of SOFA embraced rightist as well as leftist political leaders.[46] The agreement was modified once again, in December 2000. The United States agreed to give South Korea custody of soldiers accused of murder, rape, arson, drug trafficking, and eight other serious crimes as soon as they are charged.[47] But tensions over lesser crimes are likely to persist.

Third, at the governmental level, tensions over the U.S. military presence center on the extent to which South Korea should share in covering the costs of stationing American forces in Korea. "Burden-sharing" has been a hot issue in U.S.–South Korean relations since the days of Ambassador Porter. As South Korea has grown more prosperous, however, the United States has pressed more insistently for a South Korean contribution to U.S. costs much bigger than the $400 million paid in 1999. In response, Seoul has dug in its heels, arguing that its contribution is actually $2.2 billion if the value of the real estate and services provided by South Korea is taken into account.

The U.S. assumption that opposition to the American presence is limited to a small fringe of student dissidents is no longer valid, if it ever was. Popular anger cut across the political spectrum in 1999 when the Associated Press published its exposé of the Nogunri incident, in which U.S. forces killed South Korean civilians suspected of harboring North Korean agents during the Korean War. A poll conducted in 1999 by the RAND Corporation found that "Koreans are more discerning about the role of the U.S.–R.O.K. alliance and dubious about the long-term value of the U.S. regional military presence. . . . The perceived linkage between the alliance and regional stability appears to be weakening, as is support for a U.S. military presence in Korea after unification." Only 17.7 percent of the South Koreans polled wanted U.S. forces to stay at present levels after unification, and 32 percent believe that their presence "would no longer be necessary."[48]

Significantly, American public opinion studies have shown with remarkable consistency over the past twenty-five years that a majority of Americans oppose U.S. combat involvement in another Korean war. In 1975, the Chicago Council on Foreign Relations asked respondents whether they favored or opposed the use of U.S. troops if North Korea attacked South Korea. Sixty-five percent said they opposed it. In 1999, as if caught in a time warp, the council again found 66 percent opposed.[49]

CHAPTER 15

Guidelines for U.S. Policy

UNTIL NOW, most proposals for arms control and tension reduction in Korea have suffered from two basic limitations. First, they have conditioned any changes in the 1953 armistice machinery on prior confidence-building and tension-reduction steps by North Korea, instead of making such changes first to expedite arms-control negotiations. Second, they have envisaged only the redeployment or partial disengagement of U.S. forces as a quid pro quo for North Korean concessions, ruling out the possibility of complete U.S. disengagement regardless of the price that Pyongyang is willing to pay.

As I have elaborated in the preceding chapters, the replacement of the armistice machinery is long overdue. It is the sine qua non for testing whether North Korea is ready for serious arms-control negotiations, as it says, once the Korean War is formally ended. The first step in this process would logically be acceptance of the North Korean concept of a trilateral mutual security commission (North Korea, South Korea, and the United States) in place of the Military Armistice Commission. Establishment of the new trilateral body could be conditioned on the simultaneous activation of the North-South Joint Military Commission agreed upon in 1991 but never put into operation.

After these two interlinked steps are completed, the United States could then conclude peace treaties with North Korea and China, replacing the armistice, promote a separate North-South peace agreement upgrading the 1991 Basic Agreement, and terminate the U.N. Command. The three peace accords could then be submitted by the governments concerned to the U.N. Security Council, which would endorse them collectively as constituting the definitive end of the Korean War. In the same resolution, the U.N. could formally approve the termination of the U.N. Command.

The stage would then be set for negotiations within the trilateral commission and the North-South Joint Military Commission on arms-control and tension-reduction measures. To illustrate possible trade-offs, the United States and South Korea could seek an agreement providing for the pullback discussed earlier of forward-deployed North Korean forces with an offensive capability, especially heavy artillery, multiple rocket launchers, and armor, out of artillery range of Seoul. In return, U.S. and South Korean forces would also pull back from their forward positions. Given the location of Seoul, North Korea would pull back further than the United States and South Korea. As the price for an asymmetrical pullback, Washington and Seoul would be prepared to discuss the removal of weapons systems regarded by Pyongyang as offensive in character, such as Apache attack helicopters, together with the partial withdrawal of U.S. forces from the peninsula—including the withdrawal of some or all of the U.S. air forces in Korea to Japan, Guam, or Hawaii.

South Korean and U.S. military leaders warn that it would not take long for the North to move its forces forward again. For this reason, in negotiating such an agreement, Washington and Seoul should insist on two conditions. Both sides should be required to deploy their artillery in the open to facilitate inspection and to maximize the warning time that the South would have in the event of an attack. Equally important, the United States should be permitted to retain those facilities in Korea needed to provide command and control, targeting, and intelligence support of South Korean forces. Since the U.S.–South Korean Security Treaty would not be affected by the proposed accord, the United States would have a legal basis for bringing back its forces if necessary.

In order to pursue verifiable agreements with North Korea that would terminate its long-range missile program and rule out the development of nuclear weapons capabilities, the United States would have to offer a partial or complete withdrawal of its forces. As earlier chapters have explained, Pyongyang has softened its position on the U.S. presence. It would not necessarily press for a complete withdrawal if Washington shifts from its adversarial posture to that of an honest broker. But North Korea can afford to be more flexible than in the past concerning U.S. forces precisely because it is keeping its nuclear and missile options open. The reason for keeping them open is to deter a U.S. preemptive strike. Thus, it is most unlikely that Pyongyang would agree to foreclose the possible development of this deterrent capability in the absence of basic changes in the nature and mission of U.S. forces in Korea.

Once an arms-control process is started, the United States could initiate negotiations with South Korea to restructure their military relationship, replacing the U.S.–South Korean Combined Forces Command with a new, coordinated command structure patterned after the arrangements linking U.S. and Japanese forces in Japan. But since such a restructuring process would involve the end of U.S. operational control over

South Korean forces, it should not be initiated until significant progress in tension reduction has taken place.

There is a built-in dilemma in scenarios such as this one that link steps toward disengagement with progress in tension reduction. Hard-liners in both the North and South are opposed to the compromises that would be necessary for a reduction in tensions, such as a pullback agreement and, subsequently, mutual force reductions. What should the United States do if arms-control agreements prove unattainable?

My assessment is that the hard-liners in the North will lose out—*if* Washington and Seoul are prepared to put the U.S. presence on the bargaining table—because Pyongyang needs to reduce military spending for economic reasons. Should this assessment prove incorrect, the United States might not be able to find an early escape from the Korean quagmire. A more likely danger, however, is that arms-control negotiations will be sabotaged by hard-liners in the South because Seoul is under much less economic pressure than Pyongyang to cut defense spending. Suppose, for example, that the North is ready for an asymmetrical pullback zone, but Seoul throws roadblocks in the way of an agreement in order to keep U.S. forces in Korea. In such a situation, the United States should not become a hostage to South Korea. Washington could cut off military sales to push the South toward a settlement, and if this does not work, it could negotiate a unilateral arms-control agreement with the North involving a partial or complete U.S. disengagement.

The goal of the United States should be to disengage its forces gradually from the Korean civil war over a period not longer than ten years whether or not this can be done as part of a negotiated arms-control process. A phased and gradual disengagement would give the South time to fill in the major gaps in its military capabilities and would strengthen the forces in Seoul seeking an accommodation with Pyongyang for the reasons explained earlier. Although it is highly desirable and, in my view, feasible to link disengagement with arms-control trade-offs, especially relating to missile and nuclear capabilities, this linkage should not be allowed to paralyze U.S. freedom of action.

To reinforce arms-control arrangements and ensure against instability following its force withdrawals, the United States should pursue the parallel neutralization agreements with China, Russia, and Japan discussed in part 5, barring the introduction of foreign military forces into the peninsula. The stage would then be cleared, as it were, with the initiative left to Seoul and Pyongyang. Washington would have its hopes and its advice but would recede into an unaccustomed posture of detachment, ready to let the two actors make their own mistakes. In the final analysis, such a policy would be a vote of confidence in Korean nationalism and in the potential of a unified Korea as a buffer state; a policy giving importance to Korea and Koreans in their own right, at last, rather than as pawns in a never-ending game of great power rivalries.

PART IV

Toward a Nuclear-Free Korea

CHAPTER 16

The U.S. Nuclear Challenge to North Korea

ADVOCATES OF a U.S. national missile defense system depict North Korean leaders as irrational xenophobes with a mindless anti-American hatred that explains why they want nuclear weapons and why they might well use them to attack the United States. But North Korea's perception of its security environment is not irrational in the context of its embattled national history since 1945. Indeed, the North Korean effort to develop nuclear weapons and missile delivery systems was a direct response to nuclear saber rattling during the Korean War and the subsequent deployment of U.S. tactical nuclear weapons in the South for more than three decades. Other factors accelerated this effort, as I will show in the next chapter, but it was propelled, from the start, by the U.S. nuclear posture toward the peninsula.

The United States made direct or implied threats to use nuclear weapons throughout the Korean War. Declassified documents have revealed that in "Operation Hudson Harbor," B-29 bombers dropped dummy atomic bombs on Pyongyang during "simulated practice runs" in late 1951.[1] It was the U.S. threat to "use any weapon necessary" to end the war that broke the stalemate in the 1953 armistice negotiations. Soon after the truce was signed, Secretary of State John Foster Dulles proclaimed his global "massive retaliation" strategy with its threat of a nuclear response to conventional aggression anywhere. On a visit to Seoul in January 1955, Adm. Arthur W. Radford, chairman of the Joint Chiefs of Staff, made clear that the new strategy embraced Korea, declaring that the United States "would be ready to use atomic weapons, if needed," to stop any renewed Korean aggression.

By 1958, the U.S. armed forces in Korea were equipped with a variety of tactical nuclear weapons, including Honest John, Lance, and Nike-Hercules missiles that were deployed in forward positions to warn North Korea that nuclear weapons would be used in the early stages of a conflict. A former commander of U.S. forces in Korea recalled that U.S. strategy, as it evolved, envisaged the use of these weapons "at 'H + 1,' or within one hour of the outbreak of war, if large masses of North Korean troops were attacking south of the DMZ."[2] In Europe, NATO doctrine was to delay an invasion with conventional weapons and use nuclear weapons only if unavoidable as a last resort. Since the Soviet Union had nuclear weapons, the United States would risk all-out war by using them first. By contrast, in Korea, where the North did not have nuclear weapons, the United States assumed that it could use them with impunity.

To be sure, the U.S. objective was to deter a North Korean conventional attack. But as Peter Hayes has demonstrated, North Korea was "'over-deterred' by these nuclear threats," viewing the danger of an actual U.S. nuclear attack "as conceivable and even likely."

Initially, Pyongyang's reaction was to deploy its conventional forces in forward positions in a "hugging-the-enemy" strategy so that the use of nuclear weapons "would endanger friend as well as foe, civilian as well as soldier."[3] Next, Kim Il Sung announced a massive program of underground construction in 1963 to protect defense installations from bombing attacks, declaring that "we have to dig underground tunnels. We have to build factories under the ground. When we thus fortify our entire country, we can defeat those who have atomic weapons even though we do not possess them ourselves." Finally, in that same year, Pyongyang took the logical next step, asking the Soviet Union for help in developing nuclear weapons of its own.[4] Moscow refused, but to placate its ally agreed to help the North develop a peaceful nuclear energy program under international safeguards, starting with the installation of a nuclear research reactor at Yongbyon in 1965.

Three hundred North Korean nuclear scientists were trained in the Soviet Union during the next two decades. This Soviet help set in motion a two-track nuclear program in which Pyongyang did make a serious attempt to harness nuclear energy for electric power generation while at the same time laying the foundation for the pursuit of a military nuclear option. It was the Yongbyon reactor, enlarged by North Korea without Soviet help, that eventually became the focus of U.S. suspicions of a nuclear weapons effort. The North Korean missile program also originated in the 1960s after Moscow provided short-range Scud missiles that have since been upgraded and redesigned by North Korean scientists for use in developing longer-range missiles.

Throughout the cold war, the United States brandished its nuclear saber in Korea, continually strengthening the advocates of a nuclear weapons program in Pyongyang. When North Korea shot down a U.S. EC-121 spy plane over its territory in 1969, nuclear-capable B-52 bombers headed for North Korea from Guam and veered off just before reaching the thirty-eighth parallel. In most parts of the world, the Pentagon maintained a "neither confirm nor deny" policy, refusing to say where U.S. nuclear weapons were deployed. But in a controversial statement on June 20, 1975, Secretary of Defense James R. Schlesinger openly confirmed their presence in the South. "It is, I believe, known," he said, "that we have deployed nuclear weapons in Europe and Korea along with our forces, and that those nuclear weapons are available as options for the President." His reasoning for making this disclosure in the case of Korea, Schlesinger explained, was "to have an impact on North Korean calculations." He clearly succeeded in this objective, though hardly in the way that he had calculated.

The Schlesinger statement had an impact not only in North Korea but also in Japan. As Edward Seidensticker noted, a comic strip in *Asahi* several days later depicted its Sad Sack hero patiently "carrying baskets of dirt across the land, west to east, from the Japan Sea to the Pacific Ocean, to move Japan eastward. The immediate occasion for this exercise was Secretary Schlesinger's assurance that there are nuclear weapons in Korea."[5] A year later, the Pentagon unsheathed its nuclear saber once again during the 1976 "Ax Murder Incident." Without seeking prior North Korean agreement, several American and South Korean soldiers entered a forbidden neutral area of the demilitarized zone at the thirty-eighth parallel to trim a poplar tree that the United States said was blocking its surveillance northward. North Korean soldiers attempting to stop them from cutting down the tree grabbed an ax from one of the Americans and killed two U.S. soldiers. As in the EC-121 case, B-52s were dispatched from Guam and skirted close to North Korean airspace.

From 1958 until 1991, when President George Bush removed tactical nuclear weapons from the South, massive U.S. military exercises were regularly conducted with South Korean forces in which scenarios involving the use of nuclear weapons were widely advertised. The most spectacular of these exercises dramatized the deep-strike "Airland Battle" strategy unveiled in 1983. The declared U.S. goal in this strategy was not merely to defend the South in the event of an attack but to carry the war to the North and demolish the regime, using nuclear weapons "to destroy assault forces before they penetrate the main battle areas and to destroy or disrupt logistics support formations."[6] During one "Team Spirit" exercise, a B-52 bomber flew low over the valley where Defense Secretary Caspar Weinberger was observing the proceedings. A *Washington Post* reporter who was also there referred to the B-52 as "an apparent symbol of the U.S. nuclear punch that could top off any conventional defense of the South."[7]

Even after the removal of tactical nuclear weapons, the United States continued to remind Pyongyang that the U.S. nuclear umbrella over South Korea was still operative. David E. Sanger, reporting in the *New York Times* on the 1993 "Team Spirit" exercises, observed that reassurance concerning the nuclear umbrella "is what Team Spirit is all about. The United States brought the B1-B bomber and other nuclear-capable equipment to South Korea for the exercises this year, presumably to make a point, and it was exactly that which sent the North into a frenzy."[8]

After 1993, scenarios involving the use of nuclear weapons were dropped from U.S. military exercises in Korea. But the damage had already been done much earlier. The climactic phase of the North Korean nuclear weapons effort in the mid-1980s coincided precisely with the "Team Spirit" exercises trumpeting the "Airland Battle" strategy.

Despite the removal of tactical nuclear weapons from the South and from Pacific aircraft carriers in 1991, the United States has not ruled out their reintroduction and continues to deploy nuclear-armed submarines in the Pacific. Successive U.S. administrations have pledged to maintain a "nuclear umbrella" over South Korea and have threatened to use nuclear weapons first, if necessary, against North Korean forces. Pyongyang has responded with nuclear and missile programs designed both to deter any U.S. use of nuclear weapons in Korea and to neutralize the superiority of South Korean airpower over its aging Mig force. Unless the United States joins in a denuclearization of Korea and in arms-control agreements that reduce or remove the threat of a preemptive strike by U.S. aircraft, North Korea is unlikely to foreclose the development of its nuclear and missile capabilities.

CHAPTER 17

The North Korean Response

THE SHIFTING North Korean response to the U.S. nuclear challenge has reflected a broad search for security that embraces economic as well as military priorities. As this search has evolved, Pyongyang has been flexible in adapting to changing circumstances, signaling clearly that it would be willing to give up the development of nuclear weapons and missile delivery systems if its security can be assured without them.

When Moscow refused their 1963 request for help in developing a military nuclear program, North Korean scientists attempted to prepare for one on their own, drawing on the Soviet technology supplied for their civilian nuclear energy effort and the Scud missile know-how acquired through Soviet military aid. But when the cold war ended, Pyongyang quickly changed course. Faced with the cutoff of Soviet and Chinese subsidies and new opportunities to reach an accommodation with its adversaries, North Korea has used its nuclear and missile programs as bargaining chips in its continuing effort to normalize relations with the United States, Japan, and South Korea.

Like any good negotiator, Pyongyang did not put all of its chips on the table at once. Some have been held in reserve for future use in negotiating the terms of normalization and of related security assurances. Thus, in its 1994 nuclear freeze agreement with Washington and its 1999 missile-testing moratorium, North Korea did not relinquish the option of resuming its nuclear and missile programs. The freeze agreement envisions the eventual dismantling of all nuclear facilities with potential relevance to a weapons program, but only if the United States fully normalizes relations and joins in unspecified steps to achieve a "nuclear-free Korea," including "formal U.S. assurances to the D.P.R.K. against the threat or use of nuclear weapons by the United States." Similarly, Pyongyang has offered to end the testing, production, and deployment of missiles, but only as part of nuclear and conventional arms-control agreements providing for basic changes in the U.S. military posture toward Korea.

A Two-Track Nuclear Program

Critics of the freeze agreement ridicule the idea that Pyongyang was ever serious about a civilian nuclear effort. It was all just a cover, they say, for a military nuclear program. In this view, the United States made excessive concessions based on the fiction of a civilian program, especially its commitment to provide 500,000 tons of oil per year. The rationale for the oil was that it would replace the energy supplies lost as a result of the freeze, and it is true, as the critics say, that this rationale was dubious. The North Korean nuclear program was plagued with problems and might never have produced much energy. At the same time, it was not a fiction that North Korea wanted to exploit nuclear power for civilian purposes. The nature of its natural resource endowments made it logical and easy for Pyongyang to pursue a peaceful nuclear program and a military nuclear option side by side. North Korea possesses extensive reserves of the graphite and uranium needed for the gas-graphite type of reactor installed by Moscow at Yongbyon. As it happens, while this type of reactor can indeed be used to generate electricity, it is also peculiarly suited for the diversion of nuclear fuel for military purposes.[1]

Initially, given its lack of proved indigenous petroleum reserves, North Korea sought to reduce its dependence on petroleum imports by maximizing the production of coal and hydroelectric power, both of which it possesses in abundance. But it proved unable to keep up with its energy needs and became increasingly envious of Japan and South Korea with their burgeoning civilian nuclear power programs. By the mid-1970s, South Korea had three nuclear power reactors in operation and six under construction. These were light water reactors (LWRs), like those in Japan, not the gas-graphite type that the North had at Yongbyon. Light water reactors thus became a symbol of modernity in North Korean eyes. In 1985, Pyongyang persuaded Moscow to supply one of its late-model light water reactors. Soviet experts even chose a site for the reactor at Kumho, the same site later selected for the two reactors to be built under the freeze agreement. Before construction work could start, however, U.S. satellites had discovered a shutdown of the Yongbyon reactor in 1989 that offered an opportunity for the diversion of plutonium to military use. The KGB had also concluded that a nuclear weapons program was underway, prompting Soviet suspension of the Kumho project.[2]

Moscow had extended nuclear aid to Pyongyang solely for civilian use and had even pressured Kim Il Sung into signing the Nuclear Non-Proliferation Treaty (NPT) as a condition for its assistance. Subsequent events showed that North Korea was not aware of the intrusiveness—and effectiveness—of international inspection procedures under the NPT and had assumed that it could sign the treaty without jeopardizing its covert nuclear weapons effort.

Apart from the military rationale for nuclear weapons, the nuclear option was initially attractive to the North in economic terms as a cheaper route to national security than an indefinite conventional arms race with the South and high defense-spending levels that divert resources and labor from consumer goods industries. The economic rationale appeared particularly persuasive as the South's growth rates and margin of economic superiority began to soar in the 1970s. However, this rationale lost its force as the costs of the nuclear program mounted and as multiplying technical problems made it increasingly unclear when, and if, the program would ever be successfully completed in the absence of the foreign exchange needed to import vital equipment. Soviet scientists with experience in North Korea have consistently emphasized these technical problems,[3] in marked contrast to the alarmist U.S. assessments generated by the 1989 satellite findings.

The negative economic impact of the nuclear weapons effort became increasingly clear when the end of the cold war led to the end of the Soviet and Chinese food and petroleum subsidies. Pragmatists in the North argued that the only way to avert an economic collapse was to turn to the United States, Japan, and South Korea for help. The military aspects of the nuclear program should be put on hold, they argued, if Washington and Tokyo would agree in return to normalize relations and open up trade, aid, and investment links. At first, the pragmatists got nowhere, but the U.S. decision to withdraw tactical nuclear weapons from Korea on September 27, 1991, radically altered the policy debate in Pyongyang.

In reality, the removal of nuclear weapons from Korea alone did not rule out the U.S. use of nuclear weapons based elsewhere against the North. As Adm. William J. Crowe, former chairman of the Joint Chiefs of Staff, publicly acknowledged when he urged their removal, "the actual presence of any nuclear weapons in South Korea is not necessary to maintain a nuclear umbrella over the South."[4] Nevertheless, the fact that the United States was ending its provocative nuclear posture along the thirty-eighth parallel after thirty-three years greatly strengthened the pragmatists.

The debate came to a head during a meeting of the ruling Workers

Party Central Committee on December 24, 1991. In subsequent conversations with North Korean officials and diplomats, I gathered that the meeting was acrimonious and ended in an uneasy compromise. The hard-liners had argued that Washington, Tokyo, and Seoul were bent on destroying the regime. They ridiculed the idea that the North would ever get help from these unremitting adversaries. The pragmatists said in effect, "Let's test them." It was finally agreed that the nuclear program could be suspended, but not necessarily terminated, if an accommodation with Washington, in particular, could actually be reached. This compromise set the stage for a sustained diplomatic effort by the pragmatists that culminated in the nuclear freeze agreement concluded nearly three years later on October 24, 1994. As this effort proceeded, the pragmatists, led by Kim Yong Sun, then international affairs secretary of the Central Committee, faced continual rearguard attacks from their domestic opponents, who were repeatedly vindicated by U.S. rebuffs to conciliatory North Korean overtures.

Pyongyang Searches for a Compromise

Soon after the December Central Committee meeting, Pyongyang foreshadowed its readiness to explore a nuclear accommodation by agreeing to sign an inspection agreement with the International Atomic Energy Agency required under the NPT. More important, it stopped reprocessing spent fuel from the Yongbyon reactor. Another shutdown of the reactor like the one in 1989 would have permitted the diversion of spent fuel and a resumption of reprocessing. But Pyongyang pointedly avoided this fateful step. The tensions with the IAEA over inspections that soon developed centered not on evidence of an ongoing nuclear weapons program but on Pyongyang's reluctance to reveal how much plutonium it had accumulated before 1991.

Kim Yong Sun followed up the December meeting with a proposal to open negotiations with the United States, and I was one of a handful of U.S. observers who urged that Washington respond favorably. In testimony at the invitation of the Senate Foreign Relations Committee on January 14, 1992, I recommended that the United States negotiate a "package deal, spelling out clearly what economic and political benefits the North could expect if it agrees to abandon its nuclear program." My main message was that "the nuclear issue is inseparable from the broader problem of normalizing U.S. relations with the Kim Il Sung regime."

The Bush administration did agree to a meeting on January 22 between Kim Yong Sun and Undersecretary of State Arnold Kanter. This was the highest level meeting that had ever been held between the United States and North Korea. Kim came with a comprehensive proposal for normalizing relations, I was told later by participants on both sides, including an explicit statement that the North would not object to the presence of U.S. forces in Korea if relations were fully normalized. But the U.S. attitude was that having the meeting at all was a generous concession. Any future meetings would come only as a reward for North Korean compliance with its NPT obligations. There would be no "package deal." Indeed, Kanter was instructed never to use the word "normalization." Instead of engaging in diplomatic give and take, the Bush administration adopted what has been aptly described as "the crime and punishment" approach.[5]

The inconclusive New York meeting was a major setback for Kim Yong Sun and the pragmatists. What they needed to keep their domestic opponents at bay was a continuing dialogue with Washington directly linking progress toward normalization with North Korean concessions concerning the terms of IAEA inspections. In the absence of a responsive U.S. posture, they were on the defensive in Pyongyang policy struggles during the last year of the Bush administration and the early months of 1993 when Clinton and his advisers were groping for a North Korea policy. Nevertheless, they continued to prepare the way for an eventual compromise, hoping that the Washington tide would turn. In the foreground of U.S.–North Korean relations, tensions over inspections steadily escalated. In the background, the pragmatists were making conciliatory noises to all who would listen.

A revealing episode indicating that the pragmatists were looking ahead to a compromise, centering on a shift to light water reactors, occurred during the visit of a Carnegie Endowment study mission to Pyongyang in the spring of 1992. Our interest in such a shift had been stimulated by a conversation in Seoul, en route to Pyongyang, with Gen. Kim Yoon Ho, an independent-minded former chairman of the South Korean Joint Chiefs of Staff. To our surprise, he suggested that a possible way for the United States to resolve the nuclear crisis might be to give North Korea the light water type of reactors that Pyongyang had previously attempted to get from Moscow. Light water reactors were less adaptable for military purposes, he pointed out, than the gas-graphite type at Yongbyon. It was the light water type that South Korea used in its civilian nuclear program. The fact that Pyongyang had asked Moscow for light water reactors had puzzled him, General Kim said, suggesting as it did that at least some people in North Korea wanted to slow down, or stop, their nuclear weapons program.

In Pyongyang, on May 3, we asked Choe Jong Sun, foreign affairs director of the Atomic Energy Ministry, whether North Korea would be interested in getting light water reactors from the United States. "Yes, definitely," Choe immediately responded, "very interested." Less than two weeks later, Choe broached the idea of obtaining light water reactors to IAEA Director Hans Blix on his first visit to Pyongyang. This overture foreshadowed a formal request to the United States in mid-1993 that eventually proved to be the key to the nuclear freeze agreement. At the time of our 1992 visit, however, the significance of this proposal was obscured to some extent by Choe's startling revelation that reprocessing experiments had resulted in the production of "a little bit of plutonium for experimental purposes." Asked about the amount produced, he replied, "Next to nothing." But his acknowledgment for the first time that Pyongyang possessed any plutonium at all was a bombshell, leading to later CIA speculation that Pyongyang might have acquired enough plutonium for "one or two" nuclear weapons. Before leaving Pyongyang on May 4, we asked Choe again how much had been produced, and he repeated, "Oh, next to nothing." Our impression was that he had a carefully worded script intended to draw the United States into negotiations without bringing matters to the point of crisis.

In contrast to the negative attitude of the Bush administration, South Korea under President Roh Tae Woo made a serious attempt to reach out to the pragmatists during early 1992 until hard-liners in Seoul and Washington combined to subvert the process.

As his negotiator with Pyongyang Roh named Lim Dong Won, the most determined advocate of a more flexible approach to the North in the South Korean establishment. Much to the distress of the South Korean armed forces, Lim, a retired major general himself, persuaded the United States to cancel the annual "Team Spirit" military exercises with the South, which the North regarded as provocative psychological warfare. In the improved North-South atmosphere that resulted, Lim negotiated the "Agreement on Reconciliation, Non-Aggression, Exchanges and Cooperation" concluded with Pyongyang on February 19, 1992. A companion "Joint Declaration on the Denuclearization of the Korean Peninsula" provided for mutual North-South inspections of nuclear facilities. But instead of pushing immediately for nuclear inspections, as the hardliners wanted, Lim decided to seek broader follow-up agreements to improve overall relations first. He was just beginning to make progress with his North Korean counterparts, he recalled, when Gen. Robert W. Riscassi, commander of the U.S.–South Korea Combined Forces Command, announced on May 31 that the "Team Spirit" exercises would be resumed in 1993 unless the North agreed to North-South nuclear inspections.

"You could feel the change in their attitude immediately," Lim recalled later. "Direct, public pressure was certain to make them clam up. You could feel that Kim Yong Sun and his people felt betrayed and had to back off."[6] All North-South contacts were abruptly cancelled by Pyongyang. General Riscassi had made his announcement at the behest of his South Korean military counterparts, Lim said, and had not consulted the South Korean government in advance. American Ambassador Donald Gregg was also caught off guard and later called the resumption of "Team Spirit" "one of the biggest mistakes" made by the United States in dealing with the North during his tenure in Seoul.[7]

Despite this setback, Lim managed to get North-South negotiations back on track three months later when they were once again derailed, this time by his internal opponents in the KCIA. In the eighth round of the 1992 North-South dialogue, held in Pyongyang in the first week of September, the North was ready to accept the South's key demands for reunions of separated families at Panmunjom and the return of captured South Korean fishermen. In return, Pyongyang asked for the repatriation of a North Korean guerrilla hero who had been imprisoned in the South since the Korean War. Lim cabled Roh asking for approval of the deal. But the communication lines to Roh were controlled by the KCIA. The cable was never sent and a KCIA man in the South Korean delegation, Lee Dom Bok, arranged for a fabricated reply in which Roh purportedly insisted on a new demand that separated families should meet not at Panmunjom but in their home villages in the North and South. This was predictably rejected by the North, leading to the breakoff of the talks. When Lim got back to Seoul and told Roh what had happened, Lee Dom Bok was fired. But Lim was unable to restore the North-South dialogue during the remaining months of the Roh presidency and was replaced when Kim Young Sam, Roh's successor, shifted to a hard-line stance against a background of growing tensions over nuclear inspections between Pyongyang and Washington. Lim later resurfaced as Kim Dae Jung's right-hand man on North-South issues and masterminded the improvement in North-South relations symbolized by the June 2000 summit, picking up where he had left off in 1992.

WASHINGTON, SEOUL, AND THE DRIFT TO WAR

The twists and turns of the conflict over nuclear inspections that almost led to war in 1994 have been perceptively chronicled by Leon V. Sigal[8] and analyzed in my own writings during this period.[9] Underlying the U.S. failure to respond constructively to the emergence of the pragmatists were two key factors. One was that the United States played second fiddle to the IAEA, which was run by lawyers like its director, Hans Blix, who were focused on establishing legal precedents for an international nonproliferation regime, not on striking a politically viable bargain with North Korea. Sensitive to charges that he had failed to curb the Iraqi nuclear program, Blix was anxious to look tough on North Korea. An even more basic factor was frankly acknowledged by Charles Kartman of the State Department, then a middle-level official who later became the chief U.S. negotiator with Pyongyang. "We didn't really acquire much of a feel for what the North Koreans were saying to us," Kartman recalled. Before each negotiating session with the North Koreans, "We would thrash out internally what we wanted. All sorts of theology from the nonproliferation community got thrown into that. Then we would have to negotiate with the R.O.K. and thrash that out. By the time we were done with these two processes, not only were there no carrots left. There were no negotiations. We would throw this thing on the table at the North Koreans and tune out. Until Bob Gallucci really got engaged, nobody was really willing to listen to the North Koreans and adjust our positions to what they were really saying."[10]

Robert Gallucci was selected to handle North Korea when Clinton took over because nonproliferation issues fell under his jurisdiction as assistant secretary of state for politico-military affairs. But he proved to be much more sensitive to the political and diplomatic aspects of dealing with Pyongyang than most nonproliferation specialists. Gallucci immediately faced a crisis generated by U.S.–backed IAEA pressures for "special inspections" in North Korea that were designed to secure access to military facilities suspected of harboring hidden plutonium. North Korea was resisting. The atmosphere was already overheated when the United States and South Korea resumed their "Team Spirit" military exercises on March 8. Four days later, Pyongyang announced its intention to withdraw from the NPT. Under a provision of the treaty, signatories could withdraw if they gave notice three months in advance. This meant that the situation would remain fluid until June 12.

The North Korean announcement provoked a controversy in the Clinton administration and Congress over whether the United States should make a diplomatic effort to keep Pyongyang in the NPT or should apply stepped-up pressure by seeking U.N. economic sanctions. In testimony before the Senate Foreign Relations Committee on May 26, I made the case once again for a "package" approach. The way to deal with North Korea, I argued, "is to hold out the promise of clearly defined, carefully calibrated rewards linked to specific concessions on the part of Pyongyang. Pressure alone will strengthen the hard-liners there." Gallucci testified on behalf of the administration. After the hearing, we agreed to meet, and several days later, we had the first of a series of free-swinging conversations that continued until his successful conclusion of the nuclear freeze agreement in October 1994. These exchanges throw a revealing light on the evolution of U.S. policy concerning North Korea, especially the internecine debate over whether to emphasize diplomacy or pressure.

Gallucci was much more open to the views of nongovernment outsiders than many other high-level officials who were mainly interested in putting forth the official "spin." He knew little about either North or South Korea and wanted to know more. But he reacted impatiently to what he heard: that North Korean behavior was dominated by a prickly nationalistic pride; that Pyongyang could be induced to stay in the NPT, but only if it did not look like a surrender to foreign pressure; and that the United States would have to concede something in return, some token of progress toward normalizing relations and, above all, some form of security assurance acknowledging that Pyongyang perceived U.S. nuclear weapons to be a threat. He threw up his hands, describing the bureaucratic obstacles that would make adoption of such a strategy difficult. But one of his aides confided that he was hearing much the same counsel from several embattled State Department specialists with knowledge of North Korea, notably the North Korean desk officer, Kenneth Quinones, and intelligence analysts Robert Carlin and John Merrill.

Gallucci's first encounter with a North Korean diplomat came shortly after our conversation when he met with First Deputy Foreign Minister Kang Sok Ju to discuss Pyongyang's threatened withdrawal from the NPT. A joint statement with Kang on June 11 said that North Korea had "decided unilaterally" to suspend its withdrawal "as long as it considers necessary." The key to this compromise was Gallucci's decision to join in a statement supporting "the principle of assurances against the threat or use of force against the D.P.R.K., including nuclear weapons." This sounded like a mere platitude to many in Washington but was taken with the utmost seriousness in Pyongyang. Even now, North Korea harks back to this statement, berating the United States for its failure to make formal follow-up commitments explicitly ruling out the first use of nuclear weapons.

On June 12, I met Kang Sok Ju for the first time. When I congratulated him on resolving the NPT issue, he leaned forward, saying, "Tell me honestly, Mr. Harrison, what you really think. Will it appear to the world that we have given in, that we have bowed down to your country?" I replied that "suspension" of the NPT withdrawal was an ingenious formula pending further negotiations on normalization and would be recognized as such by international public opinion, adding that Gallucci was more open-minded than his predecessors and was doing his best to find a basis for a settlement consistent with political and bureaucratic realities in Washington.

On June 16, Gallucci mentioned that he wanted to drop a hint to Kang in their next round of talks concerning a possible easing of economic sanctions as part of an overall settlement of the nuclear problem. Some of his State Department colleagues saw the need for such tactical flexibility, Gallucci said, but the White House was reluctant to risk criticism from congressional hard-liners on North Korea led by Senator Richard Lugar.

At several points during this conversation he indicated that he was puzzled by the "surprisingly negative" attitude he had encountered in South Korea toward his emerging role. At one point he asked: "Do they want to solve this?" After hearing my analysis of the tensions between hawks and doves in Seoul and my conclusion that it would take strong U.S. pressure to contain the hawks, he looked disturbed, commenting, "This is something I haven't bargained for."

This exchange reflected a naïveté concerning South Korean motives on the part of many U.S. officials that led to disastrous consequences five months later. South Korean hawks controlled foreign and defense policy during the Kim Young Sam years. They were more concerned about a U.S. accommodation with North Korea than a North Korean nuclear threat because they recognized that Pyongyang was ready to trade its nuclear program for normalization with Washington. They feared that after four decades as a U.S. client, benefiting from the economic subsidy provided by the U.S. military presence, South Korea would suffer economically, as well as militarily, if the United States moved to a more symmetrical posture in Korea. Moreover, the hawks understood that normalization would help forestall a collapse of North Korea and its absorption by the South, which they wanted to promote. Their objective, accordingly, was not to help Gallucci but to do all they could to thwart him.

Many U.S. officials scoffed when Kang asked Gallucci for U.S. LWRs at their July meeting in Geneva. But Gallucci was quick to recognize that this request pointed the way to a settlement. He made a weekend dash to Washington, where he persuaded National Security Adviser Anthony Lake that the United States should not dismiss the idea out of hand. The Geneva meeting ended with a statement that "both sides recognize the desirability of the DPRK's intention to replace its graphite-moderated reactors and associated nuclear facilities with light water moderated reactors." The United States "is prepared to support the introduction of LWRs and to explore with the DPRK ways in which they could be obtained," the statement said, "as part of a final resolution of the nuclear issues."

Logically, this agreement should have led to a reduction of tensions with North Korea. But it proved to be the calm before the storm. To hard-liners in Congress and nonproliferation purists, the Geneva meeting amounted to appeasement. North Korea was still stalling on full-scale IAEA inspections and should be punished for noncompliance with the NPT, not rewarded for "suspending" its withdrawal from the treaty. The idea of giving U.S. nuclear technology to North Korea in any form and under any circumstances was inconceivable. Instead of pursuing a compromise, in this view, the United States should seek U.N. economic sanctions and apply military pressure, staging a preemptive strike to destroy the Yongbyon reactor as a last resort. Criticism of the Clinton administration was paralleled in South Korea by hard-line attacks on the Kim Young Sam government for failing to stop the drift toward rapprochement between Washington and Pyongyang.

Hard-line criticism in Seoul and Washington alike focused in particular on proposals such as mine for a "package deal" as the epitome of appeasement. On November 1, 1993, at a Brookings Institution seminar attended by several U.S. officials, I spelled out the concept in detail, listing ten economic and security concessions that would be necessary if the United States really expected North Korea to give up its nuclear program completely. Less extensive concessions would get a less definitive result. I sent a copy to Ambassador Kim Jong Su, North Korea's deputy representative at the United Nations, who telephoned me four days later to say that "I have heard from my senior colleagues in

Pyongyang. They are very interested in this proposal and find it very helpful."

On November 11, First Deputy Foreign Minister Kang Sok Ju declared in a formal statement that "the nuclear problem will be solved smoothly when an agreement is reached on the formula of a package deal solution, whereby each side should do its share. The United States is telling us to move first, but this is totally unacceptable." On November 16, Deputy Assistant Secretary of State Thomas Hubbard held an unannounced meeting with Kim Jong Su in New York and conveyed the Clinton administration's acceptance in principle of the "package deal" approach, without specifying what the contents of such a deal might be.

Word soon leaked out that the White House was considering not only a package deal but also a suspension of the 1994 "Team Spirit" exercise. With President Kim Young Sam about to visit Washington, South Korean hard-liners launched a bitter campaign against Kim. They demanded that Seoul insist on a greater voice in U.S. policymaking toward North Korea. In a table-pounding exchange with President Clinton on November 23, Kim brushed aside the agreement on a "package deal" approach that his moderate foreign minister had previously reached with U.S. officials. Before Gallucci and other State Department aides could do anything to stop him, Clinton had agreed that the United States would impose a tough new precondition on continued dialogue with North Korea. Pyongyang would first have to send an envoy to Seoul for talks on North-South nuclear inspections. Only after that would the United States suspend "Team Spirit" and resume negotiations with the North.

The predictable result of this reversal was that high-level U.S.–North Korean negotiations were not resumed. However, North Korea continued to emphasize its readiness for a package deal, and Kim Il Sung edged toward the concept of a nuclear freeze in a significant but little-noticed statement on April 19, 1994. "If the proposal for a package deal of the nuclear problem becomes a reality and the light water reactor is delivered," Kim declared, the reprocessing facility at Yongbyon "may not be needed."[11] Kim's offer did not cover the Yongbyon reactor and envisaged giving up the reprocessing facility only after "delivery" of the LWR. Nevertheless, as I argued in an intense exchange with Gallucci, it offered an opening for the United States to pursue a comprehensive freeze agreement.

The United States failed to follow up the April 19 overture from Kim Il Sung because Clinton wanted a capitulation, not a compromise. The White House continued to condition a resumption of negotiations on greater IAEA access and on North-South inspections, while Pyongyang insisted on linking such concessions to a package deal.

In an effort to strengthen its bargaining position and bring matters to a head, North Korea finally took the step that it had carefully avoided for the preceding twenty-nine months. On May 12, 1994, it started removing irradiated fuel rods from the Yongbyon reactor. Hard-liners in Washington and Seoul saw this as proof positive that the North was bent on making nuclear weapons, ignoring the fact that the reactor had not been unloaded since 1989. Senator John McCain and Brent Scowcroft, former national security adviser in the Bush White House, led the charge for preemptive air strikes to destroy the reactor and the nearby reprocessing plant.

The hysteria that pervaded Washington between May 12 and Jimmy Carter's peace initiative five weeks later focused on how much plutonium the North might have accumulated. The North itself had characterized the amount as "next to nothing" when it first revealed that it had reprocessed plutonium during my 1992 visit. Later it told the IAEA that the amount was only ninety kilograms, less than one-tenth of what would be needed for one nuclear warhead on a missile. The IAEA made no attempt to estimate how much might have been reprocessed. However, it fueled the fires of speculation when it said that reprocessing had taken place three times, in 1989, 1990, and 1991, not only in 1990 as the North insisted.

The widely quoted CIA estimate that the North might have enough plutonium for "one or two bombs" was a guess, based largely on a debatable assumption that the period of the 1989 reactor shutdown was 110 days, much longer than most expert estimates suggest.[12] Theoretically, a shutdown of this duration would have permitted the fabrication of half of the irradiated fuel rods into plutonium. But North Korea said that the reactor had been shut down for only 60 days, and that "only a few" damaged fuel rods had been removed. The reality is that no one really knew how much, if any, plutonium the North possessed. In conversations at the time, analysts in the three major intelligence agencies involved, who all had access to the same secret evidence, expressed sharply divergent conclusions. "Personally, as opposed to institutionally, I was skeptical that they ever had a bomb," observed Gen. James Clapper, who was then director of the Defense Intelligence Agency. "We didn't have smoking-gun evidence either way . . . but you build a case for a range of possibilities. . . . In a case like North Korea you have to apply the most conservative approach, the worst-case alternative."[13]

The most pressing issue confronting the United States in 1994 was not how much plutonium might have been accumulated before reprocessing was stopped in 1991. It was how much plutonium the North would accumulate if it should decide to resume its nuclear program. If completed, two big new reactors then under construction would have been able to produce enough plutonium for at least ten bombs per year. Privately, Gallucci argued that a settlement should focus on the future, not the past, and favored a resumption of negotiations. But publicly, he echoed the Clinton administration's threat to seek U.N. sanctions if Pyongyang did not permit IAEA inspectors to return and give them increased access so that they could determine how much plutonium had already been accumulated. Pyongyang responded that sanctions would be regarded as "an act of war." Tensions steadily escalated, culminating in the dangerous military confrontation during late May and early June described in part 3.

The 1994 Compromise

CAN IT SURVIVE?

JIMMY CARTER'S mission to Pyongyang saved Clinton from what could well have been the most catastrophic military crisis of his presidency. I spelled out in part 3 how close the United States came to war in 1994 and the horrendous consequences that would have ensued if the advocates of military strikes against the Yongbyon reactor had prevailed. Yet the evidence is clear that Clinton and most of his advisers, with the notable exception of Gallucci and Perry, did not want Carter to go; went along with the visit reluctantly; and were outraged, not grateful, when he negotiated a temporary nuclear freeze that undercut the U.N. sanctions policy and made a return to negotiations unavoidable.

Indeed, even in retrospect, many of them refuse to acknowledge that they were rescued from a near disaster. Former national security adviser Anthony Lake was still anxious to defend the threat to impose U.N. sanctions in a conversation on June 18, 2000. A "false debate" had arisen, he volunteered, over why North Korea had agreed to a nuclear freeze, "over whether sanctions did it or Carter did it. That's a false debate. It was both." As this chapter shows, however, the debate is not false. "Carter did it" precisely because he was not associated with the counterproductive threat of sanctions. Moreover, by the time he reached Pyongyang, the threat of sanctions was progressively losing credibility, given China's often-stated position that it would oppose a U.S. sanctions resolution in the U.N. Security Council.

THE CARTER MISSION

Carter had been invited to Pyongyang in 1991 and 1992 but had decided not to go in the face of objections from the Bush administration and South Korea. In April 1993 the Rockefeller Foundation extended a standing offer to finance such a visit. But Carter did not act on it until mid-May 1994, when he was strongly urged to go by an old Atlanta friend, James Laney, then U.S. ambassador in Seoul, who had been instrumental as president of Emory University in creating the Carter Center there. Laney was increasingly alarmed by what he felt was a needlessly confrontational U.S. policy that could well lead to war. He urged Carter to ask North Korea whether its invitation remained open and to go as soon as possible—with Clinton's blessing, if possible, without it if necessary.

On June 1, Carter recalled, he telephoned Clinton to express his concern about the situation in Korea and inform him that he might want to visit Pyongyang.[1] Clinton was preparing to go to Europe an hour later and kept the conversation short, saying that he could arrange for Gallucci to brief him at his home in Plains on June 5. Carter peppered him with questions, Gallucci recalls. "At one point, Carter asked, 'Why are we doing all of this?' He did not fully appreciate why we should be telling a sovereign state to do so many things when we ourselves possessed nuclear weapons. I reported to Lake that Carter was sympathetic to North Korean arguments and that he was going to want to go." As for his own personal feelings, "I was enthusiastic, but I was worried about what he would do. I liked Carter, and all of us were concerned at that time that we were on a track to war. I thought, if someone is going to go out there and defuse this, someone acting selflessly, as he was, God bless him."[2]

On June 6, the day after his meeting with Gallucci, Carter got a go-ahead from North Korea for a visit beginning June 15. What he did not know was that I had already been invited to visit Pyongyang starting June 4 for meetings with Foreign Ministry officials and with Kim Il Sung to discuss a concrete formula for a package deal involving a nuclear freeze. My invitation was an outgrowth of intensive conversations with Ho Jong, North Korean ambassador to the United Nations. A freeze could be negotiated, I argued, if Kim Il Sung would modify several key provisions of his April 19 offer to give up the reprocessing plant. For my part, I knew nothing of Carter's impending visit until my arrival June 4, when I was immediately asked whether I thought such a visit would help defuse tensions. I strongly urged that he be invited but had no inkling his visit would come so closely on the heels of mine.

Once it was clear that Carter intended to go, Perry recalled, "Some people, I was one, felt we should take advantage of that. Other people felt he would be an independent agent. Christopher and Lake were both apprehensive. The issue was whether he should be empowered as an agent of the president."[3]

In the end, Carter went as a private citizen, not as Clinton's emissary. But he did get Clinton's last-minute "approval," since there was no way

of stopping him anyway. Immediately after getting the green light from Pyongyang, Carter sent a message to Clinton saying "I have decided to visit North Korea" and requesting his blessing. With Clinton in Europe, Vice President Gore intercepted the message and telephoned Carter suggesting that the wording be changed from "have decided" to "am strongly inclined," which Carter accepted. Clinton then responded that he had no objection to Carter's visit as a private citizen.

On the eve of his departure, Carter came to Washington, where he had an icy meeting with Lake, Gallucci, and Daniel Poneman of the National Security Council staff, followed by a series of briefings with Pentagon, State Department, and CIA North Korea specialists. "We told him what he should know, what U.S. policy was and why," Gallucci recalled. "The president wanted our position on inspections and our seriousness about sanctions impressed on Carter at a level higher than mine. We were not talking about the terms for resuming negotiations. We wanted to fill him up with our policy."

The more Carter heard about U.S. policy, the less he liked it, and the more determined he was to make a bold move for compromise. Undersecretary of Defense John Deutch particularly rankled him with his dogmatic characterization of North Korea as a dangerous rogue state that could not be trusted. "I asked him whether he had ever been to North Korea," Carter said. "I asked all of them how they could say these things if they had never been there and didn't know the North Koreans. None of them had been there. I was more convinced than ever that we had an unrealistic approach that could well lead to war."

On the day that Carter arrived in Seoul en route to Pyongyang, June 13, the *Washington Post* front-paged an interview with me reporting Kim Il Sung's acceptance of the proposal for a nuclear freeze that I outlined in our three-hour meeting on June 9. The U.S. embassy in Seoul passed the *Post* story on to Carter, who told one of his companions on the Pyongyang trip, retired U.S. diplomat Marion Creekmore, that "had I known about that in time, I would have been in touch with him."[4] On that same day, North Korea told IAEA inspectors to leave Yongbyon.

Carter found Kim primed for their meeting. The very fact that a former U.S. president paid him homage enabled Kim to make concessions that would otherwise have looked to his people like a surrender. According to North Koreans and Americans who were present, Carter treated Kim respectfully and quickly established rapport. He persuaded Kim not only to freeze all North Korean nuclear facilities immediately but also to permit IAEA inspectors and inspection machinery to remain in place.

Carter has not made public a complete transcript of his conversation with Kim. However, he agreed to have a detailed summary prepared. In a key exchange, the summary says, Kim Il Sung recalled that North Korea had informed the United States of its desire to replace its gas-graphite reactors in July 1993, and "if the United States had helped North Korea then to acquire a light water reactor, even from a third country, the current problems could have been avoided. If the United States would now agree to a third round of talks and help the D.P.R.K. to get light water reactors, there would be no problems."[5] According to Carter, Kim had said explicitly: "If a commitment is made to furnish us with a light water reactor, then we will immediately freeze all our nuclear activities."

By persuading Kim to put a temporary freeze into effect immediately, instead of waiting to discuss a permanent freeze when negotiations with the United States were resumed, Carter opened the door for Clinton to go back to the bargaining table. The White House, however, was intent on its U.N. sanctions policy. For domestic political reasons, Clinton wanted to make it look like North Korea had backed down. Far from welcoming Carter's historic achievement, the White House reacted with undisguised shock, dismay, and anger.

Carter's breakthrough came on the morning of June 16 at the very moment when Clinton was presiding over a National Security Council meeting that had been convened to ratify a massive reinforcement of U.S. forces in South Korea. An aide rushed into the meeting to tell Clinton that Carter was calling from Pyongyang and wanted to talk to him. "He wants to speak to Bob Gallucci," Clinton said, according to Gallucci.

Carter told Gallucci that "I've got a deal that you can have with the North Koreans. We return to negotiations and they agree to freeze, not to reprocess from the fuel rods. What do you think?"

Gallucci replied, "The president, the secretary of defense and the national security adviser are in the next room. It's not my place to wing this one. Call us back." Carter agreed, adding offhandedly that he would announce North Korea's readiness for a freeze on CNN "in a few minutes." "I didn't say anything," Gallucci said, "and he promised to call back."

When he returned to the Cabinet Room and reported the conversation, the following memorable colloquy occurred:

> LAKE: "You told him not to go on CNN, I assume?"
> GALLUCCI: "He's not going to listen to me, Tony."
> LAKE: "But you did tell him, though?"

CLINTON: "You did say that this is not the right time for that, didn't you?"

"Everybody in the room was disappointed in me," Gallucci reflected, "but what was I supposed to do? I had one president in one room and another one on the telephone."[6]

Carter's CNN interview included a public denunciation of the U.N. sanctions strategy, prompting some of those at the meeting to argue that the White House should flatly repudiate his agreement with Kim. But others, including Clinton and Gore, started talking about the conditions for an acceptable freeze. Gore asked, "Can we make lemonade out of this lemon?" The United States would resume negotiations with North Korea, Carter was finally told, but only if Pyongyang agreed explicitly not to restart the Yongbyon reactor in addition to pledging not to reprocess the fuel rods. North Korea did agree. Nevertheless, four days later, many in the administration were still fuming over Carter's initiative, felt deeply embarrassed by the public impression that he had taken control of U.S. policy, and were uncertain whether negotiations should, in fact, be resumed.

On June 20, before Carter had returned, Lake invited eight non-government Asia specialists to discuss what to do next. Clinton, Perry, Secretary of State Christopher, and Gallucci attended the meeting. Such occasions have little direct impact on policymaking. For outsiders, they offer a sense of what those on the inside are thinking, and for the government, they are useful in putting out the desired "spin." The mood on June 20 was not one of jubilation but of concern that the United States was being duped. Gallucci questioned me in detail concerning precisely what Kim Il Sung had said about a freeze and seemed satisfied that my answer fit with what Carter had told him over the phone. Many of those present thought that North Korea was merely stalling for time to head off U.N. sanctions. The discussion had focused for half an hour on how to beef up U.S. forces in Seoul when I intervened, urging a resumption of negotiations immediately to follow up the Carter breakthrough. Former ambassador Donald Gregg expressed a similar view. At that point, Clinton walked into the meeting, looked at me and Gregg and said that he had heard us on the *McNeil-Lehrer News Hour* on June 14. "I agree with both of you," he declared, "that this has to be solved diplomatically, not militarily, somehow, one way or the other."

The next day Carter came to Washington to report on his trip. He had telephoned Gore from Seoul to alert him that he was coming. Gore had responded that it was "not necessary" to come, Carter said. Clinton, Gore, and Christopher all refused to see him, and Carter made his report only to Lake. "It was quite sour, a difficult meeting," Lake said, with "dueling press statements" being issued by one former and one incumbent president and Carter "not happy" that Clinton had gone to Camp David.

Carter still bristles when he recalls the snub. "They didn't believe that Kim Il Sung had really made the commitments that I said he had made," Carter reflected, "so I asked for Kim to send a letter and he did so immediately, confirming everything. It didn't dawn on me until I got there that the White House wanted to subvert what I was doing."

"I was amazed," he added with a twinkle in his eye. "I thought they'd be overjoyed."[7]

The twinkle strongly suggested that he was not really amazed. It was predictable that by going on CNN without waiting for clearance, he would make the freeze a fait accompli, generating public opinion pressures for a return to the bargaining table. It was equally predictable that his denunciation of the sanctions policy would reduce any lingering U.N. support for sanctions. He knew that the White House was still pushing a U.N. sanctions resolution and that such a resolution would have completely destroyed his understanding with Kim Il Sung. Indeed, in his press conference immediately after Carter's CNN announcement, Clinton did say that the United States would continue to push for its sanctions resolution while exploring a possible resumption of negotiations.

In reality, the U.S. sanctions effort was already dead. China's opposition was firm. For nearly a week after Carter's visit, the White House continued to hope for a last-minute Chinese decision to abstain that would have permitted a sanctions resolution to pass. But U.N. support for the U.S. sanctions position quickly faded after the Carter breakthrough and the issue never came to a vote. On July 8, the day that Kim Il Sung died, the United States and North Korea resumed negotiations.

The Freeze Agreement: Present at the Creation

The nuclear freeze agreement concluded on October, 21, 1994, known as the "Agreed Framework," was primarily a triumph of North Korean diplomacy. Carter made negotiations possible and Gallucci conducted them with sensitivity and skill. But it was the small group of pragmatists around Kim Jong Il in Pyongyang who took the initiative in pursuing a compromise with Washington and persisted steadfastly despite U.S. rebuffs and hard-line opposition in Pyongyang.

As Leon V. Sigal has pointed out, North Korea recognized that restraints on its nuclear program would have to be part of a compromise on normalization as early as 1991, when it unilaterally suspended reprocessing.[8] In 1992, Pyongyang informally expressed its interest in LWRs, thus signaling more clearly its readiness to negotiate an end to its nuclear weapons program. In July 1993 it took a step further, formally requesting LWRs in its Geneva negotiations with the United States. But Washington, at that point, consistently refused to negotiate on normalization, and Pyongyang was deeply divided over what it should give up in order to get a normalization deal—for example, what would happen to the existing gas-graphite reactor at Yongbyon and to the reprocessing plant. Thus, it was not until November 1993 that a leading spokesman of the pragmatists publicly put forward the concept of a "package deal" linking nuclear concessions with normalization.

The trade-offs that were ultimately embodied in the 1994 agreement did not begin to crystallize in specific terms until the months just before and including the meetings that Carter and I had with Kim Il Sung.

Hard-line resistance in Pyongyang to the comprehensive freeze agreement that finally emerged was apparent when Kim Il Sung suggested on April 19, 1994, that the reprocessing plant might be given up when the LWR was "delivered." Since the construction of an LWR could take six to ten years, did this mean that North Korea would continue to reprocess plutonium in the interim? The Clinton administration was not interested in finding out, as I discovered to my dismay when I urged Gallucci to explore the offer. The administration was focused single-mindedly on getting IAEA inspection access, not on identifying the elements of a freeze and a package deal, especially after North Korea unloaded the fuel rods on May 12. To the extent that the White House defined its long-term goals, it spoke only of "the dismantling and decommissioning" of North Korean nuclear facilities, not of a freeze.

My conversations with North Korean diplomats during early 1994 made clear that leading pragmatists in Pyongyang, especially First Deputy Foreign Minister Kang Sok Ju, were groping for a freeze formula that the United States would accept and that they wanted suggestions from U.S. advocates of a settlement to use in combating the hard-liners there. At the invitation of North Korean Deputy U.N. Ambassador Kim Jong Su, I met with him twice during late April to discuss what a freeze would entail. Kim Il Sung's April 19 offer could be the starting point for negotiations, I said, but it contained a fundamental flaw. The reprocessing plant would have to stop operation at the same time that the United States made a commitment to provide an LWR—not, as Kim had suggested, when the reactor was completed. It was inconceivable, I said, that the United States would make any kind of deal that permitted the production of plutonium to continue. He looked disturbed but said he would pass on what I had said. In mid-May, I was invited to visit Pyongyang beginning June 4, with strong hints that I would meet Kim Il Sung.

My first meetings there were with Kang Sok Ju and Li Hyong Chol, then director of U.S. affairs in the Foreign Ministry and later U.N. ambassador. It soon became clear that there was indeed a conflict then in progress between hawks and doves over how to handle the nuclear crisis and that the Foreign Ministry had not been consulted in advance when the fuel rods were unloaded on May 12. Kang and Li did not challenge me when I emphasized that North Korea would have to suspend its entire nuclear program as part of a package deal, including the Yongbyon reactor as well as the reprocessing plant, and that construction would have to stop on its two new reactors. Instead, they said in effect that the United States was making it difficult for them to promote a comprehensive freeze. "We know your views," Kang said. "Some of us are seriously considering them and have been thinking in such terms ourselves. But many of our colleagues won't hear of such things unless your country treats us on a basis of equality. You are trying to dig out the past history of our nuclear activities, but without a package deal. You're treating us like a criminal who has to confess. If we have a package deal on a basis of equality, you will have an opportunity to verify the present and future, and in that framework, we're prepared to discuss ways that you can determine the past. Otherwise you may lose the opportunity to verify the present and future. We have a Korean proverb, 'Don't throw the baby out with the bathwater.'"

What he had in mind, Kang added, was a multilateral agreement in which the United States would "earmark for us some portion of the assistance you are already giving to Russia and buy the light water reactors for us there." North Korean nuclear technicians had worked with Russian technicians for more than twenty years, he argued, and Moscow had already made plans for a North Korean LWR project before Gorbachev cancelled it in 1989. I pointed to the strains that still persisted in U.S. relations with Moscow and said that another way of providing the reactors would have to be found.

Kang dwelled at some length on the importance of the U.S. pledge given to him by Gallucci in June 1993, accepting the "principle of assurances against the U.S. use of force, including nuclear weapons." "If the United States would give us direct formal negative security assurances as part of a package deal," he declared, "we in our ministry will have a good argument to persuade our military scientists not to use plutonium to develop weapons. There are many in our country who don't feel as we do in our ministry."

I gathered from informal one-on-one comments that the idea of a comprehensive nuclear freeze had not yet been submitted to Kim Il Sung. This became apparent during my meeting with the Great Leader on June 9 at one of his nine summer villas, located next to his own private hot spring at Onchon about sixty miles from Pyongyang in wooded hills near the sea. Kang was present, since Foreign Minister Kim Yong Nam was out of the country.

When I suggested that we discuss how to resolve the nuclear issue, Kim began by ridiculing "what the mass media say, that we have already acquired one or two atomic bombs. That would be one or two against the ten thousand that your country has, so the odds against us would be very great. Even if we were to succeed in acquiring them, we don't have the necessary delivery systems, the airplanes, missiles, ships, and so on. So why is it necessary for us to produce one or two and become the laughingstock of the world? It gives me a headache when you continue to ask to see something we don't have. It's like dogs barking at the moon."

Then he launched into a long review of why and how North Korea had been pursuing LWRs. "We need energy and we recognize that the type of nuclear facilities we are now developing are not the best," he said. "Also, since Chernobyl, I have been deeply concerned about the safety of atomic power stations. So when I met Chernenko in 1984, I persuaded him to help us build light water reactors, and we were promised four stations, with a capacity of four hundred megawatts. We signed a contract and had a feasibility study, but Gorbachev withdrew the technicians. In this process, however, we learned about the possibilities of light water reactors, and that's why we suggested that you help us to do what we had already started to do."

At this point, I explained why I thought his April 19 offer had to be modified to reach agreement on a package deal and outlined what I considered the essential elements of a nuclear freeze: suspend operation of the reprocessing plant and reactor at Yongbyon; promise not to reload the reactor or to reprocess the fuel rods that had been removed from the reactor; stop construction of the two new reactors then underway; and permit the IAEA inspectors to return. The freeze would be part of a package deal that would set forth the terms for the normalization of relations and for the eventual dismantling of nuclear facilities. Kim looked surprised, even startled, turned to Kang, and talked with him in Korean for seven minutes. The interpreter sat silently during this exchange. Then Kim turned back to me and said: "This is very interesting and we can do this if it will help to allay your concerns. We can definitely do this, if a firm guarantee can be reached that will enable us to have light water reactors. But how can we be certain that your country will live up to your commitments? How can we be certain that you will normalize relations? My colleagues assure me that diplomats can find a way of dealing with these problems."

On the following day I met Kang, who was clearly pleased that I had elicited acceptance of a comprehensive freeze from Kim and that I intended to announce this in Beijing after my departure. My impression from Kang and his aides was that my meeting with the Great Leader had been helpful to Kang, providing, perhaps by design, a way for him to outflank his adversaries, shortcut the decision-making process, and get Kim on record in support of a comprehensive freeze. Carter then proceeded a week later to pin down the specifics of the freeze more explicitly and, most important, to persuade Kim that the freeze should start immediately in order to make negotiations with Washington possible. This idea had not occurred to me when I met Kim. My perception was that North Korea would agree to a freeze only in return for direct quid pro quos at the negotiating table. Carter's success in getting Kim to act unilaterally, at once, was the critical breakthrough that gave Clinton the political cover needed to begin negotiations.

The pragmatists in Pyongyang—led by Kang and possibly, behind the scenes, by Kim Jong Il—knew where they were going in 1994, even if the United States did not. Carter went to North Korea, he said, without any hints from the Clinton administration concerning the outlines of a compromise acceptable to the North. My discussions with Gallucci and others reinforce my conclusion that little, if any, systematic thinking had crystallized in Washington prior to the Carter visit concerning how to follow up the North's July 1993 reactor request and Kim Il Sung's April 1994 reprocessing plant offer. Gallucci acknowledged that "we hadn't thought out our terms for returning to the table" prior to the visit. It was only after Carter had reached his initial understanding with Kim Il Sung on June 16 that the White House was forced to focus on the specifics of what would constitute an acceptable freeze.

The 1994 accord is often incorrectly portrayed by both its detractors and its supporters in Washington. It did successfully freeze the operation of the Yongbyon reactor and reprocessing plant, and it did stop the construction of the two bigger reactors, all of which the detractors are reluctant to acknowledge. But it did not commit North Korea to the unconditional surrender of its nuclear weapons option, as supporters of the agreement often suggest, and it did not cover missiles. From the start of the freeze negotiations, North Korea made clear that the dismantling of the Yongbyon facilities and the termination of other activities designed to keep its nuclear option open would depend on American behavior. The nuclear option would be surrendered once and for all only after the United States fully normalizes relations and no longer poses what Pyongyang considers to be a military threat.

As one of those present at the creation of the freeze, I was vividly aware of how suspicious North Korea was that the United States might not live up to it. The interpreter during my meeting with Kim Il Sung later told me that the seven-minute conversation in Korean with Kang Sok Ju that preceded Kim's acceptance of the freeze centered on whether Pyongyang could avoid being conned by the United States, and if so, how.

Kang displayed a surprising knowledge of U.S. politics in our conversation on the day following my meeting with Kim. He correctly anticipated that there would be strong conservative opposition to a package deal and that the normalization of relations would not come easily. He made clear that if a freeze agreement could be negotiated, he would make sure that it gave North Korea the built-in leverage necessary to ensure U.S. compliance with its terms. Above all, Kang emphasized that the critical test of compliance would be whether the United States proved to be ready for full normalization, including an end to the economic sanctions imposed during the Korean War and a U.S.–North Korean peace treaty that would formally end the war and lead to a relaxation of military tensions.

Gallucci attempted to negotiate an airtight agreement that would not only freeze the North's existing nuclear facilities under strict inspection but also bar missile testing. He pressed for a binding North Korean commitment not to build new nuclear facilities. Kang did agree to a freeze of existing facilities under comprehensive inspection safeguards that have since been strictly honored. But he flatly rejected the inclusion of missiles in the agreement. On the issue of new nuclear facilities, a last-minute compromise was reached. A secret codicil prohibited the construction of new facilities to produce fissile material. But the agreement did not provide for the immediate implementation of the inspections that would have been necessary to enforce the codicil and to discover the extent of fissile material accumulations prior to the freeze. North Korea would have to accept such sweeping inspections only when construction of a "significant portion" of the two light water reactors promised in the agreement had been completed. Only when the nuclear "core" of the reactors had been installed would its existing nuclear facilities have to be dismantled. Since this was expected to take ten years or more, Pyongyang retained its freedom, in the interim, to pursue preparations for resuming its nuclear program if relations with the United States did not improve.

THE MISSILE ISSUE

As it turned out, relations quickly became embittered. North Korea had agreed to the freeze primarily because the United States promised in article 2, section 2 to phase out U.S. economic sanctions. Getting rid of sanctions was important to Pyongyang for both political and economic reasons. Politically, the sanctions symbolized the fact that the Korean War had not ended. In North Korean eyes, the only plausible rationale for sanctions was a U.S. desire to "stifle" the Pyongyang regime and bring it down. Economically, the removal of sanctions was the key to opening up the North Korean economy because they closed off the American market to products made in the North by South Korean, Japanese, and other foreign companies. But the freeze agreement had been concluded in late October, several weeks before the Republican sweep in the 1994 congressional elections. Fearful of jeopardizing congressional funding of the agreement, the Clinton administration backed off from the sanctions pledge after the elections. Many administration officials believed that North Korea would soon collapse, anyway, making it unnecessary to worry about a backlash from Pyongyang.

And indeed, at first, North Korea accepted State Department assurances that everything would soon work out if it would only be tolerant of the vagaries of U.S. politics. Pyongyang did not want to rock the boat because it badly needed the 500,000 tons of oil that it was getting annually as one of the quid pro quos for the freeze. But hard-liners in Pyongyang grew increasingly assertive as the impasse over sanctions continued. The armed forces wanted to conduct a test of the medium-range Nodong missile, which had only been tested once previously in 1993. Kim Jong Il held his generals in check for four years. He cancelled a missile test planned for October 1996 after U.S. satellites spotted preparations at the launch site and Washington warned that testing would wreck progress toward normalization. Then, in 1997, the United States began to fall behind in its oil deliveries, upsetting the already shaky North Korean economy.

In a meeting on May 9, 1998, Foreign Minister Kim Yong Nam complained bitterly that "your government takes us for granted because you think we are weak. We are losing patience. Our generals and atomic industry leaders insist that we must resume our nuclear program and develop appropriate military capabilities. If you do not act in good faith, there will be consequences." The tests of good faith, Kim said, would not only be getting oil deliveries back on schedule but "showing us that you are serious about normalization. To us, it is clear that the sanctions are intended to pressure us because you hope we will collapse. If you were serious about normalization, you would end the Korean War. How can we have normal relations if we are still at war?"

Kim Yong Nam's warning, reported in the media and conveyed to administration officials, was followed by formal diplomatic initiatives that were largely dismissed by the United States. Oil deliveries were accelerated, but Washington continued to brush off insistent North Korean demands for action on the sanctions issue and on broader steps toward normalization. Finally, on June 16, Pyongyang made a last-ditch attempt to get U.S. attention. A Foreign Ministry statement warned that "with missiles of the United States aiming at our territory, we will continue developing, testing, and deploying our own missiles to counter them." At the same time, the statement offered to discuss the "discontinuation of our missile development after a peace agreement is signed with the United States and the U.S. military threat completely removed."[9]

This warning, too, was ignored in Washington. The predictable result was a showdown between hawks and doves in Pyongyang, followed by Kim Jong Il's decision to launch a satellite that would demonstrate North Korea's potential long-range missile capabilities and, he hoped, jolt Washington into taking its concerns more seriously.

The satellite launch on August 16, 1998, did touch off a furor in Washington and Tokyo by showing that Pyongyang was much further along in its missile development than had previously been revealed. The result was Perry's mission to Pyongyang and an agreement announced by the White House on September 17, 1999, providing for the relaxation of "most" U.S. sanctions in return for a temporary North Korean moratorium on missile testing that was to remain in effect while negotiations on normalization proceeded.

As in 1994, when the United States first promised to end sanctions as part of the freeze agreement, congressional Republicans threatened to block funding for the agreement if the sanctions were actually relaxed. Once again, the United States reneged on its promise. Even so, Pyongyang honored its side of the September 17 bargain by observing the test moratorium. It was not until the Korean summit nine months later that the White House felt it had the political cover needed to go ahead with its announced relaxation of sanctions. On June 19, with caveats that only later became known, sanctions on nonstrategic trade and investment relations with Pyongang were lifted, opening the way for a rapid improvement in relations and hopeful progress toward a missile agreement during the closing months of the Clinton administration.

Four months later, Kim Jong Il sent his deputy, Vice-Marshal Jo Myong Rok, to Washington, where he was received by President Clinton. In an historic joint communiqué on October 12, Vice-Marshal Jo and Secretary of State Madeleine Albright declared that North Korea and the United States would no longer have "hostile intent toward each other." Then, in the expectation of a Clinton visit, Kim Jong Il invited Albright to Pyongyang for preliminary discussions on a missile deal. When Clinton came, Kim told Albright, North Korea would be prepared to negotiate an immediate freeze on long-range missile testing and development and to stop all exports of missiles and missile components, provided that the United States offered sufficient economic and other inducements in return, including arrangements to launch North Korean scientific research and communications satellites.

Albright recounted this explicit proposal on several occasions following her return, including a dinner at the State Department that I attended on November 2, 2000. She was more guarded concerning other, less explicit overtures by Kim that were leaked without specific attribution. Of particular importance were reports that Kim had offered to discuss a freeze on the testing and development of all missiles with a range over 320 miles, which would preclude improved versions of the medium-range Nodong missiles capable of reaching Japan and U.S. bases in Japan.

The Kim-Albright conversations led to exploratory negotiations at Kuala Lumpur, Malaysia, in mid-November that were inconclusive. Gary Samore, then senior director for nonproliferation in the National Security

Council and a U.S. negotiator at Kuala Lumpur, told me that the North Koreans were evasive. With respect to a long-range missile freeze, the most important unresolved issue was the extent of verification. On a possible medium-range freeze, it was unclear whether this could be implemented immediately, along with a long-range freeze, or would be handled in a looser, long-term "framework" agreement providing for several conditional stages during which Japan would have to become involved. Moreover, it was unclear whether the existing one hundred Nodong missiles, already deployed, would be dismantled, and it appeared probable that they would not be.

All of these issues could be resolved, North Korea said, when Clinton met with Kim Jong Il, who alone had the power to decide North Korean policy, which would be governed, in the end, by what benefits to Pyongyang Clinton would offer and how credible his promises as a lame-duck president would be.

At the time Vice-Marshal Jo visited Washington, Clinton was intrigued by the idea of going to North Korea. The official U.S. version of the October 12 Jo-Albright communiqué said that the secretary of state would visit Pyongyang in preparation for a "possible" presidential visit. The North Korean text, by contrast, omitted the word "possible." Kim Jong Il's overtures for a missile deal were predicated on expectations of a presidential visit that would carry forward the movement toward normalized relations signaled in the communiqué. Thus, when Clinton decided not to go, over Albright's objections, North Korea no longer considered itself bound by the offers that Kim Jong Il had made to Albright.

"The mere fact that certain possibilities were explored in the context of the Clinton administration, when the general environment was good, does not necessarily mean there is a basis for picking up where we left off then," Foreign Minister Paik Nam Soon said in our May 30, 2001, meeting. "Remember, there was no joint document whatsoever. We will have to take a fresh look at the whole missile issue in the context of the overall posture of the Bush administration toward us."

Clinton's eleventh-hour decision not to visit Pyongyang came in response to Republican criticism that there would not be sufficient time to nail down the specifics of a carefully negotiated missile deal and that he should not, in any case, tie the hands of a possible Republican successor. But this decision, understandable as it was in the context of U.S. politics, had a damaging impact on the policy conflict between hawks and doves within North Korea that has greatly complicated subsequent relations between Washington and Pyongyang. Since the United States had heralded the visit in the October 12 communiqué and had directly linked the Albright visit to preparations for it, Clinton's decision not to go pulled the rug out from under Kim Jong Il, undermining his ability to make concessions desired by the United States on a missile agreement and other issues.

During a debate on whether Clinton should go among the Korea specialists and former diplomats who attended the Albright dinner on November 2, I warned that a negative decision would strengthen hard-liners in Pyongyang opposed to U.S. interests and objectives. As the group disbanded, I commented to Albright that "they only want to talk about the U.S. end of it, but the real question for us is what the consequences will be in Pyongyang. I'm afraid we'll pay dearly if he doesn't go, whoever is president."

"I agree with you," she replied. "That's one of the main points I keep making when we talk about this."

CHAPTER 19

Japan and Nuclear Weapons

THE MOST astonishing literary phenomenon in the history of South Korea is the popularity of *The Rose of Sharon Has Blossomed*, a three-volume saga in which North and South cooperate in developing nuclear weapons that save the South in a war with Japan. More than five million copies of the novel have been sold since 1994, in contrast to a peak of 300,000 copies for other best-sellers in recent years.[1]

In a plot that mixes elements of historical fact with larger doses of fiction, the novel centers on a Korean-born American nuclear physicist who masterminds a secret South Korean nuclear program during the regime of the late president Park Chung Hee. The CIA, learning of the program, arranges to have the physicist killed in an auto accident. Before his death, using $65 million supplied by Park, he buys 80 kilograms of plutonium from India with the help of an Indian scientist who had been his roommate during U.S. college days. He hides the plutonium in a stone statue of an elephant in the South Korean presidential compound, sharing the secret of its location only with the Indian scientist. There it remains until the Indian reveals the hiding place to a South Korean journalist investigating rumors of a CIA hand in the auto accident.

The journalist, a fervent nationalist who dreams of reviving Park's nuclear program, persuades a fictitious later president that the South and the North must pool their plutonium and missile know-how in order to prepare for an inevitable confrontation with a nuclear-armed Japan. This time, the carefully camouflaged North-South project in the rugged South Korean Taebaek mountain range is not detected by American intelligence. Eventually Japan, alarmed by growing South Korean trade competition, does provoke a war, charging Korean incursions in contested Takeshima Island. As Japanese bombers head toward Pohang, the South's major industrial center, Seoul demonstrates its nuclear capability with a missile attack that obliterates an uninhabited Japanese island. Tokyo ignominiously backs down.

The title of the novel—*The Rose of Sharon Has Blossomed*—is the code name for the North-South nuclear program. It is also the name of a popular children's refrain celebrating liberation from Japanese colonialism. South Korea's national flower is called the Rose of Sharon because it resembles the biblical flower described in the Song of Solomon.

The most important element of historical fact in the plot is that Park Chung Hee did initiate a secret nuclear program in 1970, described in the next chapter, and was able to carry it forward without detection for four years. In 1975, armed with conclusive intelligence findings, the United States pressured Park to stop the program or face the termination of U.S. military support for the South. The program was revived during subsequent military regimes and discontinued once again under U.S. pressure.

It is also true that there was a distinguished Korean-born American nuclear physicist, Lee Hwi So, who died in an auto accident in 1977. An expert on the transmutation of atomic particles, Lee, who directed theoretical physics at the Fermi National Laboratory, was described by *Physics Today* after his death as "one of the world's leading physicists working on the theory of elementary particles." No evidence has surfaced that he helped Park's nuclear program or that his death was not accidental. But his supposed role and the CIA's complicity in his death dominate the *Rose of Sharon* and an earlier biography and novel about Lee's life.[2]

What has made the impact of the *Rose of Sharon* so powerful is the widespread and growing fear in South Korea that the prospect of a nuclear-armed Japan is not fantasy but an ever more plausible real-world danger. In the eyes of its East Asian neighbors, Japan is systematically perfecting its capacity to make nuclear weapons overnight by developing independent plutonium-reprocessing and uranium-enrichment capabilities as part of its civilian nuclear program. North Korea, describing Japan as an "associate member of the nuclear club," contrasts its own agreement in 1994 to freeze its reprocessing facilities with Japan's determined pursuit of nuclear independence.

Japan insists that its nuclear program is motivated solely by economic and energy-security considerations. Emphasizing energy security, Japanese officials point to forecasts that the world's oil will run out within four or five decades and its uranium soon thereafter. Instead of relying on imported energy sources, they say, Japan is playing it safe by developing its own autonomous nuclear fuel cycle, complete with a reprocessing capability and fast-breeder reactors that can burn plutonium to produce electricity while generating—"breeding"—still more plutonium. Moreover, they argue, memories of Hiroshima and Nagasaki make the nuclear option abhorrent and unacceptable for most Japanese, and it is settled national policy that the nation will not possess or manufacture nuclear weapons or permit their introduction by the United States in carrying out the U.S.–Japan Security Treaty.

In strategic terms, Japanese leaders maintain, Japan rules out nuclear weapons because a densely populated island nation located so close to most of its conceivable enemies would be peculiarly vulnerable to a preemptive nuclear attack. Equally important, they add, Japanese business leaders fear that nuclearization would have disastrous economic consequences, jeopardizing access to foreign markets and investment opportunities.

Opposition to the Japanese plutonium program has been growing within Japan itself, especially since a serious accident at the Monju fast-breeder reactor that led to its shutdown in 1996. Nevertheless, despite official disclaimers and growing public uneasiness over the safety of its civilian nuclear power program, there is extensive evidence that Japanese leaders do want to keep a nuclear weapons option open and deliberately opted for a plutonium-based civilian nuclear program, not only for the stated reasons but also because it can be readily converted to military purposes. Moreover, given the sophisticated character of the Japanese space program, Japan could quickly shift to the manufacture of missiles with a range and thrust comparable to the best in the U.S. arsenal. This reality confronts North and South Korea alike and will be a powerful stimulus for nuclear weapons development both before and after unification.

THE NUCLEAR DEBATE: BEHIND THE FAÇADE

Japan was one of the last countries to sign the NPT in 1970 and finally ratified it six years later only after the United States promised not to interfere with Tokyo's pursuit of independent reprocessing capabilities in its civilian nuclear-power program. When the United States first circulated drafts of the projected treaty in early 1966, Vice Foreign Minister Takeso Shimoda told a press conference that "Japan cannot agree to such a big power-centered approach, implying as it does that the nuclear powers would not be required to reduce their capabilities or stockpile, while the non-nuclear powers would be barred in this treaty from having nuclear weapons."[3] Shimoda's comments reflected widespread sentiment in the ruling Liberal Democratic Party that Japan should not foreclose its nuclear option and that it was time for the Japanese public to get over the trauma of Hiroshima.

The controversy over the NPT was intensified by a parallel debate over the terms for the projected return of Okinawa to Japan. Ironically, at the same time that U.S. arms-control officials were promoting the NPT, the Pentagon was seeking Japanese assurances that the United States could continue to keep nuclear weapons in its Okinawan bases if it gave the island back to Japan. Prime Minister Sato had made no secret of his readiness to give the United States such assurances. But he faced strong public sentiment against risking involvement in an "American war" in Korea or elsewhere in Asia that could well involve nuclear weapons. On February 5, 1968, Sato was forced to make his Diet pledge, known as the Three Non-Nuclear Principles, that Japan "will not manufacture or possess nuclear weapons or allow their introduction into this country," and on November 24, 1971, the Diet formalized this policy in a resolution.

Unknown to the Japanese public at the time, Sato commissioned a secret study on Japanese nuclear policy in late 1967 by an advisory group consisting of key government officials and scholars specializing in foreign policy and strategic issues. Political scientist Michio Royama, who revealed the existence of this study in 1994, said that Sato had specifically asked the group to examine whether it was possible and desirable for Japan to develop independent nuclear forces. The study pointed out that there were "no technical impediments" to such forces, Royama said, and that the plutonium stocks resulting from its civilian nuclear-power program would give Japan the option of making nuclear weapons. But it concluded that a nuclear-weapons program was undesirable because it would cost too much, would alarm neighboring countries, and would not have the majority support of the Japanese public.[4]

The fact that its civilian nuclear-power program would give Japan a built-in weapons option was explicitly recognized in a mid-1968 study published by the Security Research Council, a think tank sponsored by the Japanese Defense Agency. Looking ahead to Japanese defense problems in the 1970s, the study said that Japan could make twenty to thirty nuclear weapons per year if its civilian nuclear reactors discontinued power generation and were devoted entirely to the production of fissile plutonium 239.[5]

The importance of keeping the nuclear-weapons option was spelled out in a policy-planning study on Japan's foreign policy challenges in the coming decade prepared by the Foreign Ministry for internal government use in early 1969. Portions of the study were leaked to *Mainichi* in 1994 by one of the officials who had been involved. According to the study, "For the time being we will maintain the policy of not possessing nuclear weapons. However, regardless of joining the NPT or not, we will keep the economic and technical potential for the production of nuclear weapons, while seeing to it that Japan will not be interfered with in this regard."[6]

On November 21, 1969, Prime Minister Sato and President Nixon issued a communiqué in Washington confirming that the United States would return Okinawa. In addition to the publicly revealed text, the communiqué had a secret Agreed Minute that was disclosed in 1994 by Kei Wakaizumi, a Japanese scholar who accompanied Sato to Washington. Even the public text carefully left the door open for a change in the ban on the introduction of nuclear weapons. The president expressed his "deep understanding" of the "particular sentiment of the Japanese people against nuclear weapons and the policy of the Japanese government reflecting such sentiment." But the key word "policy" underlined the fact that the Three Non-Nuclear Principles were not embodied in a binding law or treaty. In the Agreed Minute, Nixon was more explicit, declaring that "in time of great emergency the United States Government will require the re-entry of nuclear weapons and transit rights in Okinawa with prior consultation with the government of Japan," as well as "the standby retention and activation in time of great emergency of existing nuclear storage locations." Sato explicitly accepted this caveat.[7]

Less than three weeks later, Sato underlined his own ambivalent attitude on the nuclear issue, sarcastically observing in an address before top leaders of the Keidanren business federation that

> we seem to be unable to possess a complete system of armament in our country, since we were the ones who were "nuclear-baptized" and the Japanese people have a special sentiment against nuclear weapons. It's regrettable, indeed, but that's where we stand just now. . . . Let me say this so that no one can misunderstand me: I do not regard it as a complete system of defense if we cannot possess nuclear weapons in the era of nuclear weapons. I will, nevertheless, adhere faithfully to the pledge I have made to the people. We will not possess, manufacture or permit the introduction of nuclear weapons; but this being so, it is inevitable, then, that we must seek our security under the U.S. nuclear umbrella.[8]

Until West Germany signed the NPT in December 1969, Japan stalled in the hope that it might be possible to fudge a decision indefinitely. But the Bonn decision and the prospect that the treaty would come into force within a matter of months brought the issue to a head. When Japan did sign the treaty on February 3, 1970, the Foreign Ministry openly expressed doubts that foreshadowed the ensuing six-year delay in ratification. In a striking departure from the cautious understatement marking most official Japanese pronouncements, the eleven-point Foreign Ministry declaration proclaimed that "this treaty permits only the present nuclear-weapon states to possess nuclear weapons. This discrimination should ultimately be made to disappear through the elimination of nuclear weapons by all the nuclear-weapon states from their national arsenals."

In the end, Tokyo agreed to ratify the treaty in 1976 only after protracted negotiations with the United States and the IAEA that left its nuclear option open. The IAEA accepted a safeguards agreement that limited its inspection to "strategic points" in the nuclear fuel cycle. The United States promised a continued supply of enriched uranium under its nuclear cooperation agreement with Japan on permissive terms not accorded to South Korea and other allies, with the exception of Britain. Tokyo would be free to develop its own uranium enrichment capability and facilities for reprocessing its spent fuel into plutonium.

Even after Japan had signed the NPT, Defense Agency Director Yasuhiro Nakasone, a longtime advocate of nuclear weapons, made clear that he had gone along with the treaty only reluctantly. In March 1970 he bitterly lamented the fact that "the two superpowers seem determined to maintain their dominance in nuclear technology in general and its military application in particular. . . . Both the 1963 partial nuclear test ban treaty and the current nuclear non-proliferation pact are primarily designed—even if covertly—to preempt, or rather deter, both Japan and West Germany from acquiring nuclear arms and thereby undermining the basis of US-Soviet nuclear hegemony.[9]

In an unprecedented ninety-eight-page *White Paper*, Nakasone's Defense Agency declared in October 1970 that "Japan should not acquire weapons which pose a threat to other countries, such as intercontinental ballistic missiles (ICBMs) and strategic bombers. As for defensive nuclear weapons, it would be possible in a legal sense to possess small-yield, tactical, purely defensive nuclear weapons without violating the Constitution. In view of the danger of inviting adverse foreign relations and large-scale war, we will follow the policy of not acquiring nuclear weapons at present."[10]

Implying as it did that the "policy" pursued "at present" could change, the *White Paper* provoked bitter protests from anti-nuclear leaders, who charged that the Pentagon and the Defense Agency were plotting a "two-key" nuclear strategy to counter emerging Chinese missile capabilities.

A revealing hint of the policy struggles within the Japanese government during the decade of debate over the NPT was offered by nuclear scientist Hiromi Arisawa, often called the father of nuclear power in Japan, who served as a member and then chairman of the Atomic Energy Commission for seventeen years.[11] When he retired in 1972, Arisawa told an *Asahi* interviewer that "we were pressed repeatedly for permission to do basic research on how to make an atomic bomb. They tried to persuade us to do so by saying that such research was permissible under the Constitution. Naturally, I always refused."[12] Arisawa did not specify who "they" were, but it is noteworthy that during part of his tenure, Nakasone was the minister of science and technology, with jurisdiction over the nuclear program.

It was not just Sato and Nakasone, both declared pro-nuclear hawks, who kept the nuclear debate alive by emphasizing the distinction between strategic and tactical nuclear weapons. Prime Minister Kakuei Tanaka, reaffirming Sato's Three Non-Nuclear Principles on March 20, 1973, added that "while we are not able to have offensive nuclear weapons, it is not a question of saying that we will have no nuclear weapons at all." In its 1980 *White Paper*, the Defense Agency once again noted, as it did in 1970, that defensive nuclear weapons would not violate the constitution, specifically mentioning Nike-Hercules air defense missiles and 203-mm howitzers.[13]

It is often assumed that Japan, as the only victim of nuclear weapons, will always have its "nuclear allergy." But memories of Hiroshima and Nagasaki are invoked by the proponents as well as the opponents of nuclear weapons. The opponents believe that Japan's unique experience has given it a special responsibility to work for the elimination of nuclear weapons. The pro-nuclear minority, in contrast, seeks to exploit the sublimated feelings of humiliation and impotent rage resulting from this "victim" self-image. Only if Japan itself acquires nuclear weapons, they argue, will the nation be able to erase the traumatic impact of the bombing from the national psyche and stand up to the United States as an equal in economic disputes and global policy decision-making.

Significantly, one of the most impassioned opponents of the U.S.–Japan Security Treaty, former *Nihon Keizai* editor Yasuo Takeyama, is a survivor of Hiroshima. In a 1992 speech implying support for a nuclear weapons program, Takeyama declared:

We Japanese have to admit very frankly with a sense of shame and regret that Japan has been a semi-independent nation under the constraints of the Japan-U.S. Security Pact and Article 9 of the U.S.-im-

posed Constitution. . . . We have to be courageous enough to restructure our post-war body politic: first by amending or enacting a new
constitution, and then by revising or rescinding the Security Pact. . . .
Even if Japan should eventually develop its own nuclear weapons,
there would be no reason for Asian countries to fear Japan. The world
has long learned to live with a nuclear-armed United States, Russia,
France, Britain, China, and perhaps even North Korea.[14]

Former prime minister Kiichi Miyazawa has warned that proposals for
a revision of article 9, the "no war" clause of Japan's constitution, could
open the way for a nuclear weapons program. Miyazawa pointed in particular to the rightist leader Ichiro Ozawa's view that Japan can only
become a "normal country" by revising its defense posture. Ozawa's plan
to send armed Japanese combat forces abroad on U.N. peacekeeping
missions would open a Pandora's box, he suggested, since

> looking ahead, if that leads to revising the Constitution and Japan has
> armed forces, before long the argument would definitely emerge that
> having nuclear weapons would be the most economical form of de-
> fense. Since conscription would be all but impossible in Japan, it would
> be necessary to rely on volunteers, but then the personnel costs would
> be quite high. Nuclear weapons armament would be much more eco-
> nomical, they would say. If there were problems about locating nuclear
> missiles on land, then pretty soon they would insist that Japan could
> deploy them on submarines.[15]

THE NUCLEAR OPTION

The controversy surrounding Japan's reliance on a plutonium-based nuclear program has focused to date primarily on two issues: whether large
plutonium stocks will accumulate and whether reactor-grade plutonium
can be used for nuclear weapons.

In November 2000 Japan had already accumulated a stockpile of separated plutonium totaling 32.8 tons, of which 5.2 tons was stored in Japan and the remainder at reprocessing facilities in Europe. Estimates by
independent experts indicate that 8 kilograms of plutonium—and possibly less, depending on the grade of plutonium, the specific weapon design, and the desired explosive yield—is sufficient fissile material for a
fission (as distinct from a fusion) weapon with a yield in the range of one
to 20 kilotons. Thus, 5.2 tons would be enough for 650 nuclear weap-

ons. Japan also has an accumulation of spent fuel that would yield another 90 tons of separated plutonium if it were reprocessed (of which 73 tons is stored in Japan), enough for 11,250 nuclear weapons.[16]

Most experts agree that reactor-grade plutonium can be used for weapons, though it has disadvantages compared with plutonium produced expressly for military purposes.[17] However, if Japan should decide to go nuclear, it would not have to rely on reactor-grade plutonium. Five other routes to a weapons program would also be available:

- Producing weapon-grade plutonium in reactors now used exclusively for generating electricity by shutting them down more frequently for refueling, thereby reducing the irradiation level ("burnup") of the fuel to weapon-grade
- Upgrading reactor-grade plutonium to weapon-grade, or producing highly enriched uranium, through use of a laser-isotope process now under experimental development at the government-operated Institute for Physical and Chemical Research at Osaka University
- Converting the centrifuges in its uranium-enrichment facilities at Rokasshomura from the production of low-enriched uranium (4.5 percent U-235) to highly enriched uranium usable in compact nuclear weapons (greater than 80 percent U-235)
- Separating the super-grade plutonium produced in the natural uranium "blankets" of its Joyo and Monju fast-breeder reactors, which has a higher degree of purity than the plutonium used in U.S. nuclear weapons
- Producing weapon-grade plutonium in a reactor specifically configured for the purpose

Producing weapon-grade plutonium in reactors designed for electric power generation would require frequent and costly shutdowns and would thus interfere with efficient electric power production. Moreover, Japan is dependent on those reactors to meet its electricity needs.

The laser-isotope process has already been successfully tested at the laboratory level, and the technology may have commercial uses in addition to its military utility. While the economics of a production-scale plant for the commercial production of low-enriched uranium fuel has yet to be demonstrated, development programs are underway in the United States and France as well as in Japan. Similarly, conversion of other enrichment technologies, such as centrifuges, for the production of highly enriched uranium would not be technically difficult. But nuclear weapons made with highly enriched uranium are bulkier than those made from plutonium. This difference could make it more difficult to develop missile warheads that are both powerful and compact.

Perhaps the most attractive option in the event of a weapons program would be separating the high-purity super-grade plutonium from the breeder blankets. This plutonium could then be used separately or blended with separated reactor-grade plutonium to create a larger supply of weapon-grade plutonium. The prototype fast-breeder reactor at Monju, which began operating in January 1995, had accumulated an estimated ten kilograms in its blanket when it was shut down after the 1996 sodium leak. When and if it is restored to operation, an additional seventy kilograms per year could be added to this accumulation, depending on the level of production. Even in the event that it is not restored to full operation, its continued use as a research or experimental facility would permit further accumulations of super-grade plutonium. The Joyo experimental fast-breeder reactor had accumulated forty kilograms in its blankets when the reactor shifted to a new design in 1994 that no longer requires blankets.[18]

In 1967, ten years before Joyo went into operation, Victor Gilinsky, then a RAND Corporation physicist and later a member of the U.S. Nuclear Regulatory Commission, warned that "it is an intrinsic property of fast breeders that about half of the plutonium produced by the breeder, the part bred in the outer 'blanket,' will have a rather low content of the troublesome plutonium 240, possibly less than five percent, even when produced in the most economical way. This material can therefore be used for military purposes with particular ease. On the other hand, the plutonium produced from economical operation of thermal reactors contains a relatively high fraction of plutonium 240 and is generally less useful for weapons."[19]

Based on French experience since 1967, Japan's super-grade plutonium would have a plutonium 240 content of only 2–3 percent—compared with 6 percent in U.S. nuclear weapons. The availability of plutonium of this high level of purity, as compared with reactor-grade plutonium, would reduce the need to conduct test explosions—a factor of great significance for Japan, with its population density and lack of suitable test sites. Moreover, less of such a pure grade of plutonium would be needed for each nuclear warhead, which would make it easier for Japan to make warheads small enough for advanced cruise missiles and ICBMs. Still another military advantage of super-grade plutonium is that in simple designs it is less susceptible than reactor-grade plutonium to premature detonation resulting from spontaneous fission.

Super-grade plutonium must be separated through reprocessing from the uranium 238 from which it is produced in the breeder blankets. With American technical help, as revealed in a Greenpeace study,[20] Japan is developing a special reprocessing plant, known as the Recycling Equipment Test Facility (RETF), designed expressly to separate super-grade plutonium in conjunction with the existing reprocessing plant at Tokai. The completion of this plant would greatly reduce the time required for the development of a nuclear weapons program. However, it is possible that the Monju reactor accident will lead to delays in the construction of the RETF and conceivably to its eventual cancellation. Japanese plans concerning this sensitive facility will be closely watched in the years ahead.

THE MISSILE OPTION

The fact that Japan already possesses, or could readily produce, substantial amounts of weapon-grade plutonium and uranium does not, in itself, mean that it could develop a significant nuclear weapons capability. It is the sophisticated character of the Japanese space program, with its convertibility to missile development, that makes Japan's potential as a nuclear power so formidable. In Tom Clancy's best-selling 1995 novel, *Debt of Honor*, which centers on a secret Japanese nuclear weapons program, Japan makes its own nuclear warheads and puts them on SS-19 ICBMs purchased from Russia.[21] But the reality is that Japan would not have to rely on any other power for missile technology. With foreign help, Japan has steadily built up its space capabilities. A controversial U.S.–Japan space cooperation agreement that remained in force from 1969 to 1984 embraced significant areas of space technology with military applications. Since the termination of this government-to-government coooperation, Japan has acquired less American technology in sensitive areas such as guidance. But a wide range of space-related private sector cooperation between the two countries has continued with U.S. government encouragement.

Japanese space agencies have successfully tested solid-fueled rocket systems that could be directly converted to intercontinental-range missiles. Both of these systems, the J-1 and the M-5, have a payload and a thrust comparable to that of U.S. ICBMs. John Pike, director of the Space Policy Project of the Federation of American Scientists, stated that "if converted to ballistic missile applications, the M-5 would seem likely to give Japan an ICBM roughly equivalent to the MX Peacekeeper, the largest currently operational U.S. ICBM, and the J-1 would probably give Japan an ICBM surpassing the performance of a Minuteman 3."[22] The range of the Minuteman 3 is about 8,000 miles, and that of the Peacekeeper, some 7,400. The J-1 was developed by marrying a solid-propellant motor from the liquid-fueled H-2 rocket to the upper stages of the MS-32, a precursor of the M-5. The H-2 has had a troubled record, with successful initial test launches and several subsequent failures. The latest version of the H-2 will be capable of carrying a three-ton payload.[23]

"By firing their existing launch vehicles at long trajectories not suitable for space launches but appropriate for missiles," Pike explained, "Japan could greatly increase the throw-weight of a missile relative to the space launch payload. For example, an intermediate-range missile capable of covering China might have a throw-weight as much as three to five times that of the satellite payload of the space launch vehicle from which it is derived."[24]

Super-grade plutonium is especially suited for the miniaturization of warheads. Since it is a more reliable explosive than grades with less purity, involving less danger of premature detonation, the other components of the warhead could be small and light. Thus, a warhead weighing 150 kilograms, containing 3 kilograms of super-grade, would be suitable for an advanced-model cruise missile with a range of 2,500 kilometers. Similarly, if Japan were to make an ICBM of the Multiple Independently Targetable Re-Entry Vehicle (MIRV) type based on technology drawn from the M-5, each warhead would weigh about 350 kilograms, and the missile would be able to carry between five and ten warheads, depending on its range.[25] The M-5 has an orbital payload capacity of 1.8 tons, which would be increased if the missile were fired on a ballistic trajectory. The U.S. Minuteman 3 and MX Peacekeeper, both MIRV-type ICBMs, can carry three and ten warheads respectively.

The Japanese space effort has entailed the development of guidance and reentry technology that could be applied to a missile program. Advanced guidance techniques were required to place and keep in orbit the unmanned space platform that was launched by the H-2 in 1995 to collect scientific data relating to research in the evolution of the universe. Japanese officials point out that targeting for a ballistic missile would require a much greater degree of precision in reentry technology than has yet been achieved. But the extent of precision required would depend on whether the missile would be designed for a "counterforce" strategy (that is, directed at missile silos or other hard targets) or for a "counter-value" (that is, "city-busting") strategy. The Orex reentry vehicle developed for the H-2 demonstrates mastery of the techniques that would be needed in pinpointing area targets such as cities. Pike estimated that the relevant reentry technology for this purpose could be perfected "in a matter of months." By contrast, he observed, it would take "three to four years" for Japan to develop the precision in reentry technology that would be needed for a "counterforce" strategy.

Japan's decision in 1999 to use its space capabilities for the development of four reconnaissance satellites with minimal U.S. technological input was a direct response to North Korea's satellite launch a year earlier and has obvious military implications. Support for this program was mobilized with explicit emphasis on its potential value in monitoring North Korean missile development. With this exception, Japan's nuclear and space programs have been sold to the public as sound economic investments that will give the country technological independence in these key sectors. Both programs are governed by legislative restrictions barring their use for military purposes.

The case for plutonium and fast-breeder reactors has been reinforced by the argument that an autonomous nuclear fuel cycle is essential for national energy security. At the same time, as we have seen, the priority accorded to both the nuclear and space programs by a succession of Japanese governments has reflected a clear recognition on the part of many key bureaucrats and political leaders that these programs give Japan the critical elements of a nuclear weapons capability.

THE THREE-CORNERED NUCLEAR DRAMA

A variety of regional and global factors that I have analyzed elsewhere will determine whether Japan decides to use its civilian nuclear and space capabilities for the development of nuclear weapons.[26] But the critical factor is likely to be whether North Korea, South Korea, or a unified Korea deploys nuclear weapons.

Japan fears that a unified Korea will go nuclear whether or not North Korea can be persuaded to give up its nuclear option. Most Japanese analysts believe that Pyongyang is using the nuclear issue to bargain for the normalization of political and economic relations with the U.S. and Japan. While not discounting the dangers posed by the North Korean nuclear and missile programs, these analysts emphasize Pyongyang's economic constraints and see a much greater potential danger from the prospect of a nuclear program combining the resources and technological prowess of both Koreas.

Tokyo, Seoul, and Pyongyang are closely eyeing each move made by the other in what has now become a three-cornered nuclear drama in Northeast Asia. North and South Korea alike see a potential military threat in Japan's plutonium stockpiling program. Whether Japan decides to pursue this program in the face of international criticism is thus likely to have a major impact on the nuclear posture of North Korea, South Korea, and a unified Korea. By the same token, advocates of a Japanese nuclear weapons program can point to nuclear hawks in Seoul as well as Pyongyang to build support for their own case in the years ahead. The goal of a nuclear-free Korea can be successfully pursued only if it is linked to broader denuclearization efforts in Northeast Asia embracing Japan and, as we will see in a later chapter, the United States.

CHAPTER 20

South Korea and Nuclear Weapons

IN 1989, THE United States made its discovery that Pyongyang was secretly attempting to develop nuclear weapons. Amid the resulting furor over the possibility of a North Korean nuclear threat, it has often been forgotten that eighteen years earlier, in 1970, South Korea had embarked on a comparable clandestine program of its own, eluding U.S. detection for nearly four years. When U.S. intelligence did find out what Seoul was up to, a bitter showdown ensued, the most serious conflict that has ever occurred in the history of U.S.–South Korean relations. The United States forced President Park Chung Hee to abandon his covert nuclear weapons effort only by threatening to cancel the U.S. security commitment to the South. Undeterred, however, Park's successors subsequently made a series of renewed attempts to acquire the technology necessary for developing both nuclear warheads and missile delivery systems. Each time, the United States found out, and each time, Seoul backed down. Far from ending the danger of a nuclear-armed South Korea, this protracted struggle between Seoul and Washington left a legacy of sublimated nationalist resentment in the South that has hardened the unresolved conflict there between moderates and pro-nuclear hawks.

The 1991 North-South denuclearization agreement formally bars both sides from making or deploying nuclear weapons and provides for mutual verification procedures that have yet to be implemented. Hopes for a meaningful inspection regime persist, and open demands in the South for an immediate nuclear weapons program subsided in the euphoric aftermath of the June 2000 North-South summit. But the 1991 agreement is the focus of a continuing sub-rosa controversy that could quickly come into the open once again if relations between Seoul and Pyongyang, or Seoul and Tokyo, should deteriorate.

The pro-nuclear hawks argue that the agreement was a sellout under U.S. pressure. It went too far, they say, by prohibiting not only the development of nuclear weapons, as such, but also the reprocessing of plutonium for use in civilian nuclear power programs. In this view, even if relations with Pyongyang do improve and the South does not need a nuclear deterrent now, both Koreas, like Japan, must possess reprocessing facilities in order to have the option of developing nuclear weapons that Japan enjoys under the terms of its nuclear cooperation agreement with the United States. Without at least the option, they warn, South Korea, North Korea, and a unified Korea would be equally defenseless if Japan should convert its civilian nuclear and space programs to military purposes.

Although American attention has been riveted exclusively on North Korean nuclear capabilities, the South Korean nuclear program, developed in close collaboration with Western companies, is technologically much more advanced than that of the North and has a much greater military potential. In 2001, Seoul had twelve nuclear power plants in operation, six more under construction, and blueprints for another twelve by 2030. It had accumulated a stockpile of twenty-seven tons of spent fuel that would be sufficient to produce enough plutonium for 3,375 nuclear warheads if the South possessed reprocessing facilities.[1] Similarly, the South Korean military-industrial complex, which has also grown up with U.S. collaboration, is technologically much more advanced than the North's Soviet-era defense industries. With this technological advantage and its nascent missile and space programs, the South could quickly develop a more sophisticated nuclear weapons capability than the North if it should seek to do so. It is this South Korean nuclear and missile potential, more than the danger of an imminent North Korean threat, that pro-nuclear hawks in Japan emphasize. Above all, the Japanese hawks warn of a nuclear-armed, unified Korea that could draw on the technological achievements of both the North and the South in a real-life replication of the *Rose of Sharon* scenario recounted in the preceding chapter.

To pursue the goal of a nuclear-free Korea effectively, in short, the United States would have to broaden its policy horizons, focusing on the South as well as the North and on the never-ending triangular cycle of suspicion over nuclear weaponry among Pyongyang, Seoul, and Tokyo.

DEATH AND RESURRECTION: THE NUCLEAR WEAPONS PROGRAM

Unlike Park Chung Hee's immediate successors, Chun Doo Hwan and Roh Tae Woo, who were ambivalent about his nuclear weapons program and made abortive efforts to resurrect it only in response to pressure from pro-nuclear hawks, Park himself was a true believer. Until his assassination in 1979, he continued to promote carefully disguised preparations for an eventual resurrection despite increasingly intrusive U.S. surveillance activities.

Park decided to seek a nuclear weapons capability partly as a way to gain military independence from Washington, partly as the key to decisive strategic superiority over the North, and partly to enhance his prestige domestically, according to Gen. Kim Yoon Ho, a former chairman of the South Korean Joint Chiefs of Staff who was a member of Park's inner circle in Blue House from 1970 to 1973. In 1968, President Nixon had served notice in the "Guam Doctrine" that U.S. allies would be expected to assume increasing responsibility for their own defense. Then came Nixon's 1970 announcement that U.S. forces in Korea would be reduced. At a time when the United States was on the defensive in Vietnam and preparing to disengage from Saigon, General Kim recalled, Park used to say that the United States "might leave us in the lurch, and it was time for us to establish our own decisive military superiority over the North so that we would not have to bow down all of the time to the Americans."[2]

General Kim was Park's intelligence adviser, responsible for maintaining a liaison between South Korean and U.S. intelligence agencies. As such, he watched for mood changes on the part of his U.S. counterparts that would betray whether they suspected that a nuclear weapons program was getting underway. When South Korea began unannounced negotiations with France in 1972 for a small-scale reprocessing plant, he said, the United States did not get wind of it. Donald Gregg, who took over as the CIA station chief in Seoul in mid-1973, told me that "we knew nothing about it at that point."[3] In early 1974, however, according to General Kim, word of a preliminary contract for the plant leaked out, triggering angry U.S. inquiries. South Korea responded by pointing out that if the United States could permit Japan to have reprocessing facilities, it should permit South Korea to do so as well. Reprocessing would help its civilian nuclear power program for the same important technical reasons that it was helpful to Japan, and the ability to reprocess did not, in itself, necessarily imply a nuclear weapons program. A South Korean investigative journalist later revealed that the 1974 contract provided for a plant that would have produced twenty kilograms of plutonium per year, enough for two or three nuclear warheads.[4]

"Naturally, they didn't want us to know what they knew," said General Kim, "but we got the impression that they knew a lot about many aspects of the program by late 1974. This is when it became very difficult to talk to each other."

In a recently declassified cable to the U.S. embassy in Seoul sent on March 4, 1975, Secretary of State Henry A. Kissinger presented the findings of an exhaustive inter-agency intelligence review of U.S. security relations with South Korea. Seoul was "proceeding with the initial phases of a nuclear weapons development program," the study concluded, and "could develop a limited nuclear weapons and missile capability within a ten-year time frame," though it would face "significant difficulties."[5] The late Richard Sneider, then U.S. ambassador to South Korea, told me that four days later he had an icy meeting with the French ambassador in Seoul. Sneider presented U.S. intelligence evidence to the French envoy establishing that the reprocessing plant about to be sold was part of a nuclear weapons program. Nevertheless, France went ahead with negotiations on credit arrangements for the sale of the plant to Seoul, prompting a formal U.S. protest to Paris in July.

American anxieties concerning South Korean intentions were intensified in early 1975 when South Korea signed a contract with Canada for a heavy water reactor. Designed to operate on natural uranium, the heavy water type of reactor is not dependent on U.S. enriched uranium supplies like the light water reactors that South Korea was then beginning to obtain from the United States. The heavy water type of reactor costs much more than light water reactors. In U.S. eyes, therefore, the reason that South Korea was seeking to decrease dependence on U.S. enriched uranium was to get more freedom to pursue its nuclear weapons effort.

Throughout late 1975 and early 1976, the United States stepped up pressure on the South in the form of increasingly explicit threats to end the U.S. security commitment and to deny Export-Import Bank financing for U.S. civilian nuclear reactors. Finally, in July 1976, Park canceled the French contract and agreed to get one Canadian heavy water reactor instead of two. This strategic retreat temporarily appeased the United States. Unknown to Washington at the time, however, Park did not disband his nuclear research apparatus or abandon his quest for reprocessing technology.

One of the key scientists involved in the French reprocessing project, Chul Kim, now a professor at Aju University, told a South Korean journalist later that Park pursued a "roundabout" approach to acquiring reprocessing technology after cancellation of the French contract. "His idea was that we would learn each aspect of reprocessing technology separately, which would not be readily detected, and then learn how to integrate them later." Under the umbrella of a new Korean Nuclear Fuels

Development Corporation, Seoul purchased factories from France for uranium concentration and conversion, for the assessment of irradiated spent fuel, and for nuclear waste treatment, using the same $20 million loan that had previously been negotiated with France for the reprocessing plant. Of these, said Chul Kim, the most important was the facility for analyzing irradiated spent fuel, known as the Post-Irradiation Examination Facility. "This facility entails determining the ratio of radioactive material in the spent fuel," he explained, "moving spent fuel from the storage pool at the reactor site to a special shelter, and the measurement and dissolution of the spent fuel through special remote control procedures. These processes are akin to the key phase of reprocessing."[6]

When South Korea resumed secret discussions with France in 1978 to revive plans for importing the reprocessing plant, the United States soon found out. President Carter blocked the deal by intervening personally with French Prime Minister Valery Giscard d'Estaing. Washington was also able to block plans for construction of a forty-megawatt research reactor that could have produced plutonium. But Seoul managed to get the Post-Irradiation Examination Facility in place before U.S. intelligence agents grasped its significance. Located at Daeduk, this facility became the scene of tense encounters between South Korean scientists and U.S. experts who made unannounced inspection visits there. Under a 1974 agreement, the United States supplied the enriched uranium used to fuel South Korean civilian nuclear reactors. The agreement entitled American inspectors to check that South Korean nuclear facilities were being used for peaceful purposes. As *Nucleonics Week* reported, U.S. inspections were much more intrusive than comparable unannounced "challenge inspections" carried out by the International Atomic Energy Agency under its safeguards agreement with Seoul.[7]

Chun Doo Hwan, who seized power in a military coup after Park's assassination, badly needed U.S. support to legitimize his regime. He stopped aspects of the nuclear program that Washington specifically singled out as suspect. At the same time, he attempted to keep on good terms with influential leaders in the armed forces and the nuclear power industry who were still seeking to prepare the way for reprocessing. In 1984, Chun authorized a secret agreement with Canada that would have enabled Seoul to recycle spent fuel into "mixed oxide" fuel, which contains weapon-grade plutonium along with uranium oxide. When a journalist revealed the agreement, Seoul argued that "mixed oxide" fuel was needed to supply plutonium for the Canadian heavy water reactor obtained in 1976, plutonium that would be used, it was said, solely for civilian power production. The United States rejected this rationale and pressed successfully for termination of the project.

"This was the second time that we tasted bitter disappointment at the hands of the United States," recalled a leading South Korean science writer, Yu Yong Won, in a 1991 study that chronicled the nuclear weapons effort.[8] Yu outlined in detail the last-ditch efforts made by nuclear scientists and key defense officials to keep the program alive during the denouement of the Chun regime and the first two years after Roh Tae Woo became president in 1987 in the South's first free election. On August 18, 1989, Yu wrote, the Joint Chiefs of Staff presented a proposal for an all-out resumption of the nuclear weapons effort known as the "Triple XXX Plan" to Defense Minister Lee Sang Hoon. According to Suh Su Jong, who was chief secretary to the director of the South Korean Central Intelligence Agency at the time, Roh did not definitively reject "Triple XXX" until mid-1991, when the United States heard about it and confronted him.[9] Under U.S. pressure, Roh ordered a mass exodus of technicians from suspect nuclear facilities in Daeduk, and in late 1991, Roh shelved the Defense Ministry plan.[10] Roh did make one concession to the pro-nuclear hawks, however, by letting them start negotiations with British and French firms to reprocess spent fuel for South Korea as they were doing for Japan. Seoul would then have received either separated plutonium or mixed-oxide fuel, which would have been essentially the same as having its own reprocessing plant. Anti-nuclear groups led by Greenpeace exposed the negotiations, triggering preemptive U.S. diplomatic moves in London and Paris.[11]

REPROCESSING AND THE NUCLEAR OPTION

In December 1991 Roh pushed through the North-South denuclearization agreement despite resistance from the pro-nuclear hawks. Although the 1991 accord has yet to be implemented, it was a landmark event, setting the stage for the 1994 nuclear freeze negotiated with North Korea by the United States. In the absence of the North-South agreement, which explicitly barred Seoul, as well as Pyongyang, from developing reprocessing facilities, the North would not have agreed to shut down its Yongbyon reprocessing plant under the freeze.

The 1991 agreement touched off a profoundly significant controversy in the South between moderates and pro-nuclear hawks that persisted until the reduction of North-South nuclear tensions following the 1994 freeze. Since 1994, this controversy has lost much of its edge, especially after the June 2000 North-South summit, but the issues that it underlined are likely to resurface in the future.

The hawks argued that the 1991 agreement could have, and should have, prohibited reprocessing plutonium for use in making nuclear weapons without ruling out reprocessing for civilian purposes. Defenders of the agreement responded that it was an unavoidable necessity in the context of a divided Korea in which North Korea was perceived to be developing a nuclear weapons capability. Both defenders and critics alike served notice that a unified Korea will demand the same treatment enjoyed by Japan and will seek a new understanding with the United States and the IAEA superseding the 1991 accord.

President Kim Dae Jung, then an opposition leader, told me in 1992 that "when Korea is reunified, we will ask the IAEA for permission to build reprocessing facilities so there is no discrimination in the treatment accorded to us and to Japan." Roh had to give up reprocessing, he declared, "as a response to circumstances, because we are still divided, but it was opposed by our nuclear scientists and I am sure that the United States and the IAEA will understand the difference in the situation when we are united."[12]

Roh Tae Woo's successor as president, Kim Young Sam, honored the 1991 accord, but he looked the other way when many of his closest lieutenants criticized it. His handpicked chairman of the National Assembly Foreign Affairs Committee, Chong Chae Mun, called for a review of the agreement on May 29, 1993. Chong declared that "we know that we could generate nuclear power at a lower cost if we had reprocessing facilities, and we cannot continue to depend on foreign countries for nuclear fuel."[13] Responding to opposition demands for a review of the agreement in a National Assembly debate, Science and Technology Minister Kim Si Chung acknowledged that "it will become unavoidable for our country to have a nuclear fuel reprocessing capability in order to dispose of nuclear waste and to secure adequate energy supplies."[14] A leading deputy in the ruling Democratic Liberal Party, Lee Woong Hee, noted that the South had paid more than $2 billion to the United States for the enriched uranium needed to operate its reactors from 1974 to 1992 and that the cost of imported reactor fuel would steadily rise. "Reprocessing," he declared, "is the key to self-sufficiency."[15]

The leading academic critic of the 1991 agreement, Kim Tae Woo, then a researcher at the government-sponsored Korean Institute of Defense Analysis, wrote that "we will suffer enormous economic and technological losses if we are unable to possess uranium enrichment and plutonium reprocessing facilities." Kim contended that paragraph 2 of the agreement, permitting the peaceful use of nuclear energy, and paragraph 3, barring reprocessing, "are not only mutually contradictory but also unreasonable." It was necessary "to prevent the use of North Korea's nuclear facilities for military purposes through international inspection. But it was not necessary to give up reprocessing facilities and to deny us in perpetuity the right to possess such facilities, which is not denied under the NPT."[16]

Kim linked the acquisition of reprocessing facilities to South Korea's dream of eventually building a fast-breeder reactor as Japan is doing. Separated plutonium is necessary to fuel breeder reactors, he said, and a breeder reactor would be a "magic lantern" for South Korean development, "the state-of-the-art resource-recycling technology that could stretch the life-span of uranium about 60 times over its usage in the light water reactors that we now have."[17] Science writer Yu Yong Won underlined the potential importance of fast-breeders in dealing with the South's nuclear waste disposal. "We suffer great losses by being unable to reprocess," he wrote. "Our nuclear fuel storage facilities are reaching their saturation point. High speed breeder reactors are in the spotlight as the next generation reactors that can maximize the use of nuclear fuel, and reprocessing facilities are essential to the manufacture of these fuels."[18]

One of the leading figures in the South Korean nuclear industry, Choi Young Myung, chief of policy research at the Korea Atomic Energy Research Institute, has made no secret of his view that the South should be permitted to reprocess. In April 1990 Choi submitted a memorandum to the IAEA, "Long-Term Policy on National Nuclear Energy Development," in the course of which he states: "Regarding the nuclear fuel cycle, reprocessing after an interim storage of the spent fuel has received increasing attention in many countries. As far as our nuclear power generation strategy is concerned, we need to upgrade our reactors from the present 1000 megawatt capacity to that of small and medium scale advanced reactors. In particular, considering that the quantity of uranium deposits will be depleted within 50 years, it is necessary to reutilize the spent fuel. In light of this situation, what do you think about your basic positions in this regard?"[19]

Choi served as chairman of the Science and Technology Subcommittee of President Roh's Commission on the 21st Century. Addressing a meeting of the commission on February 27, 1991, he declared that "the nuclear fuel cycle is one area that we must carefully consider, and all possible diplomatic efforts must be used to obtain self-sufficiency in the area of reprocessing technology, since it is an aspect of the nuclear fuel cycle essential to the fulfillment of our technological potential in nuclear energy."[20] Japan is pursuing a long-term strategy in seeking to develop a reprocessing and fast-breeder reactor capability, Choi told me in April 1992. "They want to become the regional reprocessing center for East Asia, and they are gambling that plutonium will be more economical in thirty years than it is today. But we cannot afford to be dependent on Japan in such a critical aspect of our national existence."[21]

THE MISSILE GAP

At the same time that the United States was seeking to block Park Chung Hee's nuclear weapons program, a parallel struggle between Seoul and Washington was emerging behind the scenes over South Korean efforts to develop a missile delivery system. The United States was able to contain the South Korean missile program for three decades, until growing North Korean missile capabilities provoked a South Korean drive to keep pace with Pyongyang, which remains a critical issue in U.S.–South Korean relations.

Ironically, the United States inadvertently helped Seoul acquire missile technology by letting South Korean engineers handle the maintenance of the Nike-Hercules surface-to-air missiles used for air defense by U.S. forces in Korea. As Janne E. Nolan has related, a South Korean company was set up under U.S. military auspices in 1975 to keep U.S. missiles in repair, and 161 South Korean technicians subsequently received training in missile technology from U.S. military specialists and the Raytheon Corporation. Among other things, this training program covered the inner workings of the electronic systems in the missile. Most important, the South Koreans learned what would be involved in converting the Nike-Hercules from a defensive, surface-to-air missile to a surface-to-surface missile. In a surface-to-surface mode, the missile could be used for offensive as well as defensive purposes.[22] Converting the Nike-Hercules was one of the key objectives of a covert missile development program that Park had launched under his newly established Agency for Defense Development.

The Nike-Hercules operated with a solid-fueled motor. In 1977, when the Lockheed Corporation shut down a factory in Redlands, California, that made solid-fueled rocket motors, Seoul imported the second-hand equipment in the plant for $5 million. Export control officials in Washington were apparently asleep at the switch and did nothing to stop this deal. But they did prevent Lockheed from carrying out a related plan to teach South Korean technicians how to make solid-fuel rocket propellant. Later, they blocked an audacious effort by Seoul to purchase technology related to the Atlas-Centaur, an intermediate-range U.S. missile much more advanced than the Nike-Hercules.[23]

On September 26, 1978, South Korea successfully tested a surface-to-surface version of the Nike-Hercules, naming it the NH-K. Ignoring the U.S. technology involved, the Defense Ministry proudly announced that South Korea had become one of the seven nations capable of producing its own missiles.

Washington reacted to the 1978 test by demanding that Seoul pledge not to develop missiles with a range exceeding 112 miles. This commitment was embodied in a 1979 Memorandum of Understanding that Park accepted and then proceeded to subvert. Just as he continued his nuclear weapons effort after his strategic retreat on the issue of the French reprocessing plant, so Park kept his missile program intact after the 1979 negotiations. Chun Doo Hwan, however, proved more vulnerable to U.S. pressure. In 1982, he fired 850 officials and technicians involved in advanced missile development, including the director of the program, Lee Kyong Soo, and created a scaled-down missile development agency that was ordered to honor the 1979 accord.[24] Seoul subsequently developed two upgraded versions of the NH-K that had maximum ranges within the 112-mile limit. Both of these missiles, like the Nike-Hercules, can carry nuclear warheads. The missile was initially renamed Paekkom (White Bear) and later Hyunmoo (Wise Sword).

The missile program did not again become a focus of controversy between Seoul and Washington until the United States voiced its suspicions in 1989 that North Korea had a nuclear weapons program. South Korea reacted to this revelation with a covert effort to upgrade the Hyunmoo that was detected by U.S. intelligence in its early stages and terminated after U.S. protests. Following the 1993 North Korean test, however, Seoul began pushing Washington in earnest to renegotiate the 1979 memorandum, arguing that it was unfair for South Korea to be restricted to a missile range lower than the limit specified by the U.S.–sponsored Missile Technology Control Regime (MTCR), which permits missiles capable of carrying a 500-kilogram payload up to 187 miles.

The United States was willing to upgrade the South Korean limit to

187 miles, provided that Seoul meet two conditions. One was to formalize restrictions on the export of missile-related technology, which Seoul
did in 1995. The other was to permit U.S. inspections to assure that the
MTCR limit was not being exceeded. Seoul balked at the inspection proviso, and Washington eventually backed off, agreeing not to invoke the
1979 memorandum even if Seoul did upgrade the Hyunmoo missile to
187 miles. Meanwhile, pressures were building in the South for a much
more ambitious missile program that would counter the Rodong intermediate-range missile unveiled in the 1993 test. For the United States to
upgrade the permissible range of South Korean missiles from 112 to 187
miles was a meaningless gesture, "like giving a tiny piece of biscuit to a
fully grown elephant," wrote Kim Tae Woo. Kim urged that Seoul build
a missile with a range of at least 600 miles, a missile "able to reach the
northernmost point of North Korea if fired from the southernmost part
of the South"—and although he did not say it, Japan as well.[25]

Soon after the August 1998 North Korean Taepodong I launch, U.S.
reconnaissance satellites found that South Korea had built a rocket motor
test station without notifying Washington, and in April 1999 Seoul
flight-tested an upgraded Hyunmoo. Although the missile went only
thirty miles, U.S. experts speculated that Seoul had put only enough fuel
in the tank for a short flight in order to avoid a showdown with the
United States. Based on other evidence, they concluded that it might
have a range of as much as 310 miles.[26] The missile issue dominated a
July meeting between President Clinton and South Korean President
Kim Dae Jung, who later announced that Seoul had asked Washington
for permission "to develop and test missiles with a range of 310 miles,
which would cover the border with China and give the message to North
Korea that our missiles can counter theirs."[27]

Since there is little the United States can do to stop it, Washington has
tacitly approved research and development activity that would give Seoul
the option of upgrading its missiles to 310 miles. At the same time, it has
attempted to stop South Korea from actually making prototypes of the
upgraded missile. To back up its position, the United States has imposed
restrictions on exports to South Korea of ten items relevant for advanced
missile development. Tensions between Washington and Seoul over the
missile issue had not been resolved when the June 2000 North-South
summit led South Korea to suspend the upgrade program at its own
initiative. "We've got the technical capability to go 310 miles and beyond," a high official said. "But now we must consider the summit. If we
go ahead with the missiles, it could screw up the summit track."[28]

The pace and scope of South Korea's missile development will be significantly affected by the progress of its ambitious space satellite program. In 2001, Seoul had three communications satellites and three scientific research satellites that have been periodically launched on a commercial basis by the European Space Agency and the U.S. Air Force. But Seoul has also announced a $1 billion program to put a satellite into a low-earth orbit with a domestically built rocket by 2005. South Korean officials said the satellite would be used solely for peaceful purposes such as mapping, coastal surveillance, and weather forecasting, and that the rocket would be propelled by a liquid-fueled engine, not the solid-fueled type normally used for intercontinental missiles. Since space launch technology is directly applicable to military uses, however, Seoul's development of an independent satellite capability would undoubtedly intensify the cycle of suspicion among North Korea, South Korea, and Japan.

A meaningful U.S. effort to prevent a regional nuclear arms race and to promote a nuclear-free Korea would require tightened-up restrictions on technology transfers so that the United States does not give further help to South Korean missile and space programs. It would also presuppose a coordinated approach to limiting missile testing, production, and deployment by South Korea as well as North Korea.

The key to this effort would be U.S. readiness to negotiate basic changes, discussed earlier, in the character and role of U.S. conventional forces in Korea and to join with China, Russia, and Japan in ruling out the use of nuclear weapons in Korea. North Korea's June 16, 1998, offer to discuss the terms for terminating its missile development could be the starting point for a comprehensive series of arms-control negotiations that would be mutually reinforcing. For example, if the United States agrees to play the role of an honest broker and to remove what North Korea regards as threatening aspects of its conventional force presence, in return for missile limitations, Pyongyang would be more likely than it is at present to give up its nuclear weapons option and to permit a meaningful inspection regime. With North Korean participation, in turn, the possibility of negotiating a Northeast Asian nuclear-free zone embracing Japan would greatly improve. Based on the hypothetical assumption that the United States will, in fact, eventually recognize the need for a comprehensive arms-control process, I will in the next chapter consider in specific terms what all of the powers concerned would have to do to ensure a nuclear-free Korean peninsula.

CHAPTER 21

Guidelines for U.S. Policy

> What are nuclear weapons good for? For the United States,
> they're actually a grave political handicap. It's kind of hard for
> us to say to North Korea, "You are terrible people, you are
> developing a nuclear weapon," when the United States has
> thousands of them.
>
> —General Charles Horner, former commander of the
> U.S. Space Command and commander of U.S. Air
> Forces in the Gulf War, July 15, 1995

REGRETTABLY, General Horner is atypical, one of a small number of senior retired U.S. military officers who have questioned U.S. nuclear arms-
control and nonproliferation policies.[1] Despite its own reliance on nuclear
weapons, the United States does not, in fact, find it awkward at all to tell
North Korea not to develop them. With its self-image as the "only superpower," entitled to exercise global strategic dominance, the United
States has no moral qualms in attempting to impose its inequitable nonproliferation policies wherever possible.

Reviewing the successes and failures of U.S. nonproliferation policy,
North Korea must clearly be judged a major success story. The 1994
nuclear freeze agreement between Pyongyang and Washington not only
suspended the operation of North Korea's then existing plutonium production facilities but also stopped the construction of two new reactors
with a much bigger nuclear weapons potential. India, at the other extreme, has been the most spectacular U.S. failure. What distinguishes
these two cases? India is an emerging major power, conscious of its size
and driven by its historically rooted confidence in a great national destiny.
Little North Korea, by contrast, is preoccupied with its national survival,
not its national destiny, and reacted opportunistically to U.S. nonproliferation pressures.

When the end of the cold war left it economically adrift, Pyongyang
offered up its nuclear program as a bargaining chip in exchange for economic and political benefits. However, in doing so it did not lose sight of
the inequity in U.S. nuclear policies and, in particular, of what it per-

ceives to be a security threat posed by U.S. nuclear deployments in Northeast Asia. For this reason, as earlier elaborated, Pyongyang insisted on terms in the 1994 freeze agreement that kept its nuclear weapons option temporarily open. North Korea is not required to dismantle its frozen nuclear facilities until the United States has fulfilled its own obligations under the accord.

Most attention in the United States is focused on the U.S. obligation to arrange for the construction of two new light water reactors in cooperation with South Korea and Japan. North Korea is not likely to surrender its nuclear weapons option, however, unless the United States fulfills its broader obligations to move toward a meaningful normalization of relations that eases North Korean security concerns. One of the principal tests of U.S. bonafides in North Korean eyes will be whether Washington honors article 3, section 1 of the agreement, which states that "the United States will provide formal assurances against the threat or use of nuclear weapons by the United States." Seven years after the conclusion of the accord, the language of such assurances was still a sensitive subject of dispute between Washington and Pyongyang.

Even with article 3, section 1, the 1994 accord was inherently inequitable because it left the United States free to maintain nuclear forces in Northeast Asia while requiring North Korea to dismantle its nuclear facilities and permit intrusive IAEA inspections. The North Korean moderates who promoted the accord were prepared to swallow this inequity. They argued in internecine debates that normalized relations with the United States would lead, in time, to a more benign security environment while providing immediate economic relief. But there is still significant resistance in Pyongyang to carrying out key provisions of the agreement. Many of those who were willing to freeze the nuclear weapons effort are not ready to dismantle it entirely. Above all, they are reluctant to permit IAEA inspections sweeping enough to determine how much plutonium was accumulated before 1994 and whether clandestine facilities for fissile material production have been established to replace those that were frozen.

In order to get North Korea to comply fully with the 1994 accord, the United States would first have to show that it is prepared for reciprocal denuclearization measures sensitive to North Korean security concerns. At the very least, it would have to abandon its insistence, in principle, on the right to use nuclear weapons first against conventional forces and would have to provide the explicit bilateral security assurance to North Korea envisaged in article 3, section 1. Even that might not be sufficient to foreclose the possibility of a North Korean nuclear weapons capability. In all likelihood, Washington would have to take more far-reaching steps. Durable arrangements for a nuclear-free Korea would require U.S. participation in multilateral agreements with China, Russia, and Japan that prohibit the use of nuclear weapons in the peninsula itself and set the stage for a regional nuclear-free zone. To the extent that the United States moves in this direction, the climate will become progressively more propitious for definitive implementation of the 1994 agreement.

I begin this chapter by considering the key U.S. policy changes necessary for implementation of the 1994 accord and then suggest in specific terms what other steps the United States could take to promote denuclearization in Korea and a nuclear-free Northeast Asia.

IMPLEMENTING THE 1994 AGREEMENT

Hard-line critics of the freeze agreement in Pyongyang argue in internal debates that the United States, South Korea, and Japan do not really intend to build the two new reactors promised under the accord and that North Korea should, therefore, feel free to step up its preparations for possible resumption of its nuclear weapons program. To back up this argument, they point to the fact that construction of the two reactors has moved at a snail's pace and that the end is not in sight.

The accord set a conservative target date for the completion of the reactors by 2003. In 1994, that was a realistic estimate in terms of the technical problems involved, but it failed to take into account the tenuous political and financial support for the agreement in Washington, Seoul, and Tokyo. Under the most optimistic assumptions, the reactors could now be completed by 2008. More realistic projections suggest that they might not be completed until 2015 and might never be built at all unless the United States gives a much higher priority to their completion than has so far been the case.

The Clinton administration bullied South Korea and Japan into accepting virtually complete financial responsibility for building the reactors. South Korea agreed to cover $4 billion of the cost and Japan $1 billion in the expectation that the White House would get as much money out of Congress as it could to finance the multilateral consortium created to carry out the project, the Korean Energy Development Organization (KEDO). But Clinton never asked Congress for even a token U.S. contribution to the construction of the reactors. The only U.S. financial support for implementing the accord has been paying for the 500,000 tons of oil per year promised to Pyongyang, which has cost $40 million annually but could become more expensive in the years ahead.

Japan, in particular, resents the lack of U.S. financial support for the accord because it never liked the idea of light water reactors for North Korea in the first place. I had numerous conversations in 1994 with officials of the Ministry of International Trade and Industry and the Foreign Ministry who felt that such sophisticated reactors would be unsafe in North Korea and could lead to another Chernobyl in Japan's backyard. Pyongyang's energy problems could much more expeditiously and inexpensively be resolved, they said, with systems based on natural gas, coal, oil, and hydroelectric power. Instead of directly refusing to provide the funding, Japan has artfully stalled and delayed at each stage of the way, doling out the minimum amount necessary to avoid a showdown with its allies that would make Tokyo responsible for the collapse of the accord.

South Korea, like Japan, finds it galling to bear the financial responsibility for a project controlled by the United States. North Korea saw the 1994 agreement as a step toward normalization with Washington. While it raised no objection to U.S. collaboration with others in carrying out the accord, it insisted from the start that it would deal only with an American as chief negotiator in all contacts relating to the reactor project. Thus, the United States, which pays none of the bills, plays the leading role in KEDO. This anomaly aggravates what is already "a highly politicized working environment, with strains running through all aspects of the project," according to Mitchell Reiss, a former senior KEDO official.[2] Nevertheless, South Korea sees the reactors as potentially helpful to a unified Korea and is carrying out its commitments to KEDO, albeit with time-consuming wrangling over financial issues.

The strains within KEDO, coupled with confrontational North Korean bargaining tactics in dealing with the consortium, have led to continuing delays in negotiating critical agreements relating to specific aspects of the construction process and to the eventual operation of the reactors. A dispute over the wages paid to North Korean workers made it necessary to bring in laborers from Uzbekistan as part of the workforce. Much of the infrastructure at the Kumho site had been completed by 2001, notably roads, sewage, water, an electric power plant, and homes for workers. An entire mountain had to be leveled to prepare the site, and a new port had to be constructed to facilitate the import of heavy equipment. Forty routine agreements had been concluded by 2001, but five protocols involving key issues were still stalled. These will deal with the construction timetable; the schedule for North Korean repayments; regulatory procedures to ensure safety; arrangements for transferring the spent fuel now being stored under IAEA inspection out of the country; and above all, liability in the event of a nuclear accident.

Many of the issues encompassed by the stalled protocols are likely to be resolved only if an overarching nuclear cooperation agreement is negotiated between Pyongyang and Washington, and such an agreement, in turn, would not be likely to get congressional approval until North Korea permits the IAEA to conduct the inspections envisaged in the accord as a precondition for completion of the reactors.

A nuclear cooperation agreement is necessary because the Atomic Energy Act of 1954 requires the United States to negotiate one before U.S. reactor components or nuclear materials can be exported to any other nation. To strengthen the 1954 legislation, the Nuclear Non-Proliferation Act of 1978 imposed strict standards on nuclear exports. Foremost among these standards is a commitment by the recipient nations to cooperate with the IAEA in maintaining safeguards not only on nuclear materials and equipment received from the United States but also on any other nuclear material under its control. In the case of the North Korean reactors, U.S. firms have contracted to supply such key components as coolant pumps, making a cooperation agreement mandatory.

Congressional critics of the 1994 accord have served notice that North Korea must first satisfy IAEA inspectors before Congress will approve a nuclear cooperation agreement and thus open the way for completion of the reactors. The resulting atmosphere of uncertainty has cast a pall over negotiations on many of the stalled protocols, especially the one covering liability for nuclear accidents.

Charles Kartman, executive director of KEDO, has declared that "the biggest single problem in building nuclear facilities in North Korea relates to liability," that is, who pays in the event of another Chernobyl.[3] The standard practice is for the country where the reactor is located to pay itself or to find the funding, but even if North Korea agrees to sign a liability agreement, KEDO's contractors and subcontractors are not likely to be satisfied. Chernobyl required a massive international aid effort, and one of the possible formulas for resolving the liability problem under study by KEDO would involve some form of multilateral liability agreement.

The demand that North Korea must satisfy IAEA inspectors as a precondition for U.S. approval of a nuclear cooperation agreement goes beyond the 1994 accord. The language of the accord is deliberately vague in defining how the completion of the reactors and the timing of IAEA inspections are to be orchestrated. Article 4, section 3 states only that "when a significant portion of the light water reactor project is completed, but before delivery of key nuclear components, the DPRK will come into full compliance with its safeguards agreement with the IAEA." "Full compliance," section 3 adds, will include "all steps that may be deemed necessary by the IAEA, following consultations with the Agency with regard to verifying the accuracy and completeness of the DPRK's initial report on all nuclear material in the DPRK."

As a leading South Korean critic of the accord, Lee Dom Bok, has correctly pointed out, there is no explicit reference in the agreement to the IAEA's right to conduct "special inspections." This controversial type of inspection embraces not only the nuclear facilities declared by a signatory state but also suspect undeclared facilities. "Obviously, it is Ambassador Gallucci's interpretation that the reference to 'all steps deemed necessary by the IAEA' is an expression that encompasses 'special inspections,'" Lee observed. "We do not as yet have any assurance, however, that North Korea shares Ambassador Gallucci's interpretation."[4]

The issue of special inspections is likely to be an explosive one in future IAEA relations with North Korea just as it has been in the past. It was Pyongyang's refusal to permit special inspections of two waste dumps under the control of the North Korean Army that triggered the nuclear crisis of 1993 and 1994. Pyongyang objected to special inspections in principle as an intrusion on sovereignty, pointing out that the IAEA had not previously been able to conduct such inspections even in the case of Iraq after its defeat in a war. Since 1994, the IAEA has increasingly attempted to legitimize its right to inspect all suspect nuclear facilities in signatory countries by seeking acceptance of a new type of safeguards agreement known as Model Protocol 540. Countries accepting the new agreement would have to declare a much broader range of facilities as nuclear related than in the past. The IAEA would get virtually automatic access to suspect facilities and would not have to justify obtaining such access as it must in the case of special inspections under its existing Protocol 153 agreement with North Korea. In 2001, Model Protocol 540 had come into force in ten countries, including Japan. South Korea had signed it but not ratified it. The IAEA had not invoked it in dealing with North Korea but continued to warn Pyongyang that it will sooner or later demand special inspections unless Pyongyang comes forward on its own with information relating to a wide range of unresolved issues outlined in a ten-point December 1992 questionnaire.[5]

Since the IAEA inspection process could take two years or more, the Clinton administration urged North Korea to let the inspections start immediately so that they could be completed by the time a "significant portion" of the first reactor is finished. The Bush administration ratcheted up U.S. pressure on this issue. But North Korea has resisted, pointing out that the completion of a "significant portion" is not likely before 2006 at the earliest. This contentious issue could become a dangerous focal point of tensions unless a compromise is reached. In a meeting with North Korean Foreign Minister Paik Nam Soon on May 30, 2001, I proposed step-by-step IAEA inspections contingent on progress in completing each of the eight components of a "significant portion" of the first reactor as agreed in annex 4 of the KEDO supply agreement with Pyongyang. This is "worthy of consideration," Paik replied, "but it's premature to talk of it now, since they haven't even dug a hole yet."

David Albright, in a careful analysis of the known facts, concludes that "the available information cannot establish conclusively that North Korea has enough plutonium to construct a nuclear weapon." "The most credible worst-case estimate," he says, is that Pyongyang possesses from 6.3 to 8.5 kilograms of reprocessed plutonium.[6] If the amount should, in fact, prove to be 8.5 kilograms, this would be just enough for one nuclear weapon, which would require eight kilograms. Since this would be much more than the 90 grams that North Korea declared to the IAEA, full disclosure could be profoundly embarrassing for Pyongyang. But a face-saving diplomatic solution might well be possible, with the plutonium in question destroyed or placed in IAEA custody. Pyongyang might well cooperate in the inspection process and in finding a diplomatic solution if the amount turns out to be small. The problem might be more intractable in the event that it has a significant stockpile.

Determining whether North Korea produced enough plutonium before 1994 to make any nuclear weapons and, if so, how many, is a prerequisite for defusing nuclear tensions in Northeast Asia and inducing South Korea, Japanese, and U.S. cooperation in moving toward a nuclear-free Korea. For North Korea, however, keeping other powers guessing about its nuclear capabilities has proved valuable in diplomatic as well as strategic terms. Pyongyang is likely to calibrate its cooperation with the IAEA carefully, making piecemeal concessions linked directly to progress in completing the reactors. Definitive cooperation may well depend, as suggested earlier, on whether the United States creates a favorable atmosphere by making a "no first use" declaration; by honoring article 3, section 1; and by initiating steps toward a regional nuclear-free zone, starting with a six-power agreement (the United States, China, Russia, Japan, and the two Koreas) not to use, deploy, or manufacture nuclear weapons in the peninsula.

What is necessary to prevent a gradual unraveling of the 1994 accord is a bold U.S. regional denuclearization initiative that eases North Korean security concerns, accompanied by a U.S. readiness to compensate, in some measure, for its failure to complete the reactors by the 2003 target date specified in the 1994 freeze accord. In my meeting with North Korean Foreign Minister Paik Nam Soon on May 30, 2001, he warned that Pyongyang would resume its nuclear program unless the United States, South Korea, and KEDO provide two thousand megawatts of electric power by 2003—the amount that the reactors were supposed to provide. He cited President Clinton's October 20, 1994, letter to Kim Jong Il pledging "to facilitate arrangements for the funding and implementation of interim energy alternatives for the DPRK pending completion of the first reactor." The Bush administration dismissed this as an empty threat, arguing that the Clinton letter, despite its sweeping language, referred only to the heavy oil that is being provided under the accord. But North Korea has a legitimate grievance, and the U.S. posture only strengthens North Korean hawks who want to scrap the 1994 agreement.

At the very least, the United States should encourage South Korea and KEDO to provide energy help to the North. President Kim Dae Jung promised such help in the negotiations with Pyongyang that led to the June 2000 North-South summit. Although his failure to deliver on this promise has been publicly explained in terms of technical and financial problems, American pressure has been the most important constraint on South Korean energy assistance to the North. The Bush administration, seeking to demonstrate a "tougher" approach to Pyongyang than did Clinton, has emphasized "improving the implementation of the Agreed Framework" through direct U.S. inspections going beyond the letter of the agreement, together with speeded-up IAEA inspections. South Korean energy help to the North, Washington argues, would reduce U.S. leverage by providing alternatives to the electricity that the reactors are supposed to provide.

SHOULD THE ACCORD BE RENEGOTIATED?

Apart from the obstacles and uncertainties that make it difficult to carry out the 1994 accord, many observers have questioned from the start whether it makes sense in economic and technical terms for North Korea to rely so heavily on nuclear power and, in particular, whether the antiquated and inadequate North Korean electrical transmission grid can handle the amount of power that will be produced by two reactors with a capacity of two thousand megawatts. Instead of going ahead with the reactors, in this view, the 1994 accord should be scrapped by mutual agreement with North Korea and new arrangements concluded that would help Pyongyang meet its urgent energy needs more quickly with non-nuclear power plants. The costs to foreign donors would be much less than the $5 billion required for completing the reactors, it is argued, not to mention the additional outlays that would be required to upgrade the North Korean transmission grid.

If this argument could be decided on the basis of economic and technical considerations, there is little doubt that the verdict would be in favor of non-nuclear energy solutions as the fastest and cheapest way to overcome the energy bottlenecks that paralyze the North Korean economy. Who will bear the costs of connecting the reactors to the transmission grid with a high-voltage transmission line and then modernizing the grid? But as Bradley Babson of the World Bank has noted, the 1994 agreement "was driven by a security logic, not by an economic logic."[7] North Korea agreed to freeze its nuclear weapons program in return for light water reactors. It insisted on light water reactors because South Korea and Japan have them—the same reason it had attempted to get them from the Soviet Union long before the 1994 agreement was negotiated. Like Seoul and Tokyo, Pyongyang sees nuclear power as a necessary component of a diversified approach to meeting its energy needs. Moreover, precisely because Seoul and Tokyo have them, there is a political compulsion to get them as a prestigious symbol of modernity in the eyes of the North Korean people.

Faced with the crippling impact of energy shortages on industrial and agricultural production alike, North Korea might theoretically be willing to renegotiate the 1994 accord if the United States, Japan, and South Korea made a credible offer to finance non-nuclear power plants based on coal, liquefied natural gas, or gas brought by a pipeline from Sakhalin. But the costs of such a program, while less than those of the reactor program, would not be much less, and it is far from clear that any of the countries concerned would be willing to bear these costs. Congressman Christopher Cox, chairman of the House Republican Policy Committee, did not even mention the natural gas option when he said on May 18, 2000, that "if our object is to give them electricity, certainly a coal-fired plant or a hydro plant would make a great deal of sense."[8] What he no doubt had in mind, in any case, is not that the United States should help to provide non-nuclear power for North Korea but that South Korea and Japan should shift their support to a non-nuclear KEDO energy program.

While Japan might be amenable to such an approach, South Korea would probably not be, primarily because Seoul sees two new nuclear reactors in North Korea as a contribution to the economic development and energy security of a unified Korea. It has not had doubts about the 1994 accord as such but about the inequitable distribution of the KEDO financial burden. Indeed, the South might well seek to encourage Washington, Seoul, Tokyo, and the international financial institutions to join in modernizing the North Korean electrical transmission grid in ways that would facilitate its eventual integration with the South Korean grid. By 2001, Seoul had already spent $700 million of the $4 billion it has pledged in support of the reactor project, and South Korean public and private companies had lined up contracts totaling another $2.3 billion for the construction work ahead. As a State Department official observed, "The bribes have already been paid." More important, apart from this domestic political reality, Seoul fears that any change of policy on the 1994 agreement might have a destabilizing impact on North-South relations.

Unless North Korea itself raises the issue of renegotiating the 1994 agreement, in short, the United States should not risk a possible resumption of Pyongyang's nuclear weapons program by showing any ambivalence about supplying the promised reactors. On the contrary, keeping in step with the improving relations between the North and South since the summit, Washington should take more positive leadership in greatly accelerating the construction of the reactors while offering to negotiate basic changes in its own nuclear weapons posture in Northeast Asia.

BEYOND THE "NUCLEAR UMBRELLA"

Proposals for "no first use" pledges and nuclear-free zones are often dismissed as the naïve dreams of do-gooders who do not understand the harsh realities of international politics. But the harsh reality in dealing with North Korea is that the egocentric nuclear policies pursued by the United States will simply not work. If Washington and Seoul want North Korea to surrender its nuclear weapons option, they must be prepared to negotiate an end to the concept of nuclear deterrence as the basis for the South's defense. In this concept, the United States reserves the right to use nuclear weapons first if the North should attack the South with its conventional forces.

Although the United States has removed its tactical nuclear weapons from the South, it continues to deploy ICBMs and nuclear-capable cruise missiles in its Pacific submarine fleet and nuclear-capable aircraft on its Pacific aircraft carriers. Washington has not ruled out the reintroduction of nuclear weapons to the South or to the Pacific carriers and their use in any new Korean conflict. For this reason, North Korea has repeatedly called for lifting the U.S. nuclear umbrella over the South as a prerequisite for movement toward a nuclear-free peninsula. In August 1990 Pyongyang proposed "an agreement to assure the DPRK against the use or threat of use of nuclear weapons" as the price for its compliance with NPT inspection safeguards. When Ambassador Robert Gallucci met First Deputy Foreign Minister Kang Sok Ju in June 1993, following North Korea's withdrawal from the NPT, Pyongyang agreed to suspend its withdrawal only after Gallucci accepted the "principle" of "assurances against the threat and use of force, including nuclear weapons." This pledge was strengthened in article 3, section 1 of the 1994 freeze agreement, with its direct statement that "the United States will provide formal assurances against the threat or use of nuclear weapons by the United States."

The United States could honor article 3, section 1 with a unilateral pledge not to use nuclear weapons against North Korea so long as it remains a non-nuclear weapons state. But such a unilateral pledge would be regarded as a betrayal by South Korea, since China, which still has a security treaty with the North, possesses nuclear weapons. What the United States should do is press for a six-power agreement in which it would join with China, Russia, Japan, and the two Koreas in ruling out the use or deployment of nuclear, chemical, and biological weapons in Korea by the outside powers and the development or deployment of these nuclear weapons by the two Koreas. At the same time, Washington should take two other steps. To facilitate Chinese participation in a multilateral "no use" agreement, it should accept Beijing's long-standing offer to conclude an agreement renouncing the first use of nuclear weapons against conventional forces. To honor article 3, section 1, it should also give an explicit bilateral undertaking to Pyongyang that it will not use nuclear weapons against North Korea so long as it remains a non-nuclear weapons state. Such an undertaking can appropriately be given only if it is accompanied by a six-power "no use" agreement, which has long been supported by South Korean President Kim Dae Jung.

The United States first asserted its right to initiate the use of nuclear weapons against conventional forces during the cold war, when the Soviet bloc enjoyed an overwhelming advantage in troop strength and conventional firepower in Europe. NATO warned of an irresistible "human wave" attack by numerically superior Soviet forces, and a similar rationale was used to justify the threat of "first use" in deterring North Korea. But as Morton H. Halperin, director of the State Department's Policy Planning Council during the Clinton administration, wrote in 1992, "It is time for the United States to close its nuclear umbrella and develop a new strategy in response to the end of the cold war and the collapse of the Soviet Union."[9]

In Germany, both the Social Democratic and Green Parties have long argued that the "first use" doctrine is no longer necessary. The coalition agreement between the two parties that preceded their election victory in 1998 declared flatly that "the new Federal government will advocate renunciation of the first use of nuclear weapons." After taking office, German Foreign Minister Joschka Fischer made good on this pledge, stressing two reasons why NATO should revise its nuclear policy. First, he argued, "There are no longer tank divisions along our border that can break through to the English Channel within 48 hours. The first use policy was a response to a situation that has fundamentally changed." Second, Fischer declared, "If we are serious about non-proliferation, the existing nuclear powers must create a climate of disarmament to reduce the incentive on the part of others to go nuclear." Significantly, the Foreign Affairs Committee of the Canadian Parliament supported Fischer with a report stating that NATO "could preserve its policy of deterrence yet support the need for progressively limiting reliance on nuclear weapons by declaring that it would not use these weapons to respond to a conventional attack."[10]

The German stand provoked praise from the eminent retired U.S. diplomat, George F. Kennan, who lauded "the insight and courage shown by the new German government."[11] Defense Secretary William Cohen countered that retaining the first-use option increases ambiguity, "keeping any potential adversary who might use either chemical or biological weapons unsure of what our response will be."[12] As I will elaborate later, however, this position, if sustained, would completely undermine the long-standing premise of U.S. nonproliferation policy that the United States will not use nuclear weapons against non-nuclear NPT signatories.

In the case of Korea, the United States has a crushing second-strike capability and could retaliate with a variety of nearby nuclear weapons, and nuclear-capable weapons, if Pyongyang should ever stage a nuclear first strike. Given this credible deterrent, the threat of "first use" against conventional forces is overkill, needlessly undermining efforts to negotiate meaningful denuclearization agreements with North Korea. The "first use" policy strengthens North Korean hawks who want Pyongyang to put nuclear warheads on its missiles and gives North Korea an excuse for not implementing the 1991 North-South denuclearization agreement. When I met Kim Yong Nam, chairman of the Supreme People's Assembly, on May 5, 1998, I argued that Pyongyang should sign the pending nuclear test ban treaty to show the world that it had no intention of making nuclear weapons. "How can we tie our hands like that," Kim responded, "when your country reserves the right of 'first use' against us and threatens us with your nuclear umbrella. We want a nuclear-free Korean peninsula, but on a basis of true equity and reciprocity, not on a basis of special rights for a superpower."

In the running argument with Pyongyang since 1994 over how to implement article 3, section 1, the United States has refused to go beyond a 1978 declaration that it would not use nuclear weapons against any non-nuclear weapons state party to the NPT, "except in the case of an attack on the U.S. or its allies by such a state allied to a nuclear weapons state." Since the United States is allied to the South and Pyongyang is allied to China, a nuclear weapons state, the American stand has meant, in effect, that the United States reserves the right to use nuclear weapons in Korea.

Washington retained this language in the slightly modified version of the 1978 declaration provided to Ukraine as a "security assurance" when Kiev agreed to give up its nuclear weapons and sign the NPT in December 1994. Thus, the Ukraine model is no better, in North Korean eyes, than the 1978 declaration. The prerequisite for honoring Article 3, section 1 would clearly appear to be a multilateral "no use" accord embracing China. Such an agreement would enable the United States to modify the 1978 language to which it is now wedded.

The idea of renouncing the right of "first use" anywhere in the world is anathema to U.S. military leaders. If such a commitment is made to North Korea or China, they argue, it would set a global precedent that would dangerously restrict U.S. military freedom of action elsewhere. President Clinton revealed an acute awareness of the sensitivity of this issue during the White House meeting in which I participated on June

20, 1994, described earlier, immediately following Kim Il Sung's acceptance of the nuclear freeze concept in his meetings with me and former president Carter.

When Gallucci asked me to review precisely what Kim had said, Clinton listened impassively as I responded until I referred to Kim's emphasis on the need for an explicit U.S. commitment not to use nuclear weapons against the North. "Are they really serious about that?" he suddenly interjected. "How serious will they really be about that if we have negotiations with them?" I recall clearly his intent expression when I replied that this issue would be a "deal breaker" if the United States refused to give such an undertaking. I praised Gallucci for accepting the "principle" of "assurances against the threat or use of force, including nuclear weapons" during his June 11, 1993, meeting with Kang Sok Ju. This was sufficient at the time to keep North Korea in the NPT, I said, but "we will have to go much further than that if we really expect them to give up nuclear weapons." As Clinton looked at me stonily and fidgeted, several other nongovernmental specialists present assured him that the issue could be finessed without a categorical U.S. repudiation of the "first use" option.

Six years after this exchange, Charles Kartman, who succeeded Gallucci as the chief U.S. negotiator with North Korea during the Clinton administration, told me that the United States is prepared to honor article 3, section 1 but only after North Korea has satisfied IAEA inspection requirements. Kartman's interpretation is "reasonable," Gallucci said, if article 3 is read together with article 4, which emphasizes IAEA inspections. Gallucci added, though, that in negotiating article 3, he had "deliberately left open" the question of when the United States would have to fulfill its section 1 obligations.

Based on the language of the 1994 accord, American negotiators could plausibly argue that North Korea should prove its non-nuclear bonafides before the United States will rule out the use of nuclear weapons against Pyongyang. But pointing to the same language, North Korea, for its part, is likely to insist that the United States demonstrate its own nuclear bonafides first or at least agree to a compromise based on carefully synchronized steps by both sides.

A possible scenario for such a compromise would begin with a six-power "no use" agreement that would set the stage for an unconditional U.S. pledge not to use nuclear weapons against North Korea. This would be a "post-dated" pledge that would contain language making it operative when, and if, Pyongyang has satisfied its IAEA obligations. If the language of the pledge itself is categorical, North Korea might well re-

spond with definitive action to satisfy the IAEA and to surrender its nuclear weapons option once and for all. The real question, however, is not
what North Korea will do. It is whether the United States will give up its
global "first use" theology to achieve its objectives in Korea.

The Chemical Weapons Issue

In Washington doctrinal debates over "first use," defenders of the status
quo argue that the possession of chemical and biological weapons by
potential non-nuclear as well as nuclear-armed adversaries makes unre-
stricted U.S. freedom of action necessary. Since treaty obligations prevent
the United States from countering chemical or biological weapons with
retaliation in kind, the argument goes, nuclear weapons are necessary
both to deter and respond to the use of these "weapons of mass
destruction."

The issue of how to deal with North Korean chemical and biological
weapons capabilities is inseparable from the larger unresolved issue of
whether, or to what extent, nuclear weapons are necessary for U.S. security at all. Gen. Charles Horner and Gen. George Lee Butler, former
commander of the U.S. Strategic Air Command, have made a powerful
case for the complete elimination of U.S. nuclear weapons as part of a
global denuclearization process.[13] A distinguished expert panel sponsored
by the Brookings Institution, outlining the critical first steps needed to
move toward this goal, has called for de-alerting measures accompanied
by deep cuts in nuclear weaponry that would limit all nuclear weapon
states to two hundred strategic warheads each, or fewer.[14] Janne E.
Nolan, a member of this panel, has questioned the entire concept of
nuclear deterrence that underlies U.S. nuclear strategy, urging a reassessment of "the long-standing consensus that nuclear weapons prevented
war between the two superpowers." Pointing to "detailed accounts of
episodes in which accidents or false information led to inadvertent escalation and the near use of nuclear weapons over the last four decades,"
Nolan asked to what extent it was "sheer luck and not just strategy or the
judiciousness of leaders that prevented war."[15]

True believers in its efficacy assume that nuclear deterrence has now
become more essential than ever to forestall the use of chemical and
biological weapons as well as to counter them. But as the Brookings
report demonstrated in detail, this assumption "is based on the mistaken

notion that the effects of chemical and biological weapons are morally, militarily, and politically equivalent to those of nuclear weapons."[16]

Morally, if nuclear weapons are used to destroy stockpiles of chemical and biological agents, "it is unlikely that the effects of nuclear explosions would be, and would be seen as, less hazardous than the chemical or biological contamination that would result from conventional attacks." Thus, in the short term, "nuclear attacks could turn world opinion against the United States rather than against the country that had initiated the chemical or biological attack."

Militarily, it is extremely difficult to protect people against nuclear weapons. By contrast, shelters, protective gear, vaccines, and antidotes "can be highly effective" in protecting combatants and civilians alike against chemical and biological weapons. In the case of biological weapons, maximizing their impact requires "extreme atmospheric stability," which makes their effective use "technically and operationally difficult," and "no nation is known to possess biological weapons capable of inflicting large numbers of casualties."

Politically, the Brookings report concluded, "explicit nuclear threats undermine non-proliferation goals," and "it is doubtful that any statement or policy could substantially bolster or detract from the existential deterrence that derives from the mere possession of nuclear weapons." Threatening to use nuclear weapons in response to chemical and biological attacks would shatter the existing global taboo against the use of nuclear weapons. Moreover, it would undermine the basic premise of U.S. nonproliferation policy, embodied in the 1978 security assurance and reaffirmed in 1995, that the United States would not use or threaten to use nuclear weapons against non-nuclear NPT signatories.

Contrary to common belief, the Brookings report showed, it is not clear that U.S. nuclear threats deterred the use of chemical or biological weapons during the Persian Gulf War. There is evidence that Iraq "was unable, rather than unwilling, to use its chemical weapons" as a result of the rapid and widespread destruction of Iraqi airfields, command and control systems, and lines of communication by the allied bombing campaign.[17]

Even if one believes in the efficacy of nuclear threats as a deterrent against the use of nuclear weapons, it does not follow that threats to use nuclear weapons against chemical attacks would serve U.S. interests. Indeed, the United States is hamstrung in pursuing its interest in a nuclear-free Korea by the current confusion in its nonproliferation policy over the chemical weapons issue. This confusion was illustrated when thirteen African states concluded an agreement in 1996 creating an African Nuclear Weapons-Free Zone. The United States signed a protocol pledging to respect the accord, which barred the use of nuclear weapons against any signatory state. At the same time, the White House issued a qualification stating that signing the protocol "would not limit the options available to the United States" in response to an attack by a signatory using "weapons of mass destruction." The Pentagon has repeatedly emphasized that the United States would rely on both conventional and nuclear weapons to respond to chemical aggression, and military exercises in Korea known as "Nimble Dancer" have explicitly envisaged tactical nuclear strikes in retaliation against North Korean chemical attacks against the South.[18]

In order to honor article 3, section 1 and thereby get North Korea to give up its nuclear weapons, the United States would have to resolve the ambivalence in its nonproliferation policy over the chemical weapons issue. In place of insistence on the right of "first use" in the name of countering chemical attacks, a more realistic policy would focus on persuading North Korea to join the convention barring the use of chemical weapons. Pyongyang has already signed the biological weapons convention. The United States could press for universal adherence to these conventions and their enforcement by the United Nations. The U.N. Security Council could impose sanctions against countries violating these conventions, including military action to destroy chemical and biological weapon production and storage sites. If these steps fail and the United States becomes embroiled in a conflict with a country having such weapons, the Brookings report concludes, "production and storage sites and delivery vehicles could be destroyed preemptively in the first phase of the war." Should any chemical and biological weapons survive these preemptive strikes, "massive conventional assaults against military targets could limit the scope of chemical and biological attacks" without resorting to nuclear weapons.[19]

As a practical matter, doctrine aside, would any South Korean government actually permit the United States to use nuclear weapons against the North? One of the earliest South Korean critics of the U.S. nuclear posture in the peninsula, Professor Joo Hong Nam of the National Defense College, wrote in 1987 that "the dilemma for South Koreans is whether it would be morally acceptable to see the United States use nuclear weapons against the Korean people in the North. Indeed, the South Koreans are more inclined to regard the U.S. nuclear idea as a threat rather than as a war-fighting strategy, since they have never wanted the United States to destroy their own people in the North."[20]

ASIATOM and a Nuclear-Free Zone

A six-power "no use" declaration, a U.S. " no first use" pledge, and a bilateral U.S. security assurance to North Korea are all essential first steps toward a nuclear-free Korea. But they would, after all, be mere confidence-building measures. To be more than paper promises, they should be accompanied by concrete efforts to assure that the civilian nuclear power programs being pursued by North Korea, South Korea, and Japan operate under effective multilateral safeguards trusted by all parties.

IAEA inspections alone would not be sufficient to accomplish this objective. Given the distrust of Japan resulting from the fact that it possesses reprocessing capabilities, IAEA inspections should operate in parallel with a regional inspection regime in which the two Koreas, or a unified Korea, would directly participate on an equal basis with Japan.

To break the cycle of suspicion between Japan and the two Koreas, it is necessary to establish a regional nuclear energy organization (ASIATOM) comparable to EURATOM. The purpose of ASIATOM would be to facilitate transparency, the safe operation of nuclear facilities, the safe disposal of nuclear waste material, and, above all, the coordinated management of plutonium and enriched uranium stocks held by all the member states. This is not pie in the sky. There is already significant support in both Japan and South Korea for the ASIATOM concept, driven by interest groups that want to legitimize and expand the civilian use of nuclear power. South Korea, looking to the expiration of its nuclear cooperation agreement with the United States in 2013, wants a new, revised agreement to permit both plutonium reprocessing and uranium enrichment.[21] An ASIATOM inspection regime should logically make such a change more acceptable to the United States. However, Washington has been cool to the ASIATOM concept, recognizing that it would nullify many aspects of its bilateral nuclear cooperation agreements with Tokyo and Seoul and weaken U.S. control over their nuclear programs.

Getting North Korea to join would be the biggest hurdle in establishing ASIATOM. When and if the two new reactors are built at Kumho, however, Pyongyang would be dependent on the United States and other external sources for fueling them and might become more amenable to regional cooperation. In the context of a normalization of North Korean relations with Washington and Tokyo, and of a nuclear cooperation agreement between Pyongyang and Washington, North Korean participation in ASIATOM would become a realistic objective, especially if

the United States has shown increased sensitivity to North Korean anxieties concerning the U.S. nuclear posture in Northeast Asia.

Since ASIATOM inspection safeguards would mean a definitive surrender of its nuclear weapons option, North Korean participation might well
depend on the establishment of a regional nuclear-free zone that would
bar nearby U.S. nuclear weapon deployments. The model for such a zone
could be the treaty concluded by ten Southeast Asian nations in December 1995. The Southeast Asian accord commits the signatories not to
"develop, manufacture or otherwise acquire, station or transport nuclear
weapons by any means, or test and use nuclear weapons" either inside or
outside the zone and commits them to prohibit other states from violating these restrictions within their territory. Its implementation has been
blocked by the refusal of the United States to sign a protocol pledging to
respect its provisions. China has signed such a protocol. But the United
States wants assurances that the treaty would not impede the transit of its
nuclear-armed ships and submarines. Although the treaty permits the
"innocent passage" of warships and submarines, the overflight of aircraft,
and stopovers in ports and airfields, it gives each signatory state the right
to decide whether passage in a given case is indeed "innocent" or is
related to the possible use of nuclear weapons in combat operations.

In the case of Northeast Asia, a key impediment to the establishment
of a nuclear-free zone is the fear that North Korea might use chemical or
biological weapons even if it abjured nuclear weapons. Thus, the efforts
proposed earlier to obtain North Korean agreement to global conventions barring chemical and biological weapons would greatly facilitate
progress toward a nuclear-free zone.

As an example of how a nuclear-free zone could be implemented,
Kumao Kaneko, former director of the Nuclear Energy Division in the
Japanese Foreign Ministry, has proposed that such a zone encompass a
circular area with a two thousand-kilometer radius from a central point at
Panmunjom in Korea. Japan, North Korea, South Korea, Taiwan, and
Mongolia would join in a treaty commitment not to make or acquire
nuclear weapons or to permit them on their territory. As in the Southeast
Asian accord, China, Russia, and the United States would be asked to
sign protocols affirming "respect" for the accord and pledging explicitly
not to deploy or test nuclear weapons within the treaty zone or to attack
with nuclear weapons any of the five non-nuclear signatories.[22]

Significantly, while the proposal would bar U.S. nuclear deployments
inside the treaty zone, it would not affect U.S. missile-launching submarines and other U.S. nuclear deployments outside the area, thus leaving

the United States free to use ICBMs against countries other than the five signatories.

John Endicott, former director of the Pentagon's National Institute of Strategic Studies, has mobilized the support of prominent retired military officers from potential signatory countries for an institutionalized negotiating process designed to produce a treaty less ambitious in its scope than that proposed by Kaneko. A series of conferences has mapped specific plans to establish a Northeast Asia Limited Nuclear-Free Zone Agency charged with conducting negotiations leading to the projected treaty. Endicott's proposal would define a circular zone centered at Panmunjom with a radius of twelve hundred nautical miles embracing part of China and Russia and all of Taiwan, Japan, Mongolia, and the two Koreas. The United States would pledge to respect the zone. The ultimate objective would be prohibition of all nuclear deployments within this zone. Initially, however, only tactical nuclear weapons would be prohibited.[23]

Most proposals for a Northeast Asian nuclear-free zone envisage the exclusion of nuclear weapons from parts of east and northeast China. Beijing has rejected such proposals, arguing that it would need maximum tactical flexibility in the event of a war over Taiwan and pointing to U.S. and Russian nuclear deployments in the Pacific as the basic justification for its own nuclear deployments. Chinese agreement to include parts of its territory in the zone would not be easy to negotiate under any circumstances, but if such an agreement is possible, it would require major concessions by the other powers concerned, including explicit U.S. and Russian commitments to remove nuclear deployments from the zone; a U.S. pledge to keep out of any war over Taiwan; removal of Taiwan from the scope of the U.S.–Japan Defense Guidelines adopted in 1996; and agreed limits on the character and coverage of any U.S.–Japan Theater Missile Defense (TMD) system. These concessions would be a reasonable price to pay for Chinese participation in the zone. Quite apart from the issue of a nuclear-free zone, I have spelled out in detail elsewhere the many reasons why the United States should avoid involvement in any war over Taiwan and the strong case in favor of limiting any TMD system to avoid conflict with China.[24]

In the debate between pro-nuclear and anti-nuclear forces in Japan, the anti-nuclear forces are increasingly focusing on the goal of a nuclear-free zone. Welcoming the Southeast Asian treaty, *Mainichi* said that it "raises the issue of a possible similar agreement for Northeast Asia" and called for "resilient efforts to create a chain of nuclear-free zones by na-

tions that reject the possession of nuclear weapons of their own and refuse the protection offered by nuclear umbrellas."[25] In August 1999, *Asahi* declared that "we must weaken and eventually eradicate the raison
d'etre of the nuclear umbrella by turning the Japanese archipelago, the
Korean peninsula, northeastern China, and the Russian Far East into a
nuclear-free zone." It is time, *Asahi* said, "for Japan to begin to talk to
the United States, China, and Russia about accepting this idea."[26]

This endorsement of the nuclear-free zone concept by two leading
newspapers reflects an increasing readiness in Japan to question the
premises of the U.S.–Japan security relationship. For example, former
Prime Minister Morihiro Hosokawa has asked: "How do we reconcile
our dependence on the U.S. nuclear umbrella with our purported commitment to an anti-nuclear policy? Why, in any case, are 47,000 U.S.
troops necessary in Japan?"[27] If a nuclear-free zone could be established,
Japan would no longer feel the need for its U.S. nuclear umbrella; and in
any case, the Japanese public has long questioned whether the United
States would really protect Japan in the event of a nuclear exchange with
Russia, China, or North Korea. Even at the height of the cold war, an
authoritative expert group sponsored by *Yomiuri* concluded that it would
be "highly unthinkable" for the United States to risk such an exchange
for the sake of Japan. The Communist powers could use Japan as a hostage to deter an American attack, the study said, and there would be
"little practical meaning" in the destruction of Russian and Chinese cities
after "Tokyo and Osaka had been turned into a second Hiroshima and
Nagasaki."[28] Pro-nuclear hawks in Japan have viewed the U.S. nuclear
deterrent as a temporary expedient, offering a modicum of political and
psychological protection in dealing with nuclear-armed neighbors pending the day when Japan gets its own nuclear armament. Conversely, in
the eyes of the anti-nuclear majority, the U.S. umbrella has an essentially
symbolic value as a rationale for keeping Japan non-nuclear.

Despite a growing mood of reappraisal throughout the countries of the
region, the prospects for a nuclear-free zone in Northeast Asia appear
dim in the foreseeable future. The United States is not likely to withdraw
its nuclear umbrella over Korea, unless this can be orchestrated with a
significant reduction in the danger of a conventional conflict in the peninsula and meaningful steps by North Korea to dismantle its nuclear facilities and limit its missile development. As I have shown in this and earlier
chapters, however, what the United States is itself ready to do, or not
ready to do, to modify its own military posture will largely determine
what the North and South will do. The North is likely to accept limits on

its missile program only in return for changes in aspects of the U.S. conventional military presence that it regards as threatening, and the willingness of the United States to modify its nuclear posture will critically affect whether and when Pyongyang gives up its nuclear option.

RESOLVING THE MISSILE ISSUE

The central goal of American policy should be getting North Korea to rule out the development of nuclear weapons. However, instead of focusing on the wide-ranging trade-offs necessary to achieve this goal, the United States has been preoccupied with the ancillary issue of North Korean missile capabilities. Missiles can be used as delivery systems for nuclear weapons, but even if a deal could be negotiated with North Korea curbing or ending its missile program, this would not stop Pyongyang from developing nuclear weapons delivered by other means.

North Korea's missile capabilities are important in military terms primarily because they greatly strengthen its conventional military posture in relation to South Korea and Japan. The danger of a North Korean long-range missile threat to the United States has been greatly exaggerated by proponents of a U.S. national missile defense system. It is true that the medium-range North Korean Nodong missile, which is already deployed, can reach Japan and U.S. bases in Japan. But the long-range Taepodong missile tested in 1998 is an expendable bargaining chip. Making it operational would require money and foreign help that Pyongyang does not have. More important, North Korea is keenly aware that an attack on the United States would lead to devastating retaliation and that preparation for a Taepodong launch would be readily detectable by U.S. satellites. The reason that it has pursued long-range missile development is not to commit national suicide. Rather, the military rationale for the Taepodong is deterrence, as discussed earlier, and diplomatically, it gives Pyongyang powerful leverage in dealing with Washington on security and economic issues alike, as the dialogue between Secretary of State Albright and Kim Jong Il in October 2000 demonstrated.

A careful examination of the North Korean missile program shows that the danger of a Taepodong threat to the United States is hypothetically possible but improbable. In its 1993 test, North Korea had shown that the Nodong missile had a range of 600 to 800 miles. In 1998, a much bigger Nodong missile was used as the first stage of a three-stage missile, known as Taepodong I, that overflew the northern tip of the main Japanese island of Honshu and splashed down in the Pacific Ocean 1,200 miles from its launch site.

The third stage did not ignite and the satellite was not placed in orbit, as North Korean propaganda claimed. However, the launch made clear for the first time that North Korea had acquired staging technology, which is essential for intercontinental-range missiles, since the staging of the first two stages had worked successfully. The fact that the third stage was solid-fueled was a surprise and could also prove to be important, even though this first attempt to use a solid-fuel engine failed. If Pyongyang is able to master solid-fuel technology or has access to it from foreign sources, this would be a big plus for propelling missiles to intercontinental distances.

Given its altitude, the 1998 launch did not violate Japanese airspace. But Japanese of all persuasions viewed it as provocative and threatening because it left no doubt that Pyongyang could deploy medium-range missiles capable of hitting any part of Japan with a one-thousand-kilogram (one ton) payload, the minimum requirement for a nuclear warhead. So far, the Nodong missile does not have accurate targeting. In assessing the accuracy of missiles, experts use a concept known as the "circular error of probability." They estimate the radius of a circle in which one out of every two warheads is likely to land. The radius in most Nodong estimates is three miles or more. Still, it is understandable for Japanese and U.S. military planners to assume that in time the Nodong could do significant military damage to Japan and to U.S. bases there in the event of a conflict.

In contrast to the demonstrated potential of the Nodong, it is highly debatable whether North Korea could develop long-range missiles capable of reaching U.S. territory within any predictable time frame. Yet proponents of a U.S. national missile defense system base their case largely on the specter of an imminent North Korean missile strike against the United States.

Even before the 1998 test, a congressionally mandated commission chaired by Donald Rumsfeld, later to become secretary of defense, called for deployment of such a system, warning that North Korea, Iran, and other "rogue states" might acquire the technology for long-range missiles without being detected by the United States.[29] When North Korea's 1998 test did, in fact, reveal capabilities greater than those previously detected, this warning was vindicated. The Rumsfeld Commission was justified in pointing to the limitations of U.S. intelligence. But the commission and other advocates of a missile defense system have attempted to have it both ways. On the one hand, they cite intelligence limitations as the basis for warning of a possible undetected danger. On the other, brushing aside these limitations, they project specific timetables for North Korean deployment of long-range missiles, such as three to five years, that have been largely guesswork. To incur the heavy costs and risks that would go with the proposed system on the basis of these estimates would be insupportable. Apart from the fact that some versions of the system could cost up to $240 billion,[30] and growing doubts about whether it could be counted upon to work, the destabilizing impact of such a system on existing and potential arms-control agreements with Russia and China would undermine, not enhance, U.S. security.

Most of the projections made by advocates of a missile defense system present hypothetically possible North Korean capabilities as probabilities or certainties. CIA assessments and those of independent experts differ primarily over how much emphasis should be given to the unresolved technical problems facing North Korean scientists. Thus, there is widespread agreement with the CIA estimate that if the Taepodong I were converted to a missile, it could conceivably deliver a "light payload" of twenty to thirty kilograms suitable for chemical or biological weapons to Alaska or Hawaii. The argument comes over how long it might take for Pyongyang to overcome the "important technical issues" acknowledged by the CIA and overcome the limitations of missiles as delivery vehicles for delivering chemical and biological weapons, especially biological weapons.

First, in order for North Korea to deploy the Taepodong I, the third stage would have to work. Second, as a White House spokesman said on the day after the 1998 test, even if it did work, North Korea has yet to "master the unique and fairly daunting challenges of returning a re-entry vehicle back to earth so that it can re-enter the earth's atmosphere to hit a target without burning up."[31]

The Taepodong II would have a bigger warhead and a longer range. But it is generally agreed that a two-stage Taepodong II would be able to deliver a payload of "several hundred" kilograms, at most, to Alaska or Hawaii, and an even lighter payload to the western continental United States. A three-stage Taepodong could deliver several hundred kilograms anywhere in the United States.

None of the scenarios envisaged in U.S. intelligence projections, in short, suggest that any North Korean missiles now under development would be able to hit any part of U.S. territory with a nuclear warhead. The threat posited is one of a limited chemical or biological attack.

In late 1998 the CIA estimated that the Taepodong II could be deployed "in a few years." But this is pure speculation. The pace of North Korean missile development will be governed by whether it gets foreign help.

To make a warhead small enough to be deliverable on a missile, experts say, Pyongyang would need various kinds of specialized equipment, such as high-speed X-ray cameras, necessary for testing purposes. To upgrade the accuracy of its targeting, it would need more advanced gyroscopes and other guidance and control technology than it is now believed to possess, though relatively modest improvements in accuracy might be possible without foreign help. To avoid burnup during reentry, it would need heat shields with a greater capacity to withstand stress than the two tests so far have demonstrated, such as sophisticated ceramic shields. Many of the most effective materials are not commercially available. To build a first-stage booster with enough propulsion power, it would need an engine bigger than the one used in the Taepodong I, which it could make by clustering four of its Nodong engines. To house this engine, however, the booster itself would have to be much bigger in diameter. Making this larger booster would require a new generation of lathes and other machine tools to replace the ones obtained in earlier decades for industrial purposes, mostly from Moscow.

China built its medium-range DF-3 missile with aluminum, since the distance that a missile can be propelled with a given thrust depends on its weight. In order to follow suit, North Korea would have to find a foreign supplier willing to provide a better grade of aluminum than North Korea is now able to make.

Where would foreign help come from? Suspicions of a Chinese hand abound in Washington, fed by leaks from elements in the U.S. intelligence agencies who believe U.S. China policy is too "soft." One line of speculation focuses on Pakistan and Iran as conduits for technology originally obtained from China and passed on to Pyongyang in return for North Korean help in building their own missiles. Some analysts speculate that unemployed Russian rocket engineers are now working for Pyongyang. But there is no conclusive evidence so far indicating that Pyongyang has in fact received, or is likely to receive, significant help from foreign governments.

Fears of foreign help underpin the recommendations of the Rumsfeld Commission. The commission report rejected the long-standing CIA assumption that missile development can be detected in time because it requires tests and an indigenous infrastructure exposed to satellite surveillance. Instead, the report warned that "rogue states" could get key missile components or already assembled missiles from foreign sources and launch long-range missiles without tests. This is a hypothetical possibility, but the commission offered no evidence of such foreign help that would justify incurring the costs and risks involved in deploying its proposed missile system. Most evidence suggests, on the contrary, that Pyongyang has put together the Taepodong on its own, improvising with dual-use technology picked up wherever possible on the international market.

The jerry-built character of the North Korean missile effort was underlined when a privately operated U.S. reconnaissance satellite conducted detailed studies of the site used in the 1993 and 1998 tests. "It's the mouse that roared," commented space expert John E. Pike of the Federation of American Scientists, who directed a study of the satellite imagery. The federation study declared that "this modest and underwhelming facility is barely worthy of note, consisting of the most minimal imaginable test infrastructure." Citing the absence of transportation links, paved roads, propellant storage facilities, and staff housing, the analysis concluded that "it is quite evident that this facility was not intended to support, and in many respects is incapable of supporting, the extensive test program that would be needed to fully develop a reliable missile system."[32] By contrast, the Rumsfeld Commission declared, without elaboration, that "the ballistic missile test infrastructure in North Korea is well-developed."[33]

Opponents of a U.S. missile defense system have focused on whether it would be workable. A study by the Union of Concerned Scientists has shown conclusively that such a system could easily by foiled by a variety of decoys and countermeasures.[34] Some observers have pointed out that relatively modest missile defenses based close to North Korea or other "rogue states" would be more effective than a U.S.–based system, less provocative to Russia and China, and much cheaper. But the larger question is whether Pyongyang is really hell-bent on pursuing its missile program or is ready to negotiate its "discontinuation," as it offered to do in its June 16, 1998, statement—and if so, what U.S. concessions this would require.[35]

The most intractable issue in arms-control negotiations with Pyongyang could prove to be medium-range missiles. North Korea is genuinely concerned that Japan might use its civilian nuclear reactors and its space satellite program to develop missiles with nuclear warheads. Pyongyang would no doubt seek to retain medium-range missiles to maximize its leverage in dealing with Tokyo and to deter any future U.S. military involvement in Korea.

To get North Korea to end or curtail its missile development, the United States would have to combine military concessions, such as the possible withdrawal of combat aircraft, with economic incentives. In addition to further relaxing sanctions and continuing to provide large-scale food aid, it should give top priority to negotiating the removal of North Korea from the State Department's terrorist list so that World Bank and other multilateral aid can begin. Similarly, to convince North Korea to phase out the deployment of existing Nodong missiles, Japan would have to supplement U.S. military concessions with a large financial aid package as part of its own normalization agreement with North Korea.

Faced with North Korean missiles that make its bases in Northeast Asia increasingly vulnerable, the United States should logically welcome a graceful way to disengage gradually from Korea—especially if the possibility of North Korean nuclear and missile capabilities can be foreclosed as part of the bargain and if disengagement promotes peace in Korea. But U.S. policy is hamstrung by two obsolete premises that would have to be reconsidered in order to move toward a nuclear-free Korea. The first is that U.S. forces must remain in Korea indefinitely as part of a vaguely defined U.S. role as a "stabilizer" and "balancer" in Asia. The second, and more fundamental, is that the United States is entitled to use nuclear weapons first against conventional forces and thus cannot contemplate denuclearization agreements that would include an end to the U.S. nuclear umbrella over Korea and eventually Japan.

If U.S. policy remains frozen in a cold war mold, the two Koreas and Japan appear to be headed for a nuclear and missile arms race. This outcome need not be inevitable in the context of the North-South dynamic within Korea itself, or as the next five concluding chapters show, in terms of the regional dynamics in Northeast Asia as a whole. But it is a real danger. Surveying the decades ahead, Japanese Korea specialist Hajime Izumi said in 1998 that "if North Korea does acquire nuclear weapons, we can live with such a North Korea, just as we live with a China that has at least thirty intermediate-range missiles deployed near Japan. We can live with such a North Korea, but we will need engagement to make it behave more realistically and we will, of course, need nuclear deterrence."[36]

PART V

Korea in Northeast Asia

CHAPTER 22

Will History Repeat Itself?

IN DECIDING whether to continue the American military presence and the American nuclear umbrella in Korea—and if so, for how long—the United States must consider not only American interests in Korea itself but also the broader impact of American policies on regional stability and U.S. interests in East Asia as a whole. Would the indefinite continuance of the American presence in the South promote regional stability and positive U.S. relations with Japan, China, and Russia, as its proponents argue? Or would a gradual process of disengagement, culminating in agreements to neutralize and denuclearize Korea, better serve American interests and those of the East Asian powers?

I cautioned in part 3 against an abrupt disengagement, suggesting instead a finite transitional period of perhaps ten years during which the United States would be prepared to redeploy and withdraw some or all of its combat forces in Korea, especially its combat aircraft, in exchange for North Korean pullbacks of forward-deployed forces and steps to limit or end its missile and nuclear development. The United States would seek to promote a reduction of military tensions in the peninsula during this period by adopting a more balanced posture in dealing with the North and South. I showed that past U.S. and South Korean tension-reduction proposals have been stacked against the North and proposed more equitable arms-control trade-offs that are likely to be acceptable to Pyongyang. As tensions at the thirty-eighth parallel decline and adversarial relations between the United States and North Korea come to an end, Pyongyang might well agree to the continuation of a reduced U.S. ground force presence. But the ultimate U.S. objective should be to withdraw all U.S. forces if agreements can be concluded with China, Russia, and Japan barring the future deployment of military forces in the peninsula. China and the United States would then terminate their mutual security treaties with Pyongyang and Seoul. Korea would become a neutral buffer state and, as such, would be a stabilizing force in Northeast Asia.

As I showed in part 4, U.S. denuclearization initiatives should logically accompany the neutralization of the peninsula as an arena of conventional military conflict. In the absence of such initiatives, continued uncertainty concerning North Korea's nuclear program would strengthen pro-nuclear hawks in Tokyo and Seoul, leading to a nuclear arms race.

The standard argument against neutralization and denuclearization proposals is that the withdrawal of U.S. conventional forces and the U.S. nuclear umbrella would make Korea a power vacuum and invite a repetition of the struggle between neighboring powers for dominance in the peninsula that occurred at the turn of the century. It is such a struggle, the argument runs, that could prompt a unified Korea to develop nuclear weapons. President Kim Dae Jung and other South Korean and U.S. leaders who have called for a post-reunification U.S. military presence in Korea argue explicitly that it will be needed to balance Chinese, Japanese, and Russian power.

In contrast to the South's position, the North maintains that once Korea is unified, it will not be a power vacuum but will become a strong power in its own right, able to withstand the pressures of its giant neighbors and to play an independent role as a neutral buffer. The continued presence of U.S. forces would be destabilizing, in this perspective, provoking intervention by other powers. But North Korean leaders distinguish between before and after unification. Pending unification, they say, American forces would be welcome if the United States shifts to the role of an honest broker, as discussed in part 3.

Gradual U.S. disengagement, accompanied by neutralization and denuclearization, would fit the changing geopolitical environment in Northeast Asia as the cold war recedes into history. The American military alliance with South Korea following the Korean War was a response to the North's military alliances with the Soviet Union and China. Now Moscow has nullified the operative provisions of its security treaty with Pyongyang and is selling significant military equipment and technology to Seoul. Beijing, while retaining its formal security commitment, has progressively downgraded its relations with Pyongyang in most spheres. Equally important, Russia and China have forged much more significant economic links with the South than with the North. Both Moscow and Beijing have been moving toward a symmetrical posture in dealing with the North and South and are increasingly playing the role of honest broker.

This is precisely what Washington desired when it proposed "cross-recognition" in 1988. Twice, the United States offered to link U.S. recognition of Pyongyang with Soviet and Chinese recognition of Seoul, only to renege on the offer when Moscow and Beijing did, in fact, shift to a symmetrical stance. More than a decade later, despite the basic changes that have occurred in the Korean geopolitical and strategic environment, the United States remains committed to one side in a Korean civil war that is no longer a focus of global power rivalries.

The "power vacuum" thesis rests on the assumption that history is destined to repeat itself. But does this assumption stand up to close scrutiny? In the chapters that follow I explore the historical memories that shape events today as part of a broader analysis of the dynamics of the interaction between Korea and each of its neighbors. Against this background, I seek to show why history will not necessarily repeat itself, underlining the many new factors that affect the calculus, notably economic globalization and the emergence of Korean nationalism. Finally, I consider how alternative U.S. policies in Korea will influence the future of U.S. relations with Japan, China, and Russia at both the regional and global level.

CHAPTER 23

Korea, Japan, and the United States

THE MOST striking example of the impact of historical memories on contemporary relations between Northeast Asian powers is the persistence of deep tensions between Japan and the two Koreas more than half a century after the end of Japanese colonial rule in the peninsula.

Most Japanese look down on Koreans as crude country cousins who imitated but never absorbed Chinese culture. In the Japanese self-image, Japan took the best of Chinese culture, created a distinctive Japanese cultural amalgam, and then turned to face the new challenge from the West, using Western technology to modernize, but not Westernize, Japan. In Japanese eyes, the Korean failure to organize itself as Japan did during the Tokugawa period resulted from its inherent inferiority to Japan, which justified the colonization of the peninsula as part of an effective Asian response to Western power. By contrast, Koreans see themselves as the first and most authentic heirs of a Chinese cultural legacy that Japan copied and then corrupted. In Korean eyes, by annexing the peninsula, the Japanese revealed themselves to be amoral, nouveau-riche opportunists who dishonored a Confucian heritage that they owed to Korea. Far from uniting Asia to face the Western challenge, Japan had divided it, using Western technology for its own aggrandizement at the expense of a neighboring Asian country that was also part of the Confucian cosmos.

It is the underlying resentments and cultural tensions left over from history that make the danger of a nuclear arms race between Japan and the two Koreas, or a unified Korea, worthy of serious attention. Public opinion polls consistently show a deep mutual distrust and animosity between the two countries, with each identifying the other as the "most disliked."[1]

The clear and present Chinese nuclear threat to Japan is much more significant than the hypothetical possibility of a future threat from North Korea, South Korea, or a unified Korea. In political and psychological terms, however, it is not easy for the advocates of a nuclear-armed Japan to arouse Japanese public fear of China. Apart from a profound, ingrained cultural respect for China, many Japanese accept China's argument that its nuclear deployments are not directed at Japan but are in large part a response to the U.S. and Russian nuclear presence in East Asia. By contrast, even a hypothetical nuclear danger from Korea arouses a visceral negative reaction. Japanese cultural contempt for Korea and Koreans makes the idea of a militarily superior Korea psychologically intolerable, apart from the security threat involved.

THE LEGACY OF COLONIAL RULE

Historians agree that Japanese colonial rule was unusually harsh and explain its severity partly as an extension of ingrained feudal attitudes that influence the behavior of Japanese toward each other even today. Once having assigned Koreans to an inferior status, it came naturally for Japanese colonial administrators to apply the hierarchical standards of their own society with exaggerated zeal. The oppressive character of Japanese colonial rule was accentuated by the fact that it was administered to a great extent by generals who established a virtual military dictatorship, with army officers installed as local police chiefs. Suspected anti-Japanese activists were imprisoned and tortured in an intermittent reign of terror that culminated in the bloody repression of a nationwide movement for independence in March 1919. The historical consensus is that some 7,500 Koreans were killed and 46,000 injured during the ensuing twelve months alone. March 1, the day on which the organizers of the movement issued a declaration of independence, is one of two major national holidays celebrated in Korea today, the other being the day that Japanese rule ended.

International protests and a phase of political liberalization in Japan led to a moderation of the Japanese colonial administration during the next decade. However, when Japan embarked on its expansionist policy with the takeover of Manchuria in 1931, Korea became the forward logistical base for Japanese forces. This led to a tightening of Japanese rule from 1931 until V-J Day in which Japan intensified its effort to wipe out the Korean language and other manifestations of Korean identity. A 1938 edict banned the use of Korean in schools, made Japanese language instruction compulsory for adults as well as children, and prohibited the publication of Korean-language newspapers. In 1939, Koreans were ordered to change their monosyllabic names to multisyllabic Japanese-sounding names; to recite the Japanese "Oath of Imperial Subjects," bowing down to the imperial palace; and to worship at Shinto shrines.

Faced with a manpower shortage that had crippled the war effort, Japan conscripted 208,000 Koreans into the Japanese armed forces and some two million Koreans for hard labor in mines, factories, and construction projects dispersed in Japan, Sakhalin, and the South Pacific. As Chong Sik Lee has recalled, "The Korean workers were essentially slaves, huddled into what amounted to concentration camps guarded constantly by Japanese men and dogs."[2] Recent disclosures concerning "comfort women" who were forcibly recruited to travel with Japanese forces have rekindled Korean anger over the colonial period. In Korean eyes, Japan's expressions of regret for its colonial excesses were both grudging and inadequate until the 1998 visit of President Kim Dae Jung to Japan, when Prime Minister Keizo Obuchi, in a joint declaration with President Kim, "humbly accepted the historical fact that Japanese colonial rule inflicted unbearable damage and pain on Korean people and expressed remorseful repentance and a heartfelt apology for the ordeal." But this carefully negotiated gesture did not calm anti-Japanese feeling in South Korea for long because a variety of Japanese politicians were quick to disown Obuchi's sentiments. Moreover, the word for "apology" used in the Japanese text of this declaration, *owabi*, is weaker and more ambiguous than *shojai*, the word that Seoul had suggested. The traumatic impact of the colonial decades will in all likelihood continue to be a powerful force shaping both Japanese and Korean attitudes for many years to come.

PROMOTING A SEOUL-TOKYO AXIS

In addition to poisoning relations between Japan and the two Koreas, the legacy of the colonial decades profoundly affects how Japan views its own interests and responsibilities, and those of the United States, with respect to the defense of South Korea and the unification of the peninsula.

Japan's attitudes toward the American role in Korea are inextricably mingled with its lingering bitterness over its defeat in World War II and its expulsion from Korea and Taiwan. The 1998 Japanese motion picture *Pride*, a sympathetic portrayal of wartime Premier Hideji Tojo, is a dramatic reminder that Japan is deeply ambivalent concerning its role in the prewar decades and in the war itself. The older generation of conservative politicians, in particular, believes that Japan was a liberator, not an aggressor, and has had some success in instilling nationalistic attitudes in the younger generation.[3]

Significantly, American policy dating back to the occupation has supported the Japanese right wing at the expense of the Socialists, who consistently advocated an acknowledgment of Japanese war guilt and forthright apologies to Korea and China. The United States in effect absolved Japan's wartime leaders of guilt by permitting the emperor to remain on his throne. "Since the war was fought in the name of the Emperor," points out Robert M. Orr, vice president of the American Chamber of Commerce in Japan, "how could soldiers carrying out the will of the Emperor be guilty if the Emperor himself was innocent?"[4] Moreover, the decision to exonerate Hirohito was followed by a related decision with even greater practical significance: the release of imprisoned Japanese war leaders. This was a critical step in facilitating the establishment of a right-wing government that could be counted on to support the United States in the cold war. Initially, the U.S. occupation authorities had intended to make the purge of prewar and wartime rightist leaders permanent by writing a clause to that effect into the final treaty returning Japan to sovereign status. But this idea was dropped once it became clear that the United States and Japan would be cold war allies.

Japan's ambivalence concerning its colonial past and its wartime role explains why it has resisted the inclusion of Korea within the scope of the U.S.–Japan military alliance. The underlying attitude of Japanese conservative leaders is that the American-Soviet division of the peninsula made matters much worse for Korea and the rest of Asia than would have been the case if Japanese rule had continued. Thus, when the United States has periodically asked Japan during and after the cold war to make commitments concerning joint military responsibilities relating to Korea, successive Japanese governments have balked. Edward Seidensticker, analyzing conservative attitudes, explains that "to such Japanese, it does not seem fair that Tokyo should be asked now to repair the damage wrought by Washington" when it took over Korea, displaced Japanese colonial rule, and joined with the Soviet Union in the partition. "Such Japanese," Seidensticker recalls, "remember how America started having second thoughts about a disarmed Japan when trouble came up in Korea, and in a somewhat hypocritical manner told Japan that although naturally the 'peace constitution' and the disarmed Japan which it called for were here to stay, it would be all right for Japan to have a 'police reserve.' In that police reserve was the beginning of Japanese rearmament, and to be told now that rearmament should go the whole distance because trouble is once again brewing in Korea is too much. It was not for them, thank you."[5]

The American position has consistently been that Japan is obliged by its security treaty with the United States to join in the defense of the South in the event of Northern aggression. In countering this position, Japanese leaders have generally cited the pacifism of the Japanese public and have argued that the intensity of anti-Japanese sentiment in Korea would undermine military cooperation with Seoul. But the governing factor in the Japanese attitude is, in actuality, the belief that the United States should properly bear the responsibility for maintaining the peace in Korea because it helped to divide the peninsula in the first place. It is not the Japanese style to say this to the United States or to challenge the American position directly. Instead, when American pressures have made it unavoidable, Japanese leaders have sought to appease Washington with cosmetic gestures, while parrying American efforts to pin them down with respect to whether, or to what extent, Japan would join with the United States militarily in the defense of the South.

Japan's skill in avoiding military commitments relating to Korea has been demonstrated repeatedly in ambiguous joint statements by the leaders of the two countries. Thus, in their 1969 communiqué formalizing the reversion of Okinawa, President Richard M. Nixon and Premier Eisaku Sato said that the security of South Korea "is essential to the security of Japan." This phrase was inserted at the insistence of the United States as a Japanese quid pro quo for the U.S. agreement to make the future use of its bases in Okinawa conditional on U.S. "prior consultation" with Japan. In American eyes, the reference to Korea in the joint communiqué went hand in hand with the more explicit Sato statement in a National Press Club speech pledging "prompt and positive" Japanese action on any U.S. request for the use of its bases in Japan to wage combat operations in the event of "an armed attack against the Republic of Korea." Defending what he had done back in Japan, however, Sato disavowed the English expression *positive*, explaining that the Japanese phrase he had used in his Press Club address, *mao mukini*, could more accurately be translated as "in a forward-looking way." "When we say that we shall determine our attitude 'in a forward-looking way,'" Sato told a Diet questioner, "we mean that we say 'yes' in a forward-looking way or we say 'no' in a forward-looking way. I cannot say under what conditions we will say 'yes' or we will say 'no.'"[6] By April 1974, Foreign Minister Toshio Kimura had further explained that what was "essential" to Japan was not "the security of the Republic of Korea" but "the peace and security of the Korean peninsula in its entirety." By August, Kimura had taken another step in the direction of greater symmetry with his controversial statements that there is "no threat" from the North and that "the government of the Republic of Korea is not the only lawful government in the Korean peninsula."[7]

When Prime Minister Takeo Miki visited Washington in 1975, he sought to avoid a reaffirmation of the 1969 language, proposing that his joint communiqué with President Ford state only that "the maintenance of peace on the Korean peninsula is necessary for peace and security in East Asia, including Japan."[8] As Miki's pro-Seoul critics were quick to point out, it was clear that Sato's "ROK clause" had become a broader "Korea clause."[9] This same formulation was employed in the 1977 communiqué issued by Prime Minister Takeo Fukuda and President Jimmy Carter and in the joint declaration following the 1983 summit between Prime Minister Yasuhiro Nakasone and South Korean President Chun Doo Hwan.

Throughout the cold war, the United States has unsuccessfully attempted to promote military cooperation between Japan and South Korea under the U.S. aegis. To set the stage for such cooperation, Washington began by pressing Tokyo and Seoul to normalize their relations and to open up trade and investment contacts. For more than a decade after the Korean War, South Korean leaders resisted American pressures to negotiate a normalization treaty with Japan because they feared that it would open the way for potential Japanese economic dominance in the South. Syngman Rhee, in the words of one of his closest associates, "sincerely believed that we could not afford to fall into the Japanese lap economically without perpetuating the division. . . . Our national survival requires that we do not get mixed up with the Japanese pending unification."[10] Writing in 1964, as U.S. pressure for a normalization treaty mounted, Professor Hahm Pyong Choon, later South Korean ambassador to Washington, warned that "the inevitable outcome of economic cooperation with Japan is that our economy will become an appendage of the Japanese economy."[11]

The United States was not able to push Seoul to the negotiating table with Japan until the advent of the Park Chung Hee military regime in 1961. Park had served as an officer in the Japanese forces in Manchuria during the colonial period and was not among the Korean officers with nationalistic views who deserted to join the anti-Japanese Korean Liberation Army in Chungking, a fact repeatedly emphasized by his political opponents. In 1965, he agreed to conclude a normalization treaty, forcibly suppressing massive opposition protests, and obtained significant campaign contributions in the years thereafter from Japanese companies in return for favored economic treatment.[12]

Japan, for its part, was happy to have American help in opening up trade and investment in the South but also had to be pressured by the United States into concluding of the 1965 accord. The Japanese objective of gaining economic access to the South would have been satisfied by a joint declaration, as against a formal treaty that required at least a partial bow in the direction of recognizing Seoul as the only exclusive sovereign in Korea. Prime Minister Hayato Ikeda had strongly suggested on many occasions that Japan could not ignore the existence of North Korea and the treaty language finally chosen was deliberately open-ended. Pointing to the carefully ambiguous language in the treaty, Foreign Minister Etsusaburo Shiina flatly assured the Diet on August 5, 1965, that "the problem of North Korea is still in a state of carte blanche. The area of the treaty application is limited only to the area where the present jurisdiction of South Korea extends."

The American role in pushing through the 1965 normalization treaty provides a painful illustration of the law of unintended consequences. Although the treaty did not bring Japan and South Korea together militarily, as the U.S. had envisioned, the influx of Japanese trade and investment resulting from the accord has indeed made South Korea an "appendage of the Japanese economy" as anticipated by Rhee and Hahm-Pyong Choon. In the myopic U.S. perspective of 1965, Japanese investment in the South was desirable because it would reduce the need for U.S. economic aid to Seoul. Washington was totally unprepared for the scope and thrust of the ensuing Japanese drive for leverage over the South Korean economy, just as it was unprepared for the dynamism of worldwide Japanese economic expansion at the expense of the United States itself during the decades thereafter. The result of American intervention in Japanese relations with South Korea has been to reinforce the enmities left over from the colonial period with new and ever-growing economic tensions.

The 1965 agreement opened the way for a dependent South Korean economic relationship with Japan that has consistently led to trade deficits with Tokyo. In 1996, the deficit reached $15 billion, three-fourths of South Korea's total trade deficit. In theory, the principal advantage of foreign enterprise is that the host country gets a steady trickle of new technology as ancillary domestic industries grow up to supply the foreign enterprise with more and more of its components. But the trickle-down concept does not hold true when already developed technologies are brought in for predetermined export markets and already manufactured components are shipped in for assembly merely to take advantage of low wage rates. In the absence of the domestic "product cycle," there is a built-in necessity to keep up a high rate of imports in order to maintain export growth. Thus, exports contribute little to the balance of payments, leading not only to steadily larger trade deficits but also to steadily rising indebtedness to sustain industrial as well as other imports. In the case of South Korea, this was a key factor leading to the foreign exchange crisis of 1997.

Encouraged by the United States, which was motivated by cold war strategic considerations, the Park Chung Hee regime adopted economic policies consciously designed to give priority to rapid economic expansion regardless of the political costs incurred in the form of dependence on Japan. Japanese companies, in turn, did their part to make South Korea dependent on Japanese technology, rather than other foreign technology, by establishing informal control over South Korean enterprises through dummy partners and technical assistance or licensing agreements, as distinct from equity investment. As a result, in the machinery sector alone, 58.6 percent of South Korean imports between 1962 and 1995 came from Japan. In some industrial classifications, such as motor vehicle parts and machine tool parts, South Korean manufacturers rely on Japanese suppliers for more than 60 percent of their imported components. "In effect," concludes Karl Moskowitz, "by supplying components, Japanese companies are capturing much of the value added in Korea's manufactured exports."[13]

JAPANESE POLITICS AND NORTH KOREA POLICY

The American policy of promoting a Seoul-Tokyo axis was opposed by a significant minority of Japanese leaders who favored a symmetrical Japanese posture toward Seoul and Pyongyang. Three Liberal Democratic prime ministers during the decade following the Korean War—Ikeda, Yukio Hatoyama, and Tanzan Ishibashi—had suggested on many occasions that Japan should seek to establish friendly relations with North Korea as part of an overall rapprochement with the Communist powers, only to encounter strong resistance from LDP hard-liners. Opposition leaders argued more vociferously that a one-sided involvement with Seoul could prove to be dangerous for Japan, making it easier for the

United States to involve Tokyo militarily in Korea if a new war should break out. Given the continuing tensions over Korea between Japanese hawks and doves, Japanese policy toward Pyongyang was incoherent and opportunistic during the cold war. It fluctuated erratically in accordance with changes in domestic political alignments, shifts in regional geopolitical currents, the twists and turns of the North Korean line, and, above all, American pressures. Whenever the doves seemed to be gaining ground, the United States lobbied intensely within the bureaucracy and ruling party to block any change in the Japanese posture.

Reviewing the history of Japanese relations with North Korea, Masao Okonogi has observed that "Tokyo-Pyongyang relations had made relatively smooth progress" until the 1961 military coup in Seoul, followed by the 1965 Seoul-Tokyo normalization treaty. Pyongyang concluded after the treaty that there was no hope for an early normalization agreement of its own with Tokyo and angrily shifted for the next seven years to a hard line toward what was officially branded as "the revival of Japanese militarism."[14] Tokyo, during this period, concentrated on forging its new ties with the South. However, in 1972, sensitive to the improvement of U.S. and Japanese relations with China then developing, Pyongyang returned to a soft line. Compensation for the injuries inflicted during the colonial period did not have to be part of a normalization agreement, Pyongyang said, but could come after unification, a position that contrasted markedly with its subsequent insistence on the inclusion of "reparations" in a normalization accord. Of more immediate relevance, Tokyo would not have to repudiate the 1965 agreement with Seoul as a precondition for normalization.

Despite strong signals of U.S. displeasure, Japan responded to this reversal of North Korean policy by stepping up two-way trade from a 1972 level of $57 million to $250 million three years later. In the Japanese Diet, the Dietman's League for the Promotion of Japan–North Korea Friendship claimed 300 members in 1975, embracing both the ruling party and the opposition Socialists, as against 243 in the rival pro-Seoul grouping. By 1977, bilateral trade was expected to reach $400 million. But the North defaulted on nearly $600 million in debts to Japanese creditors in 1976 as a result of excessive foreign exchange outlays based on exaggerated expectations of increased prices for its raw material exports. The 1976 default dampened Japanese economic interest in North Korea, and it was not until 1985 that two-way trade reached the $400 million level. North Korean terrorist adventures, notably the Rangoon bombing in 1983 and the 1987 explosion of a Korean Air Lines plane, further soured Japanese attitudes toward Pyongyang. South Korea, meanwhile, was steadily widening the margin of its economic and military superiority over Pyongyang, prompting a newly confident posture toward the North that led to a softening of North-South tensions.

"As long as out and out antagonism between Seoul and Pyongyang remained unchanged," explains Akio Watanabe, "there was little room for Japanese diplomacy towards North Korea."[15] President Roh Tae Woo's Nordpolitik policy permitted a more flexible Japanese posture. Moreover, as the seniormost Japanese intelligence analyst dealing with North Korea observed in September 1998, Japan wanted "to prevent the gap between North and South from widening too much. That would create an unstable situation that could be dangerous for us."[16] Once again ignoring objections from Seoul and Washington, Japan started to soften its policy toward the North in 1989 with a statement expressing "deep regret and repentance" concerning the colonial period. This gesture was followed by a high-level bipartisan mission to Pyongyang in 1990 that paved the way for an abortive normalization dialogue ending in 1992.

Reversing its 1972 stance on the terms for normalization, North Korea demanded the immediate start of payments that it called "reparations" and that Japan called an "economic cooperation" program. This led to an impasse over how much Japan would have to pay, which has continued to block a normalization agreement. In 1965, Seoul had received $800 million in loans and grants. As a matter of pride and face, Pyongyang wants to get a comparable sum, taking into account changes in exchange rates and the value of the dollar. Japan is ready to provide roughly $5 billion, but the North has demanded more, asking for $11 billion on one occasion.

"Instead of seeking a fifty percent solution, which is usual in diplomatic negotiation," wrote Watanabe with undisguised bitterness, "Pyongyang appeared to seek a one hundred percent solution, insisting on the complete justice of its claim, while demanding an unconditional surrender, so to speak, by the Japanese."[17] To strengthen its bargaining position, Japan has emphasized other issues, notably the alleged North Korean abduction of eleven Japanese citizens during the Park Chung Hee period for use in intelligence operations and the North's refusal to permit the Japanese wives of North Koreans to revisit Japan. But the size of the compensation package is likely to be the real stumbling block to an agreement when and if serious negotiations are resumed.

The breakdown of the normalization dialogue in 1992 coincided with a significant change in the balance of forces within Japan resulting from the rout of the Socialists in the 1993 Diet elections. Right-wing elements were more strongly entrenched than ever when the 1994 nuclear crisis with North Korea erupted. Significantly, however, this increase in rightist strength did not affect Japan's determination to avoid involvement in any U.S. military action in Korea. Despite strong U.S. pressure at the height of the crisis in May and June 1994, Japan refused to cooperate in imposing sanctions against North Korea and to prepare for a possible naval blockade to enforce sanctions.

Ironically, the shift to the right in Japanese politics since 1993, coupled with the 1994 U.S. nuclear freeze agreement with North Korea, has produced a complete reversal of the bargaining relationship between the U.S. and Japan over Korea policy. During the cold war years, with the Socialists pushing for normalization, the United States did its best to snuff out any signs of a softening of Japanese policy toward Pyongyang. After 1994, the United States began to pursue a policy of limited engagement with Pyongyang in order to sustain the nuclear freeze and has sought Japanese support for food aid to North Korea as well as for financing of the nuclear freeze. But Japan, for its part, has hardened its terms for normalization with Pyongyang since 1994 and has resisted American pressure for economic engagement with Pyongyang no less tenaciously than it resisted earlier U.S. pressure for military cooperation in the defense of the South.

This hardening of the Japanese posture toward the North has primarily reflected the increased freedom of action enjoyed by hawkish politicians and bureaucrats no longer constrained by a powerful Socialist opposition. At the same time, it has been greatly facilitated by a sea change in Japanese popular perceptions of North and South Korea that began with the 1987 Seoul Olympics and has increased since the 1994 death of Kim Il Sung. In earlier decades, the two Koreas were lumped together in Japanese imagery, but now they are sharply differentiated. North Korea has become the focus of the animosity and contempt previously directed at all Koreans. The Olympics dramatized a striking economic gap between the South and the North that has been underlined by the food shortages and other economic difficulties in the North since Kim Il Sung's death. Many Japanese, like many Americans, see North Korea as an economic basket case and assume that it will collapse. In this image, Kim Jong Il is either too weak or too doctrinaire to reform his failed socialist system rapidly enough to avert a collapse, and his totalitarian, military-based rule enables a small elite to live in luxury while large segments of the population starve. This differentiation between a "bad" North Korea and a more benign South was reinforced in Japanese eyes when Pyongyang flaunted its missile capabilities by launching a satellite over Japan in August 1998.

DOES JAPAN WANT TO KEEP KOREA DIVIDED?

South Korea and North Korea alike share the perception that Japan does not want Korea to be reunified. In Korean eyes, Japan is plotting to reassert its hegemony and is thus determined to forestall the consolidation of a neighboring state of seventy million people that could become an economic competitor and even a military adversary. This Korean perception assumes that Japan has arrived at a settled assessment of its long-term interests and objectives in Korea and has consciously designed its policies to keep the peninsula divided. In reality, however, Japanese policies toward Korea have been and continue to be opportunistic, reactive, and devoid of any long-term vision based on a clearly defined national consensus. To the extent that a consensus exists in Japan concerning Korea, it is simply that Japanese economic and military burdens there should be kept to a minimum. Whether or not Korea is unified matters less, in itself, than whether unification, when and if it comes, proves to be disruptive and costly for Japan and whether a unified Korean state would be more or less difficult to handle both economically and militarily than two Koreas, one of which, North Korea, now pursues a militantly nationalistic posture toward Tokyo.

During the cold war, as we have seen, Japan adapted comfortably to a divided Korea, profiting handsomely from Korean War contracts and later from its U.S.–sponsored trade and investment access to the South. However, as Australian scholar Denny Roy has observed, Japan's "natural inclination" after the Korean War ended was to pursue a more balanced "two Korea" policy than the pro-Seoul posture demanded by the United States, "exploiting trade possibilities in both countries and maintaining enough political influence in both capitals to discourage another inter-Korean war."[18] In contrast to Washington, Tokyo did not demonize Pyongyang, and recurrent American warnings that the North might make a new attempt to unify Korea by force were not taken very seriously. In 1979, a Japanese *Defense White Paper* declared that "conditions on the Korean peninsula" are a major factor threatening regional peace and stability. But it did not point the finger of blame at North Korea, noting only that "severe North-South tension remains unabated." What worried

Japan was not a North Korean military adventure but rather that American tensions with China and the Soviet Union might spill over into the peninsula and that Korea would become the battleground for a superpower proxy war in which Japan, as a U.S. ally, would be engulfed.

For example, in 1975, Kei Wakaizumi, in a review of the U.S.–Japan alliance that typified the views of mainstream Japanese analysts, did not acknowledge any North Korean military threat to Japanese interests as such but expressed his "profound apprehension" that a new Korean conflict might draw Japan into a confrontation with China and the Soviet Union.[19] Similarly, Kiichi Miyazawa, who was serving at that time as foreign minister, discounted the Japanese security stake in Korea itself but voiced concern that a new war could lead to a flood of refugees and "routed troops" who might seek shelter in Japan, adding to the existing tensions between the Japanese people and their Korean minority.[20]

The concerns expressed by Wakaizumi and Miyazawa in 1975 were remarkably similar to the concerns that now shape Japanese thinking about the future of Korea in the aftermath of the cold war. The few Japanese analysts who have discussed the unification issue in print focus not on the pros and cons of unification for Japan but on how specific unification scenarios might affect Japanese interests.

Masao Okonogi, disputing the South Korean belief that Japan is opposed to unification, writes that "most Japanese do not have a concrete image formed about a unified Korea and Japan's relations with it. What most Japanese are vaguely concerned about is not unification itself but about the immense confusion that may occur in the process of unification, especially a sudden North Korean collapse leading to a second Korean War." If Korea is unified by war, he warns, Japan will face a "torrent of refugees" as well as international pressures to share "not only the costs and risks of the war but also the costs of postwar reconstruction."

While the fighting is going on, the United States will insist on Japanese "rear area" military cooperation that will "make Japan the target of North Korean missile attacks and subversive activities." To some extent, Japan would profit from the war, he notes, since "as in the Korean War of 1950 to 1953, a second Korean conflict would bring about a large wartime demand for various things, stimulating Japanese exports." But the economic benefits of a new war would be "negligible" compared with the large-scale financial help that Japan would be expected to provide after the war to make a unified Korea economically viable.

Given the costs and risks of a collapse scenario, Okonogi concludes, it would be less expensive and less dangerous for Japan to help finance economic reform and liberalization in North Korea and a process of gradual, peaceful unification.[21] This is also the view of other academic supporters of a "soft landing" policy, such as Akio Watanabe, who argues that "everything depends on how unification takes place and what kind of Korea will emerge after unification." Watanabe calls on Japan to "promote 'Operation Soft Landing' by providing financial assistance, together with other friendly nations, both before and after unification."[22] In Japan as in the United States, however, the concept of a "soft landing" has been challenged by those who believe that a collapse in Pyongyang is not only inevitable but desirable. This view has been strengthened by the persistent economic difficulties in North Korea since the death of Kim Il Sung, leading to a paralysis of policymaking in Tokyo as well as Washington.

Japan agreed only reluctantly in 1994 to join with the United States and South Korea in financing the U.S.–negotiated nuclear freeze agreement with Pyongyang. Since then, Japanese foot-dragging has been a major factor delaying implementation of the accord. To the extent that Tokyo has come up with funds, usually at the eleventh hour, this has not been as part of a long-range Japanese Korea policy but as an unavoidable obligation to Washington. On the one issue most important for the survival of the Pyongyang regime, food aid, Japan has lagged far behind the United States in contributing to international relief efforts despite the fact that it has had warehouses bulging with surplus rice stocks. When good harvests pushed the surplus over three million tons, Tokyo finally pledged to give 200,000 tons of rice in 2000 and 500,000 tons in 2001, hoping to limit a drop in the price of domestically produced rice that was hurting its farmers.

The North Korean launch of a satellite over Japan in 1998 has hardened opposition to Japanese financial support for policies designed to promote a "soft landing." Strictly speaking, given its altitude, the launch was not a violation of Japanese airspace. However, Japanese of all persuasions viewed it as provocative and threatening, since it demonstrated clearly for the first time Pyongyang's ability to deploy medium-range missiles capable of hitting any part of Japan. This display of missile capabilities, coupled with suspicions that Pyongyang might be secretly developing nuclear weapons in violation of the freeze, has given new ammunition to Japanese hawks who believe that Japan should have its own nuclear and missile arsenal. In a departure from the conscious Japanese cold war policy of not demonizing North Korea, the Japanese right wing now has a vested interest in fanning fears of a North Korean military threat in order to strengthen popular support not only for a nuclear and missile buildup but also for other programs that would enhance Japan's military autonomy, notably reconnaissance satellites built and operated independently by Japan.

Cutting across the debate over Korea policy in Japan is a widespread belief that Japan can adapt to whatever happens in Korea and should not waste much money trying to influence whether and how Korea is reunified. The result will be a market economy, in this perspective, whether North Korea adopts gradual reforms and survives for some time or is absorbed by the South after a breakdown of the existing system. To make this transformation serve Japanese interests and minimize Korean economic competition, Japan should seek to maintain the inequities in its economic relations with South Korea, keeping South Korean industries dependent on Japanese spare parts, raw materials, and components. At the same time, Japan should continue to encourage the United States to assume responsibility for a stable environment in the peninsula conducive to Japanese trade and investment.

As for the danger of a security threat from Korea, this reasoning goes, Japan could face such a danger from either a divided or a unified Korea. North Korea already poses a potential nuclear and missile threat, and it is only American pressure that has stopped South Korea from developing nuclear weapons or, at the very least, from emulating Japan by developing a reprocessing capability that would give it the option of making nuclear weapons. Nevertheless, many Japanese do foresee several ways in which a unified Korea could prove to be more dangerous for Japan in security terms than the status quo. One is the possibility that a strong upsurge of nationalist feeling following unification would lead Korea to sever its U.S. military ties, or that the United States itself would take the initiative to end a U.S. military presence no longer needed to deter a Northern invasion. To promote their own agenda, pro-nuclear hawks in Japan argue that a unified Korea without a pledge of U.S. nuclear protection would inevitably develop its own nuclear capability, combining the existing nuclear and missile capabilities of North and South. This view is challenged by many Japanese analysts who contend that a unified Korea would adopt a non-aligned foreign policy and defense posture without nuclear weapons if Japan, the United States, China, and Russia would move toward a nuclear-free Northeast Asia, starting with an agreement ruling out the use or deployment of nuclear weapons in Korea.

The greatest postunification nightmare in Japanese eyes is that Korea and China might conclude a military alliance with a nuclear dimension designed to offset Japanese power. "Many Japanese do have worries in a vague sense about a rise of extreme nationalism in a unified Korea," writes Masao Okonogi, "fearing that this might be directed toward Japan. For example, if an emotional conflict occurs between Japan and Korea, the possibility of a unified Korea turning toward China to counter Japan cannot be denied."[33] Yoichi Funabashi, the diplomatic correspondent of *Asahi Shimbun*, echoes this assessment, pointing to the sharp criticism of Japan's past militarism by Chinese President Jiang Zemin and former South Korean President Kim Young Sam in their November 1995 joint press conference in Seoul. "In that criticism," observes Funabashi, "Japan saw anti-Japanese sentiment in Korea and China amalgamating to portend a troubling geopolitical future, especially with the prospect of Korean unification."[24]

CHAPTER 24

Korea, China, and the United States

ONE OF THE key issues in the debate over the future of the American military presence in Korea is what impact a U.S. withdrawal would have on the relations between China and a unified Korea. The case for a pos-tunification U.S. military presence frequently includes a warning that China would move into the "vacuum" resulting from a U.S. withdrawal by concluding a military alliance with Korea, complete with a nuclear umbrella, linked with preferential status for Korea in trade and invest-ment relations. The rationale for such an alliance, it is argued, would be the perception of a common threat to both countries from Japan. But this warning rests on a line of analysis that distorts the historical record of Sino-Korean relations, ignores the emergence of Korean nationalism dur-ing the past half century, and underrates the strength of the divisive fac-tors that are already beginning to emerge in Sino-Korean relations.

Warnings of a Sino-Korean military alliance reflect a Sino-centered his-torical perspective in which it is assumed that China has exercised hege-mony over Korea for most of its history and would only be reasserting a traditional pattern of relations. It is true that China had tributary rela-tions with successive Korean dynasties from the sixth century until the Japanese annexation of Korea in 1910. In Chinese eyes, these were rela-tions between an elder brother and a younger brother. Then as now, China perceived Korea as a buffer state critical to Chinese security. It assumed that its seniority would guarantee military cooperation in time of crisis. From the Korean vantage point, however, the ceremonial obei-sance rendered to China by Korean kings only signified their cultural respect for China as the center of what was then the civilized world. It was precisely because China carefully refrained from interfering with Ko-rean political autonomy that this obeisance was acceptable and that Ko-rea did intermittently cooperate with China militarily to defend what it perceived as Korean interests.

In the contemporary context, Korean cultural respect for China and the power of the Confucian legacy reinforce the powerful economic fac-tors that draw Korea to Beijing and could well make Korean relations with China closer than those with any other power. But the historical, cultural, and economic pull of China is offset by a growing sense of Korean nationalism in both North and South that had not yet coalesced in earlier centuries. This new nationalism lies behind the uneasiness in South Korea concerning the prospect of an indefinite U.S. military presence. By the same token, the upsurge in nationalist sentiment likely to follow unification would make subordinate status as a military ally of China psychologically unacceptable. Given this heightened national self-consciousness, a U.S. withdrawal would not leave a "vacuum," since a unified Korea would assert its own interests as a regional power. For example, in dealing with China, a unified Korea would be likely to adopt a militant posture in jurisdictional disputes over seabed petroleum resources and in a latent territorial conflict over three border provinces of northwestern China with historical and ethnic links to Korea.

In this chapter I will seek to present a balanced assessment of the historical record and of the other factors relevant to an analysis of the future of Sino-Korean relations. I will then consider how this assessment defines U.S. policy options in Korea and how alternative U.S. policies would affect U.S. interests in Northeast Asia.

THE LIMITS OF TRIBUTE

The development of Chinese relations with Korea has evolved in four stages marked by a delicate balance between Korean acceptance of subordinate status and a steadily growing desire for national autonomy. For Korea, the rationale for tributary status was primarily cultural, but both sides recognized its security significance from the outset and cooperated militarily when Japan attempted to use Korea as an invasion corridor in the seventeenth century.

In the earliest stage, when China was unified and Korea was not, Chinese military power spilled over into border territory that later became part of the emerging Korean state. In the second stage, starting in the sixth century A.D., a newly unified Korea expelled Chinese military power and established tributary relations with China that were steadily extended during the next eight centuries. The tributary relationship was fully institutionalized during the third stage from the fourteenth through the nineteenth centuries. Finally, in the fourth stage, China and Korea alike failed to modernize as rapidly as Japan did, thus opening the way for Japanese colonial rule.

Korean nationalists today trace the origins of Korean national identity to the kingdom of Choson, which covered a relatively small area of what is now northwestern Korea beginning at least five centuries before Christ and, according to legend, much earlier. With this localized exception, however, Korea was a congeries of warring principalities when the Chin and early Han dynasties were unifying China during the four centuries beginning in 221 B.C. The emerging Chinese state was strong, confident, and bent on expansion, sending its armies far and wide to consolidate and, where possible, extend its frontiers. In the case of Korea, after invading Choson by land and sea, China set up four military fiefdoms that extended as far South as Seoul. This Chinese control of much of Korea endured until the last half of the second century A.D., when factionalism began to weaken the Han dynasty and the Korean fiefdoms, like other Chinese border satrapies, drove out the invaders. The ouster of the Chinese was followed by the coalescence of three warring dynasties in Korea delimited along regional lines, Silla, Paekche, and Koguryo.

Significantly, in the seventh century, the Silla dynasty enlisted the help of the Tang dynasty in China to subdue its Paekche rivals, who were being supported by a Japanese expeditionary force. After the Silla victory, however, the Chinese generals involved sought to exact their reward by lopping off a slice of Korean territory. This led to five years of fighting in which a defeated Koguryo general helped the Silla victors drive out the Chinese once again in A.D. 676.

During the "Period of the Three Kingdoms" that preceded unification, the dominant Silla kingdom ruled all of the peninsula except for pockets in the southwest and northwest, where the Paekche and Koguryo dynasties continued to hold their ground. The Koguryo domain and later that of an allied state known as Parhae, claimed by some historians to have been ethnically Korean, extended far into adjacent areas of Manchuria for five to seven centuries, a fact cited increasingly by Korean nationalists today. It was a Koguryo general who emerged as the unifier of Korea in the tenth century, establishing the Koryo dynasty, which ruled from 918 to A.D. 1392.

Even during the period of dynastic rivalries, the Korean elite had started to import things Chinese on a large scale. The process gained momentum during the Koryo period, leading to the formalization of tributary relations, and reached its climax during the early centuries of the ensuing Yi dynasty (1392–1910), which coincided with the flowering of art and culture in China during the Ming dynasty. The Korean elite looked increasingly toward China during the Ming period not only as a powerful neighbor to be placated but as a cultural mentor to be imitated.

The Yi leaders were drawn to China in the same way that Renaissance Europe was attracted to Greece as the citadel of civilization and culture in what was then the known world. As Hae Jong Chun has observed, the Korean monarchy and ruling class also promoted the tributary system because they recognized that it would be a source of legitimacy "helping to preserve their status and power."[1] In time, however, during the period of the Ming dynasty, it was China that took the initiative in expanding tributary ties, primarily for commercial reasons. Three large Korean royal delegations traveled to China every year with caravans full of commercial cargo and gifts that cost ten times more than the gifts bestowed by China on the visiting Koreans. In return, China sent delegations representing the emperor to confer his formal blessing on the occasion of the investiture of Korean kings.

"The Chinese," writes historian Carter Eckert, "undoubtedly read more in the way of political subservience into these formalities than did the Koreans themselves. When the Koreans talked about 'revering China,' what they really meant was revering this cosmopolitan culture that ultimately transcended the spatial and temporal boundaries of particular dynasties. . . . To the pre-modern Korean elite, 'revering China' was the measure of their own greatness."[2] China's relationship to Korea, Bruce Cumings adds, was "widely called a 'suzerainty,' but it was not one that amounted to much. . . . The Sino-Korean tributary system was one of inconsequential hierarchy and real independence, if not equality. Absolutely convinced of its own superiority, China assumed that enlightened Koreans would follow it without being forced." Among themselves, Cumings said, the Chinese dismissed Koreans as *gaoli bangzi* (Korean country hicks), breeding underlying resentment on the part of the Koreans and a determination to maintain their independence.[3]

The military component of the tributary system was dramatically demonstrated when the unification of Japan in the sixteenth century led to a Japanese invasion of Korea intended to set the stage for the conquest of China. A Japanese attack force landed at Pusan in 1592 but was soon bottled up in a coastal enclave by the combined onslaught of Chinese forces that were rushed to Korea by the Ming dynasty, Korean guerrilla bands that sprung up throughout the countryside, and a Korean naval fleet of the world's first armored warships, armed with a primitive type of missile. The Korean naval forces, commanded by the remarkable Admiral Yu Sun Shin, cut off Japanese supply lines, prompting Japan to send a second expeditionary force five years later. In a momentous battle, however, Admiral Yi, with only twelve ships, destroyed some three hundred

Japanese ships after trapping them in a narrow strait, one of the most celebrated episodes in Korean history. Korean historians attribute the subsequent Japanese retreat to the bravery of Admiral Yi and Korean guerrilla fighters, but the role of Chinese ground forces in blocking the initial Japanese invasion appears to have been significant.

The tributary system lost much of its meaning for Korea after the Manchu overthrow of the Ming dynasty in China and the establishment of the Ching dynasty. In contrast to its admiration for Ming China as the exemplar of the culture to which Korea paid tribute, the Yi elite looked on the Manchus with contempt as "barbarian" and saw Korea as the guardian of the Ming tradition. Moreover, the factionalism and debauchery of the Ching government during the nineteenth century sapped its political and military vitality and its ability to defend China's preferential position in Korea. What had been China's most valued tributary became a cockpit of intrigue between contending foreign powers and eventually the arena of two major wars between Japan and its major rivals for hegemony in Korea—China and Russia.

For China, its decisive defeat by Japan in 1894 and its subsequent exclusion from Korea was a profound humiliation. Then came the intrusion of U.S. and Soviet power into the peninsula following World War II at a time when China was once again factionalized and immobilized, this time by the civil war between Nationalists and Communists. Once China had reestablished its unity, it was not surprising that the new People's Republic acted decisively in the defense of Chinese interests during the Korean War when the North Korean Army proved unable to stop the American advance toward the Yalu River. China took the fateful step of crossing the Yalu boundary and confronting the United States militarily despite the fact that the Communist regime, then barely a year old, was just beginning to rebuild national, political, and economic institutions after the long years of civil conflict. Ultimately, Beijing committed 2.5 million combat troops to the Korean War, of which 115,000 were killed and 221,000 were wounded. The Chinese decision to intervene has often been interpreted as demonstrating the unity of the Sino-Soviet bloc during the early years of the cold war. But it had more to do with China's historic security stake in Korea and the self-image of the Communist leadership as the defenders of Chinese nationalism who had mobilized national resistance to the Japanese occupation of northern China from 1937 to 1945. At bottom, Chinese intervention did not reflect cold war Communist solidarity but rather China's bedrock national interest in drawing a line that would set the limits of American influence in Korea.

CHINA AND NORTH KOREA: UNEASY ALLIES

China's basic interest during and after the cold war has been to make certain that no other power ever again acquires a dominant position in the peninsula. This called initially for a substantial economic and military aid role in North Korea that would offset the influential position enjoyed by the Soviet Union in Pyongyang as a result of its key role in installing the Kim Il Sung leadership.

When the Korean War ended, Beijing wrote off all war debts to China. For the next three decades, Beijing and Moscow competed for influence in Pyongyang, with North Korea skillfully playing off the two Communist powers against each other. Moscow had greater financial resources available for its aid programs than China did and was more advanced technologically. Thus, Soviet aid inputs exceeded those of China. By 1976, Soviet grants and loans to Pyongyang totaled $1.53 billion, against $967 million from China. However, in addition to its economic aid, Beijing gave Pyongyang preferential treatment in trade relations.

China became North Korea's principal source of crude oil, building a pipeline that brought oil directly from its nearby Taching oilfield to North Korea. As part of trade agreements concluded in 1982 and 1986, China provided an average of one million tons of crude oil per year through this pipeline at a "friendship price." It also helped Pyongyang construct oil refineries, petrochemical plants, and other industrial facilities. By the late 1980s, however, with the Soviet system on the verge of economic and political collapse, China no longer faced much competition from the Soviet Union as an aid donor. Moscow told Pyongyang in 1990 that North Korea would have to begin repaying its $4 billion debt to the Soviet Union and would have to pay in hard currency for all subsequent imports, including crude oil, for which it would have to pay the world price. North Korean imports of Soviet oil, which totaled 440,000 tons that year (against 1.1 million from China), promptly dropped to 40,000 tons in 1991.

Since the end of Soviet aid competition, China has faced conflicting policy priorities in Pyongyang. On the one hand, the economic pragmatists now dominant in Beijing would like to deal with North Korea on a businesslike basis. They recognize that Chinese aid often subsidizes economic inefficiency rooted in overcentralization and ideological rigidity. On the other, China's long-term national interests make it essential to maintain greater influence there than any other power or combination of powers, especially the United States, Japan, and the Russian Federation. Equally important, China wants to forestall an economic breakdown in North Korea that could lead to political instability, a refugee influx into China, and a possible military conflict with South Korea involving American forces.

The tension between economic pragmatism and geopolitical priorities in China's posture toward North Korea was apparent following the 1990 Soviet decision to stop subsidizing Pyongyang. At first Beijing followed suit, demanding hard currency payment at world market prices for all imports, including oil. But urgent North Korean entreaties, including a personal pilgrimage by Kim Il Sung to solicit help from Deng Xiao Ping, soon led China to reschedule or forgive North Korean debts and soften trade terms temporarily. North Korean imports of crude oil and coal remained relatively constant for several years thereafter. China's share of North Korea's total foreign trade rose from 24 percent in 1991 to 37 percent in 1994, accounting for 37 percent of its oil imports and 80 percent of its food grain imports. In 1995, however, rising domestic demand for food grains within China led to spiraling food price inflation that prompted the Chinese government to cut off grain shipments to North Korea as part of a broader decision to stop all grain exports. This left Pyongyang in the lurch just when two successive years of flood and drought damage in 1995 and 1996 ravaged North Korean agriculture. It was the temporary cutoff of Chinese food grains that made the food shortage following the floods so severe until international aid efforts partially mitigated the crisis.

Reversing course in early 1996, China extended 120,000 tons of emergency food grains aid and signed a five-year agreement with Pyongyang to provide 500,000 tons of grain annually, half of it as a grant and half at concessional prices. To the dismay of Pyongyang, most of this food aid has consisted of corn, not rice, which is the traditional mainstay of the North Korean diet. For example, out of 570.2 million tons provided during the 1996–97 fiscal year, 463.9 million tons was corn and only 75.9 million tons was rice. China does not announce its food aid, but most evidence suggests that the value of its aid has exceeded $800 million on the basis of world market prices, compared to $1.68 billion contributed as of January 2001 by the United States and other foreign governmental and nongovernmental donors.

Both China and North Korea are often secretive concerning the extent and terms of their trade and aid dealings. A Chinese embassy spokesman in Washington would say only that grant aid in 1999 would not exceed

$150 million, including food and fuel. Other food and fuel supplied to Pyongyang, he said, involves some form of repayment. Since 1995, there have been periodic signs of tension between Beijing and Pyongyang resulting from China's insistence on hard currency transactions and from its pressure on North Korea to adopt economic reforms modeled on the Chinese experience. Although China gives North Korea long-term credit and "preferential" prices that are lower than world market prices, these prices are much higher than the earlier "friendship" prices. As a result, North Korean crude oil imports from China dropped from the one-million-ton level reported in 1994 to 503,000 tons in 1997. In late 1998, Beijing made an emergency donation of 80,000 tons of crude oil to avert a shutdown of the North Korean transportation system and in early 2000, 500,000 tons of coal. China carefully calibrates its aid to Pyongyang, in short, providing just enough to head off an economic collapse but no more.

In addition to its economic support, China has also supplied substantial military assistance to North Korea. The lion's share of military aid received by Pyongyang during the cold war came from the Soviet Union, primarily because China itself was dependent on Soviet military technology until the 1980s and had relatively little to offer that Pyongyang could not obtain from Moscow. But the Chinese role has been important to North Korea as an offset to complete dependence on the Soviet Union. After the armistice of 1953, Chinese forces stayed in North Korea until 1958, and as a parting gift they handed over large quantities of American, Japanese, and Kuomintang small arms that had been captured during World War II and the Chinese civil war. Between 1958 and 1964, as China began to produce its own weapons with Soviet guidance and support, Beijing was able to give Pyongyang Mig-15, Mig-17, and Mig-19 jet fighters, Il-28 bombers, and other weaponry, with an estimated value of $432 million. China itself does not publish statistics relating to its arms transfers, but data compiled by the U.S. Arms Control and Disarmament Agency (ACDA) suggest that between 1964 and 1994, China transferred military equipment and spare parts to North Korea with a value of $1.54 billion, less than one-tenth the $11.2 billion total for the Soviet Union during the same period.[4]

Bates Gill has shown that the ups and downs of Chinese military aid to North Korea often correspond to developments in the Sino-Soviet rivalry. For example, when North Korea criticized Soviet behavior in the Cuban missile crisis, Moscow cut off military assistance, and China quickly stepped into the breach. Beijing sent 390 Mig-15s, Mig-17s, and other aircraft to Pyongyang in 1963 alone, only to cut back military hardware shipments abruptly following the North Korea–Soviet rapprochement in 1965. Similarly, when China feared that Pyongyang might give Moscow a naval base at Najin or Nampo in the early 1980s, Beijing launched a military aid offensive during the ensuing decade that reflected the growing sophistication of its indigenous defense manufacturing capabilities.[5] The most important aspect of this offensive was the upgrading of the quality of the aircraft provided to the North Korean Air Force. In addition to 108 of its more advanced Q-5 and F-6 fighters, between 1975 and 1992 Beijing also provided 14 Romeo-class submarines, together with the technology for manufacturing them.

Little definitive information is available concerning Chinese transfers of missile technology, a topic of growing speculation in the context of North Korea's surprisingly rapid progress in developing long-range ballistic missiles. Pyongyang has relied almost entirely on Soviet Scud missile technology in designing its Nodong and Taepodong missiles. However, Beijing has licensed the production of several varieties of air defense missiles, including its solid-fuel propelled HQ-2, which might have contributed to Pyongyang's development of the solid-fuel technology demonstrated in the third stage of its unsuccessful 1998 attempt to orbit a satellite. The fact that the Taepodong I has a diameter very close to that of the Chinese DF-3 missile has fueled suspicions of a covert Chinese role in the North Korean missile program. But Beijing angrily denies such a role, pointing out that Pyongyang's missile development has stimulated support for a theater missile defense system, which China strongly opposes. Beijing countercharges that the bulk of Taepodong equipment comes from Japanese technology obtained by North Korea from third countries.

By the end of the 1980s, Chinese military aid gradually tapered off as Soviet military aid competition declined and as Chinese military policy toward the Korean peninsula increasingly emphasized the reduction of military tensions. The 1990 South Korean *Defense White Paper* might have been too categorical when it said that "China stopped supplying arms to North Korea in the mid-1980's as part of its policy of encouraging military stability on the peninsula." Significantly, while ACDA statistics also indicated a tapering off during the 1980s, they did show $90 million in military aid from 1985 to 1994, primarily in the form of spare parts and replacement items needed to keep existing hardware in operation, not complete new weapons systems. China continues to maintain military advisers in Pyongyang, and Chinese and North Korean military leaders exchange regular high-level visits that are invariably accompanied by fulsome North Korean expressions of gratitude for the intervention of Chinese forces during the darkest days of the Korean War.

CHINA AND SOUTH KOREA: AN ECONOMIC BONANZA

In contrast to its exclusive alignment with Pyongyang during the first two decades of the cold war, Beijing has gradually shifted to greater symmetry in its relations with the North and the South since the early 1970s. The fundamental precondition for this shift was the relaxation of cold war tensions in Asia that began with the Nixon visit to China in 1972. Another factor that enabled China to change its posture in Korea was the decline of the Soviet Union as an aid competitor and its collapse in 1991. As Chae Jin Lee has observed, however, economic, not geopolitical, factors played the "central role" in promoting the transition to what was at first a de facto and then a de jure two-Korea policy.[6]

In 1978, China made its historic decision to remove the ideological straitjacket that had impeded its economic development and to adopt major reforms in both its domestic and foreign economic policies. This led to a liberalization of restrictions on foreign trade and investment designed to attract an increased influx of foreign capital and technology. Opening up the economy, in turn, necessitated the normalization of diplomatic and economic relations not only with the United States and Japan but also with China's immediate neighbor, South Korea, which had been steadily widening its margin of economic superiority over North Korea.

Beijing opened unofficial trade with Seoul gradually beginning in 1979. This was followed by the first official diplomatic contact between Beijing and Seoul in 1983 when a hijacked Chinese airliner landed in Seoul. China's decision to support the simultaneous entry of North and South to the United Nations in 1991, despite the initial objections of Pyongyang, made clear that Beijing had basically altered its Korea policy. Formal diplomatic relations with Seoul came soon thereafter in 1992.

In an effort to minimize the damage to its relations with Pyongyang, Beijing had continued to channel most of its trade with the South through third-party intermediaries in Hong Kong until the normalization of diplomatic relations, accompanied by the conclusion of a formal trade agreement. Nevertheless, Chinese–South Korean trade had grown steadily from $434 million in 1984 to $3.087 billion in 1988 and $5.8 billion in 1991. Even during periods of economic slowdown in China, South Korea had continued to increase its purchases of Chinese goods whether or not China was in a position to reciprocate, reflecting its frankly political objective of weaning Beijing away from its exclusive economic ties with Pyongyang. Once a trade agreement was concluded, the level of two-way trade rapidly increased to $11.6 billion in 1994 and a peak of $23.5 billion in 1997 before a drop to $15.1 billion in the first ten months of 1998 resulting from the Asian financial meltdown.

The imbalance of this trade in South Korea's favor has been striking, rising steadily from $130 million in 1984 to $1.2 billion in 1993 and $3.4 billion in 1997. This gap has reflected an explosive rate of economic growth in China that has generally been higher than that in South Korea. However, in the case of some Chinese exports, such as agricultural products and light industrial goods, it has also resulted from South Korean protectionism, leading to trade-related political tensions.

Despite large trade imbalances, South Korea is an attractive economic partner for China because its intermediate technology is in many cases better suited to China than the more expensive high technology of the United States, Japan, and Western Europe. China needs this intermediate technology at this stage of its development and has been eager to obtain it from South Korea not only through trade but above all through investment. For China and South Korea alike, geographic proximity makes investment ties not only convenient but also desirable in economic terms, since it reduces transportation costs and barriers to communications. Chae Jin Lee also offers an interesting psychological insight concerning Chinese–South Korean relations that accords with my own observations. The Chinese feel "more comfortable with the sociable and outgoing South Koreans," Lee writes, "than with the Japanese, who are still under close scrutiny because of their past colonial ambitions and who frequently assume an air of economic superiority."[7] The element of tension in Chinese relations with Japan has not stopped Beijing and Tokyo from gradually enlarging their economic cooperation, but the more relaxed climate of Chinese–South Korean relations does help explain the intensity and speed that has marked the growth of economic ties between Beijing and Seoul.

By 1994, the cumulative total of South Korean investment in China reached $1.1 billion, and by 1998 it had passed $2 billion. By contrast, Chinese investment in South Korea has been negligible. For small and medium-sized South Korean companies, in particular, China is a much more desirable investment locale than alternatives like the United States and other countries with higher labor costs. The productivity of Chinese workers is lower than that of South Korean workers, but the average wage for both managers and unskilled laborers in China is generally one-tenth as high as the comparable wage in South Korea. Readily available raw materials and cultural similarities, including the availability of bilingual workers of Korean ancestry, have also made China attractive for South Korean investors. Perhaps the key factor that has drawn South Korean investors to China is the geographic proximity of China's northern and northeastern regions. The three northeastern provinces of Liaoning, Jilin, and Heilongjiang are located just across the Yalu and Tumen Rivers and have had close historical ties with Korea that have resulted in large concentrations of ethnically Korean settlers. These three provinces alone have attracted 26 percent of South Korean investment in China, and the four adjacent provinces along the Bo Hai Gulf to the south account for another 61 percent.

Manchuria, "Greater Korea," and Yellow Sea Petroleum

Although China benefits from the influx of South Korean investment into northeast China, Beijing is disturbed by the nationalistic political undercurrents that accompany this influx, especially a well-organized movement in South Korea to draw Manchuria into a Korea-centered regional economic bloc, a "Greater Korea" comparable to the economic networks among southeastern China, Hong Kong, and Taiwan often described as "Greater China." This is one of several small shadows that impart an element of uncertainty to the future of relations between China and a unified Korea. Another potential source of conflict lies in unresolved jurisdictional disputes over seabed petroleum deposits in the Yellow Sea.

The three northeastern provinces are of great strategic importance to China, situated as they are close to the southern part of the Russian Maritime Provinces as well as to North Korea. An estimated two million Koreans live in these provinces, nearly half in the Yanbian Autonomous Region of Jilin province. They have resisted cultural absorption by China and maintain a strong sense of Korean identity. The official language of government, education, and the media in Yanbian is Korean. Since Korean immigrants introduced rice farming to Manchuria, Korean farmers now monopolize the rice trade in northeast China and are better-off than rural Chinese in this region; and in the cities of the northeast, too,

Koreans have a higher educational and economic level than the Han Chinese. As a Hudson Institute study observed, "The potential for the 're-Koreanization' of Chinese citizens of Korean descent, who are rediscovering their Korean heritage, is a problem for China."[8] During the 1988 Seoul Olympics, it was no secret to Beijing that the large delegations of ethnic Koreans from China attending the games cheered South Korean, not Chinese, athletes.

What has made the dynamism of its Korean minority worrisome to Beijing is the linkage between the Koreans of northeast China and a politically tinged movement in South Korea known as the Damul Institute. A king named Damul is depicted in many Korean historical accounts as the most powerful monarch of the Dangoon Chosun kingdom, which ruled southern Manchuria and what is now northern Korea for an undetermined period ending in the second century B.C. and marked the start of Korean nationhood, setting the stage for the Koguryo dynasty. Koguryo, Silla, and Paekche ruled Korea during the period of the "Three Kingdoms" that preceded unification under the Koryo dynasty in the tenth century.

"Damul" means "reclaim all," and the founder of the Damul Institute, Ki Joon Kang, writes of "the Korean people's fervent hopes to recover our lost land." In a book detailing the historical rationale for his movement, Kang seeks to show that Damul's realm at its height embraced more than 800,000 square miles, reaching even beyond Manchuria to the west. Although subsequent Dangoon Chosun rulers were driven back to Korea, he maintains, a succession of Korean patriots have made recurring attempts to regain the lost territories, notably the brief reconquest of Liaoning and Jilin in southern Manchuria in the third century A.D. by the Koguryo king Gwangkaeto. Although the Silla dynasty was able to expel marauding Chinese forces from Korea in the seventh century, "sadly, it failed to recover Manchuria." During the next five centuries, however, a new Korean dynasty with Koguryo roots established the Parhae kingdom in areas of Manchuria formerly part of the Koguryo realm, which "remains a very vital part of Korean history" acknowledged in standard school textbooks. Finally, Kang recalls, the Koryo dynasty staged at least three unsuccessful forays into Manchuria, culminating in a protracted struggle during King Sejong's fifteenth-century reign in which ten Korean fortresses in Jilin held their ground for several decades until China prevailed.

Calling for Korea to "form a cultural and economic 'bloc' with Manchuria," Kang argues that "China needs only to lend Manchuria, and a Korea-Manchuria bloc can be launched based on China's manpower and

Korean technology and capital." Manchuria is not really Chinese, he says, since there are eight ethnic groups living there and Manchuria feels "spiritually, economically and culturally 'ownerless'." These people are "Chinese only on paper. They continue to pursue their unique ways of life as Northerners. They would not feel guilty of deserting China by forming a bloc with Korea."

At one point Kang talks of Siberia as part of a Korea-centered economic grouping. "A small country like Korea," he explains, "is bound to get lost in the shuffle between the major powers. That is why Koreans must persuade Manchuria and Siberia to join hands with them—not in terms of territory or military force but of economics and culture. Territorial nationalism would precipitate needless disputes with neighboring countries."[9]

The Damul Institute regularly takes well-financed delegations consisting largely of South Korean businessmen on tours of northeast China designed to stimulate an awareness of the area as part of the Korean heritage and a good place for Korean investment. More than one hundred thousand people have gone on these tours since the establishment of diplomatic relations between Beijing and Seoul in 1992. A *Wall Street Journal* reporter who accompanied one of these delegations in 1995 was struck by its militantly nationalistic flavor, complete with frequent singing of a patriotic Damul anthem during visits to tombs, museums, ancient fortresses, and the former Koguryo capital city of Jiban, where guides reconstructed memories of a Korean golden age. Outlining plans for an economic federation that would include North Korea, South Korea, and Manchuria, Damul's president told the *Journal* that "Northeast Asia is one bloc, and it's Korean. Reuniting Manchuria with Korea is not only desirable, it's critical for our country." A Hyundai Heavy Industries manager explained that "Manchuria was ours but was taken away. That's why we came here, for investment reasons. Maybe one day it will be ours again."[10]

The vigor of the Damul movement, which claims fifty thousand members, led Chinese Prime Minister Li Peng to lodge a protest against its activities in a 1995 meeting with visiting South Korean Premier Lee Hong Koo. Damul spokesmen are now more circumspect, emphasizing their cultural objectives and denying any irredentist political goals. Nevertheless, a leading Japanese strategic analyst, Shunji Taoka of the *Asahi Shinbun*, has argued that postunification military tensions between Korea and China over Manchuria are more likely than the often-predicted tensions between Korea and Japan.[11]

The possibility of jurisdictional disputes over seabed petroleum deposits in the Yellow Sea has been underlined by the economic problems besetting both the South and the North. The South Korean economy is even more energy-intensive than that of Japan, and crude oil imports impose an onerous burden on the South Korean balance of payments. Until the 1997 Asian financial crisis, South Korean energy imports cost three times as much as Japan's as a fraction of gross national product, with oil demand increasing at a rate of 20 percent per year. South Korea was using ten times as much oil per capita as China. The necessity to cut back crude oil imports since 1997 has been a key factor contributing to the recession in the South and has revived interest in Yellow Sea petroleum exploration, which was suspended after jurisdictional conflicts with Beijing. In the case of the North, the loss of subsidized Soviet and Chinese oil at the end of the cold war has led to virtual economic paralysis that has stimulated serious oil exploration efforts for the first time, including seabed exploration.

South Korean and foreign interest in Yellow Sea petroleum was triggered by a 1968 United Nations seismic survey that reported a "great potential" for oil and gas deposits there.[12] In April 1969, Gulf Oil was awarded the first two offshore concessions granted by Seoul, both of them in Yellow Sea areas along the west coast. This was followed by Shell and Texaco concessions in January and February 1970. At first, China made little effort to interfere with U.S. and European seismic survey ships that crisscrossed the Yellow Sea during the 1969–72 period. As this survey work grew more intense, however, Chinese naval craft began to harass survey vessels operating relatively far from the Korean coast in a potentially disputed middle zone of the Yellow Sea.

In Chinese eyes, Seoul had acted provocatively in allocating concessions unilaterally without first reaching a boundary agreement with Beijing or Pyongyang or both. China does not yet clearly accept the median-line principle in law of the sea discussions and could well insist on geological criteria for sea boundaries more favorable to its interests. Such criteria, in turn, could lead to substantial Chinese claims extending into what South Korea regards as its side of the Yellow Sea. More important, even if it did agree to negotiate a median line with Seoul, this would not automatically make it easy to agree on a boundary settlement. Median-line boundaries are fixed in accordance with the particular islands, or "base points," designated by the countries concerned as defining their coastal limits. In the case of the Yellow Sea, Chinese maps have delineated implicit base-point claims that were ignored in the initial concession boundaries laid down by South Korea.

Beginning in 1971, China conveyed its displeasure over these boundaries by sending lightly armed fishing vessels into the vicinity of survey operations. The floating tracer cables used in seismic studies were systematically cut on at least four occasions. Later, when Gulf conducted drilling operations from February to June 1973 in one of its two concession areas, Peking escalated its response by encircling the Gulf drilling rig with gunboats. By late March, Gulf had capped the well it had been drilling, and by June it had terminated its Yellow Sea operations. A report by Gulf geologists prepared for a technical conference in late 1974 made clear that the most promising parts of the zone in geological terms were the Kunsan Basin and the western Yellow Sea Subbasin, both located at the western end of the concession area where Chinese and South Korean claims overlapped.[13]

The danger of a conflict over sea boundaries between Beijing and Seoul is aggravated by the fact that the most promising geological structures in the Yellow Sea are located either in a shadowy middle zone between Korea and China that has yet to be demarcated in accordance with agreed base points, or in areas geologically linked with more extensive structures still closer to China. At first, when U.S. companies decided not to risk a confrontation with Beijing, Seoul talked of "going it alone." But South Korea's attitude toward Yellow Sea oil gradually became intertwined with its efforts to get Chinese diplomatic recognition and economic cooperation. Seoul has put this issue on the shelf temporarily while periodically sounding out Beijing on cooperative exploration efforts.

North Korea, for its part, has awarded oil exploration concessions in recent years to three small foreign oil companies: Snyder, the British subsidiary of a Texas firm; Beach Oil of Australia; and Taurus of Sweden. Snyder and Taurus are drilling or planning to drill in undisputed areas close to the Yellow Sea coast, but if initial drilling proves successful, their interest in disputed areas further offshore is likely to intensify.

Seabed petroleum development in the Yellow Sea would become more practicable if the two Koreas would adopt an agreed position concerning Korean median-line claims vis-à-vis China. A median-line agreement with China would enable North and South Korea to launch cooperative seabed exploration and development efforts that are now paralyzed by jurisdictional disputes and eventually to join with China in such efforts in those seabed areas where geological structures overlap the median line. As North Korea and South Korea explore the prospects for economic cooperation in the aftermath of their June 2000 summit meeting, they are likely to focus increasingly on the need for cooperation in Yellow Sea petroleum development, starting with the adoption of an agreed median-line position vis-à-vis China.

China and the American Military Presence

Significantly, while Beijing has shifted to a more symmetrical posture in its dealings with the two Koreas, its new posture remains conspicuously asymmetrical in one critical aspect. China continues to maintain its 1961 treaty commitment to intervene militarily in the event of an attack against North Korea. Article 2 of the Sino–North Korean 'Mutual Aid and Cooperation Friendship Treaty' declares that "the two signatory nations guarantee to adopt immediately all necessary measures to oppose any country or coalition of countries that might attack either nation." Each signatory, the treaty adds, "must spare no effort to supply the other with military or any other support." Abrogation of the treaty is not easy. The right to abrogate can be invoked only at specified five-year intervals, and each party must give advance notice of one year. The Sino–North Korean treaty constitutes a more binding and unqualified commitment than the U.S.–South Korean Security Treaty, which conditions U.S. intervention on consultations with Congress. The Soviet Union also had a security treaty with Pyongyang with a binding intervention clause, but in 1996 the Russian Federation said that this clause was "inoperative," and a revised treaty adopted in 1999 provided only for "consultation" in the event of external threats to the security of either country.

Despite its treaty obligations, Beijing has signaled with increasing clarity that its central objective in Korea is to encourage a relaxation of North-South tensions, promote stability, and avoid involvement in another Korean war that would divert energy and resources from its economic priorities. Banning Garrett and Bonnie Glaser, in a systematic 1995 survey of Chinese elite perceptions of policy options in Korea, found that "Chinese leaders would be likely to consider military intervention only if they perceived Chinese security to be directly threatened or if the war had begun as a clear-cut case of unprovoked aggression by Seoul or the United States. Under other circumstances, they would probably reject any intervention to save the North Korean regime in a conflict with the South."

Garrett and Glaser conclude that China would have "few ideological concerns" about the loss of a Communist ally through Korean unification. The consensus of analysts is that North Korea is "unlikely" to collapse during the next decade and that reunification will eventually take place in a gradual and peaceful way. What worries these analysts is not the prospect of unification as such but the possibility that unification will occur in a destabilizing fashion and, above all, the genuine danger that it will lead to diminished Chinese influence in the peninsula relative to that of other powers.[14]

When Garrett returned to interview ten key Korea specialists in Beijing in 1998, his assessment of basic Chinese interests largely echoed what he had heard three years earlier. In 1998, however, he found new apprehensions that the United States might ignite a war in Korea by overreacting to North Korea's missile development and greatly exaggerating the danger of a covert nuclear weapons program. "The Chinese are alarmed," he wrote, "by the prospect of military conflict on the Korean peninsula, worried that the U.S. might be too eager to threaten and use force to resolve its differences with the D.P.R.K., and uncertain how China would react to the use of force by the United States." Several analysts pointed with particular alarm to U.S. media accounts of a new U.S. military contingency plan, cited in part 3, in which the U.S. goal in the event of another Korean war would no longer be limited to the defense of the South but would extend to the destruction of the North Korean regime and occupation of the North by South Korean forces. The new plan would go into operation, according to these accounts, not only if North Korea actually attacked but also if the U.S. detected what it regarded as "unambiguous signals" of a North Korean intention to attack, in which case "preemptive strikes" would be possible.[15]

My own intensive exchanges with Chinese officials and analysts concerning Korea, including conversations during 2001, parallel and extend the findings of Garrett and Glaser. China was indeed alarmed by reports of the new U.S. contingency plan and communicated its concern through diplomatic channels to the United States. While reserving judgment on U.S. intentions in Korea and carefully avoiding threats of Chinese retaliation in the event of U.S. involvement in another Korean war, Chinese diplomats pointedly warn that it would be difficult for the United States to contain military operations within North Korea in such a war, since U.S. and South Korean forces would be tempted to engage in "hot pursuit" of North Korean forces and refugees fleeing across the Chinese border.

North Korea is important to China, in the final analysis, mainly as a buffer against a U.S., Japanese, or Russian military presence in Korea. By the same token, China would not be opposed to the unification of Korea if it occurs peacefully and if a unified Korea maintains a neutral foreign policy and defense posture in which foreign military forces are excluded from the peninsula.

The principal focus of Chinese concern is that the United States will seek to carry over its military alliance with South Korea to a unified Korea. In the absence of the American military presence, most Chinese observers believe, a neutral, unified Korea, while freewheeling and jealous of its independence, would be closer to China than to any other power, psychologically bound not only by their historic ties but also by shared fears of Japanese expansionism. A formal military alliance would not be necessary, in the Chinese perspective, because Korea and China share deep fears of Japanese expansionism that could quickly be translated into joint action in the event of a military crisis. Conversely, the purpose of a U.S. military presence in Korea, linked to a U.S. alliance with Japan, would be to bring Korea into a regional U.S. strategy designed to contain Chinese influence.

South Korea, for its part, has carefully kept all of its options open. When Chinese President Jiang Zemin and South Korean President Kim Young Sam met in Seoul on November 14, 1995, they told a joint news conference that they had an "in-depth" discussion about Japan. Protesting Japan's refusal to acknowledge adequately the atrocities committed during its colonial rule in Korea and its wartime occupation of North China, Jiang said that "we agreed that not forgetting the past is a necessary lesson for the future." The Japanese newspaper *Yomiuri* reported on the following day that China and South Korea "found common ground in chastising Japan for its perceptions of history. Some observers say that they have formed an alliance, but it would be an exaggeration to call them 'allies'."[16] In contrast to Kim Young Sam, President Kim Dae Jung avoided an anti-Japanese posture during his 1998 visit to Beijing and made unprecedented concessions to Japan on trade issues and fishing rights when he visited Tokyo in order to win a stronger apology for its colonial occupation than Japan had previously made. At the same time, Kim Dae Jung is seeking to establish high-level military contacts with China, which Beijing has so far resisted.

Tao Bing Wei, the leading North Korea specialist in the Chinese Foreign Ministry, has openly expressed Chinese suspicions that the emerging U.S. relationship with Pyongyang is the first step in a long-term U.S. plan to preempt Chinese influence in Korea. Warning Washington not to use North Korea as an anti-China beachhead, he said obliquely but pointedly at an international conference in 1996 that "if one country should attempt to use its development of relations with the D.P.R.K. as a means to promote certain strategies of its own, it will inevitably add complex new factors to the solution of the Korean issue."[17] This anxiety is not surprising in view of the repeated North Korean efforts to promote U.S. interest in better relations by arguing explicitly that close ties with Pyongyang would help Washington contain both Chinese and Japanese influence in Korea. One instance of such North Korean efforts came in 1995 when Kim Byong Hong, who holds a rank equivalent to a U.S. assistant secretary of state, said that Pyongyang wanted close ties with the U.S. to offset the power of its immediate neighbors. While Japan is Korea's principal potential adversary, he said, "China and Russia are also big powers on our borders, and it is in your interest to help us balance this power until we can build up the strength of our unified nation."[18]

In a conversation following his defection to South Korea, Hwang Chang Yop, former international secretary of the ruling Workers Party, emphasized that Koreans in the North and South alike share a desire to forestall a restoration of the hegemonic position that China enjoyed in Korea until the nineteenth century. "The Chinese have been trying to pull Kim Jong Il into their sphere," he said, "but he doesn't tell them a damn thing and has even been openly critical of them. What I'm worried about is that if the food problem and economic stagnation go on and on, he will bow down to China to get the help he needs. He'll be forced to knuckle under."[19]

Advocates of a continued postunification U.S. military presence in Korea often misrepresent the Chinese position, suggesting that China would be content to see U.S. forces remain in Korea indefinitely. "After the normalization of Sino-American relations," writes Professor Yang Li Wen of Beijing University, "there emerged an argument in the United States that China 'tacitly approved' or even 'welcomed' the continued stationing of U.S. troops in South Korea in order to oppose the Soviet Union. This is a serious distortion of China's Korea policy and quite contrary to facts." In reality, Yang said, China wants the United States to withdraw its troops from Korea "as soon as possible" because their presence "prolongs the division of Korea and will lead to the perpetual U.S. mastery of South Korea."[20] This view has frequently been echoed by other Chinese spokesmen.[21] The *Beijing Review* has called regularly for a U.S. withdrawal "at the earliest possible date,"[22] and Ye Ruan, a key Foreign Ministry official, declared shortly after the collapse of the Soviet Union that "the United States should speed up its force withdrawal from Korea in the light of new circumstances."[23]

As these statements indicate, it is a gross overstatement to say that China has "welcomed" or even "tacitly approved" the U.S. military presence in Korea. At the same time, a distinction should be made between the way that China views the American presence in the context of a divided Korea and the way that it would view a postunification presence. With Korea divided, Chinese officials say privately, a precipitate U.S. withdrawal could be destabilizing. Thus, many Chinese analysts have soft-pedaled demands for a rapid withdrawal in recent years, suggesting instead a phased disengagement process linked to North and South Korean force reductions and redeployments. Once Korea is unified, however, Chinese officials and analysts agree, the United States could no longer argue that its forces are needed to keep the peace, and the only plausible rationale for their continued presence would be the containment of China.

As I indicated in part 3, North Korea is ready for a phased U.S. disengagement process extending over a period as long as ten years, during which the United States would shift to the role of an honest-broker. This would be acceptable to China. Only time will tell whether Pyongyang and Beijing would desire or tolerate a continued U.S. presence when and if a Korean confederation is established. In such a transitional situation, falling short of complete unification, the North and South would continue to maintain separate armed forces and the possibility of military conflict would continue to exist.

Some American advocates of a continued U.S. military presence acknowledge that China would prefer to have a complete withdrawal of U.S. forces following unification but argue that Beijing could be induced to accept a partial withdrawal. Thus, Morton H. Halperin writes that many Chinese express a readiness to acquiesce in a U.S. presence if American forces and bases remain south of the thirty-eighth parallel.[24] The late Paul H. Kreisberg cited conversations indicating that Beijing would insist on the removal of all ground forces but would not object to a continued security treaty link that would permit the reintroduction of U.S. forces in specified circumstances.[25] Citing conversations with Chinese diplomats, Rear Adm. Eric A. McVadon, a former U.S. defense attaché in Beijing, states that China would not object to the continued presence of U.S. forces in both Korea and Japan if their role is "limited to actions involving just the U.S. and the host country." Many in the

United States, he points out, want U.S. forces to be "the core of a quick reaction force to deter or confront regional contingencies." Thus, "if China adheres to this recently presented formulation, Washington and Beijing will find themselves at odds."[26] By contrast, Robert Scalapino finds it "very unlikely that China would accept willingly an American military presence on its border. After nearly fifty years, the Korean War would have been lost. Perhaps a Korean-American security agreement could be achieved without ground forces in the area—but even an adjustment of this nature would likely cause complications with China."[27]

My own conclusion after exhaustive discussions of this issue with Chinese officials over the years is that postunification U.S. military links of any kind with Korea would become a bitterly divisive issue in Sino–U.S. relations unless these links were part of an anti-Japanese alignment with Seoul and Beijing. In Chinese eyes, the argument that such links would help "stabilize" Northeast Asia is a thinly veiled rationale for a strategy actually designed to contain China in cooperation with Japan and prevent the regional hegemony that China expects by virtue of its size and power.

CHAPTER 25

Korea, Russia, and the United States

CZARIST RUSSIA, the Soviet Union, and now the Russian Federation have all regarded the Korean peninsula as the focal point of their geopolitical and strategic interests in Northeast Asia. Moscow is dismayed by the marginalization of Russian influence in Korea that has taken place since the end of the cold war and is likely to seek a restoration of its role as a major player there in future decades.

In Russian eyes, the United States has done its best to make sure that the Russian Federation is marginalized by building American policy in Northeast Asia around China and Japan and by excluding Moscow from diplomatic initiatives related to Korea that affect Russian interests, notably the 1994 nuclear freeze agreement with North Korea. While it is true that the United States has ignored Russian concerns in Korea during the past decade, the principal reason for the decline in Russian influence there is not what the United States has done but rather what Russia has failed to do. Weakened by its internal economic and political turmoil, the Federation has been unable to project significant economic and military power in the peninsula. Nevertheless, in fashioning its future policies, the United States will face insistent pressures from Russia for recognition of its right to have a voice in major power decisions relating to Korea. Indeed, in the absence of Russian cooperation, the United States would be unable to implement the proposals for denuclearization and neutralization of the Korean peninsula put forward in earlier chapters.

THE TRAUMA OF 1905

In contrast to China and Japan, with their ancient cultural and political ties to Korea, Russia did not become deeply involved in the peninsula until 1860, when Czar Alexander II acquired the Maritime Territories from China. This extension of the empire gave Moscow an eleven-mile common border with Korea. Initially Russia focused only on commercial objectives, seeking to control gold mining and other mineral concessions in the northern part of the peninsula. But its ambitions gradually expanded as the disintegration of the Ching dynasty in China and factional strife in the Yi dynasty in Seoul made Korea increasingly vulnerable to Japanese encroachments. When its new Meiji rulers took over in 1868, Japan moved aggressively to replace China as the dominant external power in Korea. In 1876, Japanese emissaries, backed up by a series of naval attacks, pressured King Kojong into signing a treaty in which he acknowledged Korea to be an "autonomous" state, thus formalizing the end of its status as a tributary of China. This opened the way for an intense jockeying for position between competing foreign powers during the next three decades that culminated in the Russo-Japanese War. Russian, American, British, French, and Japanese representatives were all active in Seoul during this period, enlisting local allies. France supported Russia. The United States and Britain, which admired the Meiji effort to modernize Japan, gave Tokyo a free hand while concentrating on the pursuit of their commercial interests.

Russia aligned itself with King Kojong and traditionalist forces. Japan, pressing Korea to emulate the Meiji reforms, found allies among some of the indigenous Korean reformers who were seeking to modernize the monarchy, but many of the Korean modernizers resisted both Russian and Japanese incursions. When King Kojong called on China in 1894 to quell the populist Tonghak rebellion, Japan saw a golden opportunity to force China out of Korea once and for all and sent in its own forces for the purported purpose of protecting Japanese nationals. The resulting confrontation led to clashes between Chinese and Japanese troops over their respective rights in Korea that soon escalated into the year-long Sino-Japanese war.

Japan's easy victory over China enabled Tokyo to install compliant officials in Seoul who pushed an ambitious reform agenda. King Kojong initially made no effort to confront the Japanese, but Queen Min quietly encouraged popular resistance. Some of the reforms, such as the introduction of a Western-style calendar, provoked a relatively mild reaction. But when pro-Japanese officials issued edicts requiring Korean men to emulate Western-style clothing and hairstyles, removing their traditional "top-knot," armed bands roamed the country killing Japanese and Korean officials regarded as Japanese sympathizers. As Vipin Chandra observes, "The top-knot order was viewed by many as an assault on the cardinal Confucian virtue of filial piety itself, for the top-knot had long been a visible, symbolic expression of the duty of a son not to sully the integrity of the body that linked him to his ancestors."[1]

King Kojong seized this opportunity to assert himself, purging the responsible officials and reversing a wide range of the Japanese-sponsored reforms. Tokyo quickly struck back in 1896 by sending a band of thugs to murder and burn Queen Min in a bungled operation that was supposed to be accomplished in secret but was witnessed by Russian and American observers in the palace. Fearing his own assassination, the king, with the help of Russian agents, disguised himself as a woman and made his escape to the Russian Legation riding in one of the cloistered sedan chairs that frequently go in and out of the palace. This bold Russian challenge to Japan prompted urgent negotiations in which Moscow and Tokyo explored a possible division of the peninsula into clearly defined spheres of influence. But the negotiations failed, and the king returned to his palace a year later.

With the king now firmly on their side, the Russians grew increasingly bold, not only in Korea but also in neighboring Manchuria, where Russia and Japan were both seeking to move into the vacuum resulting from the collapse of the Ching dynasty. In 1897, Moscow succeeded in ousting Japan from its role in training the Korean Army, opening the way for Russian and then French advisers in place of the Japanese. In 1898, Russian forces won out in Manchuria after a series of military skirmishes with the Japanese. In 1901, Russia obtained exclusive rights to coaling stations and other port facilities in Masanpo and Yongampo harbors. Finally, in February 1904 Japan made a last-ditch effort to stop Russian inroads by seeking once again to negotiate a division of the peninsula into spheres of influence. When this effort failed, Tokyo declared war against Moscow in February 1904 and compelled Seoul to permit Japanese forces to march through Korea en route to Manchuria and to the Russian border in the north. It took only a year for Japan to overrun Russian outposts in the Maritime Territories, capture the Russian naval base at Port Arthur in Manchuria, and decimate the rest of the Russian Navy in the famous battle of the Tsushima Strait.

The humiliating defeat suffered by Moscow in 1905 has seared into the Russian psyche deeply embedded historical memories. Nearly a century later, Russia remains acutely conscious of its strategic vulnerability in Northeast Asia and of how important it is to deny the use of Korea militarily to potential enemies or, if possible, to secure Korean military cooperation. The most conspicuous aspect of this vulnerability is the vast distance separating Russian bases in the Far East from Moscow and other centers of industrial production. In time of war, the Trans-Siberian and Baikul-Amur railways can easily be disrupted. Apart from the logistical problems posed by exposed transportation and communication arteries, Moscow faces topographic factors that limit the areas suitable for Far

Eastern bases, together with climatic conditions that have severely restricted the utility of these bases. Vladivostok freezes over for three months every year and averages at least eighty days of fog. Sovietskaya Gavan is also icebound for four months and is fogbound even in summer. Petropavlovsk, isolated in the Kamchatka peninsula, is difficult to supply. Moreover, none of these bases has direct access to the open sea. Ships must pass through one of three straits connecting the Sea of Japan to the Pacific Ocean and can thus easily be bottled up if they are not already in the open sea when and if hostilities erupt.

RUSSIA AND NORTH KOREA: ALLIES NO MORE

Memories of 1905 led the Soviet Union to serve notice at the Yalta and Potsdam conferences that it would demand recognition of its interests in Korea as a key part of a postwar peace settlement with the Allies. When the Russians learned of the impending Japanese surrender before the United States did by intercepting a decoded diplomatic cable, they were quick to declare their entry into the Pacific War. This enabled them to demand a role in accepting the Japanese surrender and thus to move Soviet forces into the northern part of the peninsula while the United States was landing troops in the south. In contrast to the vagueness of the United States concerning its objectives in Korea, Moscow was clearly pursuing the division of the peninsula that it had failed to obtain half a century earlier. As South Korean historian Cho Soon Sung writes, the lack of well-defined American goals during the critical months at the end of World War II "amounted to a tacit invitation to the Russians to occupy Korea, setting in train the events that led to the division."[2]

Anticipating its cold war confrontation with the United States and Japan, Moscow moved purposefully to establish a government in Pyongyang that it hoped would be a close military ally. What the Soviet Union did not anticipate was a split with China that would lead to competition with Beijing for influence in Pyongyang and would make North Korean military cooperation especially critical if the worst-case scenario of a war with China should materialize. North Korea was able to play off Moscow and Beijing against each other throughout the cold war precisely because it understood that the use of airfields and missile bases in North Korea would increase China's exposure to Soviet bombs and land-based missiles and that the use of North Korean naval bases would greatly reduce the distance required by the Soviet Pacific fleet to reach Chinese territory.

Kim Il Sung was only thirty-three when he made his appearance in Pyongyang with the Soviet occupation army in 1945 after more than a decade as an anti-Japanese guerrilla leader in Manchuria closely allied with the Chinese Communists. The details of his shift from Chinese to Soviet sponsorship are a subject of continuing controversy. Most evidence indicates that he spent the last three years of the war in the Soviet armed forces after taking refuge from an advancing Japanese column in Siberia with his guerrilla followers in 1941. Some sources state that Kim rose to the rank of major in the Soviet forces. At the National Revolutionary Museum in Pyongyang, one of the exhibits shows a proclamation dated August 1939 ordering Kim's guerrilla units to help defend the Soviet Union in the face of a Japanese attack along the Soviet-Mongolian border. This is followed by a photo in which a smiling Kim is shown in August 1945, side by side with Soviet troops arriving in North Korea.

Taking full advantage of his initial Soviet backing, Kim and his coterie of close friends from Manchurian days quickly took control of the Workers Party created to run the new North Korean state. They systematically elbowed aside leading figures in the Communist organization that had existed in Korea while they were in Manchuria. Initially, Kim's regime had a "made-in-Moscow" taint. This was not only because he and his inner circle were viewed as creatures of the Soviet occupation. It also reflected the fact that the Russians had brought with them a group of trusted "Soviet-Koreans" who held Soviet citizenship and had risen through the ranks of the Communist apparatus in the Soviet Union itself as representatives of a sizable Korean minority. Moscow put leading "Soviet-Koreans" in key positions in the Workers Party and the government apparatus, giving them a controlling role in the newly created police and intelligence agencies.

As I suggest in the opening chapter of this book, the original assumption that Moscow was responsible for starting the Korean War has been increasingly undermined by historical research. On the contrary, most evidence suggests that it was Kim Il Sung who proposed the idea to Moscow. The most explicit and credible recent evidence to this effect is the account of a prominent Soviet-era military insider, Gen. Dimitri Volkogonov, who has cited secret files on the war showing that it was Kim who first raised the question of a "military reunification" of Korea on January 19, 1950.[3] In any case, whether Stalin or Kim took the initiative, Moscow lost its position as the dominant external power in Pyongyang as a result of the Korean War. Chinese intervention in the war led to Chinese co-sponsorship of the Pyongyang regime. In the aftermath of the conflict, with de-Stalinization beginning in Moscow, Kim purged the "Soviet-Koreans," consolidated his personal control of the Workers Party, and began to articulate his policy of *juche*, or self-reliance, as a rationale for his increasingly freewheeling posture in dealing with both Moscow and Beijing.

Even during the war, tensions had begun to develop between North Korea and the Soviet Union in mid-1951 when Pyongyang wanted to escalate the conflict and Moscow refused. Soviet concurrence in the armistice was seen as a betrayal of the North Korean cause. The resulting disenchantment with Moscow was intensified by strains over the terms of Soviet aid, especially when Moscow pressed North Korea in 1956 to accept the concept of a "division of labor" within the Communist bloc by joining COMECON (the Communist Council for Mutual Economic Assistance), and Pyongyang refused. Seeking to shape the North Korean economy to serve Soviet economic priorities, Moscow did its best to frustrate Pyongyang's decision to emphasize heavy industry and to create its own machine-building capability. This led to North Korean efforts to attract Chinese aid as an offset to Soviet dependence, accompanied by ideological attacks on Moscow for what Pyongyang considered the "revisionist" appeasement of the United States exemplified during the Cuban missile crisis.

Moscow reacted to a continuing barrage of ideological assaults by abruptly suspending economic and military aid to North Korea in 1962, recalling all of its technical advisers. Aid was eventually resumed at reduced levels following a post-Kruschchev turnabout in Soviet policy in late 1965. It was soon after the restoration of aid that Pyongyang formally rejected the concept of a "leading party" in the international Communist movement in a manifesto on August 12, 1966, "Let Us Declare Our Independence." Asserting that "all fraternal parties are equal and independent," the Workers Party organ *Rodong Shinmun* summed up North Korean policy as one of "*Juche* in ideology, independence in politics, self-reliance in economy and self-defense in national defense."

Kim Il Sung consistently refused to modify his economic priorities as the price for a renewal of Soviet aid and continued to use Moscow as a nationalist whipping boy, charging that "the modern revisionists . . . brought economic pressure upon us, inflicting tremendous losses upon our socialist construction." The basic objective underlying Kim's effort to maximize economic self-sufficiency was a desire to create the base for an independent defense production capability and thus increase his freedom of action in dealing with South Korea. This led to tensions with Moscow over military as well as economic aid, with Pyongyang seeking access to sophisticated military technology that Moscow was unwilling to provide. The Soviet Union did provide an estimated $835 million in military aid from 1964 to 1978, but Pyongyang openly complained to visitors that it was not being treated as well as other Soviet allies.

Soviet–North Korean relations were cool throughout this period, in contrast to a steady improvement in North Korean relations with Beijing, including infusions of Chinese military aid. Warning that it did not want to get involved in another war in Korea, Moscow criticized Pyongyang for seizing the U.S. spy ship *Pueblo* in 1968 and for shooting down a U.S. EC-121 reconnaissance plane in 1969. Soon after the EC-121 incident, President Nixon made his often-quoted comment that "perhaps more than any other nation in the Communist bloc,"[4] North Korea is "completely out of the control of the Soviet Union and Communist China."

By 1979, the continuing deterioration of Sino-Soviet relations had reached its climax with Beijing's abrogation of its "unequal" 1950 treaty with Moscow. This formally brought to an end the special Soviet military rights in Manchuria that Stalin had demanded as the price for helping the new Communist regime in Beijing during its early years. Faced with an increasingly assertive China that had normalized its relations with the United States and Japan, Moscow decided in 1984 to prepare for the worst-case scenario of a military conflict with Beijing by strengthening its ties with Pyongyang. Prime Minister Konstantin Chernenko invited Kim Il Sung to Moscow for his first state visit in seventeen years, paving the way for a major escalation of Soviet military aid to Pyongyang.

During the years immediately thereafter, North Korea received Mig-23, Mig-29, and SU-25 aircraft; Scud and SA-3 surface-to-air missiles; AT-3 anti-tank missiles; T-62 tanks; and help in building a helicopter factory. It was this influx of costly sophisticated equipment that pushed the grand total of Soviet cold war military aid to Pyongyang to $11.2 billion. Moscow also agreed to defer North Korean debt repayments and promised to provide four nuclear reactors that North Korea wanted for its civilian nuclear power program, the light water type of reactor that was later to figure in the 1994 nuclear freeze agreement between North Korea and the United States. In return, North Korea agreed to sign the NPT and Soviet TU-16 reconnaissance aircraft were permitted to fly over North Korean territory on intelligence missions enroute to Vietnam,

Manchuria, and areas of the Bo Hai Gulf and the Yellow Sea where China conducts its largest naval exercises. For the first time since 1953, Soviet naval units were given access to the North Korean port of Wonsan.

Paradoxically, North Korea received its most significant influx of Soviet military hardware during the very years when the Soviet Union was undergoing an internal political transformation that was destined to produce a profound change in Moscow's posture toward Pyongyang. Recalling his 1986 meeting with the newly ascendant Mikhail Gorbachev, Kim Il Sung told me during our 1994 meeting that "all of this talk of Glasnost and Perestroika deeply alarmed us. We knew it would lead to disaster and to big problems for us, and it did. That man destroyed overnight what it had taken seventy years to build."[5]

Gradually, as Gorbachev consolidated his power base in Moscow, it was clear that he wanted to move to a more balanced Soviet posture in the peninsula that would be consistent with his efforts to improve relations with the West. His objective was to retain a foothold in Pyongyang while opening relations with Seoul. In 1988, the Soviet Union participated in the Seoul Olympics despite Pyongyang's protests, and by 1990, Moscow and Seoul had established diplomatic relations. Gorbachev did not stop Soviet military aid to Pyongyang during his tenure. However, he did stall on fulfilling Chernenko's nuclear reactor commitment, reflecting a new emphasis on nonproliferation that led to pressures on Pyongyang to permit IAEA inspection of North Korean nuclear facilities.

The collapse of the Soviet Union in 1991, the downfall of Gorbachev, and the emergence of Boris Yeltsin led in swift succession to a termination of Soviet military aid to Pyongyang, Russian cancellation of the operative clauses of the 1961 Soviet security treaty with North Korea, pressures for repayment of Pyongyang's $3.5 billion debt to Moscow, and insistence on hard currency repayment in all trade transactions. The reactor deal Kim had made with Chernenko was formally canceled. Perhaps the most serious blow of all for North Korea was the cutoff of most Soviet oil deliveries resulting primarily from Pyongyang's lack of hard currency, which crippled fertilizer factories, tractors, and irrigation pumps, setting the stage for the food shortages of later years.

In contrast to Gorbachev's efforts to retain a foothold in North Korea while opening ties with the South, Yeltsin virtually wrote off Russian interests in Pyongyang during his first four years as president, focusing single-mindedly on forging a new relationship with Seoul. As a leading Foreign Ministry functionary later put it, "The leaders of the new anti-Communist regime in Moscow felt nothing but contempt for Communists both inside and outside of Russia, and North Korea, with its pure Stalinist-type dictatorship, seemed the worst possible case. It was assumed that all remaining Communist regimes in the world were doomed and that Russia should distance itself from a decaying international pariah, especially since economic cooperation with North Korea was simply not profitable."[6] The attitude prevailing in Moscow at this time was epitomized by the information minister of the Yeltsin government, visiting Tokyo in 1992, who advised Japan not to pay reparations to North Korea as part of any normalization of relations, as it had done with Seoul, "so as not to prolong this repressive, obsolete regime."[7]

As economic problems in Russia itself led to the decline of reformist elements and an upsurge of nationalist and Communist forces in the 1992 and 1995 elections to the Duma, Korea policy, like other aspects of Yeltsin's foreign policy, became a focus of controversy in Moscow. A significant pro–North Korea lobby emerged, embracing right-wing elements in the Duma, prominent officials in Yeltsin's own Ministry of Foreign Affairs, leading generals with ties to defense industries, and Russian diplomats and technicians who have served in Pyongyang. Their central argument for restoring ties with North Korea is that Russia has a continuing strategic stake in the peninsula and should seek to become a major player there once again, primarily to offset a potentially expansionist Japan that may acquire nuclear weapons. To regain its influence, this argument holds, Russia should seek to balance its relations with Seoul and Pyongyang, as China has done. While not advocating new military aid or the sale of offensive weapons, proponents of this view favor the sale of "defensive" weapons and spare parts for Russian equipment already in the North Korean armory, if Pyongyang is able to pay in hard currency or to offer attractive barter terms, such as payment in minerals or other raw materials. This view had prevailed by the time Kim Jong Il visited Moscow in late 2001, when President Vladimir Putin agreed to provide spare parts and components, but only on a cash basis.

Pressures for a reassessment of Russian policy have been reinforced by what Moscow sees as a deliberate American policy of excluding Russia from the peninsula, reflected in a series of U.S. rebuffs: first, the summary U.S. dismissal of the Russian proposal in early 1994 for a ten-power conference to resolve the nuclear crisis with Pyongyang; next, U.S. rejection of subsequent Russian requests for a role in implementing the 1994 U.S.–North Korean nuclear freeze agreement; and finally, the exclusion of Russia from the four-power talks (North and South Korea, China, and the United States) on a peace process in the peninsula that have been in progress since 1997.

Economic as well as strategic arguments have been advanced by advocates of reengagement. Given the extent of the resources that the Soviet Union invested in the economic development of North Korea, it is argued that Moscow should do what it can to minimize Russian losses to the greatest extent possible. Instead of completely writing off the $3.5 billion North Korean debt, in this view, Moscow should seek to restore trade ties that would enable Pyongyang to pay some of the debt back, exporting Russian products that are not competitive in the international market but would be acceptable to a hard-pressed North Korea. Even if the main focus of Russian economic interest in Korea will be Seoul, not Pyongyang, this argument runs, some of the most important joint projects under discussion with Seoul would require North Korean cooperation, notably the proposed gas pipelines from Siberia or Sakhalin to South Korea, which would have to cross North Korean territory.

In Moscow, as in Washington and Tokyo, the debate over Korea policy has hinged largely on the issue of whether or not a collapse is likely in Pyongyang. As a consensus has developed that Kim Jong Il is securely in power and that prospects for a collapse are minimal, Moscow has begun to take modest steps to reengage with Pyongyang. A package of economic agreements in 1996 envisaged Russian help in getting Soviet-built factories back into operation through the provision of spare parts and technicians, together with steps by North Korea to begin repaying its debt, partly through reinstitution of the barter method of payment. More recently, Moscow has made clear that it now favors the normalization of North Korean political and economic relations with both Washington and Tokyo. Most important, Moscow has gradually edged toward a resumption of arms sales. In 1994, Stephen J. Blank of the U.S. Army War College cited evidence that support for a resumption of sales is "gaining in the government."[8] In 1997, Alvin Z. Rubenstein wrote that Russia was providing "some arms, primarily of a defensive character, and some spare parts."[9] In 1999, Pyongyang made a covert deal with Kazakhstan to obtain Russian military equipment, including early-model Mig aircraft. Russia continued to maintain a military advisory mission in Pyongyang in 2000. No overt support exists in Moscow for a resurrection of the 1961 mutual security treaty, which has been converted to a nonmilitary Treaty of Friendship and Cooperation similar to the one that Moscow has concluded with Seoul. However, when President Vladimir Putin visited

Pyongyang in July 2000, his joint communiqué with Kim Jong II pledged that Pyongyang and Moscow "would contact each other without delay if there is a danger of aggression against the D.P.R.K. or Russia, or a need to consult and cooperate in the event that peace and security are threatened."[10]

RUSSIA AND SOUTH KOREA: HIGH HOPES

The debate in Moscow over whether to seek a restoration of Russian influence in Pyongyang has reflected in part a realization that the economic benefits of the new Russian relationship with Seoul are not likely to be as grandiose as originally anticipated. When Mikhail Gorbachev braved North Korean wrath by opening diplomatic relations with Seoul in 1990, he expected a massive influx of South Korean credits and investment that would help to rescue the faltering Soviet economy and stimulate the economic development of Siberia and the Far East republics. By 1999, however, South Korean companies had invested a cumulative total of only $151.4 million in the entire Russian Federation, including $138.8 million in the Far East. Trade has proved to be mutually beneficial to Moscow and Seoul, with Russian exports to South Korea totaling nearly $1 billion in 1998 out of a bilateral trade total of $2.1 billion. But the level of trade has remained relatively constant after an initial period of growth and most projections indicate that Russian exports to South Korea are not likely to expand much in the foreseeable future.

For his part, President Roh Tae Woo expected the normalization of relations with the Soviet Union to facilitate an improvement of South Korean relations with Pyongyang. "The road between Seoul and Pyongyang is now blocked," he said after his first meeting with Gorbachev. "We must therefore choose an alternative route to the North Korean capital by way of Moscow and Beijing."[11] Thus, when the Soviet Union collapsed and Moscow turned its back on Pyongyang, the strategic importance of the opening to Moscow sharply declined in South Korean eyes.

Roh and Gorbachev inadvertently created a built-in source of discord in the Seoul-Moscow relationship by negotiating an agreement providing for a series of South Korean loans to Moscow totalling $3 billion. From the outset, Moscow was unable to keep up repayments, and Seoul suspended further disbursements in 1991 after extending $1.47 billion in credits. The Russian Federation, which inherited the debt, proved to be even more delinquent and was $451 million in arrears by the end of 1993.

As it became increasingly clear that the loan agreement would have to be renegotiated, defense-related industries in Moscow saw an opportunity for Russia to prepare the ground for future arms sales to Seoul by including military equipment in a debt repayment package. In August 1993, Vice Premier Alexander Shobkin made the first formal Russian offer to provide advanced weapons systems in repayment of the debt. Directly challenging South Korean reliance on the United States as the principal source of its military hardware, Shobkin urged Seoul to accept the Russian SA-12 missile defense system as part of a repayment package instead of buying U.S. Patriot missiles.[12] This provoked strong U.S. pressures on Seoul to steer clear of military involvement with Moscow and an initially cool South Korean response to the Russian proposal. When the debt was renegotiated in 1995, however, Seoul did agree that $650 million of the debt could be repaid in military hardware, with another $730 million in raw materials and $70 million in helicopters. Subsequent follow-up agreements resulted in the delivery of $225 million in military hardware by early 1999, including such state-of-the-art items as T-80 main battle tanks, BMP-3 infantry fighting vehicles, AT-3 anti-tank guided missiles, and SA-16 surface-to-air missiles, plus 25 out of 55 promised helicopters.

When the 1997 Asian financial crisis forced South Korea to scale down its plans for the domestic production of military aircraft, Moscow offered the latest version of its SU-35 fighter aircraft, to be assembled in factories in South Korea, complete with the most advanced Russian jet engine and phased grid radar. Russia is also pressing Seoul to accept its submarines instead of proceeding with a pending French purchase. However, the United States has continued to throw cold water on military links between Seoul and Moscow. Former secretary of defense William Cohen has repeatedly declared that it would be a political and military mistake for South Korea to buy Russian air defense missiles in place of the Patriot, going so far as to warn that Russian SA-12 missiles might accidentally threaten U.S. jets in any new Korean war. Cohen has also questioned the interoperability of the SA-12 with the F-15 and other U.S. supplied military aircraft now in the South Korean inventory.[13] American opposition is likely to stop or severely restrict the further acquisition of additional Russian weaponry. Moreover, South Korean defense officials echo the American argument that interoperability is a serious concern.

There is a conflict over Russian arms acquisitions between economic officials in Seoul, who want to get the debt paid off, and defense officials, who fear the loss of already budgeted funds for defense procurement if Russian military hardware becomes available. Russia is anxious to find some acceptable form of repayment so that the debt issue does not damage the overall growth of economic relations with Seoul and has offered to provide military technology to Korean defense industries in place of actual weapons systems. If repayment in military hardware is unacceptable, Moscow told Seoul in March 1999, South Korea should extend the repayment period from eight to twenty-five years and write off a large portion of the $1.7 billion, including interest, still outstanding.

Apart from tensions over repayment of the debt, the potential for significant increases in South Korean investment in the Russian Federation is likely to be limited in the short-term future by continuing political and economic instability in Moscow and resulting uncertainties in the investment environment. Stringent taxation, conflicting national and local laws, demands for protection money by organized criminal gangs, and a deteriorating infrastructure have discouraged South Korean companies from investing in many parts of the Federation. One notable exception is eastern Siberia, where South Korean investors are attracted by unusually low wage rates, such as 56 cents per hour in the textile industry, compared with $2.69 in South Korea. A growing number of South Korean textile and electronic firms have set up factories in Vladivostok and nearby towns and are shipping "Made in Russia" apparel to the United States, thus circumventing U.S. restrictions limiting the level of imports from South Korea. The Nakodhka Free Economic Zone is also attracting the interest of South Korean companies seeking wage rates lower than those in more developed parts of the Federation.

Looking ahead, South Korean investment could well grow substantially when and if the Federation revives economically and Russian consumers become more affluent. Moreover, even if the Russian economy remains moribund, Moscow's vast, largely unexploited petroleum resources—in eastern Siberia, the Sakha Republic directly to the north of Korea, and Sakhalin Island—are likely to attract increasing South Korean interest.

Until 1997, Seoul and Moscow were actively exploring a $20 billion project to build a natural gas pipeline with Japanese participation from Yakutsk in the Sakha Republic to South Korea and Japan, capable of carrying up to thirty billion cubic meters of gas annually. The pipeline would have to go through North Korea, which would receive a supply of gas in return for its cooperation. But Russia's unwillingness to make a significant financial commitment has made it less attractive to Seoul and Tokyo than another less costly projected pipeline project originating near Irkutsk in eastern Siberia, which would cross into China through Mongolia or directly to the east of the Sino-Mongolian border and would then proceed through North Korea to the South and later by an undersea pipeline to Japan. In 1997, Russia and China signed an agreement to pursue this project that envisaged financial support from British Petroleum; the China National Petroleum Corporation; and South Korean and Japanese companies. Under the agreement, the $10 billion pipeline would carry at least twenty billion cubic meters of gas annually over a thirty-year period from the already developed Kovyktinskoye gas field and possibly much more from nearby fields, depending on economic and geological studies not yet completed.

Keun Wook Paik, an energy specialist at the Royal Institute of International Affairs in London, has proposed multilateral cooperation to break the financial and political bottlenecks that obstruct development of a regional pipeline network. Paik cites the "invisible competition" of existing suppliers of liquefied natural gas to Northeast Asia as a key factor obstructing agreement on such a network.

Japanese foot-dragging on the development of Sakhalin and Siberian resources is also linked to the unresolved territorial dispute between Moscow and Tokyo over the Kurile Islands and the fact that the projected pipelines would cross through North Korea. A Royal Institute survey of Japanese and South Korean companies conducted by Paik in 1995 found that 66 percent of the Korean respondents "strongly favored" the idea of a pipeline passing through North Korea, while 55 percent of the Japanese respondents opposed it. "This is a strong reflection," Paik observed, "of Korea's desire for reunification between the two Koreas. But in reality, no financing will be available for the route passing through North Korea owing to the confrontation between the two Koreas."[14]

When the June 2000 intra-Korean summit relaxed North-South tensions, interest in a pipeline route crossing North Korea resurfaced. With Sakhalin natural gas production about to begin and a pipeline link from Sakhalin to Khabarovsk in prospect, Paik proposed the extension of the pipeline directly southward from Khabarovsk through adjacent North Korea to South Korea. South Korea, he said, should provide the $1 billion required for the extension. Apart from the profound economic and political impact that the pipeline would have on North-South cooperation, he argued, Seoul would quickly recover its investment by reducing its dependence on more costly energy imports from the Persian Gulf and other distant sources.[15]

MARGINALIZING MOSCOW

The American effort to minimize South Korean military procurement from Russia reflects a broader, albeit unstated, regional goal: perpetuating the status of the United States as the dominant outside power in the peninsula. Given this goal, Washington has repeatedly ignored Russia's contention that it has an inherent right to participate in international decisions relating to Korea by virtue of its geographical position as a neighboring state located directly adjacent to Korean territory.

The most conspicuous American affront to Russian interests in Korea was the exclusion of Moscow from the resolution of the 1994 nuclear crisis with North Korea. During the preceding decades, Moscow had worked cooperatively with Washington to promote nonproliferation in Korea by successfully pressuring Pyongyang to sign the NPT in 1985 and to permit IAEA inspection of North Korean nuclear facilities in 1992. With its historically rooted fears of an expansionist, rearmed Japan that might have territorial designs in Sakhalin Island and Siberia, Russia shares the American desire to prevent North Korea from acquiring a nuclear weapons capability that could strengthen pro-nuclear hawks in Japan.

When Gorbachev assumed power, he was quick to recognize that Chernenko's promise to give Pyongyang four light water nuclear reactors could complicate his efforts to improve relations with Washington. Gorbachev delayed implementation of this pledge despite pressures from supporters of the project in the Russian nuclear power industry. However, to fend off the nuclear lobby, he permitted a feasibility study at the potential reactor site in Kumho, the same location eventually chosen by the Korean Energy Development Organization (KEDO) for the construction of the two reactors to be built under the 1994 U.S.–North Korean nuclear freeze agreement. Eventually, Yeltsin canceled the reactor deal in 1993 amid growing tensions between Washington and Pyongyang over the North Korean nuclear program. Yeltsin knew that the Russian nuclear lobby would protest. But he expected the criticism leveled against him in Moscow to be offset by American gratitude for this contribution to U.S. nonproliferation objectives, an expectation that proved to be illusory.

During U.N. Security Council debates from March to June 1994 over whether to impose an economic embargo against North Korea, Russia proposed a ten-power conference (the five permanent members of the Security Council plus the U.N. secretary general, the director-general of the IAEA, Japan, and the two Koreas) to seek ways of defusing the crisis. The United States and South Korea brushed aside this proposal and two subsequent proposals for multilateral negotiations including Russia. When the United States put forward a sanctions resolution, Moscow threatened a veto, charging Washington with bad faith. Foreign Minister Andrei Kozyrev said that the resolution contradicted an agreement "to work out a draft resolution jointly" that would include "both the idea of sanctions and specific ideas on an international conference."[16] In the end, facing resistance from Japan and China in addition to Russia, the United States dropped the idea of sanctions after the Pyongyang visit by former president Jimmy Carter in June opened the way for the freeze agreement.

To my surprise, the issue of Russian participation in a settlement of the U.S. nuclear controversy with Pyongyang came up immediately when I proposed a freeze of their nuclear facilities to North Korean leaders in June 1994. First Deputy Foreign Minister Kang Sok Ju told me that he liked the basic concept of a North Korean freeze in return for economic and political concessions by the United States, including the construction of light water reactors to replace the existing graphite-based reactors to be covered by the freeze. But Kang immediately objected when I outlined a scenario in which the new light water reactors would be obtained from the United States, South Korea, or Japan. As I noted in part 4, he made clear from the start that North Korea wanted Russian reactors. Recalling the Kumho feasibility study, he said during a three-hour meeting on June 6 that the United States should extend aid to Russia that would enable Moscow, in turn, to provide the reactors to North Korea. "You are helping them these days," he said, "so you should be able to do this." I replied that Washington would be cool to such an arrangement, pointing out that U.S.–Russian relations were not as cozy as he seemed to think. "It would be much more difficult to carry out if you involve South Korea and Japan," he said. "Our nuclear technicians know the Russians after working with them for so many years and it would be much easier to do it that way."

Carter persuaded Kim Il Sung to initiate a freeze immediately in order to set the stage for a diplomatic dialogue with Washington. It was not until five months later that the nuclear freeze agreement was concluded in October and not until June 1995 that North Korea yielded to U.S. insistence that South Korea would build the new reactors, with financing to be provided by Seoul, Tokyo, and, to a much lesser extent, Washington. During this year-long interval, Russia lobbied vigorously for a share in the reactor project. Foreign Minister Kozyrev offered to cancel an $800 million Russian contract for the construction of a light water reactor and power plant in Iran, to which Washington objected, in exchange for a less lucrative contract to build one of the new reactors for North Korea.[17] Initially Pyongyang encouraged Moscow, but in the end Pyongyang acceded to the U.S. argument that only Seoul and Tokyo were prepared to put up the financing needed for the $4 billion reactor venture. *Izvestia* observed bitterly that Russia had voluntarily canceled its bilateral reactor contract with Pyongyang as a show of solidarity with the United States, "but our efforts to 'lend a hand' have been disregarded and we will have to scrap our hopes for a role in helping to modernize the North Korean nuclear energy complex, a prospect we were very much counting on. It turns out that Russia is being squeezed out of the nuclear market. We have become an 'outsider' in Asia."[18]

Russia asked to be represented on the board of the U.S.-Japanese-South Korean consortium formed to build the reactors for North Korea, KEDO, but after protracted negotiations, the Russian overture was rejected because Moscow was unable to make the required financial contribution.

While Russia was still smarting over its exclusion from the nuclear settlement with Pyongyang, it received another slap in the face in April 1996 when President Clinton and President Kim Young Sam proposed four-power talks (the two Koreas, the United States, and China) to discuss the replacement of the 1954 armistice with a permanent peace structure. Georgiy Kunadze, the Russian ambassador to Seoul, commented that as one of the two powers that divided Korea in 1945, Moscow had a right to participate in such discussions.[19] Three years later, after four inconclusive rounds of the four-power talks at Geneva, Kunadze's successor, Evgeny Afanasiev, suggested in early 1999 their expansion into a six-party dialogue including Russia and Japan.[20] Foreign Minister Igor Ivanov added in a Moscow interview that "we want Russia's voice to be heard in a settlement of the most explosion-prone problem of the Asia-Pacific, that is, the Korean problem, and to this end we will pursue a balanced policy toward both Korean states."[21] Russian pronouncements have consistently envisaged a gradual process of reunification, starting with a confederation accompanied by the phased withdrawal of foreign forces. Equally important, Russia launched a vigorous campaign of economic diplomacy in 2001 designed to promote cooperation between

North and South Korea. The Russian Railroad Company wants to extend the Trans-Siberian Railroad to North Korea, where it would link up with the South Korean rail system to make possible a major expansion of container trade between Europe and Asia. Confident that this would become profitable, the Russian Company, a state monopoly with swollen coffers, has offered to finance the required renovation of the North Korean system. As negotiations with Pyongyang and Seoul over managerial issues proceeded in 2001, Russia was also accelerating efforts to promote natural gas pipelines from western Siberia and Sakhalin Island that would go through North Korea to South Korea.

In negotiating the future of the peninsula with Stalin during the closing months of World War II, President Franklin D. Roosevelt clearly recognized that Russia had traditionally regarded Korea as the focal point of its geopolitical and strategic interests in Northeast Asia. At the time of his death, he was seeking to promote U.S.–Soviet cooperation in administering a united Korea under a multilateral trusteeship. As Bruce Cumings has observed, Roosevelt wanted "to involve the Russians in a joint administration of Korea, to embrace them and their interests in a country that touched their borders," and thus "to forestall unilateral solutions." But Roosevelt's death in April 1945 came before negotiations on a trusteeship had crystallized. In August, on the eve of the Japanese surrender, the new Truman administration, hoping "to assure a predominant American voice in postwar Korean affairs" and doubtful that a trusteeship would do so, hastily divided the peninsula, tactily inviting the Red Army to occupy the North and setting the stage for the installation of a U.S. client regime in the South.[22]

When the cold war ended and Seoul normalized its relations with Moscow, former secretary of state James A. Baker made an abortive move in 1991 to include Russia in a six-power dialogue on Korea. "The process of reconciliation and, eventually, reunification on the Korean peninsula needs to be based on Korean initiatives," he wrote in *Foreign Affairs*. Nevertheless, "the four major powers—the United States, the Soviet Union, China and Japan—have important interests that intersect there. As the North-South dialogue progresses, we will explore the possibilities for a forum for the two Koreas and the four major powers in Northeast Asia that will support the dialogue, help in the easing of tensions, facilitate discussion of common security concerns and possibly guarantee outcomes negotiated between the two Koreas."[23]

North and South Korea both objected to the inclusion of Japan, and Baker never pursued his proposal. Seoul might not be as inflexible on this issue now, but until Japan and North Korea normalize their relations, Pyongyang is not likely to join in a six-power forum involving Tokyo. Given this reality, the United States should demonstrate in other ways its recognition that Moscow will be a key player in promoting a secure, nuclear-free Korea.

As noted earlier, the proposals for a military neutralization of Korea and a six-power denuclearization agreement presuppose Russian participation. Exploratory negotiations on these proposals could be initiated through bilateral channels or through the inclusion of Russia in the four-power talks at Geneva, in parallel with a U.S. transition to the role of an honest broker and tripartite (North Korea-South Korea-United States) arms-control negotiations under the aegis of the Mutual Security Commission proposed by Pyongyang.

The American policy of marginalizing Russia in Korea is consistent with an overall approach toward Russia that oscillates between two extremes: on the one hand, condescension toward Moscow as the loser in the cold war, a basket case no longer entitled to superpower status; on the other, half-hearted efforts to help forestall an economic collapse that could lead to a right-wing nationalistic backlash at the expense of the United States. The expansion of NATO, U.S. intervention in Kosovo, the projected abrogation of the Anti-Ballistic Missile Treaty, and the American effort to minimize Russian participation in the development of Central Asian petroleum resources are fueling a xenophobic anger in Moscow that could indeed prove damaging to American interests, especially if Russia recovers its economic vitality and political cohesion. Yet the opportunity still exists for constructive cooperation based on a recognition that the Russian nuclear arsenal makes Moscow an indispensable partner in promoting global security, especially the reduction and elimination of nuclear weapons envisaged in article 6 of the Nuclear Non-Proliferation Treaty. In the case of Korea, Russian cooperation would be essential for the achievement of the militarily neutralized Korea free of nuclear weapons envisaged in earlier chapters.

CHAPTER 26

Then and Now

THE CASE FOR A NEUTRAL KOREA

THE CASE for the indefinite continuation of the American military presence in Korea rests on a questionable set of assumptions: first, that U.S. disengagement would create a power vacuum; second, that China, Japan, and Russia would move into this vacuum, competing for dominance as they did from 1894 to 1905; and finally, that a reunified Korea without U.S. protection would either seek a military alliance with one of its neighbors, probably China, or would develop its own independent nuclear capability.

These assumptions exclude the possibility that a reunified Korea could play the independent, non-nuclear buffer role envisaged in the proposals for a militarily neutralized peninsula and a nuclear-free Northeast Asia presented earlier. Yet a variety of factors make this possibility a realistic goal in an emerging regional environment that differs fundamentally from that of a century ago.

The critical difference between then and now is that Korea at the turn of the century was not yet politically sensitized and mobilized. Still largely a feudal, rural society with a limited educational infrastructure, it had not achieved the universal literacy that the North and South have today. It had not developed a broadly based nationalist consciousness and was not yet seeking to assert its identity in the community of nation-states. The powerful spirit of Korean nationalism emphasized in part 1, aroused by four decades of peculiarly brutal Japanese colonialism and five decades of division, has introduced a new and potentially decisive element into the situation.

Nationalism is now a driving force in both the North and South. It will make any form of unified regime much less vulnerable to foreign manipulation than the politically quiescent and economically underdeveloped Korea of a century ago. Once the division is ended, in short, there will be no power vacuum for outsiders to fill. Korea will emerge as a power in its own right, making its own decisions concerning the nature and size of its military capabilities on the basis of what others do or do not do. For example, in the absence of some form of regional agreement that would rule out a Japanese nuclear capability and the use of American, Chinese, and Russian nuclear weapons in Korea, it is possible that a unified Korea would develop an independent nuclear deterrent. But a U.S. disengagement, in itself, need not lead to this outcome.

It is precisely because Korean nationalism is so strong that pressures for U.S. disengagement have been building up in recent years and are likely to intensify following a confederation or full unification. The enduring impact of Japanese colonial rule as a stimulus to Korean nationalism has been emphasized in an earlier chapter. But the United States, too, is a focus of Korean nationalist sentiment, given the American role in imposing the division of the peninsula in 1945. Throughout the colonial decades, Koreans had looked ahead hopefully to the moment when the Japanese departed as the occasion for their national entry onto the world stage, only to find themselves trapped between American- and Russian-installed regimes when the moment arrived. Reflecting a superpower perspective, the conventional wisdom in the United States during the cold war was that a balance of power existed in East Asia among the United States, Japan, China, and Russia. This thinking lingers even today. But this "balance" exists at the cost of a divided Korea, a cost unacceptable to the Koreans themselves.

The assumption that there would be a power vacuum in a reunified Korea if U.S. forces withdraw reflects insensitivity to this new reality of a dynamic Korean nationalism. Similarly, the assumption that Japan, China, and Russia would not respect a military neutralization of Korea reveals both a misreading of history and a blindness to the changes that have taken place in Northeast Asia during the past century.

In contrast to the European experience, the unification of Korea would not be perceived by its neighbors as inherently threatening. Germany in the first flush of its unification during the nineteenth century was expansionist, but in the case of East Asia, Japan was the expansionist power and Korea the victim of its colonial oppression. Moreover, Korea became the focus of external contention a century ago precisely because at that time a power vacuum did exist in Seoul, where the Yi dynasty was collapsing. The vulnerability of Korea coincided with a decline of Chinese power that tempted a newly assertive Japan to move into the vacuum. By contrast, there is no such power imbalance between China and Japan today. Neither would risk a military confrontation over Korea except in the face of the gravest provocation, and it would be much more difficult for either to manipulate internal factional divisions in a unified Korea than it was in the late nineteenth century.

The assessment presented in the three preceding chapters supports the view that a militarily neutral Korea would be respected by each of its immediate neighbors if it is also respected by the United States and other extra-regional powers.

As we have seen, Japan looks down on Korea and still nurses a deep-seated bitterness over its expulsion from the peninsula as a result of its defeat in World War II. But far from wanting to reestablish its hegemony there, Tokyo has attempted during and since the cold war to avoid economic and military responsibilities in Korea that it feels should rightly be assumed by the United States as the price for having expelled Japan and for using Korea as a cold war outpost of American power.

In Japanese eyes, Korea is a place to make money, not to spend it. For Tokyo, the Korean War was a timely opportunity to obtain lucrative procurement contracts that accelerated its postwar economic recovery. Later, when the United States bulldozed South Korea into normalizing relations with Japan, Tokyo did nothing to discourage American hopes that its 1965 normalization treaty with South Korea would be the precursor of a Seoul-Tokyo axis. In reality, Tokyo had no intention of becoming involved militarily in Korea but was only too happy to have American help in establishing what have proved to be unusually profitable—and unusually exploitative—Japanese economic relations with South Korea.

Throughout the cold war, the United States repeatedly failed in its efforts to commit Japan to a meaningful role in the defense of South Korea. American pressures did successfully block intermittent efforts by Japanese doves to promote a normalization of relations with Pyongyang. Washington obtained only cosmetic concessions, however, when it pressed Tokyo for explicit agreement on the military responsibilities that Japan would assume in the event of a new Korean conflict.

Since the end of the cold war, Japan has continued to resist pressures for military commitments relating to Korea. Much has been made of the defense guidelines that President Clinton and Prime Minister Hashimoto pledged to adopt in their 1996 Tokyo summit. But the two leaders were merely using this pledge to paper over significant differences on both trade and security issues that have since intensified. Japan made no significant new commitments relating to Korea in the protracted negotiations over the guidelines. Indeed, the guidelines make no reference to Korea, Taiwan, or any other specific locale of possible conflict. In a masterpiece of calculated ambiguity, they pledge "appropriate measures in response to situations in areas surrounding Japan, including diplomatic efforts to prevent further deterioration of such situations," stressing that "the concept, 'situations in areas surrounding Japan,' is not geographic but situational."

On two key issues of special importance to American negotiators, Japan diluted the language proposed by Washington. The United States wanted Japan to pledge direct participation in any U.S. naval blockades on the high seas in the event of a war with North Korea or China. The preliminary draft of the guidelines envisaged cooperation in "activities to ensure the effectiveness of economic sanctions," including "the inspection of ships and related activities." But at Japan's insistence, the final draft called for cooperation in the inspection of ships "based on United Nations Security Council resolutions," adding that such cooperation should be carried out "in accordance with each government's own criteria." Another vaguely worded provision relating to Japanese help in minesweeping carefully sidestepped any reference to where such help could be provided. However, Foreign Minister Yukihiko Ikeda told the Diet on June 12, 1997, that Japan intended this clause to apply only to minesweeping in Japanese territorial waters, except in cases where U.N. resolutions specifically called for military action on the high seas.

The Pentagon puts a positive spin on the guidelines by pointing to clauses reaffirming Japanese readiness to provide access to U.S. and Japanese bases in Japan during a military emergency. Although these clauses are more detailed and more explicit than similar promises in the past, they deal only with "rear area" logistical support, and their implementation would be contingent in crucial respects on the approval of local civilian authorities.

The goal of a Seoul-Tokyo military axis still preoccupies many U.S. military planners even though it proved elusive throughout the cold war. A 1996 RAND report to the Pentagon, outlining possible forms of U.S.–Korean defense cooperation following unification, indicated a preference for a "regional security structure" linking Seoul and Tokyo as U.S. allies. The new structure "would focus primarily on projecting security outward elsewhere in Northeast Asia and, to the extent appropriate, into more distant locales in the Asia-Pacific region."[1] Such proposals find little or no acceptance in Japan, where public opinion increasingly favors diluting the alliance and phasing out the presence of U.S. combat forces for reasons explained in part 5. More important, in Korea, with its memories of Japanese colonialism still fresh, the concept of a military partnership with Japan would be politically indigestible; and in Beijing, it would be perceived as an anti-China alignment, intensifying Chinese opposition to a postunification U.S. military presence in Korea.

Based on its experience since 1945, the United States should at long last accept the reality that Japan is not prepared for significant military cooperation in relation to Korea. More broadly, Japan will seek to keep the major financial as well as military responsibility for peace and stability in Korea pinned squarely on Washington for as long as possible. Tokyo's reluctance to support the 1994 U.S. nuclear freeze agreement with North Korea has exemplified what is a conscious Japanese effort to minimize burdens in Korea that it feels the U.S. should properly assume.

For the most part, Japanese leaders do not share the apocalyptic U.S. view of the dangers posed by North Korea. This was illustrated by the differing reactions in Washington and Tokyo to the North Korean satellite launch in 1998. To Washington, the launch posed a serious and imminent military challenge. But many Japanese leaders recognized that Pyongyang was primarily motivated by a desire for greater leverage in negotiating economic and political normalization with the United States and Japan. The fury of the Japanese reaction did not reflect fear alone but a more complex psychological chemistry driven by the historically based perception of a culturally inferior Korea discussed earlier. In Japanese eyes, it was intolerable effrontery for an economically bankrupt Korean regime that should, by all rights, be deferential to subject them to such brazen pressure tactics.

To be sure, there is an element of fear in the Japanese public's perception of Pyongyang, a feeling that Kim Jong Il is an unstable dictator who might do anything. But most Japanese leaders are relatively sanguine. They know that Tokyo has launched numerous satellites of its own much more sophisticated than the abortive one launched by Pyongyang in 1998 and could convert its satellite capabilities overnight to make missiles comparable in range and thrust to the most advanced U.S. missiles. They know that the United States deploys overpowering nuclear capabilities in its Pacific submarines that would be available for use against North Korea under the U.S.–Japan Security Treaty even if U.S. combat forces in Japan should be phased out. They know that advocates of a missile defense system in the United States have exaggerated the North Korean missile threat to bolster their case. Japanese hawks have deliberately fanned public fears of Pyongyang in order to unlock support for long-desired military expansion programs that have less to do with North Korea than with China and, above all, with moving toward military independence from the United States. The most significant of such programs, hurriedly pushed through in 1999, is the development of Japanese-controlled reconnaissance satellites that will be capable of conducting intelligence monitoring operations all over China.

Looking ahead, Japan is prepared to adapt to whatever happens in

Korea, either a continuation of the status quo or a collapse in Pyongyang leading to the absorption of the North by the South. The Japanese preference would be for an indefinite U.S. military presence in the South that would help freeze the division and stabilize the climate for Japanese investment there. However, Japanese enthusiasm for the American presence is tempered by concern that the United States might get into a war with the North in which it would seek to involve Japan. If the United States should withdraw its forces from Korea, Japan would in all likelihood let matters take their course, avoiding military entanglements in the peninsula and normalizing relations with North Korea as it had started to do in the early years of the cold war until the United States objected.

Although normalization would entail some financial settlement with Pyongyang comparable to what Japan gave the South in 1965, Tokyo would not be likely to provide continuing large-scale economic help to the North designed to forestall a collapse. The Japanese assessment is that Korea will end up with a market economy whether North Korea adopts gradual reforms, survives for some time and is integrated peacefully with the South, or is absorbed by Seoul in a violent convulsion. Similarly, Tokyo foresees a possible nuclear threat from Korea whether or not it is reunified, since the South Korean technical potential for nuclear weapons and missiles is even greater than that of the North.

In the unlikely event of a collapse, it would be extremely unrealistic to expect Japan to foot a major share of reconstruction costs. A proposal by Gen. William Odom, former director of the National Security Agency, typifies the illusory hopes of many observers for what he calls "a major Japanese-Korean-American deal over Korean unification." In this proposal, Tokyo would "provide abundant capital assistance to Seoul whenever reunification eventually occurs" and pledge to keep a significant U.S. military presence in Japan in return for a South Korean commitment not to acquire nuclear weapons, including "a promise to dismantle Pyongyang's program if it falls into their hands," together with a commitment to maintain "indefinitely at least a modest U.S. presence after unification." China and Russia, Odom conceded, "may not like all aspects of this deal," but it would serve their interests because a continued American presence would keep Japan and Korea non-nuclear. In addition, he concludes, a continued U.S. presence would keep peace between Korea and Japan and between Japan and China."[2]

Scenarios such as this are out of touch with realities in Northeast Asia and would be counterproductive. Even if Japan were ready to underwrite postunification Korean reconstruction costs, which it is not, such a Korean dependency on Japan would destabilize the region by fueling China's fears of a Japan-Korea alignment designed to contain its influence. Linking such a dependency to a continued U.S. military presence in Korea and Japan would add to Chinese anxieties. The prospect of a continued U.S. presence after reunification would prompt Beijing to do exactly what Tokyo most fears: seek a military alliance with Seoul. Yet Beijing has respected Korean autonomy historically and appears ready to honor the neutrality of a unified Korea without U.S. forces. As for the danger of a Korean nuclear weapons capability, no Korean regime is likely to surrender its sovereign nuclear option unless Japan, too, is prepared to do so, especially since Japan, unlike South Korea, has already developed plutonium reprocessing facilities that could be quickly converted to military purposes.

Odom assumes that the U.S. nuclear umbrella would remove the danger of a nuclear arms race between Japan and Korea. As I have elaborated elsewhere, however, U.S. promises of nuclear protection are no longer credible in Asia, if they ever were.[3] There are few Koreans and Japanese who seriously believe that the United States would intervene with nuclear weapons in a conflict between Japan and Korea or Japan and China.

If it is possible to head off a nuclear arms race between Japan and Korea, the most promising way to do so would be to negotiate a series of declaratory regional denuclearization agreements that would set the stage for the long-term pursuit of a broader regional nuclear-free zone agreement with verification machinery. One such declaratory agreement, proposed in part 3, would bar the use or deployment of Chinese, Russian, American, and Japanese nuclear weapons in Korea. Another would commit Korea, the United States, China, and Russia not to use nuclear weapons against Japan in return for a formal Japanese commitment not to develop nuclear weapons.

As the price for forswearing nuclear weapons, Japan would no doubt insist on significant steps to honor article 6 of the NPT. In article 6, the existing nuclear powers pledged to phase out their own nuclear weapons in return for the commitment by non-nuclear NPT signatories to remain non-nuclear. Japan pressed for steps to implement article 6 at the 1995 NPT Review Conference and would likely pursue this issue in earnest once again before joining in regional denuclearization agreements.

Assuming that Japan is willing to take part in such agreements and that Korea is denuclearized, negotiations could proceed over time on the complex issues that would be involved in establishing a meaningful nuclear-free zone with verification machinery. These issues could well prove insoluble in the absence of progress toward global nuclear arms control and the resolution of the Taiwan issue. For example, in return for pulling back deployments of missiles capable of reaching Japan and Korea, China could well insist on the inclusion of U.S. and Russian nuclear deployments within the area covered by the zone and the exclusion of Taiwan and adjacent Chinese coastal areas from the zone. Such concessions would be bitterly resisted in Washington and Moscow, but they would be well worth considering to avert the danger of a nuclear arms race between Tokyo and Seoul.

Russian cooperation would clearly be necessary for the success not only of regional denuclearization initiatives but also of broader efforts to promote and maintain peace in Korea. Significantly, as noted earlier, at the time of his death, President Franklin D. Roosevelt envisaged Russian-American cooperation that might have avoided the division of the peninsula and the resulting cold war confrontation there between Moscow and Washington.

Since the end of the cold war, the U.S. desire to minimize Russian influence in Korea has reflected a recognition that Moscow, like Beijing, is opposed to the postunification presence of American forces in Korea. But U.S., Russian, and Chinese objectives could well converge as support for the American presence gradually declines in Korea itself during the transition period leading up to unification. It will then become increasingly clear to the United States that what matters most in Korea is not keeping its own forces there but making sure that no other power steps into its shoes.

For its part, Russia has no desire to station its own forces in Korea and wants to see U.S. forces withdraw under multilateral neutralization arrangements that would bar the future introduction of American, Chinese, and, above all, Japanese forces in the peninsula. In contrast to the ambivalence of Beijing and Tokyo concerning the reunification of Korea, Moscow is confident that it would serve Russian interests. "If history is properly considered," writes the Russian scholar Gennady Chufrin, "a unified Korea would be close to us, which would improve our bargaining position against Japan."[4] In a similar vein, Alvin Z. Rubinstein concludes that "of the involved powers—China, Japan, the United States and Russia—Russia has the least to lose politically, militarily or economically from unification." Indeed, he adds, Korea's "historic animosity toward Japan and suspicion of China would prompt it to cultivate closer relations with Russia, and as a major industrial producer, it would find a natural complementarity in Russia's markets, energy and raw materials."[5] This assessment was vindicated when President Kim Dae Jung actively encouraged Russian initiatives that would be economically beneficial to both the North and the South and would promote their economic integration, notably the extension of the Trans-Siberian Railroad to Korea and the construction of natural gas pipelines to Korea from Siberia and Sakhalin Island.

Russia's 1994 proposal for a ten-power conference, with its broad agenda, evoked little enthusiasm in either the South or the North, both of whom object viscerally to anything that smacks of collusive foreign interference in intra-Korean affairs. However, both Seoul and Pyongyang do acknowledge the need for the participation of external powers in dealing with security issues with which they are directly involved. Thus, China, as a signatory to the 1954 armistice, is a necessary participant in discussions on a peace treaty and has properly been included in the Geneva four-power talks on replacing the armistice, while Russia has not. Looking beyond discussions on a peace treaty, however, both Russia and China, as neighboring states with nuclear weapons and a long record of military involvement in Korea, would be necessary participants in discussions with the United States on a nuclear-free and militarily neutralized peninsula. The idea of Japanese participation proved controversial in the case of former secretary of state James A. Baker's proposal for a six-power forum on Korea, but it would, in all likelihood, be acceptable in the context of discussions focused more narrowly on security issues, since Koreans on both sides of the thirty-eighth parallel regard a rearmed Japan as their major potential security threat.

For the United States, the immediate challenge during the years ahead will be to negotiate a gradual, orderly transition from its present adversarial role on one side of a civil war to a more balanced role designed to stabilize North-South relations. At the end of the suggested transition process spelled out in part 3, all U.S. combat forces would be withdrawn, but noncombat logistics forces and bases could remain and the U.S.–South Korean Security Treaty would continue in force to permit the reintroduction of combat forces if necessary. The U.S. security treaty with Seoul would be terminated only if China terminates its security treaty with Pyongyang and Russia pledges not to restore its former security commitment. Therefore, during the transition period, the United States should actively prepare the way for its disengagement not only by moving to a new role as an honest broker between North and South but also by initiating a broader Korean security dialogue with China, Russia, and Japan.

The central goals of this dialogue should be a four-power agreement not to intervene in Korea with conventional forces and a six-power agreement with North and South Korean participation ruling out the manufacture, use, or deployment of nuclear weapons in Korea. Stable progress toward unification and enduring peace in Korea will be a realistic possibility, in the long run, only if the peninsula can be insulated from the historic rivalries of its powerful neighbors.

Notes to the Chapters

OVERVIEW

1. In 1994 Russia made available to scholars 216 previously classified documents on the Korean War totaling 548 pages, covering the period 1949–53, adding significantly to previously available archival sources. Kathryn Weathersby, who has done the most extensive translation of these and earlier documents into English, concludes that the Soviet role was "essential, but it was as facilitator rather than initiator." See the following works by Weathersby: "Soviet Aims in Korea and the Origins of the Korean War," Cold War International History Project working paper no. 8, Washington, D.C., Woodrow Wilson International Center for Scholars, 1993; "New Findings on the Korean War," Cold War International History Project *Bulletin* (Fall 1993): 1, 14; "To Attack or Not to Attack?" *Bulletin* (Spring 1994): 1–9; letter in response to Adam Ulam, *Bulletin* (Fall 1994): 21; and

"New Russian Documents on the Korean War," *Bulletin* (Winter 1995–96): 30–84. See also Dimitri Volkogonov, *Autopsy for an Empire* (New York: Free Press, 1999), pp. 155, 418. For earlier evidence supporting the conclusion that Moscow was a facilitator rather than an initiator, see Nikita Khrushchev, *Khrushchev Remembers*, ed. Strobe Talbott (Boston: Little Brown, 1970), pp. 367–69; Charles E. Bohlen, *Witness to History* (New York: W. W. Norton, 1973), pp. 288–304; Robert R. Simmons, *The Strained Alliance* (New York: Free Press, 1975), pp. 107–10; Karunakar Gupta, "How Did the Korean War Begin?" *China Quarterly* (fall 1972); and Sergei N. Goncharov, John H. Lewis, and Xue Litai, *Uncertain Partners* (Stanford, Calif.: Stanford University Press), 1993.

2. This figure has been compiled primarily from the annual tables from 1972 to 1977 in *World Armaments and Disarmament* (Stockholm: Almquist and Wiksell), the yearbook published by the Stockholm International Peace Research Institute (SIPRI), and from the annual tables from 1963 to 1975 in *World Military Expenditures and Arms Transfers*, published by the U.S. Arms Control and Disarmament Agency. These estimates were based on intelligence sources and media reports in addition to the limited published Soviet and Chinese data. Credible fragmentary evidence from my own intelligence sources and a wide variety of published sources was also taken into account (e.g., the *Defense White Papers* of the Republic of Korea, especially those for 1989 and 1990).

3. See Chung Il Kwon, interview by the John Foster Dulles Oral History Project, Princeton University Library, October 12, 1965, p. 3. For the most authoritative historical accounts of this controversial period, see Chang Il Oh, "The 1953 Armistice Negotiations," in *Korea and the Cold War*, ed. K. C. Baum and J. I. Matray (Claremont, Calif.: Regina Books, 1993), pp. 220–25; *Foreign Rela-*

tions of the United States, 1952–54, vol. 15: *Korea* (U.S. Department of State: Washington, D.C., 1984), 1368–69; and Max Hastings, *The Korean War* (New York: Simon and Schuster, 1987), p. 325.

4. *Foreign Military Sales, Foreign Military Construction Sales and Military Assistance Facts*, Department of Defense, September 30, 1998, pp. 53–54. Fiscal year 1998 data provided by the Arms Sales Monitoring Project, Federation of American Scientists. For fiscal year 1999, see the statement of Gen. Thomas A. Schwartz, commander, U.S. forces in Korea, Senate Armed Services Committee, March 7, 2000.

CHAPTER I
THE PARALYSIS OF AMERICAN POLICY

1. R. Jeffrey Smith, "U.S. Accord with North Korea May Open Country to Change," *Washington Post*, October 23, 1994, p. A36.

2. Jim Hoagland, "The Trojan Horse at North Korea's Gate," *Washington Post*, August 2, 1995, p. A25.

3. Jim Mann, "U.S. Watches North Korea for Signs of Collapse," *Los Angeles Times*, February 12, 1996, p. 1.

4. This was recounted in a presentation titled "New Prospects for Dialogue with North Korea" at a meeting of the North Korea Working Group, U.S. Institute of Peace, Washington, D.C., March 31, 1998.

5. James Bennet, "Under the Spotlight in China, Gore Lacked Luster," *New York Times*, March 30, 1996, p. 14.

CHAPTER 2
NATIONALISM AND THE "PERMANENT SIEGE MENTALITY"

1. Tokuma Utsonomiya, *Hankyo Ideologie Gaiko o Haisu* (I oppose anti-Communist ideological diplomacy) (Tokyo: Iwanami Shoten), 1966, pp. 48, 54.

2. Carter Eckert, "Korean Reunification in Historical Perspective" (paper prepared for a conference on Korean reunification sponsored by *Seoul Shinmun*, February 3, 1996), p. 7.

3. Callum A. MacDonald, *Korea: The War before Vietnam* (London: Macmillan, 1986), p. 234.

4. Army Command Reports, 1949–54, cited in Callum A. MacDonald, "'So Terrible a Liberation': The U.N. Occupation of North Korea," *Bulletin of Concerned Asian Scholars* 23, no. 2 (1991): 17.

5. W. Karig, M. W. Cagle, and F. A. Manson, *Battle Report: The War in Korea* (New York: Farrar and Rinehart, 1952), pp. 111–12, cited in MacDonald, "'So Terrible a Liberation,'" p. 16.

6. Cited in Bruce Cumings, "It's Time to End the 40-Year War," *The Nation*, August 23, 1993, p. 206.

7. Stephen Endicott and Edward Hagemann, *The United States and Biological Warfare: Secrets from the Early Cold War and Korea* (Bloomington: Indiana University Press, 1998), esp. pp. 1–26, 88–106.

8. MacDonald, "'So Terrible a Liberation,'" esp. pp. 6–15.

9. *Chosun Ilbo*, September 27, 1963, p. 1. See also *Official Biography*, Ministry of Culture and Information, Republic of Korea, April 1969, p. 5.

10. O Yong Jin, *Hana ui Chunyon* (One witness account) (Pusan: Kungmin Sasang Chidowan, 1952), p. 141.

11. Kyung Hyun Kim, "Fractured Cinema: The Discourse of Nation in Sea of Blood" (University of Colorado, 1997), p. 3.

12. Bruce Cumings, "The Corporate State in North Korea," in *State and Society in Contemporary Korea*, ed. Hagen Koo (Ithaca: Cornell University Press, 1993), p. 213.

13. Han S. Park, "The Nature and Evolution of Juche Ideology," in *North Korea: Ideology, Politics, Economy*, ed. Han S. Park (Englewood Cliffs, N.J.: Prentice-Hall, 1996), p. 12.

14. Eckert, "Korean Reunification in Historical Perspective," p. 40.

15. Bernard Krisher, "Report from North Korea," *Gekkan Asahi*, September 1991, p. 15.

16. Nicholas Kristof, "Great Leader to Dear Leader," *New York Times Magazine*, August 20, 1989, pp. 45–46.

17. Kim Il Sung, interview by Rev. Kwon H. Hyung, Seoul, May 3, 1998.

18. Kim Il Sung, *With the Century: 1* (Pyongyang: Foreign Languages Publishing House, 1992), pp. 106–7.

19. Cumings, "The Corporate State in North Korea," p. 209.

20. K. A. Namkung, "The American Role in Korean Reunification" (an address at the Institute for National Strategic Studies, National Defense University, May 28, 1996).

21. Kim Jong Il, "Our Sovereignty Must Be Our Priority," Korean Central News Agency, October 10, 1998.

CHAPTER 3
THE CONFUCIAN LEGACY

1. Thomas Hosuck Kang, *Why the North Koreans Behave As They Do* (Washington, D.C.: Center for Dao-Confucianism, 1994), p. 123.

2. Gregory Henderson, *Korea: The Politics of the Vortex* (Cambridge, Mass.: Harvard University Press, 1968), pp. 29–32, 312–33.

3. Bruce Cumings, "The Corporate State in North Korea," in *State and Society in Contemporary Korea*, ed. Hagen Koo (Ithaca: Cornell University Press, 1993), pp. 199–200.

4. Masao Maruyama, *Thought and Behavior in Modern Japanese Politics* (New York: Oxford University Press, 1969), p. 36.

5. Cumings, "The Corporate State in North Korea," p. 204.

CHAPTER 4
REFORM BY STEALTH

1. Marcus Noland, "Why North Korea Will Muddle Through," *Foreign Affairs* 76 (July–August 1997): 115–16.

2. George M. McCune, *Korea Today* (Cambridge, Mass.: Harvard University Press, 1950), p. 140.

3. Harrison Salisbury, *To Peking—And Beyond: A Report on the New Asia* (New York: Quadrangle, 1973), pp. 200, 199.

4. United Nations Development Program, *Monthly Report*, New York, September 1987, p. 10.

5. *Kulloja*, Pyongyang, November 1987, p. 8.

6. Frank Zeigler, interview by the author, Koryo Hotel, Pyongyang, September 26, 1987.

7. John Merrill, "North Korea's Halting Efforts at Economic Reform" (paper delivered at the Fourth Conference on North Korea sponsored by the Institute of East Asian Studies, University of California, and the Korean Association of Communist Studies, Seoul, August 7–11, 1989).

8. Ibid.

9. Kim Jong U, "North Korea's External Economic Policy" (paper prepared for a conference titled "Korea: Prospects for Economic Development," sponsored by the Sigur Center for East Studies, George Washington University, Washington, D.C., April 22–23, 1996), pp. 3–6.

10. Damon Darlin, "Reporter's Notebook: Pyongyang Lets Visitors Roam Free—Within Limits," *Wall Street Journal*, May 13, 1992, p. A10.

11. Bradley O. Babson, interview by the author, Washington, D.C., April 3, 1998.

12. Edwin Truman, assistant secretary of the Treasury for International Affairs, quoted by Agence France Press, May 7, 2000.

13. "U.S. Denies A.D.B. Visas," *Chosun Ilbo*, April 29, 2001, p. 10.

14. Bradley O. Babson, "Vietnam and North Korea: Seven C's for Comparison" (paper delivered at the Woodrow Wilson School, Princeton University, April 24, 1998), p. 4.

15. UNDP *Thematic Roundtable on Agricultural Recovery and Environmental Protection in the Democratic People's Republic of Korea*," Pyongyang, May 1998, p. 4, a report prepared for a conference on North Korean agricultural self-sufficiency sponsored by the UNDP, Geneva, May 28–29, 1998.

16. Bradley O. Babson, "The North Korean Economy Today" (paper delivered at the U.S. Institute of Peace, January 4, 1999).

17. "President Says North Korea Taking First Steps toward Openness," *Korea Herald*, October 1, 1998, p. 2.

18. Lee Ho Chul, "Recent Changes in North Korea and Its Information Technology Revolution" (paper prepared for the Eleventh U.S.–Korea Academic Symposium, "The Korean Peninsula in the Twenty-First Century," sponsored by the Korea Economic Institute of America, Washington, D.C., September 18–19, 2000), p. 20.

19. Ibid. See also pp. 14, 23.

20. Yoon Jung Ho, "North Korea Joins Intelsat," *Chosun Ilbo*, May 29, 2001, p. 2.

21. Li Hyung Cho, "Seoul to Help North Korea Build Satellite-Based Internet Access System," *Korea Herald*, June 28, 2001, p. 5.

22. Ibid., p. 35.

23. Tao Bing Wei, "Some Views on the Question of the Korean Peninsula," (paper delivered at a seminar on North Korea sponsored by the Kim Dae Jung Peace Foundation, Seoul, November 26, 1996), p. 46.

24. Erich and Marilyn Weingartner, "North Korea: Is Aid the Answer?" (The Dorothy and David Lam Lecture, University of Victoria, British Columbia, October 15, 1999). See abridged version in *NAPSNet*, published by the Nautilus Institute, December 13, 1999, p. 2.

25. Ri Dong Gu, "Some Thoughts on the Adjustment of Farmers Market Prices," *Kim Il Sung University Gazette* 44, no. 33 (1998): 14.

26. Jee Hae Bom, "North Korea to Introduce Farmers' Contract," *Chosun Ilbo*, March 3, 2001. Datelined Beijing, this report cites Chinese government sources.

27. Adrian Buzo, *The Guerrilla Dynasty* (Boulder, Colo.: Westview, 1999), pp. 246–47.

28. Aidan Foster-Carter, ed., *North Korea Report*, Seoul, October 1996, p. 12.

29. Park Choon Ho, interview by the author, Seoul, May 6, 1999.

30. Kim Mun Song, "The Foreign Economic Policy of the D.P.R.K." (address at the Council on Foreign Relations, New York, January 26, 1998).

31. Marcus Noland, *Avoiding the Apocalypse: The Future of the Two Koreas* (Washington, D.C.: Institute for International Economics, 2000), pp. 93–95.

32. For accounts of the negotiations between North Korea and a consortium of Western banks in 1987 and 1988, see Stephen Fidler, "Banks at Odds over North Korean Deal," *Financial Times*, July 19, 1988, p. 25; and Fidler, "Bank Launches Court Action on North Korea," *Financial Times*, June 4, 1990, p. 20. The negotiations collapsed when Australian and west European banks split over the terms of the settlement. See also Robert Steiner, "A Few Fund Managers See Value in Pyongyang Debt," *Asian Wall Street Journal*, November 29, 1993, p. 10.

CHAPTER 5
GOLD, OIL, AND THE BASKET CASE IMAGE

1. Bruce Cumings, *The Origins of the Korean War*, vol. 2 (Princeton: Princeton University Press, 1990), pp. 141–52, esp. p. 143. See also Fred Harvey

Harrington, *God, Mammon and the Japanese* (Madison: University of Wisconsin Press, 1966), pp. 144–65; and Cumings, *Korea's Place in the Sun* (New York: W.W. Norton, 1997), pp. 24–27.

2. "Mining in the DPRK: Prospects for Sectoral Opening" (report of a seminar sponsored by the National Mining Association in cooperation with the Atlantic Council of the United States, August 19, 1997), p. 46.

3. Alex Stewart, "Glimmers of Hope Seen in North Korean Basins, Markets," *Oil and Gas Journal*, January 4, 1999, pp. 62–65. The author has also conducted continuing discussions with Jae Nang Sohn of the Hyundai Engineering and Construction Company, who is concerned with North Korean oil prospects, and Myong In Sung, a Houston-based energy consultant who is assisting North Korea in finding foreign exploration partners.

4. Lee Kyo Kwan, "North Korea Produces Crude Oil," *Chosun Ilbo*, May 27, 2001, p. 1.

5. *Carbohydrate Potential of the DPRK West Bay Basin*, a confidential report by Busuph Park, president, Global Oil Survey Company, Beijing. The author wishes to thank Busuph Park for making this report available and sharing his insights on petroleum prospects in North Korea.

6. "Hyundai Sees Oil Prospects," *Chosun Ilbo*, September 18, 1998, p. 4.

CHAPTER 6
KIM JONG IL AND HIS SUCCESSORS

1. *Chosun Ilbo*, August 17, 2000, p. 2.

2. Doug Struck, "Albright Visit Brings Red Carpet," *Washington Post*, October 25, 2000, p. 2.

3. Jim Hoagland, "The Week That Was," *Washington Post*, October 15, 2000, p. A23.

4. *Hankyoreh Shinmun*, Seoul, June 14, 2000, p. 5. The luncheon was held on August 12. Translations from the South Korean media were done for the author by Kim Tae Kyung of *Hankyoreh Shinmun*. A transcript of the luncheon dialogue prepared by the participating editors was reported by the Yonhap News Agency, Seoul, and translated by the Foreign Broadcast Information Service on August 14 (KPP20000814000035).

5. *Hankyoreh Shinmun*, June 14, 2000, p. 5. See also *Chosun Ilbo*, June 16, 2000, p. 13.

6. *Kookmin Daily*, June 24, 2000, p. 6.

7. *Shin Dong: A Monthly*, Seoul, September 2000, p. 6.

8. John Burton, "Mr. Kim's Dazzling Debut," *Financial Times*, June 17/18, 2000, p. 19.

9. Antonio Betancourt, interview by the author, Washington, D.C., May 3, 1992.

10. Elaine Sciolino, "Blurred Images of North Korea's 'Junior'," *New York Times*, July 17, 1994, p. 1. See also an interview with Baeli by Tetsuo Sakamoto in *Sankei Shimbun*, Tokyo, October 17, 1992, morning edition, p. 4.

11. Nayan Chanda, "Vital Signs," *Far Eastern Economic Review*, March 14, 1996, p. 16.

12. Li Nam Ok, interview by Maeng Ho Choi, *Dong A Ilbo*, Seoul, March 20, 1997, p. 20.

13. Li Nam Ok, interview by Ray Suarez, National Public Radio, *Talk of the Nation*, October 7, 1997.

14. Li Nam Ok, interview by Maeng. See also Flammetta Rocco, "Why I Had to Flee My Country," *Daily Telegraph*, London, September 30, 1997.

15. *Bungei Shunju*, Tokyo, February 10, 1998, pp. 274–92.

16. The CIA English-language text made available to me by the author, dated November 30, 1987, never published, was titled *The Kingdom of Kim Jong Il*. The Korean edition was titled *Choguk-un Chohanul Chomolli* (Diary: The motherland is beyond the sky and far away) (Pacific Palisades, Calif.: Pacific Artist Corporation, 1988).

17. K. A. Namkung, interview by the author, Washington, D.C., June 8, 1996.

18. I interviewed Hwang at his safe house under the protection of the National Intelligence Service in Seoul on May 1, 1998, and May 3, 1999.

19. Wada Haruki, *Kita Chosen: Yugekitai Kokka No Genza* (North Korea: The guerrilla unit state) (Tokyo: Iwanami Shoten, 1998), p. 230.

20. "Our Party's Policy of Giving Priority to the Army Is Invincible," joint article published by *Rodong Shinmun* and *Kulloja*, organs of the Central Committee of the Workers Party of Korea, in *Rodong Shinmun* (press release no. 34, DPRK Permanent Mission to the United Nations, June 17, 1999).

21. Hwang Chang Yop's transcript of Kim's speech on December 7, 1996, was published in *Chosun Ilbo*, October 10, 1997.

22. *Hankyoreh Shinmun*, June 14, 2000, p. 5.

23. Carter Eckert, "Korean Reunification in Historical Perspective" (paper prepared for a conference on Korean reunification sponsored by *Seoul Shinmun* [now renamed *Pae Han Maeil Shinmun*], February 3, 1996), p. 20.

24. Vipin Chandra, *Imperialism, Resistance, and Reform in Late Nineteenth Century Korea* (Berkeley: Institute of East Asian Studies, University of California, 1995), pp. 43–72.

25. Jane Perlez, "Visit Revises Image of North Korean," *New York Times*, October 26, 2000, p. A12.

26. Hwang, interview.

27. Li, interview by Suarez.

28. *Washington Post*, September 26, 1993, p. 16; William Perry, interview on *The News Hour with Jim Lehrer*, Public Broadcasting System, September 17, 1999.

CHAPTER 7
TRADING PLACES

1. See Selig S. Harrison, *The Widening Gulf: Asian Nationalism and American Policy* (New York: Free Press, 1978), pp. 210–44.

2. Kim Dae Jung, "The Once and Future Korea," *Foreign Policy* 86 (spring 1992): 45.

3. Cited in Harrison, *The Widening Gulf*, p. 20.

4. Erik H. Erikson, *Identity: Youth and Crisis* (New York: W. W. Norton, 1968), pp. 21–22.

5. Bernard B. Fall, "Sociological and Psychological Aspects of Vietnam's Partition," *Journal of International Affairs* (July 1964): 179–80.

6. Cited in Roy Richard Grinker, *Korea and Its Futures: Unification and the Unfinished War* (New York: St. Martin's Press, 1998), p. 85.

7. Ibid., pp. 79–81. For a perceptive discussion of *han*, see Michael Shapiro, *The Shadow in the Sun: A Korean Year of Love and Sorrow* (New York: Grove-Atlantic, 1990), pp. 140–45.

CHAPTER 8
CONFEDERATION OR ABSORPTION?

1. "Socialist Constitution of the Democratic People's Republic of Korea," *Korea Today*, Pyongyang, July 1973, p. 24.

2. Edward J. Baker, "A Glimpse of North Korea," Yenching Institute, Harvard University, November 10, 1988, p. 3, an English version of an article published in Korean in *Hankyoreh Shinmun*, Seoul, October 23, 1988.

3. Han made this statement at a symposium in his honor at the Carnegie Endowment for International Peace, Washington, D.C., June 5, 1991.

4. Ibid.

5. Ibid.

6. "Ten-Point Program of Great National Unity of the Whole Nation for Reunification of the Country," presented at the Fifth Session of the Ninth Supreme People's Assembly, Pyongyang, April 7, 1993 (press release no. 13, DPRK Permanent Mission to the United Nations, April 8, 1993, p. 2).

7. "Observations on Ways of Korea's Reunification Corresponding with the Current International Developments and the Trends of the Times," an undated analysis provided to the author by Kim Byong Hong, policy planning director, Foreign Ministry, on a visit to Pyongyang, September 27, 1995, p. 3.

8. Kim Byong Hong, interview by the author, Pyongyang, May 5, 1998. See also *Rodong Shinmun*, Pyongyang, February 10 and 23, 1998.

9. U.S. Senate Committee on Foreign Relations, *Report on the Far East*, 86th Cong., 2d sess., 1960, p. 7.

10. See the interview with coup leaders in *Dong-a-Ilbo*, Seoul, May 26, 1961, p. 4. See also *Chosun Ilbo*, April 26, 1962, p. 1, for a summary of *The History of*

the Korean Revolutionary Trials, a detailed account of the circumstances and attitudes leading to the coup.

11. Selig S. Harrison, "Two-Germany Talks Spur Similar Ideas in Korea," *Washington Post,* May 12, 1970, p. 4.

12. "Decade of Confidence and Achievement," the president's annual New Year's press conference for 1971 (Ministry of Culture and Information, Republic of Korea), p. 13.

13. "Inaugural Speech by President Park Chung Hee," July 1, 1971, pp. 4–5.

14. Address by President Roh Tae Woo at the opening session of the 147th National Assembly, Seoul, September 11, 1989, reprinted in *Dialogue with North Korea* (Washington, D.C.: Carnegie Endowment for International Peace, 1990), appendix E (61–63). See also "Korean National Community Unification Formula: An Outline," Ministry of Foreign Affairs, Seoul, September 11, 1989.

15. Kim Dae Jung, "The Once and Future Korea," *Foreign Policy* 85 (spring 1992): 47.

16. Han Wan Sang, "The Kim Young Sam Government's Unification Policy" (keynote address at the Ninth U.S. Forum on the Problems of the Korean Peninsula, Arlington, Virg. July 16, 1993), p. 6. Han Wan Sang was then the deputy prime minister and minister of national unification of South Korea.

17. Kim Chang Ki, "Kim Young Sam Rejects Unconditional Unification," *Chosun Ilbo,* July 7, 1993, p. 3.

18. American Embassy cable to the secretary of state, Ref. 3724, R0708 10Z, August 1998. See text reproduced in Bill Gertz, *Betrayal* (Washington, D.C.: Regnery Publishing, 1999), p. 262.

19. *Aesop's Fables (Complete and Unabridged)* (New York: Lancer Books, 1968), pp. 130–31.

20. *The News Hour with Jim Lehrer,* Public Broadcasting System, June 9, 1998.

21. Kim Dae Jung, interview by Tetsuya Chikushi, Tokyo Broadcasting System Television Network, 1354 GMT, February 2, 2000. For an English translation, see FBIS JPP 20000210000029, February 10, 2000. See also Lee Chang Sup, "President Kim Describes Kim Jong Il as a Pragmatist," *Korea Herald,* February 12, 2000, p. 1, reporting an interview in *Der Spiegel,* the Germany weekly, in which Kim Dae Jung said that Kim Jong Il is "a pragmatist and appears to be in full control of North Korean affairs.".

22. Conversation with Hajime Izumi, Tokyo, June 10, 2001. Izumi, a professor at Shizuoka University, is an adviser to the Japanese Foreign Ministry and attributed this information to informed Japanese government sources.

23. Kim Dae Jung, interview by the author, Seoul, June 7, 2001.

24. Hwang Won Tak, who participated in the summit as President Kim Dae Jung's national security adviser, used this term in briefing Korea specialists in Washington on June 17, 2000. Kim Dae Jung used it in a dinner meeting with Korea specialists at the Waldorf Astoria Hotel, New York, on September 7, 2000.

For the text of the June 14 joint statement by Kim Jong Il and Kim Dae Jung, referring to "common factors," see Associated Press dispatch in the *New York Times*, June 15, 2000, p. 15.

25. Dinner meeting with Korea specialists, New York, September 7, 2000.

26. "Seoul Says Reunification of Koreas to Take Time," Reuters dispatch published in the *Korea Herald*, October 1, 2000, p. 3.

27. Reuters, March 7, 2001.

28. David Reardon, senior representative for exploration, British Petroleum, and Kim Chong Ku, commercial counselor, interviews by the author, North Korean Embassy, Moscow, October 17, 2001.

29. Unification Ministry press release, March 10, 2000.

30. "Samsung to Develop Computer Software in North," *Korea Herald*, April 3, 2000, p. 4.

31. Ko Yun Hee, "North Korean Taedong River Complex Increasing Production," *Joongang Ilbo*, April 17, 2000, p. 3; "Hanvit Bank Moves North," *Korea Times*, July 10, 2000, p. 10; and Kim Kwang Ki, "First Delivery of South-North Korea Cigarette Arrives in Inchon," *Joongang Ilbo*, March 23, 2000, p. 1.

32. Kim Ji Ho, "First Inter-Korean Motor Rally in Mount Kumgang," *Korea Herald*, April 18, 2000, p. 4.

33. Seo Jang Soo, "Korea-Made Blue Jeans to Be Shipped to North," *Joongang Ilbo*, December 2, 1999, p. 2.

34. "Republic of Korea: Time to Reform the National Security Law," Amnesty International, International Secretariat, London, February 1999 (AI Index, ASA, March 25, 1999).

35. "Democracy in the Republic of Korea," Korea Information Service, Seoul, June 1999, p. 7.

36. Bae Jin Young, "The Fiscal Burden of Korean Reunification and Its Impact on South Korea's Macroeconomic Stability" (paper prepared for the U.S.–Korea Academic Symposium, "Economic and Regional Cooperation in Northeast Asia," Seoul, November 1997), p. 199.

37. Yun Kun Young, "Korean Unification and Property Ownership in North Korea" (paper prepared for a conference titled "Two Koreas: Towards One Economy," sponsored by the Korea-America Economic Association and the Korea Society, Washington, D.C., October 4–5, 1999), pp. 14, 16, 18.

38. Marcus Noland, "Some Unpleasant Arithmetic Concerning Unification" (APEC working paper 96–13, Institute for International Economics, Washington, D.C., 1996). See also Marcus Noland, Sherman Robinson, and Li Gang Liu, "The Costs and Benefits of Korean Unification" (paper delivered at the Institute for International Economics, Washington, D.C., 1998).

39. Yong Sun Lee, "The Costs and Financing of Korean Unification" (paper prepared for a conference titled "Two Koreas: Towards One Economy," sponsored by the Korea-America Economic Association and the Korea Society, Washington, D.C., October 4–5, 1999), pp. 11–12.

40. Lawrence H. Summers, "The Unified German Economy and Its Implications for a Unified Korean Economy," *Newsletter of the Research Institute of National Unification*, Seoul, October 1992, p. 9. This is the transcript of a lecture delivered on August 26, 1992, at the institute.

41. Gifford Combs, "Some Economic Factors in German Reunification," *Security Dialogue* 24, no. 4 (December 1993): 310–20.

42. Helmut Schmidt, "Lessons of the German Reunification for Korea," *Security Dialogue* 24, no. 4 (December 1993): 402.

43. Kim Dae Jung, interview by Cable News Network, January 2, 2000, reported by Agence France Press, January 3, 2000.

44. Norman Levin, *The Shape of Korea's Future* (Santa Monica, Calif.: RAND Corporation, 1999), p. 10. This is the report of a public opinion poll conducted jointly by the RAND Center for Asia-Pacific Policy and *Joongang Ilbo*.

45. Roy Richard Grinker, *Korea and Its Futures: Unification and the Unfinished War* (New York: St. Martin's Press, 1998), pp. 10, 23. See also preface, pp. 11–48, 73–98.

46. Ibid., pp. 257–71.

CHAPTER 9
THE UNITED STATES AND REUNIFICATION

1. Cited by U.S. Ambassador Donald Gregg in an address before the Korean Council on Foreign Relations, Seoul, November 21, 1990.

2. Cho Soon Sung, *Korea in World Politics, 1940–50: An Evaluation of American Responsibility* (Berkeley: University of California Press, 1967).

3. Cho Soon Sung, "Hanguk ui yangdan kwa miguk ui chaegim" (The division of Korea and America's responsibility), *Sasanggye* (July 1960): 57.

4. Gregory Henderson, *Korea: The Politics of the Vortex* (Cambridge, Mass.: Harvard University Press, 1968), pp. 126–29. For another eyewitness account, see Harold R. Isaacs, *No Peace for Asia* (Cambridge, Mass.: MIT Press, 1967), pp. 93–94.

5. Yi Yong Gun, "8/15 Kaiho Zengo no Souru" (Seoul before and after the August 15 liberation), *Toitsu Chosen Shimbun*, Tokyo, August 15 and 31, 1970.

6. Bruce Cumings, *The Origins of the Korean War*, vol. 1 (Princeton: Princeton University Press, 1981), pp. 71–91.

7. Ibid., p. 86.

8. Cited in Richard E. Lauterbach, *Danger from the East* (New York: Harper, 1947), p. 201.

9. A former associate of Yo Un Hyong stated that five members of the original seven-man executive committee of the Republic of Korea named on August 17, 1945, were conservatives or non-Communists of other hues: Chairman Yo, Vice Chairman An Chae Hong, General Affairs Chairman Ch'oe Kun U, Finance Chairman Yi Kyu Gap, and Security Director Kwon T'ae Sok. Two of these,

Ch'oe and Yi, a former Buddhist priest, were outspokenly anti-Communist. The two other members, Organization Director Chong Paek and Public Relations Director Cho Tong, were described as "moderate Communists." See Yi, "8/15 Kaiho Zengo no Souru," August 15, 1970.

10. Henderson, *Korea: The Politics of the Vortex*, pp. 126–29. See also pp. 115–19.

11. "South Korea's 'Other Side,'" *Far Eastern Economic Review*, June 18, 1965, pp. 593–95.

12. Transcript of an interview with Paek Tu Jin, Seoul, September 28, 1965, John Foster Dulles Oral History Project, Princeton University Library, pp. 11, 15. See also the transcript of an interview with Chung Il Kwon, Seoul, September 29, 1964, ibid., esp. pp. 29–35, and the interview with Son Won Il, Seoul, September 29, 1964, ibid., esp. pp. 11, 14–15.

13. *Chosun Ilbo*, November 6, 1963, p. 4.

14. Hahm Pyong Choon, "Korea's 'Mendicant Mentality'?" *Foreign Affairs* 43 (October 1964): 169.

15. Cha Chi Chol, "Implementation of the 'Brown Memo,'" *Dong A Ilbo*, September 20, 1966, p. 2.

16. Lauterbach, *Danger from the East*, p. 201.

17. Henderson, *Korea: The Politics of the Vortex*, pp. 336–37, 342. See also Ko Chong Hun, *Kun* (Army) (Seoul: Tongbang Sowon, 1967).

18. "U.S. May Have Forced Chun to Cancel Summit," *Korea Herald*, August 20, 1998, p. 2, citing a report in the September issue of *Minju Choson* quoting Chun as saying, "I suppose there was pressure from the United States." This explanation was also confirmed by Jae Nang Sohn, then an assistant director of the Korean Central Intelligence Agency, in an interview with the author, Seoul, May 10, 2000.

19. Airport arrival statement by Dr. Billy Graham, March 31, 1992, p. 2.

CHAPTER 10
TRIPWIRE

1. "Nobody Can Slander the DPRK's Missile Policy," Korean Central News Agency, June 16, 1998, monitored by the Foreign Broadcast Information Service (ID FTS 1998061600035).

2. The verbatim text of the minutes was given to the author by Maj. Gen. (Ret.) Lim Dong Won, then national security adviser to President Kim Dae Jung, Seoul, May 4, 1998.

3. Among my interlocutors have been President Kim Il Sung, interviewed on June 26, 1972, and June 9, 1994; Lt. Gen. Kwon Jung Yong, then deputy army chief of staff for strategy, disarmament, and foreign affairs, interviewed on May 2, 1992, and June 7, 1994; Col. Gen. Ri Chan Bok, chief North Korean representa-

tive in the Military Armistice Commission, interviewed on September 28, 1995, and May 3, 1998; President Kim Dae Jung of South Korea, interviewed on May 1, 1998, and May 2, 1999; Maj. Gen. (Ret.) Lim Dong Won, interviewed on May 1, 1992, when he was vice-minister of unification, directing South Korean participation in the North-South dialogue, and on eleven subsequent occasions, including May 1, 1998, and May 2, 1999, during his tenure as national security adviser to President Kim Dae Jung; Maj. Gen. Park Yong Ok, then director of policy planning in the South Korean Ministry of Defense, interviewed on May 2, 1992, and his successor, Maj. Gen. Yong Koo Cha, interviewed together with Major General Park on May 5, 1999, in Seoul.

4. "Kim Dae Jung Peace Foundation Secretary General Lim Dong Won Discusses the Four-Party Meeting and Comprehensive Peace Agreement," *Kim Dae Jung Peace Foundation on Record*, no. 3 (July 1996): 6–9, reporting on the Unification Forum of the Institute of Far Eastern Studies, Kyungnam University, June 14, 1996.

5. William Perry, interview by the author, Stanford University, Palo Alto, California, May 16, 2000.

6. Don Oberdorfer, *The Two Koreas* (Reading, Mass.: Addison-Wesley, 1997), p. 306.

7. Richard Halloran, "South Korea, U.S. Draft Deadly Response Plan," *Washington Times*, November 19, 1998, pp. 1, 13; Halloran, ". . . But Carry a Big Stick," *Far Eastern Economic Review*, December 3, 1998, pp. 26–28; Halloran, essay published on "Global Beat" website, November 14, 1998.

8. "A Combined PSI Warfare Command," *Chosun Ilbo*, January 15, 1999, p. 10. See also *Korea Herald*, January 14, 1999, p. 1; and U.S. Forces, Korea, news release no. 99-01-06, January 13, 1999.

9. For example, see "Right to Preemptive Strike Does Not Rest Entirely with Enemies," Korean Central News Agency, Pyongyang, December 6, 1998; and "The United States Must Clearly Know Its Opponent," *Rodong Shinmun*, Pyongyang, December 4, 1998.

10. Lt. Col. (Ret.) John H. Cushman, interview by the author, Washington, D.C., June 1, 1999.

11. "South Korea Rejects the Idea of Preemptive Strikes on North Korea," Dow-Jones Newswires, March 5, 1999.

12. "Defense Minister Urges Cooperation between ROK, Japan Armed Forces," *Korea Herald*, March 6, 1999, p. 2.

13. James R. Asker, "Washington Outlook," *Aviation Week and Space Technology*, March 8, 1999, p. 25.

14. William Perry, interview by the author, Stanford University, Palo Alto, California, May 16, 2000.

15. "'Sunshine' or Moonshine?" *Wall Street Journal*, March 2, 1999, p. A18.

CHAPTER 11
THE UNITED STATES AND THE MILITARY BALANCE

1. Choe Won Ki, "Report on the Assessment of the Fighting Capability of the North Korean Military Prepared by the Intelligence Staff of the Eighth Army," *Wolgang Chungang*, October 1, 2000, pp. 140–47, translated by the Foreign Broadcast Information Service, October 1, 2000 (ID KPP20000921000058).

2. U.S. Department of Defense, *2000 Report to Congress: Military Situation on the Korean Peninsula*, September 12, 2000, p. 3; Stephen Fidler, "Threat from North Korea 'Has Grown,'" *Financial Times*, March 28, 2001, p. 10.

3. Ministry of National Defense, Republic of Korea, *Defense White Paper, 1999*, pp. 69–84. See also "On the Defense," *Newsreview*, Seoul, October 3, 1998, p. 10; and "Pulling out the Stops," *Newsreview*, Seoul, October 16, 1999, p. 8.

4. Defense White Paper, 1999. Assistance with respect to U.S. and ROK airpower was provided by Brig. Gen. (Ret.) James F. Grant, a former director of intelligence of U.S. forces in Korea.

5. Lee Sung Yul, "Seoul to Buy Spy Planes to Beef Up Intelligence," *Korea Herald*, August 8, 1999, p. 1. See also "A.D.D. to Develop Spy Satellite," *Chosun Ilbo*, November 3, 1998, p. 1.

6. For example, see Edward W. Desmond, "If the Shooting Starts, Who Will Win?" *Time*, April 4, 1994, pp. 19–21; Lonnie Henley, "A War Scenario: Korea Cataclysm," *Washington Post*, May 4, 1997, pp. C1–4; and Col. Trevor N. Dupuy, *Future Wars* (New York: Warner Books, 1996), pp. 196–205.

7. Michael O'Hanlon, "Stopping a North Korean Invasion: Why Defending South Korea Is Easier Than the Pentagon Thinks," *International Security* 22, no. 2 (spring 1998): 137–39, 148–53, 159–61.

8. Desmond, "If the Shooting Starts," p. 20.

9. Dupuy, *Future Wars*, p. 203.

10. *Defense White Paper, 1999*, p. 83.

11. Kim Tae Woo, "The South Korean Perception of the Nuclear Threat" (paper presented at "The Western Powers and Regional Perspectives on the Nuclear Future" conference sponsored by the International Institute for Strategic Studies, London, December 2, 1999), pp. 8–9.

12. O'Hanlon, "Stopping a North Korean Invasion," pp. 139, 161–66.

13. Brian Cloughley, "The Korean Flashpoint Waits to Be Ignited," *Jane's International Defense Review* (September 1996): 27.

14. This is based on an interview with General Grant on April 11, 2000, Washington, D.C., and a text of talking points for speeches to defense industry groups provided to the author by General Grant, executive vice president of Zel Technologies.

15. Brig. Gen. (Ret.) John C. Bahnsen, "The Kaleidoscopic U.S. Army," *Armed Forces Journal* (November 1985): 81–82.

16. Gen. (Ret.) Robert W. Sennewald, interview by the author, Washington, D.C., April 27, 2000.

17. Ministry of National Defense, *Yisip Il Se Gi Eui Gugga Ambowa Guk-bangbi* (National defense in the twenty-first century and the defense budget), March 3, 2000, pp. 43–46. Translated for the author by Lee Gong Soon. See also Kang Seok Jae, "Government Calls for Substitute Force in Event of U.S. Military Pullout," *Korea Herald*, March 6, 2000, p. 1.

18. Don Kirk, "South Korea: A Record Defense Budget," *New York Times*, June 20, 2001, p. 10.

19. Nicholas Eberstadt and Judith Bannister, *The Population of North Korea* (Berkeley: Institute of East Asian Studies, University of California, 1992), p. 30.

20. Robert G. Liotta, "Offset: A Factor in Korean Defense Industry Development" (paper prepared for a conference sponsored by the Council on U.S.–Korean Security Studies, November 30, 1987), p. 1.

21. Hwang Dong Joon, "South Korea's Defense Industry: An Asset for the U.S.," Heritage Foundation Backgrounder no. 38, December 10, 1985. See also Yong Sook Lee and Ann Markusen, "The South Korean Defense Industry in the Post Cold War Era" (working paper no. 150, Project on Regional and Industrial Economics, Hubert Humphrey Institute of Public Affairs, University of Minnesota, September 1999), p. 13. See also Federation of American Scientists, *Arms Sales Monitor*, Washington, D.C., October 1999.

22. Lee and Markusen, "The South Korean Defense Industry," p. 14.

23. Guo Hongjun, "ROK Working for Developing and Producing Weapons for Itself," *People's Liberation Army Daily*, November 28, 1999, p. 5.

24. Chul Hwan Kim, "Defense Industrial Cooperation and Technology Transfer between Korea and the U.S.," June 1999. Dr. Kim is a professor in the Korea National Defense College, Seoul.

CHAPTER 12
NEW OPPORTUNITIES FOR ARMS CONTROL

1. International Institute for Strategic Studies, *The Military Balance: 1999–2000* (London: Oxford University Press, 2000), p. 176. For 1993 data, see Bae Jin Yong, "The Costs of National Defense" (paper prepared for the U.S.–Korea Academic Symposium, "Economic and Regional Cooperation in Northeast Asia," Seoul, November 10–12, 1997), pp. 5–6.

2. Nicholas Eberstadt and Judith Bannister, "North Korea: A Statistical Glimpse into a Closed Society," *Journal of Korean Reunification* 2 (March 1993): 54.

3. Selig S. Harrison, "Kim Seeks Summit, Korean Troop Cuts," *Washington Post*, June 26, 1972, p. 1.

4. *Choguk t'ongil e kwanhan widaehan suryong Kim Il-song tongji ui munhon*

(Documents of the Great Leader Comrade Kim Il Sung on the unification of the fatherland) (Pyongyang: Samhaksa, 1975), p. 144.

5. Kim Il Sung attributed this statement to Lee Hu Rak in a conversation with Japanese Diet member Tokuma Utsonomiya. Cited in "Details of the Meetings between Premier Kim Il Sung and Representative Tokuma Utsonomiya: Second Meeting, North Korea and the United States," August 9, 1974, p. 6. See also Utsonomiya's "The Relaxation of Tensions and Korean Unification" (paper presented at the Conference of Japanese and U.S. Parliamentarians on Korean Problems, Washington, D.C., September 19, 1977), p. 23.

6. For the texts of the 1987 and 1988 proposals, see Selig S. Harrison, *Dialogue with North Korea* (report of a seminar on tension reduction in Korea) (Washington, D.C.: Carnegie Endowment for International Peace, 1989), appendix B (pp. 47–50). See also "On Easing the Tension on the Korean Peninsula and Creating a Peaceful Climate for National Reunification: Disarmament Proposal for the Korean Peninsula," press release no. 30, DPRK Permanent Observer Mission to the United Nations, June 2, 1990; and "Keynote Speech by Premier Yon Hyong Muk in Seoul," press release no. 41, September 6, 1990.

7. Harrison, *Dialogue with North Korea*, p. 8.

8. "U.S. Relations with North Korea," a symposium by the Carnegie Endowment for International Peace, Washington, D.C., June 5, 1991.

9. Selig S. Harrison, "Get a Food for Peace Deal with North Korea," *International Herald Tribune*, May 14, 1997, p. 10.

10. Yunjoo Jung, "Minister Han Offers Pullback," *Hankyoreh Shinmun*, May 15, 1997, p. 1.

11. "Gist of the Opening Statement by Kang Young Hoon, Prime Minister of the Republic of Korea, at the First South-North High Level Meeting on 5 September 1990," Embassy of the Republic of Korea, Washington, D.C., September 8, 1990.

12. Brig. Gen. Jin Kim Ryoo, "Opening Remarks," subcommittee on tension reduction, sixth plenary session, the four-party talks, Geneva, August 6, 1999, p. 4.

13. Lim Dong Won, "Conditions for Arms Control between South and North Korea," *Chosun Ilbo*, October 10, 1989, esp. pp. 4–5.

14. Lim Dong Won, "Next Steps in Arms Control," in *Restarting the Peace Process in the Korean Peninsula*," ed. Kongdan Oh and Craig. S. Coleman, report on a conference sponsored by the *Korea Times*, Los Angeles, June 8, 1994, pp. 135–36, published by the *Korea Times*, Los Angeles, September 1994.

15. Yong Sup Han, *Designing and Evaluating Conventional Arms Control Measures: The Case of the Korean Peninsula* (Santa Monica, Calif.: RAND Corporation, 1993), publication no. N-3411, pp. 120–24. This was previously published as a RAND Graduate School Dissertation no. N-34111-RGSD, July 1991.

16. Lee Chang, "Setting National Priorities: Welfare vs. Defense," *Korean Social Science Journal* 16 (spring 1990): 27–47.

17. Yong, *Designing and Evaluating Conventional Arms Control Measures*, p. 119.

18. Pedro Almeida and Michael O'Hanlon, "Impasse in Korea: A Conventional Arms Accord Solution?" *Survival* 41, no. 1 (spring 1999): 58–72, esp. p. 60.

19. "Summary of Nuclear Portion of Conversation between Former President Carter and Then President Kim Il Sung, Pyongyang, North Korea, June 16, 1994: Prepared by Marion Creekmore and Reviewed by President Carter," September 20, 2000, p. 3.

20. "The Future of Inter-Korean Relations" (conference report of the KIDA-CSIS Study Group on ROK–US Policy toward North Korea, Rapporteur Michael J. Mazarr, published by the Center for Strategic and International Studies, Washington, D.C., January 1991), pp. 8–9.

21. "Challenges of Building a Korean Peace Process" (special report of a United States Institute of Peace working group, Washington, D.C., June 1998), pp. 2, 13–14.

22. William Perry, interview by the author, Stanford University, Palo Alto, California, May 16, 2000.

CHAPTER 13
ENDING THE KOREAN WAR

1. Gen. Ri Chan Bok, interview by the author, Pyongyang, May 5, 1998.

2. "Nobody Can Slander the DPRK's Missile Policy," Korean Central News Agency, June 16, 1998, monitored by the Foreign Broadcast Information Service.

3. Col. Jack Pritchard, deputy director for East Asian and Pacific affairs in the National Security Council, speaking at a seminar sponsored by the American Enterprise Institute for Public Policy Research, Washington, D.C., February 19, 1998, said that "our objective is to steer the four-party talks at Geneva back into the model of the North-South Basic Agreement of 1991 so that the armistice can be replaced by an agreement between North and South.".

4. Chang Il Ohn, "The 1953 Armistice Negotiations," in *Korea and the Cold War*, ed. K. C. Baum and J. I. Matray (Claremont, Calif.: Regina Books, 1993), p. 218.

5. Ibid., p. 220.

6. Ibid., pp. 220–26.

7. *Foreign Relations of the United States, 1952–54*, vol. 15: *Korea* (Washington, D.C.: Department of State, 1984), pp. 1368–69.

8. Ibid. See also Walter S. Robertson to John Foster Dulles, June 26, 1953, top secret file 797.00/6-2653, declassified by the State Department under the Freedom of Information Act, case no. 391 (cited in Ohn, "The 1953 Armistice Negotiations," pp. 222–24).

9. Letter from the Joint Chiefs of Staff to Gen. John E. Hull, October 10, 1953, JCS Records, RG 218, CCS 383.2, Korea, sec. 137, NA. See also Ohn, "The 1953 Armistice Negotiations," pp. 224–25.

10. Max Hastings, *The Korean War* (New York: Simon and Schuster, 1987), p. 325.

11. Bruce Cumings and Jon Halliday, *Korea: The Unknown War* (New York: Viking/Penguin, 1988), p. 210.

12. Ibid., p. 211.

13. Transcript of an interview with Paik Too Chin, Seoul, September 28, 1965, John Foster Dulles Oral History Project, Princeton University Library, pp. 11, 15. See also transcript of an interview with Son Won Il, Seoul, September 29, 1965, pp. 14–15, and an interview with Chung Il Kwon, Seoul, October 12, 1965, p. 3, both in Dulles Oral History Project.

14. Bruce Cumings, *Korea's Place in the Sun* (New York: W.W. Norton, 1997), p. 479.

15. John Barry Kotch, *The United Nations Command in Historical Perspective: Anatomy and Legacy of a U.N. Collective Security Enforcement Action* (Seoul: Hanyang University Press, 1990).

16. Trygvie Lie, *In the Cause of Peace* (New York: Macmillan, 1954), p. 334.

17. Patrick M. Norton, "Ending the Korean Armistice Agreement: The Legal Issues," *Nautilus Institute Policy Forum Online*, March 3, 1997, no. 97-03 (*http://www.nautilus.org/fora/security/2a—armisticelegal—norton.html*). Mr. Norton is special counsel in the law firm O'Melveny and Myers, based in Shanghai.

18. National Security Council Decision Memorandum 251, National Security Council, Washington, D.C., cited by Kotch, *The United Nations Command in Historical Perspective*, appendix 8, p. 323.

19. "Kim Dae Jung Peace Foundation Secretary General Lim Dong Won Discusses 'The Four Party Meeting and a Comprehensive Peace Agreement,'" *Kim Dae Jung Peace Foundation on Record* no. 3 (July 1996), 6–7. This is the text of a presentation at the Unification Forum of the Institute of Far Eastern Studies, Kyungnam University, Seoul, June 14, 1996.

20. Richard Stilwell, "Challenge and Response in the Northeast Asia of the 1980's: The Military Balance," in *Strategy and Security in Northeast Asia*, ed. R. Foster (New York: Crane Russak, 1979), p. 99.

21. "Kim Dae Jung Peace Foundation Secretary General Lim Dong Won Discusses 'The Four Party Meeting and a Comprehensive Peace Agreement,'" p. 8.

22. Lt. Gen. John H. Cushman, interview by the author, Washington, D.C., May 4, 1997.

23. "Memorandum for Ambassador Porter," February 19, 1971, p. 3. Underhill provided a copy of this memorandum to the author on January 10, 1991, following his retirement from the Foreign Service after service as ambassador to Malaysia.

24. Jimmy Carter, interview by the author, Atlanta, June 14, 2000.

25. Robert Gallucci, interview by the author, Washington, D.C., June 16, 2000.

26. Letter to the author from Col. Carl J. Kropf, public affairs officer, headquarters, U.S. forces, Korea, May 11, 1999.

27. Li Hyong Chol, interview by the author, New York, October 29, 1996.

28. William J. Perry, *Review of United States Policy toward North Korea: Findings and Recommendations*, Office of the North Korea Policy Coordinator, U.S. Department of State, October 12, 1999, p. 8.

29. Stephen Bosworth, interview by the author, Seoul, May 4, 1999.

30. "President Kim Reaffirms Kim Jong Il's Approval of U.S. Troops Here," *Korea Times*, August 17, 2000. See also *Hankook Ilbo*, Seoul, August 17, 2000, p. 2.

31. John Burton, "Seoul Marks War Anniversary," *Financial Times*, June 26, 2000, p. 4.

32. Jane Perlez, "Albright Says U.S. Pullout Isn't Planned in South Korea," *New York Times*, June 24, 2000, p. 6.

33. "Early Bird News Service," Department of Defense, August 10, 2000.

34. *Beijing Review*, July 24, 2000, reported by Agence France Press, July 26, 2000.

35. Kenneth Quinones, "The Korean Peninsula: Preserve the Past or Move toward Reconciliation?" (paper prepared for the Council on Foreign Relations Task Force on Managing Change in the Korean Peninsula, Washington, D.C., October 1997–May 1998).

CHAPTER 14
THE TAR BABY SYNDROME

1. William J. Porter, interview by the author, Seoul, April 16, 1971.

2. "Memorandum for Ambassador Porter," February 19, 1971, p. 2. Underhill provided a copy of this memorandum to the author on January 10, 1991, following his retirement from the Foreign Service after service as ambassador to Malaysia.

3. Joel Chandler Harris, *The Complete Tales of Uncle Remus* (Boston: Houghton Mifflin, 1983), pp. 6–8.

4. Francis Underhill, interview by the author, Seoul, May 10, 1971.

5. James Laney, interview by the author, Atlanta, June 14, 2000.

6. Senate Committee on Foreign Relations, *United States Security Agreements and Commitments Abroad: The Republic of Korea*, Hearings before the Subcommittee on U.S. Security Agreements and Commitments Abroad, 91st Cong., 2d sess., 1970, pt. 6, pp. 1561–62, 1592–94.

7. *Korea and the Philippines: November, 1972*, staff report prepared for the Senate Committee on Foreign Relations, (Washington, D.C.: GPO, 1973), p. 47.

8. House Committee on Appropriations, Subcommittee on Defense Appropriations, *Department of Defense Appropriation Bill, 1975*, 93d Cong. 2d sess., 1974, H. Rept. 93-1255, pp. 33–4, 39–49.

9. Selig S. Harrison, "One Korea?" *Foreign Policy* no. 17 (winter 1974–75): 35–62.

10. Jimmy Carter, interview by the author, Atlanta, June 14, 2000. See also Don Oberdorfer, *The Two Koreas* (Reading, Mass.: Addison-Wesley, 1997), p. 103.

11. "It's Time to Loosen the Grip on Korea," *Business Week*, September 5, 1988, p. 114.

12. Senator Carl Levin, *Report on a Trip to Korea, Japan and the U.S. Pacific Command*, presented to the Senate Foreign Relations Committee, June 2, 1989, p. 5.

13. Mark Clifford and Shim Jae Hoon, "Welcome Wears Thin," *Far Eastern Economic Review* 145, no. 28 (July 13, 1989): 28.

14. Department of Defense, *A Strategic Framework for the Asian Pacific Rim: Looking toward the Twenty-First Century*, April 19, 1990, p. 4. See also Charles R. Larson, "An American Umbrella for Asian Storms," *Asian Wall Street Journal*, April 16, 1993, p. 1.

15. Statement made by President Bill Clinton at a news Conference with President Kim Young Sam of South Korea, Seoul, July 27, 1995.

16. Charles William Maynes, "The Limitations of Force" (paper prepared for the Aspen Strategy Group Conference, Aspen, Colorado, August 1994), pp. 9–10.

17. David E. Brown, "The United States and South Korea" (paper prepared for "South Korea, North Korea and the United States," conference sponsored by Southern Methodist University, Dallas, March 21, 1997), p. 3.

18. James Lilley, interview by the author, Washington, D.C., June 20, 2000. The recreational and other perquisites of life at the ten major U.S. military installations in South Korea are detailed in *U.S. Forces Travel Guide to Overseas U.S. Military Installations* (Falls Church, Va.: Military Living Publications, 1999), pp. 106–18.

19. Dana Priest, "A Four-Star Foreign Policy?" first in a series of three articles titled "The Proconsuls," *Washington Post*, September 28, 2000, p. 1.

20. Doug Bandow, *Tripwire* (Washington, D.C.: Cato Institute, 1996), p. 71.

21. Ibid.

22. Ibid. p. 72.

23. *Japan Times*, October 27, 1989, p. 1.

24. "Target Date 2010," *Korea Herald*, November 10, 1999, p. 1.

25. Bandow, *Tripwire*, p. 74.

26. Ted Galen Carpenter, "Ending South Korea's Unhealthy Security Dependence," *Korean Journal of Defense Analysis* (winter 1995): 181.

27. Ibid., p. 182.

28. James Laney, interview by the author, Seoul, May 28, 1994.

29. Lee Sang Hoon, Interview by the author, Seoul, October 10, 1991.

30. Gen. Thomas A. Schwartz, commander, U.S. forces, Korea, testimony before the Senate Armed Services Committee, March 6, 2000.

31. "Cutting Unnecessary Military Spending: Going Further and Faster," *Defense Monitor* 21, no. 3 (1993): 2. See also Stephen Daggett and Kathleen Hicks, "Defense Budget: Alternative Measures of Costs of Military Commitments Abroad," supplement to the *Defense Monitor*, June 16, 1995, p. 1.

32. Earl C. Ravenal, *Designing Defense for a New World Order* (Washington, D.C.: Cato Institute, 1992), p. 51.

33. Cited in Don Oberdorfer, *The Two Koreas* (Reading, Mass.: Addison-Wesley, 1997), p. 311.

34. William W. Kaufmann and John D. Steinbruner, *Decisions for Defense: Prospects for a New Order* (Washington, D.C.: The Brookings Institution, 1991), p. 46.

35. Steve Glain, "Seoul's Weapons Buildup Suffers Loss of Credibility," *Asian Wall Street Journal Weekly*, January 3, 1994, p. 1; and Glain, "U.S. Officials Question South Korean Readiness to Fight the North: Defense Ministry Fears Japan More than Pyongyang as Long-Term Threat," *Wall Street Journal*, January 17, 1995, p. 1.

36. U.S. Congress, *Moving United States Forces: Options for Strategic Mobility* (Washington, D.C.: Congressional Budget Office, 1997), pp. xviii, 25–26, 29–30.

37. Mark Thompson, "What Will Be the Weapons of the Future?" *Time*, May 22, 2000, p. 102.

38. Selig S. Harrison, *The Widening Gulf: Asian Nationalism and American Policy* (New York: Free Press, 1978), pp. 377–78.

39. Congress, *Moving United States Forces*, p. 33.

40. William J. Taylor and Michael J. Mazarr, "R.O.K.–U.S. Defense Cooperation in the Context of Arms Control" (paper presented at "Comprehensive Security in Northeast Asia," conference sponsored by the Center for International Studies and the Korean Institute for Defense Analysis, Seoul, November 5–6, 1990), p. 21.

41. For an extended discussion of the use of Korea as a rationale for U.S. military budgeting, see Leon V. Sigal, *Disarming Strangers: Nuclear Diplomacy with North Korea* (Princeton: Princeton University Press, 1998), p. 233.

42. Jim Wolfe, "Powell Sees Opportunity for U.S. to Reduce Military Strength," *Defense News*, April 8, 1991, p. 1.

43. Nicholas Kristof, "Police and Demonstrators Battle in Seoul." *New York Times*, July 9, 1987, p. 3.

44. Hyun Hong Choo, "Korean Perceptions of America," *Shin Dong A Monthly*, (February 1995): 32.

45. Seong Ok Chol, "Prostitution on U.S. Military Bases," *Korea Report*, Washington (January–February, 1989), pp. 10–11.

46. John Burton, "Koreans Not So Comfortable on America's Sofa," *Financial Times*, July 15, 2000, p. 4.

47. Sang Hun Choe, "Seoul Gets More Power in Crimes Involving G.I.'s," *Washington Post*, December 29, 2000, p. 10.

48. Norman D. Levin, *The Shape of Korea's Future* (Santa Monica, Calif.: Center for Asia-Pacific Policy, RAND Corporation, 1999), pp. xv, 33.

49. For the 1975 findings, see Michael Getler, "Troops in Korea Stir Concern," *Washington Post*, May 24, 1975, pp. A13–14. For 1999, see Chicago Council on Foreign Relations, *American Public Opinion and U.S. Foreign Policy*, ed. John Rielly (Chicago: Chicago Council on Foreign Relations, 1999), fig. 6-4, p. 38. See also figs. 2-5, p. 13, 4-6, p. 28.

CHAPTER 16

THE U.S. NUCLEAR CHALLENGE TO NORTH KOREA

1. Conrad C. Crane, "To Avert Impending Disaster: American Military Plans to Use Atomic Weapons during the Korean War," *Journal of Strategic Studies* 23, no. 2 (June 2000): 79–80. See also Bruce Cumings and Jan Halliday, *Korea: The Unknown War* (London: Viking/Penguin, 1988), p. 165.

2. Bruce Cumings, *Parallax Visions: Making Sense of American-East Asian Relations at the End of the Century* (Durham: Duke University Press, 1999), p. 131.

3. Peter Hayes, "American Nuclear Dilemmas in Korea" (paper delivered at a conference sponsored by the U.S. Korea Security Studies Council, December 3, 1987), pp. 14, 43. See also Hayes, *Pacific Powderkeg: American Nuclear Dilemmas in Korea* (Lexington, Mass.: Lexington Books, 1990), pp. 123–52.

4. John W. Lewis, then director of the Stanford University Arms Control and Disarmament Program, speaking at a Carnegie Endowment for International Peace seminar on October 10, 1993, described his meetings with Soviet nuclear scientists who had received these overtures from North Korea.

5. Edward Seidensticker, "Japan after Vietnam," *Commentary* (September 1975): 56.

6. *Concept for Nuclear Operations in a Nuclear Environment*, Defense Nuclear Agency Technical Report DNA-TR-81-133, Washington, D.C., June 1982, p. 19, cited in Hayes, *Pacific Powderkeg*, p. 91.

7. Michael Getler, "Weinberger, South Korean President Observe Exercises," *Washington Post*, April 18, 1982, p. 20.

8. David E. Sanger, "North Korea Bars Inspectors," *New York Times*, March 14, 1993, p. E18.

CHAPTER 17

THE NORTH KOREAN RESPONSE

1. Peter Hayes, "Should the United States Supply Light Water Reactors to Pyongyang?" (paper prepared for a conference on North Korea sponsored by the Carnegie Endowment for International Peace, November 16, 1993), pp. 3–6.

2. Alexander Zhebin, "A Political History of Soviet-North Korean Cooperation," in *The North Korean Nuclear Program*, ed. James Clay Moltz and Alexander Mansourov (New York: Routledge, 1999), p. 35.

3. Ibid. See also Georgiy Kaurov, "A Technical History of Soviet-North Korean Nuclear Relations," in *North Korean Nuclear Program*, ed. Moltz and Mansourov, pp. 52–53.

4. Adm. William J. Crowe, "North Korea: U.S. Policy Issues" (paper prepared for a conference on Korea sponsored by the Summit Council on World Peace, Washington, D.C., September 11, 1993), p. 2.

5. Leon V. Sigal, *Disarming Strangers: Nuclear Diplomacy with North Korea* (Princeton: Princeton University Press, 1998), p. 60.

6. Lim Dong Won, interview by the author, Seoul, April 29, 1998. *Stars and Stripes*, May 31, 1992, reported General Riscassi's statement, prompting a comment in *Dong-A-Ilbo*, June 2, 1992, p. 1, that "since General Riscassi's statement may provoke North Korea to assume a hardline position of its own, his words may have the effect of blocking further progress in the inter-Korea relationship.".

7. Cited in Don Oberdorfer, *The Two Koreas: A Contemporary History* (Reading, Mass.: Addison-Wesley, 1997), p. 273.

8. Sigal, *Disarming Strangers*.

9. For example, see "Breaking the Nuclear Impasse: Paths to Cooperative Security in Korea" (paper prepared for a conference on Northeast Asian Security cosponsored by the Brookings Institution and the Institute of Foreign Affairs and National Security, Washington, D.C., November 1–2, 1993); "The North Korean Nuclear Crisis: From Stalemate to Breakthrough," *Arms Control Today* (November 1994): 22–25; "Three Myths May Foil Progress," *New York Times*, June 24, 1994, p. A27; "Package Incentives for Forswearing Nuclear Arms," *Washington Post*, January 30, 1994, p. A29; and "North Korea and Nuclear Weapons: Next Steps in American Policy," testimony presented before the Subcommittee on East Asian and Pacific Affairs, Senate Foreign Relations Committee, May 26, 1993.

10. Sigal, *Disarming Strangers*, p. 109.

11. "North Korea's Kim Calls Nuclear Talk 'Fictitious,'" *Washington Times*, April 19, 1994, p. A17.

12. David Albright, "How Much Plutonium Did North Korea Produce?" in *Solving the North Korean Nuclear Puzzle* (Washington, D.C.: Institute for Science and International Security, 2000), pp. 114–19.

13. Sigal, *Disarming Strangers*, pp. 93–94.

CHAPTER 18
THE 1994 COMPROMISE: CAN IT SURVIVE?

1. Jimmy Carter, interview by the author, Carter Center, Atlanta, June 14, 2000.

2. Robert Gallucci, interview by the author, Washington, D.C., June 15, 2000.

3. William Perry, interview by the author, Palo Alto, California, May 16, 2000.

4. Marion Creekmore, interview by the author, Carter Center, Atlanta, May 16, 2000.

5. "Summary of Nuclear Portion of Conversation between Former President Carter and Then President Kim Il Sung, Pyongyang, North Korea, June 16, 1994: Prepared by Marion Creekmore and reviewed by President Carter," September 20, 2000, p. 2.

6. Gallucci, interview.

7. Carter, interview.

8. Leon V. Sigal, *Disarming Strangers: Nuclear Diplomacy with North Korea* (Princeton: Princeton University Press, 1998), p. 32.

9. "Nobody Can Slander the DPRK's Missile Policy," Korean Central News Agency, June 16, 1998, monitored by the Foreign Broadcast Information Service.

CHAPTER 19
JAPAN AND NUCLEAR WEAPONS

1. *Mugunghwa Kk'Och'i P'iossumnida* (The Rose of Sharon has blossomed), (Seoul: Haenaem Publishing Company, 1994), sold 1.3 million sets of the complete trilogy and 4.1 million copies of separate volumes. It has not been translated into English.

2. *Physics Today* (September 1977): 76. *Haek Mulli Hakja Lee Hwi So* (Nuclear physicist Lee Hwi So) (Seoul: Puri), a biography by Kong Suk Ha, a professor at Doksong Women's College, appeared in 1989. The same author's novel, *Lee Hwi So Sosol* (Lee Hwi So the novel), also published by Puri, appeared in 1993. Neither work contained factual evidence linking Lee to Park's program. However, Kong stated that he had interviewed Park's family and Lee's family in preparing his novel. The novel depicts Lee as helping the nuclear program, and the biography contains a photo of a National Service Medal posthumously awarded to Lee by Park praising his "contributions to Korean scientific achievement."

3. Press Conference, Foreign Ministry, Tokyo, February 17, 1966.

4. "Nuclear Armament Possible But Unrealistic: Secret Reports," *Asahi*, November 13, 1994, p. 1.

5. "Nuclearization Possible Technically," *Mainichi*, July 12, 1968, p. 4.

6. "The Capability to Develop Nuclear Weapons Should Be Kept: Ministry of Foreign Affairs Secret Document in 1969," *Mainichi*, August 1, 1994, p. 1.

7. "Agreed Minute to Joint Communiqué of United States President Nixon and Japanese Prime Minister Sato Issued on November 21, 1969" (top secret), Washington, D.C., two pages. See Kei Wakaizumi, *Tasaku Nakarishi o Shinzemu to Hossu* (I want to believe there was no other alternative) (Tokyo: Bungeishunju Limited, 1994).

8. This is based on a tape recording of Sato's comments to business executives at Keidanren headquarters in Tokyo on December 8, 1969, translated for me by

Seiji Yamaoka of the *Washington Post*. See Selig S. Harrison, "Japanese Wary of Nuclear Treaty," *Washington Post*, December 15, 1969, p. 3.

9. Yasuhiro Nakasone, "The International Environment and the Defense of Japan in the 1970's" (address delivered at the Harvard Club of Japan, June 30, 1970), p. 8.

10. Selig S. Harrison, "Japan To Be 'Medium-Rank' Power," *International Herald Tribune*, October 21, 1970, p. 1. See also "Gist of White Paper on Defense," *Japan Times*, October 25, 1970, p. 20.

11. His formal title was acting chairman. The honorific chairmanship is held concurrently by the minister of state for science and technology, a political appointee. Arisawa served under a succession of seven ministers.

12. "Ningen No Chie Nante Asahaka Na Manodesu" (Humanity's wisdom is a shallow thing), *Asahi*, September 12, 1972, p. 6. Arisawa's revelation was recalled by a columnist on the occasion of his death, "Kyo No Mondai" (Topic of the day), *Asahi*, March 9, 1988, p. 55.

13. *Asahi*, October 15, 1980, p. 8.

14. Yasuo Takeyama, "Japan and Its Role in Asia" (address at the 1992 Taipei YPO World Conference, April 27–May 1, 1992), pp. 15–16, 19.

15. "Nichibei Kankei 'Taitoo Na Kankei' to iu Ukareta Hanashi de Wa Nai" (Is 'a normal country' the path toward nuclear armament?), interview with former prime minister Miyazawa, *AERA*, published weekly by the *Asahi Shimbun*, March 21, 1994, pp. 18–19.

16. Selig S. Harrison, *Japan's Nuclear Future: The Plutonium Debate and East Asian Security* (Washington, D.C.: Carnegie Endowment for International Peace, 1996), pp. 18–21.

17. For example, see J. Carson Mark, "Explosive Properties of Reactor-Grade Plutonium," *Science and Global Security* 3 (1992): 1–13.

18. Jinzaburo Takagi states in a memorandum dated March 22, 1996, that the Joyo accumulation in the radial blanket was officially reported to have been twenty-two kilograms. He estimates that there are an additional eighteen kilograms in the axial blanket. The blankets are now in storage.

19. Victor Gilinsky, "Fast Breeder Reactors and the Spread of Plutonium," memorandum RM-5148–PR (Santa Monica, Calif.: RAND Corporation, 1967), pp. vii, 28.

20. *The Unlawful Plutonium Alliance: Japan's Supergrade Plutonium and the Role of the United States* (Amsterdam: Greenpeace International, 1994), p. 10.

21. Tom Clancy, *Debt of Honor* (New York: G. P. Putnam's Sons, 1994), esp. pp. 205–18.

22. John Pike, interview by the author, Washington, D.C., January 10, 1996.

23. Gen. Toshiyuki Shikata, "Can Japan Take the Lead in Nuclear Weapons?" (paper prepared for a conference sponsored by the Center for International Strategy, Technology, and Policy, Georgia Institute of Technology, Hakone, Japan, October 3, 1999), pp. 709.

24. Pike, interview.

25. Harrison, *Japan's Nuclear Future*, esp. pp. 33–40.

26. Ibid.

CHAPTER 20
SOUTH KOREA AND NUCLEAR WEAPONS

1. *Plutonium Watch*, Institute for Science and International Security, Washington, D.C., October 2000 issue, p. 6.

2. Gen. Kim Yoon Ho, interview by the author, Seoul, May 2, 1992.

3. Donald Gregg, telephone interview with the author, September 11, 2000.

4. Kapchae Cho, "Nuclear Game on the Korean Peninsula," *Wolgang Choson*, Seoul, April 1990, pp. 220–55 (translated for the author by Taewoo Kim).

5. Department of State Telegram 048673, Control 859Q, March 4, 1975, 11:40 P.M., secs. 1, 4.

6. Kapchae, "Nuclear Game," p. 14.

7. Mark Hibbs, "Legacy of Secret Nuclear Program Led U.S. to Blunt R.O.K. Cooperation," *Nucleonics Week* 40, no. 1 (January 7, 1999): 10.

8. Yu Yong Won, "Korea Must Obtain Nuclear Armament Capability," *Wolgang Choson*, Seoul, October 1991, pp. 222–37 (FBIS-EAS-91-016, October 29, 1991, p. 13).

9. Paul Shin, "U.S. Said to Stop South Korea's Nuke Bomb Plans," *Washington Times*, March 29, 1994, p. A11.

10. Ibid. See also Yu, "Korea Must Obtain Nuclear Armament Capability," p. 10.

11. See the letter from Bridget Goodman to British Nuclear Fuels, Greenpeace-United Kingdom, March 15, 1993, provided by Greenpeace.

12. Kim Dae Jung, interview by the author, Seoul, May 1, 1992.

13. "Denuclearization Policy under Fire," *Newsreview*, Seoul, November 6, 1993, p. 5.

14. Yonhap News Service, October 9, 1993, cited in FBIS-EAS-93-195, October 12, 1993, p. 36.

15. "Denuclearization Policy under Fire."

16. "Korea's Nuclear Dilemmas," *Korea and World Affairs* (summer 1992): 274.

17. Ibid., p. 278.

18. "Korea Must Obtain Nuclear Armament Capability," p. 12.

19. Choi provided a copy of this memorandum to the author in a meeting with a delegation representing the Carnegie Endowment for International Peace Study Group on Nuclear Weapons and the Security of Korea, Seoul, April 20, 1992.

20. Text provided by Choi, ibid.

21. Ibid.

22. Janne E. Nolan, *Trappings of Power: Ballistic Missiles in the Third World* (Washington, D.C.: Brookings Institution, 1991), pp. 49–50. See also Peter Hayes, "The Two Koreas and the International Missile Trade," in *The International Missile Bazaar*, ed. W.C. Potter and H. W. Jencks (Boulder: Westview Press, 1993), pp. 136–38.

23. Peter Hayes, "Early Indicators: ROK Long-Range Missile Capabilities," *NAPSNet*, published by the Nautilus Institute, Berkeley, California, November 17, 1999, p. 2.

24. Lee Sung Yul, "U.S. Pressured Chun Doo Hwan to Scuttle Missile Development Program," *Korea Herald*, June 10, 1999, p. 3.

25. Kim Tae Woo, "ROK–US Missile Accord Should be Scrapped," *Korea Post* (October 1998): 26–27. See also Kim Tae Woo, "South Korea's Missile Dilemmas," *Asian Survey* (May/June 1999): esp. p. 19.

26. James Risen, "South Korea Seen Trying to Extend Range of Missiles," *New York Times*, November 14, 1999, p. A1.

27. "Kim: This Is Basically a Win-Win Policy," *Washington Times*, October 19, 1999, p. A13.

28. Doug Struck, "As Relations Thaw, Seoul Suspends Arms Plan," *Washington Post*, June 25, 2000, p. A20. See also Son Key Yong, "U.S. Halts Exports of Missile Parts to Korea," *Korea Times*, January 12, 2000, p. 3, and Phillip Finnegan, "South Korea, U.S. Slowly Advance to Missile Pact," *Defense News*, June 5, 2000, p. 1.

CHAPTER 21
GUIDELINES FOR U.S. POLICY

1. "'Scrap Nuclear Arsenal,' General Says," *Los Angeles Times*, July 17, 1994, p. A12. See also the address by Gen. Lee Butler to the State of the World Forum convened by the Mikhail Gorbachev Foundation, San Francisco, October 2, 1996, and *An Evolving U.S. Nuclear Posture*, report of the project on eliminating weapons of mass destruction sponsored by the Henry L. Stimson Center, December 1995, of which Gen. Andrew J. Goodpaster, former Supreme Allied Commander in Europe, served as chairman.

2. Mitchell Reiss, "KEDO and the DPRK: Problems and Prospects on the Road Ahead" (paper presented at "The Perry Report, the Missile Quagmire, and the North Korea Question: The Quest for New Alternatives," conference sponsored by Keio University, Tokyo, October 22, 1999), p. 4.

3. Comments before a conference on Korea sponsored by the Korea Society, Metropolitan Hotel, New York City, June 20, 2001, p. 4. For other discussions of the liability issue, see Steven Mufson, "U.S. Lauds Korean Talks, Says More Work Ahead," *Washington Post*, June 16, 2000, p. A25. See also General Accounting Office, *Nuclear Non-Proliferation: Implementation of the U.S./North Korea Agreement on Nuclear Issues*, October 1996, p. 13.

4. Lee Dom Bok, "Beyond Geneva: Risks versus Opportunities" (paper prepared for "Nuclear Non-Proliferation in 1995: Renewal, Transition or Decline," conference sponsored by the Carnegie Endowment for International Peace, Washington, D.C., January 30, 1995), p. 6.

5. David Albright, *Solving the North Korean Nuclear Puzzle* (Washington, D.C.: Institute for Science and International Security, 2000), pp. 274–75. For details concerning Model Protocol 540, see Michael May, ed., *Verifying the Agreed Framework* (Stanford: Center for International Security and Cooperation, Stanford University, 2001), pp. 24–25.

6. Albright, *Solving the North Korean Nuclear Puzzle*, pp. 117–26, esp. pp. 124–25.

7. Bradley O. Babson, "The North Korean Economy Today" (paper prepared for a roundtable on the North Korean economy sponsored by the U.S. Institute of Peace, January 4, 1999), p. 7.

8. This statement was made on May 18, 2000, during a debate on amendment no. 3 offered by Cox to the National Defense Authorization Act for Fiscal Year 2001, changing the language of section 1205, *Congressional Record*, p. H3360.

9. Morton H. Halperin, "Let's Close the Nuclear Umbrella," *Christian Science Monitor*, January 23, 1992, p. 18.

10. The coalition agreement between the Social Democratic Party and the Green Party was concluded at Bonn on October 20, 1998. Joschka Fischer called for a change in NATO policy on the first use of nuclear weapons in interviews with *Suddeutsche Zeitung*, Munich, November 27, 1998, p. 9, and *Der Spiegel*, Hamburg, November 23, 1998, p. 84. His speech to the NATO Council presenting his views is reported in David Buchan, "Bonn Doubts over NATO N-Weapons," *Financial Times*, London, December 9, 1998, p. 3. The Standing Committee on Foreign Affairs and International Trade, House of Commons, Canada, presented a similar view in *Canada and the Nuclear Challenge: Reducing the Political Value of Nuclear Weapons for the Twenty-First Century*, December 10, 1998 (see esp. p. 78).

11. George F. Kennan, "Back to the Nuclear Question," *Washington Post*, December 16, 1998, p. A31.

12. *Morning Edition*, National Public Radio, December 3, 1998.

13. General Butler and General Horner were among fifty-nine retired senior military officers in the United States and other countries who called for the United States to take the lead in pressing for the global elimination of nuclear weapons in a statement on December 4, 1996 ("Joint Statement on Reduction of Nuclear Weapon Arsenals: Declining Utility, Continuing Risks," Washington, D.C.). See also General Butler's speech at the Henry L. Stimson Center when the center awarded him its 1996 Award for Public Service on January 8, 1997, and General Horner's speech before an audience of journalists specializing in defense issues, reported in the *Los Angeles Times*, July 17, 1994.

14. Harold A. Feiveson, ed., *The Nuclear Turning Point* (Washington, D.C.: Brookings Institution Press, 1999), esp. pp. 151–53.

15. Janne E. Nolan, *An Elusive Consensus* (Washington, D.C.: Brookings Institution Press, 1999), pp. 111–12.

16. Feiveson, *The Nuclear Turning Point*, pp. 35–41, esp. p. 36.

17. Ibid., p. 39.

18. Nolan, *An Elusive Consensus*, p. 100.

19. Feiveson, *The Nuclear Turning Point*, p. 40.

20. Joo Hong Nam, "U.S. Forces in Korea: Their Role and Strategy," *Korea and World Affairs* (summer 1987): 275–76. See also Joo, *America's Commitment to South Korea: The First Decade of the Nixon Doctrine* (Cambridge: Cambridge University Press, 1980).

21. Kim Dae Jung, interview by the author, Seoul, May 1, 1992.

22. Kumao Kaneko, "Japan Needs No Umbrella," *Bulletin of the Atomic Scientists* (March/April 1996): 46–51.

23. Details of the Endicott effort can be found in the report of a conference sponsored by the Center for International Strategy, Technology and Policy, University of Georgia, *Toward a Limited Nuclear Free Zone in Northeast Asia: Senior Panel's Deliberations on a Draft Initial Agreement*, Atlanta, February 24, 1995. The signatories of this statement were Gen. Kim Jaechang, former Vice Chairman of the Joint Chiefs of Staff, Republic of Korea Army; Lt. Gen. Toshiyuki Shikata, former commander of the Northern Army, Japan Ground Self-Defense Force; Maj. Gen. V. N. Bunin, former director of Far Eastern affairs, Russian General Staff; and Prof. Xuetong Yan, deputy director, China Institute of Contemporary International Relations.

24. Selig S. Harrison, "China and the United States in Asia: Putting the 'Threat' in Perspective," in *China's Future*, ed. Ted Galen Carpenter (Washington, D.C.: Cato Institute, 2000). See also Selig S. Harrison and Clyde V. Prestowitz, Jr., *Asia after the 'Miracle': Redefining U.S. Economic and Security Priorities* (Washington, D.C.: Economic Strategy Institute, 1998), pp. 71–73.

25. "For a Chain of N-Free Zones," *Mainichi*, December 18, 1995, p. 10.

26. "Lift the Nuclear Umbrella," *Asahi*, August 27, 1999, p. 13.

27. Morihiro Hosokawa, address to Council on Foreign Relations, Washington, D.C., March 11, 1996.

28. Kobayashi Yosaji, ed., *1970: An Approach to Revisions of the Security Treaty* (Tokyo: Yomiuri Shimbun, 1966), pt. 2, chap. 2, pp. 109–10.

29. *Report of the Commission to Assess the Ballistic Missile Threat to the United States* (Washington, D.C.: Systems Planning Corporation, 1998), esp. p. 12.

30. William D. Hartung and Michelle Ciarrocca, *Tangled Web: The Marketing of Missile Defense, 1994–2000* (New York: Arms Trade Resource Center Special Report, World Policy Institute, 2000), p. 1. Even at the research stage, Hartung and Ciarrocca show, the missile defense program has been lucrative for defense

contractors. The ten contractors receiving the largest share of missile defense spending in 1998 and 1999 alone received $2.87 billion (table A, p. 18).

31. Statement by Mike McCurry, White House spokesman, August 13, 1998.

32. Space Imaging, Inc., of Thornton, Colorado, operated the Ikonos satellite that obtained photos of the North Korean site at Nodong in North Hamgyong province. The Federation of American Scientists study, *Nuclear Forces Guide: Nodong*, was released on the FAS website on January 2, 2000. See also William J. Broad, "Spy Photos of Korea Missile Site Bring Dispute," *New York Times*, January 11, 2000, p. 10.

33. *Report of the Commission to Assess the Ballistic Missile Threat to the United States.*

34. *Countermeasures: A Technical Evaluation of the Operational Effectiveness of the Planned U.S. National Missile Defense System* (Cambridge, Mass.: Union of Concerned Scientists and the MIT Security Studies Program, 2000).

35. Russian President Vladimir Putin said that Kim Jong Il had made another offer to discuss discontinuing missile production in a meeting on July 18, 2000. According to Putin, Kim "voiced an idea under which North Korea is even prepared to use exclusively the rocket equipment of other countries for peaceful space research if they offered it" (Michael R. Gordon, "North Korea Reported Open to Halting Missile Program," *New York Times*, July 20, 2000, p. 10). Inconclusive efforts to pin down what Kim had in mind and how this idea might fit into a U.S.–North Korea missile settlement were made during Secretary of State Albright's visit to Pyongyang in October 2000 and in subsequent working-level discussions in Kuala Lumpur, Malaysia, two weeks later.

36. Hajime Izumi, address at a conference on Korean reunification sponsored by *Hankyoreh Shinmun*, Seoul, May 5, 1999.

CHAPTER 23
KOREA, JAPAN, AND THE UNITED STATES

1. For example, in a 1988 poll, 54 percent of Japanese said they disliked Koreans most and 51 percent of Koreans said they disliked Japanese most. R. M. March, "Face to Face," *Korea Business World* (October 1988): 36. See also Chong Sik Lee, *Japan and Korea: The Political Dimension* (Stanford: Hoover Institution Press, Stanford University, 1985), p. 2.

2. Chong, *Japan and Korea*, p. 15. Bruce Cumings, in *Parallax Visions: Making Sense of American–East Asian Relations at the Turn of the Century* (Durham: Duke University Press, 1998), p. 74, shows that "millions of Koreans were forcibly relocated to Japan, Manchuria and northern Korea for hard labor in mines and factories." At the same time, he documents the positive economic role that Japanese colonial economic policy played in initiating Korea's industrial revolution.

3. For an example of this ambivalence, see "'Pride' Highlights Flawed Trials,"

by Hisahiko Okazaki, a prominent retired diplomat and foreign policy commentator, reprinted from the *Japan Times* in the *Korea Herald*, July 15, 1988, p. 1.

4. Robert M. Orr, Jr., "The Rape of History," *J.P.R.I. Critique* 2 (July 1998): 1.

5. Edward Seidensticker, "Japan after Vietnam," *Commentary* (September 1975): 56.

6. This is cited in Kwan Ha Yim, "Korea in Japanese Foreign Policy" (paper prepared for the 1973 Annual Meeting of the American Political Science Association, New Orleans, September 4–8, 1973), p. 12.

7. Kimura's statements and the controversy surrounding them can be found in the *Japan Times*, Tokyo, August 31, 1974, and *Asahi Shimbun*, Tokyo, October 2 and December 9, 1974. See also Eiichi Imagawa, "Japan's Peaceful Coexistence Policy toward Korea" (paper prepared for the Conference of Japanese and U.S. Parliamentarians on Korean Problems, Washington, D.C., September 19–20, 1977), p. 29.

8. "Delicate Differences between U.S. and Japan," *Nihon Keizai*, August 8, 1975, p. 2. See also "We Urge Formulation of Korean Peninsula Policy Which Will Not Leave Behind Roots of Trouble for Future," an editorial in *Nihon Keizai*, on August 2, 1975. As examples of Japanese press coverage underlining the divergence in the U.S. and Japanese positions on the communiqué language, see editorials in *Mainichi* ("U.S.–Japan Summit Talks Leave Doubts") and *Tokyo Shimbun* ("Different Evaluation of Japan on Japan–U.S. Summit Talks") on August 8, 1975 (translated in U.S. Embassy Press Translations).

9. "'R.O.K. Clause' Changed to 'Korean Clause,'" *Sankei*, August 7, 1975, p. 2.

10. Yung Tai Pyun, Rhee's prime minister (1953) and foreign minister (1953–55), interview by the Dulles Oral History Project, Princeton University, Seoul, September 29, 1964, pp. 8, 20. See also Admiral Sohn Won-yil, interview by the Dulles Oral History Project, ibid., p. 11.

11. Pyong Choon Hahm, "Korea's 'Mendicant Mentality'?" *Foreign Affairs* 43, no. 1 (October 1964): 171.

12. For details concerning Park's relations with the Japanese colonial regime, see Selig S. Harrison, *The Widening Gulf: Asian Nationalism and American Policy* (New York: Free Press, 1978), pp. 215, 246. The author covered Park's fundraising and political activity as Northeast Asia bureau chief of the *Washington Post* from 1968 to 1972.

13. Karl Moskowitz, "Korean-Japanese Economic Relations," in *Korea's New Challenges and Kim Young Sam*, ed. C. J. Sigur (New York: Carnegie Council on Ethics and International Affairs, 1993), p. 60. See also Walter Hatch, "Grounding Asian Flying Geese: The Costs of Depending Heavily on Japanese Capital and Technology," *Policy Report* no. 3 (April 1998), entirety, published by the National Bureau of Asian Research, Seattle.

14. "The Revival of Japanese Militarism," Korean Central News Agency,

Pyongyang, January 10, 1966. See also Masao Okonogi, "The Political Dynamics of Japan-North Korean Relations," *Korea and World Affairs* (summer 1989): 333.

15. Akio Watanabe, "Japanese–North Korean Relations and Korean Reunification" (paper prepared for a symposium at Hanyang University, Seoul, September 27, 1994), p. 13.

16. Ichiro Uchiyama, Cabinet Research Office, Japan's counterpart to the CIA National Intelligence Council, interview by the author, Tokyo, September 9, 1988.

17. Watanabe, "Japanese–North Korean Relations and Korean Reunification," p. 15.

18. Denny Roy, "Japan's North Korea Policy," *Asian Survey* 28, no. 12 (December 1988): 1287–88.

19. Kei Wakaizumi, "Japan's 'Grand Experiment' and the Japanese-American Alliance" (paper delivered at the Woodrow Wilson International Center for Scholars, October 9, 1975), p. 33.

20. "Foreign Minister Refers to Inflow of Refugees and Routed Troops as Effect of 'War in R.O.K.' upon Japan's Security," *Yomiuri*, August 23, 1975, p. 1.

21. Masao Okonogi, "The North Korean Crisis and Japan's Choice" (paper prepared for a conference on Korean reunification sponsored by the Kim Dae Jung Peace Foundation, Seoul, March 10, 1997), p. 10.

22. Watanabe, "Japanese–North Korean Relations and Korean Reunification," p. 11.

23. Okonogi, "The North Korean Crisis and Japan's Choice," p. 16.

24. Yoichi Funabashi, "Tokyo's Depression Diplomacy," *Foreign Affairs* 77, no. 6 (November/December 1998): 30. See also Masao Okonogi, "Beyond the Status Quo: A View from Japan" (paper prepared for "Kim Dae Jung's Sunshine Policy," conference at Georgetown University, Washington, D.C., May 17, 1999); and Hajime Izumi, "Recent Developments on North Korea and the Perry Initiative" (paper prepared for "The Future of North-South Relations" conference sponsored by the Kim Dae Jung Peace Foundation, Seoul, February 24, 2000).

CHAPTER 24
KOREA, CHINA, AND THE UNITED STATES

1. Hae Jong Chun, "Sino-Korean Tributary Relations in the Ching Period," in *The Chinese World Order: Traditional China's Foreign Relations*, ed. John King Fairbank (Cambridge, Mass.: Harvard University Press, 1968), p. 111.

2. Carter J. Eckert, "China and Korea in Historical Perspective," in *Historical Perspectives on Contemporary East Asia*, ed. Merle Goldman and Andrew Gordon (Cambridge, Mass.: Harvard University Press, 2000), pp. 120–22.

3. Bruce Cumings, *Korea's Place in the Sun* (New York: W. W. Norton, 1997), p. 100.

4. This figure has been compiled primarily from the annual tables from 1972 to 1977 in *World Armaments and Disarmament*, the yearbook published by the Stockholm International Peace Research Institute (SIPRI) (Stockholm: Almquist and Wiksell), and from the annual tables from 1963 to 1975 in *World Military Expenditures and Arms Transfers*, published by the U.S. Arms Control and Disarmament Agency. These estimates were based on intelligence sources and media reports in addition to the limited published Soviet and Chinese data. Credible fragmentary evidence from my own intelligence sources and a wide variety of published sources was also taken into account (e.g., the *Defense White Papers* of the Republic of Korea, especially those for 1989 and 1990).

5. R. Bates Gill, *Chinese Arms Transfers* (Westport, Conn.: Praeger, 1992), esp. chap. 2.

6. Chae Jin Lee, *China and Korea: Dynamic Relations* (Stanford: Hoover Institution Press, 1996), pp. 70–72.

7. Ibid., p. 81.

8. Robert Dujarric, *Korea: Security Pivot in Northeast Asia* (Indianapolis: Hudson Institute, 1998), p. 66.

9. Ki Joon Kang, *Damul Koe Yuksa Wa Eu Yaksok* (Damul and its promise to history) (Seoul: Damul Press, 1997), pp. 48–52. See also *Damul Minjok Hagkyo* (One who rules East Asia rules the world), a brochure describing the goals of the Damul Institute, and the institute's monthly magazine, *Buksori* (The sound of the drums). Selections from Ki Joon Kang's book were translated for the author by Jihyun Kim. For a discussion of ethnic Koreans living in China, see Han S. Park, "Koreans in China: Political Implications" (paper prepared for the Korea Seminar, Columbia University, March 15, 1985).

10. Steve Glain, "After 1,300 Years, White-Collar Armies Target Manchuria," *Wall Street Journal*, October 9, 1995, p. A1.

11. Shunji Taoka, "Japanese Maritime Self-Defense Forces in the Next Century," *Sekai No Kansen* (December 1995): 31–37 (translated in FBIS-EAS-96-068).

12. K. O. Emery, "Geological Structure and Some Water Characteristics of the East China Sea and the Yellow Sea," *CCOP Technical Bulletin* (Bangkok: United Nations Economic Commission for Asia and the Far East, 1969), p. 41.

13. Selig S. Harrison, *China, Oil and Asia: Conflict Ahead?* (New York: Columbia University Press, 1977), pp. 129–36. See also S. B. Frazier, "Marine Petroleum Exploration of the Huksan Platform: Korea" (paper delivered at the Circum-Pacific Energy and Minerals Resources Conference, Honolulu, August 26–30, 1974), pp. 3, 13–14 and figs. 1–4. See also Chong Su Kim, "The Petroleum Potential of the Korean Offshore" (paper delivered at the Circum-Pacific Energy and Minerals Resources Conference, Honolulu, August 26–30, 1974), pp. 9–10 and fig. 4.

14. Banning Garrett and Bonnie Glaser, "How China Views Korea and Its Future," *Asian Survey* 35, no. 6 (June 1995): 544. See also "Report on a Study Mission to Beijing," June 10, 1995, p. 4.

15. Banning Garrett, "Chinese Views of the North Korean Situation and U.S. Korea Policy: Key Findings" (discussion outline prepared for a Brookings Institution seminar on January 14, 1999, based on discussions in Beijing, December 8–11, 1998).

16. "Toward Unshakable Japan–ROK Ties," *Daily Yomiuri*, November 16, 1995, p. 17. See also "Jiang, Kim Hold Joint Press Conference," BBC Summary of World Broadcasts, November 20, 1995 (EE/D2461/D), reporting Korean Broadcasting System radio report, 0500 GMT, November 14, 1995; and John Burton, "Jiang Cements Ties with Seoul," *Financial Times*, November 15, 1995, p. 4.

17. Tao Bingwei, "Some Views on the Question of the Korean Peninsula" (paper presented at "The North Korea Policies of the U.S., Russia, China and Japan," symposium sponsored by the Kim Dae Jung Peace Foundation, November 26, 1996), p. 48.

18. Kim Byong Hong, interview by the author, Pyongyang, September 29, 1995.

19. Hwang Chang Yop, interview by the author, Seoul, May 4, 1999.

20. Yang Li Wen, "The Korean Peninsula Situation in the Eyes of the Chinese Media (1978–1988)" (paper prepared for a conference on China at the Carnegie Endowment for International Peace, Washington, D.C., March 10, 1990), pp. 16–17.

21. For example, see Jia Hao and Zhuang Qubing, "China's Policy toward the Korean Peninsula," *Asian Survey* 32, no. 12 (December 1992): 1154.

22. For example, see "The United States and Korea," *Beijing Review*, September 5, 1987, p. 7.

23. Ye Ruan, "The Historical Transformation of the Korean Peninsula and China's Concerns" (paper presented at the Workshop on Security and the Korean Peninsula in the 1990s, Australian National University, Canberra, March 25–27, 1992), p. 8.

24. Morton H. Halperin, "U.S. Security Objectives after Korean Reunification" (paper prepared for a conference sponsored by the Century Foundation, March 3, 1998), p. 3.

25. Paul H. Kreisberg, "Korea and Asia in the Twenty First Century" (paper prepared for a conference at the Naval War College, March 10, 1997), p. 10.

26. Eric A. McVadon, "Chinese Military Strategy in the Korean Peninsula," in *China's Military Faces the Future*, ed. James R. Lilley and David Shambaugh (Washington, D.C.: M. E. Sharpe for the American Enterprise Institute, 1999), p. 276.

27. Robert A. Scalapino, "Korean Security after Unification" (paper prepared for a conference on Asian security in the twenty-first century, East-West Center, Honolulu, November 1, 1996), p. 21.

CHAPTER 25
KOREA, RUSSIA, AND THE UNITED STATES

1. Vipin Chandra, *Imperialism, Resistance and Reform in Late Nineteenth Century Korea* (Berkeley: Institute of East Asian Studies, University of California, 1988), p. 46.

2. Cho Soon Sung, *Korea in World Politics: An Evaluation of American Responsibility* (Berkeley: University of California Press, 1967), p. 45.

3. Dimitri Volkogonov, *Autopsy for an Empire* (New York: Free Press, 1998), p. 418.

4. Richard Nixon, statement at press conference, April 18, 1969.

5. Kim Il Sung, interview by the author, Pyongyang, June 9, 1994.

6. Evgeniy Bajanov, "Russia and North Korea," (paper presented at "The North Korea Policies of Russia, China, Japan and the United States," conference sponsored by the Kim Dae Jung Peace Foundation, Seoul, November 26, 1996), p. 68.

7. Evgeniy Bajanov and Natasha Bazhanova, "The Evolution of Russian-Korean Relations," *Asian Survey* 34, no. 9 (September 1994): 792–93.

8. Stephen J. Blank, *Russian Policy and the Korean Crisis* (Strategic Studies Institute, U.S. Army War College, 1994), p. 19.

9. Alvin Z. Rubinstein, "Russia's Relations with North Korea," in *Imperial Decline: Russia's Changing Role in Asia*, ed. Stephen J. Blank and Alvin Z. Rubinstein (Durham: Duke University Press, 1997), p. 173.

10. "Joint Declaration, V. V. Putin, President, the Russian Federation, and Kim Jong Il, Chairman, National Defense Commission, Democratic People's Republic of Korea," July 19, 2000, para. 2.

11. Bajanov, "Russia and North Korea," p. 63.

12. Ibid., p. 65. See also Shim Jae Hoon, "Russia Returns," *Far Eastern Economic Review*, January 13, 2000, p. 21.

13. Chikahito Harada, *Russia and Northeast Asia*, Adelphi Paper 310 (London: International Institute of Strategic Studies, 1997), p. 70.

14. Keun Wook Paik, "Pipeline Gas in Northeast Asia: Recent Developments and Regional Perspective," briefing paper no. 39, (London: Royal Institute of International Affairs, 1998), p. 6.

15. Keun Wook Paik, "Revitalizing North Korea's Energy through the Pipeline Gas Option," *Financial Times Asia Gas Report*, London, September 2000), p. 4.

16. Alessandra Stanley, "Moscow Miffed by U.S. Draft on Korea," *New York Times*, June 17, 1994, p. 3.

17. Carla Ann Robbins, "An Iran-North Korea Swap?" *Wall Street Journal*, May 5, 1995, p. 14.

18. Leonid Mlechin, "We Are Being Squeezed Out," *Izvestia*, October 29, 1994, p. 3.

19. Robert Dujarric, *Korea: Security Pivot in Northeast Asia* (Indianapolis: Hudson Institute, 1998), p. 110.

20. Jun Kwan Hoo, "Year of the Moscow-Seoul Ties," *Newsreview*, Seoul, January 9, 1999, p. 6.

21. "Russia Must Be Active in the Asia-Pacific Region," *Nezavisimaia Gazeta*, February 23, 1999, p. 6. For surveys of Russia's response to U.S. policy in Korea, see Dujarric, *Korea*, pp. 108–12; Rubinstein, "Russia's Relations with North Korea," pp. 175–83; and Ralph A. Cossa, *The Major Powers in Northeast Asian Security*, McNair Paper 51 (Washington, D.C.: Institute for National Strategic Studies, National Defense University, 1966), pp. 41–51.

22. Bruce Cumings, *Korea's Place in the Sun* (New York: W. W. Norton, 1997), p. 188.

23. James A. Baker, "America in Asia," *Foreign Affairs* 71 (winter 1991–92): 13.

CHAPTER 26

THEN AND NOW: THE CASE FOR A NEUTRAL KOREA

1. Jonathan D. Pollack and Young Koo Cha, *A New Alliance for the Next Century* (Santa Monica, Calif.: National Defense Research Institute, RAND, 1996), esp. pp. 68–69.

2. W. E. Odom, *Trial after Triumph: East Asia after The Cold War* (Indianapolis: Hudson Institute, 1996), pp. 134–35. See also Odom, *Korean Unification and After: The Challenge for U.S. Strategy* (Indianapolis: Hudson Institute, 2000), esp. p. 35.

3. Selig S. Harrison, *Japan's Nuclear Future: The Plutonium Debate and East Asian Security* (Washington, D.C.: Carnegie Endowment for International Peace, 1996), pp. 24–25.

4. Gennady Chufrin, "Korea and Russia: Looking Ahead" (paper presented at "The North Korea Policies of Russia, China, Japan and the United States," conference sponsored by the Kim Dae Jung Peace Foundation, Seoul, November 26, 1996), p. 10.

5. Alvin Z. Rubenstein, "Russia's Relations with North Korea," in *Imperial Decline: Russia's Changing Role in Asia*, ed. Stephen J. Blank and Alvin Z. Rubenstein (Durham: Duke University Press, 1997), p. 175.

Index